Grade 11

D0899817

Grammar for Writing

Senior Series Consultant

Beverly Ann Chin
Professor of English
University of Montana
Missoula, MT

Series Consultant

Frederick J. Panzer, Sr.
English Dept. Chair, Emeritus
Christopher Columbus High School
Miami, FL

Series Consultant

Charlotte Rosenzweig, Ed. D.
English Dept. Chairperson
Long Beach High School
Long Beach, NY

Series Editor

Phyllis Goldenberg

Acknowledgments

Excerpts from the *Common Core State Standards for English Language Arts* © Copyright 2010, National Governors Association Center for Best Practices and Council of Chief State School Officers. All rights reserved.

Printed in the United States of America

Teacher's Edition: ISBN: 978-1-4217-1131-7
Student Edition (s/c): ISBN: 978-1-4217-1121-8
Student Edition (h/c): ISBN: 978-1-4217-1111-9
2 3 4 5 6 7 8 9 RRDW 20 19 18 17 16

For additional online resources, go to www.grammarforwriting.com and enter the Teacher Access Code: TTYUMDNJKF

CONTENTS

Available at www.grammarforwriting.com:

For Teachers

✔ password-protected supplemental Answer Keys

✔ teacher notes to portfolio projects

✔ professional development videos and full-length articles by experts in the field

✔ Answer Key to Student Test Booklet

✔ planning and pacing guide

For Students

✔ additional practice for grammar lessons

✔ step-by-step portfolio projects

✔ interactive SAT/ACT worksheets for additional standardized test preparation

✔ peer review form

For more information about *Grammar for Writing* Online Components, see page T18.

Introduction to the Common Core Enriched Edition

The Common Core State Standards (CCSS) for English Language Arts represent a broad-based collaborative effort of educators, administrators, and experts to provide consistent benchmarks for learning, from kindergarten through high school. The standards, which are research- and evidence-based, demand an increase in complexity and rigor at each grade level. They set forth what knowledge and skills students need for success in school and prepare them for the challenges they'll later face in college and in the workforce.

The English Language Arts standards encompass five major strands: Reading, Writing, Speaking and Listening, Language, and Media and Technology. Each strand presents its own clear and consistent framework. Taken together, the five strands represent an integrated model of literacy for the twenty-first century.

Grammar for Writing, Common Core Enriched Edition, is designed as an effective tool to address the grade-specific goals of the writing component and language conventions of the standards. ***Grammar for Writing*** weaves the study of language conventions into a range of writing applications, including meeting the critical goal of writing to sources.

Grammar for Writing, Grade 11, focuses students on using precise language, discipline-specific vocabulary, consistent style, and appropriate transitions to

- produce *arguments* that state a claim about a substantive text or issue supported by logical reasoning and sufficient evidence;

- write *informative/explanatory* texts that examine complex ideas and information, using effective organization and concrete examples;

- compose *narratives* about real or imagined experiences using key narrative techniques to engage readers.

Grammar for Writing, Grade 11, develops grammar by helping students

- demonstrate command of standard English grammar and usage;

- exhibit command of standard English capitalization, punctuation, and spelling;

- apply knowledge of language to vary syntax effectively and consult grammar references for guidance as needed.

Each grammar or writing lesson identifies the CCSS it covers and signals when the standards are integrated.

CCSS notes in the side column highlight for teachers the lessons that offer the most targeted, in-depth instruction for covering Grade 11 standards.

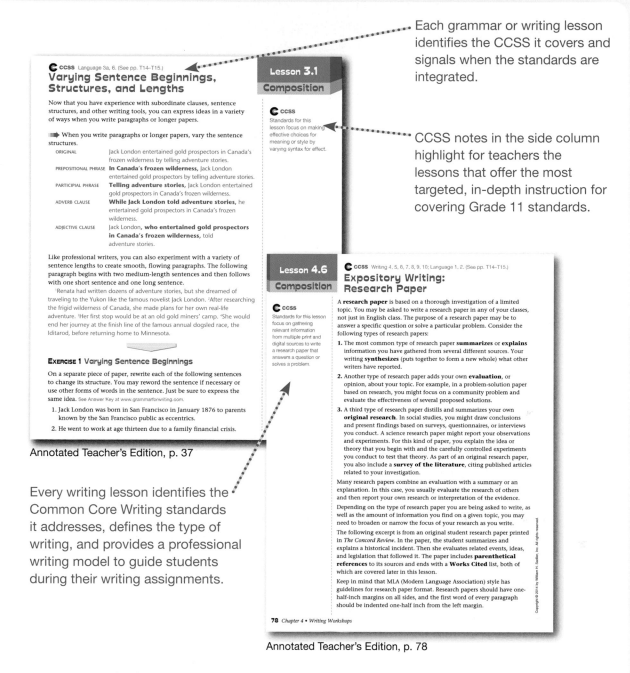

Annotated Teacher's Edition, p. 37

Annotated Teacher's Edition, p. 78

Every writing lesson identifies the Common Core Writing standards it addresses, defines the type of writing, and provides a professional writing model to guide students during their writing assignments.

The following table shows the full text of Grade 11 Writing standards 1–10 and Language (conventions) standards 1–3. The left-hand column shows where each standard is covered in *Grammar for Writing, Common Core Enriched Edition.* Relevant Reading and Speaking and Listening standards are included in the CCSS correlations that appear at the top of each lesson. For CCSS correlations for the entire *Grammar for Writing* program, visit www.grammarforwriting.com.

WRITING STANDARDS
Text Types and Purposes

Chapter and Lesson
(See key below.)

1. Write arguments to support claims in an analysis of substantive topics or texts, using valid reasoning and relevant and sufficient evidence.	2.3, 4.2, 5.2, 5.7, 6.1, 6.6, 6.7, CR6, 7.2, 7.4, CR7, 8.6, 9.5, CR10, 11.1, 12.2
a. Introduce precise, knowledgeable claim(s), establish the significance of the claim(s), distinguish the claim(s) from alternate or opposing claims, and create an organization that logically sequences claim(s), counterclaims, reasons, and evidence.	4.2, 4.3
b. Develop claim(s) and counterclaims fairly and thoroughly, supplying the most relevant evidence for each while pointing out the strengths and limitations of both in a manner that anticipates the audience's knowledge level, concerns, values, and possible biases.	4.2, 4.3
c. Use words, phrases, and clauses as well as varied syntax to link the major sections of the text, create cohesion, and clarify the relationships between claim(s) and reasons, between reasons and evidence, and between claim(s) and counterclaims.	4.2, 4.3
d. Establish and maintain a formal style and objective tone while attending to the norms and conventions of the discipline in which they are writing.	4.2
e. Provide a concluding statement or section that follows from and supports the argument presented.	4.2, 4.3
2. Write informative/explanatory texts to examine and convey complex ideas, concepts, and information clearly and accurately through the effective selection, organization, and analysis of content.	4.4, 4.7, 13.1
a. Introduce a topic; organize complex ideas, concepts, and information so that each new element builds on that which precedes it to create a unified whole; include formatting (e.g., headings), graphics (e.g., figures, tables), and multimedia when useful to aiding comprehension.	2.3, 4.4
b. Develop the topic thoroughly by selecting the most significant and relevant facts, extended definitions, concrete details, quotations, or other information and examples appropriate to the audience's knowledge of the topic.	2.2, 4.4
c. Use appropriate and varied transitions and syntax to link the major sections of the text, create cohesion, and clarify the relationships among complex ideas and concepts.	2.3, 4.4
d. Use precise language, domain-specific vocabulary, and techniques such as metaphor, simile, and analogy to manage the complexity of the topic.	4.4
e. Establish and maintain a formal style and objective tone while attending to the norms and conventions of the discipline in which they are writing.	4.4
f. Provide a concluding statement or section that follows from and supports the information or explanation presented (e.g., articulating implications or the significance of the topic).	4.4
3. Write narratives to develop real or imagined experiences or events using effective technique, well-chosen details, and well-structured event sequences.	4.1, 8.1
a. Engage and orient the reader by setting out a problem, situation, or observation and its significance, establishing one or multiple point(s) of view, and introducing a narrator and/or characters; create a smooth progression of experiences or events.	4.1
b. Use narrative techniques, such as dialogue, pacing, description, reflection, and multiple plot lines, to develop experiences, events, and/or characters.	4.1
c. Use a variety of techniques to sequence events so that they build on one another to create a coherent whole and build toward a particular tone and outcome (e.g., a sense of mystery, suspense, growth, or resolution).	4.1
d. Use precise words and phrases, telling details, and sensory language to convey a vivid picture of the experiences, events, setting, and/or characters.	4.1
e. Provide a conclusion that follows from and reflects on what is experienced, observed, or resolved over the course of the narrative.	4.1

Production and Distribution of Writing

4. Produce clear and coherent writing in which the development, organization, and style are appropriate to task, purpose, and audience.	1.2, 2.4, 2.5, 4.1–4.7
5. Develop and strengthen writing as needed by planning, revising, editing, rewriting, or trying a new approach, focusing on addressing what is most significant for a specific purpose and audience.	1.1–1.4, 4.1–4.6
6. Use technology, including the Internet, to produce, publish, and update individual or shared writing products in response to ongoing feedback, including new arguments or information.	4.3, 4.5, 4.6

RW Revising and Editing Worksheets   EW Editing and Proofreading Worksheets   CR Chapter Review   CuR Cumulative Review

Research to Build and Present Knowledge

	Chapter and Lesson
7. Conduct short as well as more sustained research projects to answer a question (including a self-generated question) or solve a problem; narrow or broaden the inquiry when appropriate; synthesize multiple sources on the subject, demonstrating understanding of the subject under investigation.	4.6
8. Gather relevant information from multiple authoritative print and digital sources, using advanced searches effectively; assess the strengths and limitations of each source in terms of the task, purpose, and audience; integrate information into the text selectively to maintain the flow of ideas, avoiding plagiarism and overreliance on any one source and following a standard format for citation.	4.6
9. Draw evidence from literary or informational texts to support analysis, reflection, and research.	4.6
a. Apply *grades 11–12 Reading standards* to literature (e.g., "Demonstrate knowledge of eighteenth-, nineteenth- and early-twentieth-century foundational works of American literature, including how two or more texts from the same period treat similar themes or topics").	4.5
b. Apply *grades 11–12 Reading standards* to literary nonfiction (e.g., "Delineate and evaluate the reasoning in seminal U.S. texts, including the application of constitutional principles and use of legal reasoning [e.g., in U.S. Supreme Court Case majority opinions and dissents) and the premises, purposes, and arguments in works of public advocacy (e.g., The Federalist, presidential addresses]").	4.7
10. Write routinely over extended time frames (time for research, reflection, and revision) and shorter time frames (a single sitting or a day or two) for a range of discipline-specific tasks, purposes, and audiences.	2.2, 2.3, 2.5, 3.4, 4.1–4.7, 5.2, 5.5, 5.6, 5.7, 6.1, 6.6, 6.7, CR6, 7.2, 7.4, 7.5, CR7, 8.1–8.4, 8.6, 9.5, 9.6, 10.3, 10.4, CR10, 11.1, 12.1, 12.2, 13.1, 13.3, 14.1, 14.2, 14.3, 14.5, 15.2, CR15, 16.4

LANGUAGE STANDARDS
Conventions of Standard English

	Chapter and Lesson
1. Demonstrate command of the conventions of standard English grammar and usage when writing or speaking.	1.4, 3.2, 3.3, 3.4, RW3, 4.1–4.7, 5.1–5.8, RW5, CR5, 6.1–6.8, RW6, CR6, 7.1–7.5, RW7, CR7, 8.1–8.6, RW8, CR8, CuR5–8, 9.1–9.6, RW9, CR9, 10.1–10.5, RW10, CR10, 11.2–11.6, RW11, CR11, 12.1, 12.2, 12.4, 12.5, RW12, CR12, CuR9–12, 13.6, EW13, EW14, EW15, EW16
a. Apply the understanding that usage is a matter of convention, can change over time, and is sometimes contested.	11.1, 11.3, 12.3, 12.5
b. Resolve issues of complex or contested usage, consulting references (e.g., *Merriam-Webster's Dictionary of English Usage, Garner's Modern American Usage)* as needed.	11.3, 12.5
2. Demonstrate command of the conventions of standard English capitalization, punctuation, and spelling when writing.	1.4, RW3, 4.1–4.7, RW5, 6.1, 6.5, RW6, RW7, RW8, RW9, RW10, 11.1, RW11, RW12, 13.1–13.6, EW13, CR13, 14.1, 14.2, 14.4, 14.5, 14.6, 14.7, EW14, CR14, 15.1–15.4, EW15, CR15, EW16, CR16, CuR13–16
a. Observe hyphenation conventions.	5.1, 5.4, 14.7, 16.2
b. Spell correctly.	12.1, 16.1–16.4, CR16, CuR13–16

Knowledge of Language

3. Apply knowledge of language to understand how language functions in different contexts, to make effective choices for meaning or style, and to comprehend more fully when reading or listening.	3.5, 3.6, 6.4, 8.6, CR8, 9.5, 14.3, CR14
a. Vary syntax for effect, consulting references (e.g., Tufte's *Artful Sentences)* for guidance as needed; apply an understanding of syntax to the study of complex texts when reading.	3.1

RW Revising and Editing Worksheets   EW Editing and Proofreading Worksheets   CR Chapter Review   CuR Cumulative Review

Five Ways to Use *Grammar for Writing, Common Core Enriched Edition*

Flexible and versatile, **Grammar for Writing** can facilitate a variety of instructional purposes. Teachers may opt to use the program as the core vehicle for delivering language arts instruction, or they may choose to use it as a supplement to meet specific curricular goals and students' needs.

Instructional Use	Key Features and Support
1. **Complete Course**	• Comprehensive coverage of CCSS for writing and language conventions • Research-based instructional approaches • Thorough explanations and abundant examples • Instruction, practice, assessment, and reteaching • Full array of components
2. **Reference Tool**	• Easy two-part organization of chapters and lessons • Complete index of grammar and writing concepts • List of Commonly Confused Words • Online reference tools
3. **Guide for Independent and/or Small Group Learning**	• Clarification of lesson topics • Explanatory charts and graphic organizers • Annotated Professional Models and Student Writing Models • Activities for Working Together • Strategic hints, tips, and reminders
4. **Source of Review and Practice**	• Engaging and effective exercises for every lesson • Meaningful student-centered online practice • Writing Workshops, including writing to sources • Chapter Review activities • Revising and Editing Worksheets • Editing and Proofreading Worksheets • Cumulative Review activities
5. **Test Preparations**	• SAT/ACT practice section • Tests in standardized-test formats • Practice Test in every Chapter Review • Additional assessment online and in Test Booklet • Test-taking tips

Program Components—Print

Student Edition

The Student Edition of this comprehensive grammar and writing program helps all learners meet Common Core State Standards (CCSS) for English Language Arts. Its chapters provide an organized path to help students master increasingly sophisticated core skills in grammar, usage, punctuation, capitalization, and spelling—all in service to effective written communication.

Key features of the print edition include:

- Teaching of the fundamental steps of the Writing Process

- Varied Writer's Workshop Assignments that clearly define task, audience, and purpose

- Sidebar tips, writing models, and editing worksheets

- Frequent assessment options to evaluate ongoing progress via Chapter Review and Cumulative Review exercises

Annotated Teacher Edition

The Annotated Teacher Edition that accompanies the program is a rich source for CCSS instruction, convenient on-page answers and annotations, as well as helpful tips and strategies for efficient lesson planning, classroom management, and assessment.

Key elements of the ATE include:

- CCSS-targeted instructional notes and standards

- Writing Process guidelines

- Support for English Language Learners and Striving Learners

Test Booklet (separate purchase)

The Test Booklet extends testing and assessment opportunities that parallel the chapters in the Student Edition. It includes comprehensive chapter tests that follow typical standardized test formats: error recognition and correction. A Diagnostic Test helps teachers identify problem areas and address individual needs; a Mastery Test augments the assessments found in the Student Edition. A separate Test Book Answer Key is provided online for ease of scoring.

Extra Practice Exercise Pages present lesson-by-lesson exercises similar to those that appear in the print version. Teachers may assign these to individuals or groups as needed for practice, homework, or assessment.

Student Edition Answer Keys exist for each chapter. In cases where answers may vary, full sample answers or written responses appear.

A **Writing Rubric** is a checklist that can help identify students' performance levels. Note that the rubric is generic so that it can be applied to all types of essays. The rubric is based on a six-point scale, but you may find that, in your own classroom, a four-point scale, beginning at Level 4, is more suitable. At the beginning of the semester, share this rubric with your students as a handout they can use to guide their writing.

Extra Practice
Exercises,
Lesson 10.3

Portfolio Projects are multiple-step assignments designed to give students further practice with research, writing, grammar, usage, and mechanics. Each chapter-based project begins with a research component as students use credible Web sites to find information on their topic. Then students work through each step of the writing process, including prewriting, drafting, revising, editing, proofreading, and publishing. For some portfolio projects, students will be expected to work independently. For others, students may be required to work with a writing partner or in small groups.

Interactive SAT/ACT Worksheets are sets of questions that serve as a guide for students to use as they prepare to take these standardized tests. These worksheets provide extra practice for grammar-based ACT questions and SAT topics, such as Identifying Sentence Errors, Improving Sentences, and Improving Paragraphs.

The **Pacing Guide** offers teachers a plan for using *Grammar for Writing, Common Core Enriched Edition,* as a complete course.

The Role of Grammar in Improving Students' Writing

by Beverly Ann Chin, Ph.D.

Grammar is the sound, structure, and meaning system of language. All languages have grammar, and each language has its own grammar. People who speak the same language are able to communicate because they intuitively know the grammar system of that language—that is, the rules of making meaning. Students who are native speakers of English already know English grammar. They recognize the sounds of English words, the meanings of those words, and the different ways of putting words together to make meaningful sentences.

However, while students may be effective speakers of English, they need guidance to become effective writers. They need to learn how to apply their knowledge of grammatical concepts from oral language to written language.

Effective grammar instruction shows students what they already know about grammar, and it helps them apply this knowledge of language and its conventions as they write. By connecting their knowledge of oral language to written language, teachers can demystify abstract grammatical terminology so that students can write—and read—with greater competence and confidence.

What Does Research Say About Grammar and the Teaching of Writing?

Strong research evidence suggests that the most beneficial way of helping students improve their mastery of grammar in writing is to use students' writing as the basis for discussing grammatical concepts. Researchers agree that it is more effective to teach punctuation, sentence variety, and usage in the context of writing than to approach the topic by teaching isolated skills (Calkins, 1980; DiStefano and Killion, 1984; Harris, 1962).

As students revise and edit their writing, teachers can provide grammar instruction that guides students in their attempts to identify and correct problems in sentence structure and usage. For example, if a teacher sees that many students are writing sentences containing misplaced modifiers, the teacher can present a minilesson on this concept using examples from student writing. The teacher can have students edit their own and each others' drafts for this problem.

Integrating grammar instruction into the revising and editing process helps students make immediate applications, thus allowing them to see the relevance of grammar in their own writing.

To What Specific Aspects of Writing Does Grammar Contribute?

Because writing is a complex activity for many students, teachers should focus on the grammatical concepts that are essential for the clear communication of meaning.

Research on the teaching of grammar since the early 1900s shows that grammar instruction that is separate from writing instruction does not improve students' writing competence (Braddock and others, 1963; Hillocks, 1986). In addition, research indicates that the transfer of formal grammar instruction to writing is not applicable to larger elements of composition. Through detailed studies of students' writing, Shaughnessy (1977) concludes that the best grammar instruction is one that gives the greatest return for the least investment of time. Shaughnessy advocates four important grammatical concepts: the sentence, inflection, tense, and agreement. She recommends that teachers encourage students to examine grammatical errors in their own writing. She also cautions teachers not to overemphasize grammatical terminology to the detriment of students' ability to understand and apply the concepts.

Weaver (1998) proposes a similar approach to teaching grammar in the context of writing. She writes, "What all students need . . . is guidance in understanding and applying those aspects of grammar that are most relevant to writing."

In a chart as reproduced here, Weaver proposes five grammatical concepts that enable writers to show improvement in sentence revision, style, and editing.

A minimum of grammar for maximum benefits

1. Teaching concepts of subject, verb, sentence, clause, phrase, and related concepts for editing
2. Teaching style through sentence combining and sentence generating
3. Teaching sentence sense through the manipulation of syntactic elements
4. Teaching both the power of dialects and the dialects of power
5. Teaching punctuation and mechanics for convention, clarity, and style

(Weaver, 1998, pp. 21–23)

Rather than striving to teach all grammatical concepts to all students, teachers should prioritize and provide instruction on the grammatical elements that most affect their students' ability to write effectively. Teachers should also be sensitive to individual students' readiness to learn and apply grammatical concepts.

How Does Sentence-Combining Improve Writing?

Sentence combining is the strategy of joining short sentences into longer, more complex sentences. As students engage in sentence-combining activities, they learn how to vary sentence structure in order to change meaning and style. Numerous studies (Mellon, 1969; O'Hare, 1973; Cooper, 1975; Shaughnessy, 1977; Hillocks, 1986; Strong, 1986) show that the use of sentence combining is an effective method for improving students' writing. The value of sentence combining is most evident as students recognize the effect of sentence variety (beginnings, lengths, complexities) in their own writing.

Hillocks (1986) stated that "sentence combining practice provides writers with systematic knowledge of syntactic possibilities, the access to which allows them to sort through alternatives in their heads as well as on paper and to choose those which are most apt" (150). Research also shows that sentence combining is more effective than freewriting in enhancing the quality of student writing (Hillocks, 1986).

Hillocks and Smith (1991) show that systematic practice in sentence combining can increase students' knowledge of syntactic structures as well as improve the quality of their sentences, particularly when stylistic effects are discussed as well. Sentence-combining exercises can be either written or oral, structured or unstructured. Structured sentence-combining exercises give students more guidance in the ways to create the new sentences; unstructured sentence-combining exercises allow for more variation, but they still require students to create logical, meaningful

sentences. Hillocks (1986) reports that, in many studies, sentence-combining exercises produce significant increases in students' sentence-writing maturity.

Given Noguchi's (1991) analysis that grammar choices affect writing style, sentence combining is an effective method that helps students develop fluency and variety in their own writing style. Students can discover sentence variety, length, parallelism, and other syntactic devices by comparing their sentences with sentences from other writers. They also discover the decisions writers make when they revise sentences for their effect on readers.

Teachers can design their own sentence-combining activities by using short sentences from student writing or other appropriate sources. For example, teachers who notice many choppy sentences in students' writing can place these sentences on an overhead for all their students to read. Teachers can then ask different students to combine orally the short sentences in a variety of ways. As students share their different sentence combinations, their teacher can show students how they are naturally applying grammatical concepts such as clauses, phrases, modification, conjunctions, appositives, antecedents, and verb forms.

By participating in oral and written sentence-combining activities, students discover the relationships among meaning, sentence structure, usage, and punctuation. When presented as a revising strategy, sentence-combining activities help students identify short, choppy sentences in their own writing, leading them to combine their ideas in more fluid and sophisticated ways. As students generate more complex sentences from shorter sentences, they discover how the arrangement of phrases and clauses affects meaning and their readers.

What Strategies Can Teachers Use to Teach *Grammar for Writing*?

Grammar instruction is most naturally integrated during the revising, editing, and proofreading phases of the writing process. After students have written their first drafts and feel comfortable with the ideas and organization of their writing, teachers may wish to employ various strategies to help students see grammatical concepts as language choices that can enhance their writing purpose.

For example, teachers can help students revise for effective word choices in a writing conference. As the teacher and student discuss the real audience(s) for the writing, the teacher can ask the student to consider how formal or informal the style of writing should be. The teacher can remind the student that all people vary their level of language (formal to informal) in oral conversations, depending on their listeners and the speaking context. The teacher can then help the student identify words that change the level of formality of the writing.

Teachers can help students revise boring, monotonous sentences by having a partner read aloud the writing to the student writer. As the partner reads the writing aloud to the writer, both the partner and the writer can recognize when too many sentences begin with "It is" or "There are." Both the partner and the writer can discuss ways to vary the sentence beginnings. After the writer revises the sentences, the partner can read the sentences aloud, and both can discuss the effectiveness of the revision.

Teachers can help students edit from passive voice to active voice by presenting a minilesson. In editing groups, students can exchange papers and look for verbs that often signal the passive voice, such as "was" and "been." When students find these verbs, they can read the sentence aloud to their partners and discuss whether the voice is passive and, if so, if the sentence might be strengthened with an active-voice verb. The student writer can decide which voice is most effective and appropriate for the writing purpose and audience.

Teachers can help students become better proofreaders through writing groups. Based on the writing abilities of students, teachers can assign different proofreading tasks to specific individuals in each group. For example, one person in the group can proofread for spelling errors, another person for agreement errors, another person for fragments and run-ons, and another person for punctuation errors. As students develop increasing skill in proofreading, they can become responsible for more proofreading areas. Collaborating with classmates in writing partner groups helps students improve their own grammar skills as well as understand the importance of grammar as a tool for effective communication.

As teachers integrate grammar instruction into writing instruction, they should use the grammar terms that make sense to the students. By incorporating grammar terms naturally into the processes of revising, editing, and proofreading, teachers help students understand and apply grammar purposefully to their own (student) writing. Strategies such as writing conferences, partnership writing, grammar minilessons, and peer response groups are all valuable methods for integrating grammar into writing instruction.

How Does the Teaching of Grammar Relate to the Common Core State Standards?

The Common Core State Standards Initiative (2010) published the *Common Core State Standards for English Language Arts & Literacy in History/Social Studies, Science, and Technical Subjects* to "help ensure that all students are college and career ready in literacy no later than the end of high school" (p. 3). The standards offer an integrated model of literacy through Reading, Writing, Speaking and Listening, and Language strands. Specifically, Writing and Language standards combine writing and grammar skills to help students demonstrate literacy and communicate effectively across content areas:

Writing 4: Produce clear and coherent writing in which the development, organization, and style are appropriate to task, purpose, and audience (p. 46).
Language 3: Apply knowledge of language to understand how language functions in different contexts, to make effective choices for meaning or style, and to comprehend more fully when reading or listening (p. 54).

According to the standards:

To be college- and career-ready writers, students must take task, purpose, and audience into careful consideration, choosing words, information, structures, and formats deliberately. They need to know how to combine elements of different kinds of writing . . . to produce complex and nuanced writing. (p. 41)

To be college and career ready in language, students must have firm control over the conventions of standard English. At the same time, they must come to appreciate that language is at least as much a matter of craft as of rules and be able to choose words, syntax, and punctuation to express themselves and achieve particular functions and rhetorical effects. (p. 51)

Based on an initiative by the Council of Chief State School Officers and the National Governors Association, the Common Core State Standards seek not only to develop college and career readiness, but also to "lay out a vision of what it means to be a literate person in the twenty-first century" (p. 3).

In other words, these standards prepare students to use their grammar and writing skills in college, the workforce, and beyond.

References

Braddock, R., Lloyd-Jones, R., & Schoer, L. *Research in Written Composition.* Urbana, IL: National Council of Teachers of English, 1963.

Calkins, L. M. "When Children Want to Punctuate: Basic Skills Belong in Context." *Language Arts* 57 (1980): 567–73.

Cooper, C. "Research Roundup: Oral and Written Composition." *English Journal* (1975): 64, 72.

DiStefano, P. & Killion, J. "Assessing Writing Skills Through a Process Approach." *English Education* 16, no. 4 (1984): 203–7.

Harris, R. J. "An Experimental Inquiry into the Functions and Value of Formal Grammar in the Teaching of Written English to Children Aged Twelve to Fourteen." Ph.D. diss., University of London, 1962.

Hillocks, G., Jr. *Research on Written Composition: New Directions for Teaching.* Urbana, IL: ERIC Clearinghouse on Reading and Communication Skills and the National Conference on Research in English, 1986.

Hillocks, G., Jr., & Smith, M. "Grammar and Usage." In *Handbook of Research on Teaching the English Language Arts*, edited by J. Flood, J. M. Jensen, D. Lapp, & J. R. Squire, 591–603. New York: Macmillan, 1991.

Mellon, J. C. *Transformational Sentence-Combining: A Method for Enhancing the Development of Syntactic Fluency in English Composition.* NCTE Research Report No. 10. Urbana, IL: National Council of Teachers of English, 1969.

National Governors Association Center for Best Practices and Council of Chief State School Officers. *Common Core State Standards for English Language Arts & Literacy in History/Social Studies, Science, and Technical Subjects.* Washington, D.C.: National Governors Association Center for Best Practices and Council of Chief State School Officers. 2010.

Noguchi, R. R. *Grammar and the Teaching of Writing: Limits and Possibilities.* Urbana, IL: National Council of Teachers of English, 1991.

O'Hare, F. *Sentence-Combining: Improving Student Writing Without Formal Grammar Instruction.* Urbana, IL: National Council of Teachers of English, 1973.

Shaughnessy, M. P. *Errors and Expectations: A Guide for the Teacher of Basic Writing.* New York: Oxford University Press, 1977.

Strong, W. *Creative Approaches to Sentence Combining.* Urbana, IL: ERIC and the National Council of Teachers of English, 1986.

Weaver, C. *Lessons to Share on Teaching Grammar in Context.* Portsmouth, NH: Heinemann, 1998.

Additional full-length, research-based articles and professional development videos by Beverly Ann Chin, Ph.D., are available at www.grammarforwriting.com.

Writing for College and Career Readiness

Mastery of the Common Core State Standards for Writing and Language enables students to communicate effectively in college and the workforce. For students, this means exhibiting the ability to produce a range of writing products, while demonstrating a strong command of the conventions of standard English. College- and career-ready students need to be able to demonstrate the following criteria.

Work Independently

Students can work independently to prepare for and complete a variety of writing tasks. They can examine and convey complex information, use narrative techniques to develop real or imagined experiences, and build a convincing argument that presents evidence-based claims and relevant counterclaims fairly. They are able to find and use a range of resources, including teachers, peers, and print and digital reference materials, as support during the writing process.

Adapt Writing

Students can recognize the appropriate style, audience, and purpose for each task and adjust their writing accordingly. They can effectively use different kinds of evidence based on the assignment's mode and purpose.

Students are also prepared to combine elements from different modes as they write. For instance, an argument may use a narrative technique to effectively persuade readers.

Incorporate Text Evidence

Students can cite specific and relevant text evidence to support their own ideas and to show proficiency in new content areas. They can use sound reasoning to gather information, evaluate sources, and synthesize source material accurately and effectively as they write to sources.

Use Technology Wisely

Students can use technology, including the Internet and digital media, to enhance their research and writing. They can efficiently use online search engines and recognize credible Web-based resources. They are able to integrate digital and print sources strategically and appropriately to support their own ideas.

Step-by-Step Revising, Editing, and Proofreading

Many students might be satisfied with turning in their first draft as a final paper. Help them to understand that the revising, editing, and proofreading stages in the writing process raise the standards for their own writing. What they learn from repeated practice in revising and editing sticks; over the course of a year, students produce better-organized, better-written first drafts based on what they have learned through revising and editing.

Note that this series distinguishes between revising and editing—two steps that many teachers lump together as revising. We have separated these steps because it is hard for students to look critically at a piece of writing and see everything at once. Encourage students to create and use a checklist for each stage of the revising, editing, and proofreading process.

Revising

To be college and career ready, students must be able to objectively evaluate and revise their own writing. Revising is concerned with ideas and unity, organization and coherence, sentence variety, and word choice (see the four-step strategy for revising

> **CCSS** Writing 5; Language 6. (See pp. T14–T15.)
>
> ## Revising
>
> ➤ When you **revise**, you shape your draft into its almost-final form.
>
> When you revise a draft, you reshape and rewrite your material to make it clearer, more focused, and easier to understand. Revision may involve adding new content, deleting redundant thoughts or phrases, or changing the organization of your information.
>
> Reread your paper four times—once for ideas and unity, once for organization and coherence, once for sentence variety, and once for word choice. Use the strategies that follow as a checklist to make sure your ideas and presentation are clear.
>
> ### REVISING STRATEGIES
>
> 1. **Ideas and Unity** Does your paper adequately summarize your main ideas? Do you need to add or cut supporting details? Do you need more background information? Is everything relevant, or related, to your main idea(s), or have you wandered off track?
>
> 2. **Organization and Coherence** Do you grab the reader's attention with an interesting opening sentence? Is information presented in a logical order—that is, an order that makes sense to the reader? If not, change the order of paragraphs to present information differently. Would adding transition words help? Does the last sentence bring closure to the writing?
>
> 3. **Sentence Variety** Do your sentences read smoothly? (Try reading them aloud.) Have you varied sentence beginnings, lengths, and structures? Can you combine sentences with related ideas within a paragraph? Are ideas expressed clearly?
>
> 4. **Word Choice** Have you used words that are too general or vague? If so, replace them with more precise words. Have you used a cliché or an overworked word (such as *great*, *nice*, or *bad*)? If so, find fresh words to express your ideas. (You might want to use a thesaurus to find synonyms.) Does your writing sound stilted with too many difficult vocabulary words? Have you used appropriate vocabulary for your intended audience? Have you explained or defined any technical terms?
>
> **Lesson 1.3**
> **Composition**
>
> **CCSS**
> Standards for this lesson focus on improving writing by revising and rewriting, focusing on changes appropriate to purpose and audience.
>
> **Enriching Your Vocabulary**
>
> The adjective *redundant* means "using more words than needed; wordy; unnecessary to the meaning." It comes from a Latin word, *redundare*, meaning "to overflow," and it has a connotation of overwhelming readers with unnecessary and irrelevant information.
>
> *Chapter 1 • The Writing Process* **15**

Annotated Teacher's Edition, p. 15

on p. 15). The revising stage encourages students to read through their drafts four separate times, concentrating on only one of these issues with each reading.

As students revise, encourage them to keep their audience, task, and purpose in mind. Ask them to think about whether their development, organization, and style are appropriate and effective. A writing partner or revising checklist may help students see their own writing more objectively.

Editing

Students must be able to demonstrate a firm command over the conventions of standard English both in college and in the workplace. The editing stage involves recognizing and correcting mistakes in grammar and usage (see the editing questions on p. 18). Students should be prepared to edit their own writing and the drafts of their writing partners.

Suggest that students let their first draft sit a while so they can approach it with "fresh eyes." Before they share their drafts with one or more writing partners, encourage them to do a round of self-editing. Remind students that the grammar and usage lessons in this book can serve as a guide as they identify and correct their own errors.

Proofreading

To demonstrate readiness for college and career, students need to be skilled in applying their knowledge of language through careful proofreading. Proofreading refers to checking for and correcting errors in spelling, capitalization, and punctuation (encourage students to use the proofreading symbols on p. 19). Over the course of the year, students will practice this skill by

proofreading their own drafts and those of their peers.

Remind students that proofreading is usually the final step before publishing, or sharing their writing with others. Students should focus on each word and punctuation mark of each sentence as they read. Encourage them to team up with a writing partner or form small writing groups to check for any errors they may have missed in their own writing.

EXERCISE 24 Organize and Draft Your Essay

Start writing anywhere in the essay, focusing on two or three of your most important points. Don't concentrate on writing perfect sentences. Just get your ideas down in sentence and paragraph form so you'll have something to revise. Feel free to add new ideas as you write. You can sort out ideas, reorganize, and add or delete words, phrases, and sentences later. Answers will vary. Students should refer to Lesson 1.2 for drafting strategies.

EXERCISE 25 Revise and Title Your Essay

Let the draft sit for awhile. After you reread your essay, develop a title that leads the reader to your claim or simply states the name of the play. Then use the four-step revising strategy suggested in Lesson 1.3. Read for ideas and unity, organization and coherence, sentence variety, and appropriate word choice for your purpose and audience. As you and your writing partners revise your draft, ask questions such as those that follow.

Is the essay coherent, well organized, and easy to follow? Are the general statements clear and concise? Do you cite specific lines from the play to back up each point you make in the essay? Does every point you make in the essay bolster your claim? Is everything unified (directly related to the claim)? Answers will vary.

EXERCISE 26 Edit and Publish Your Essay

Double-check each quotation for accuracy, including punctuation. When you are satisfied that you have corrected all errors in grammar, usage, punctuation, capitalization, and spelling, exchange papers with a partner to check for any errors you may have missed.

- If you and several of your classmates write about the same play—or plays in the same genre or historical period—form groups to read your classmates' essays, and then comment on them. After one of you reads an analysis to the group out loud, elicit questions and disagreements from your audience.

- You may wish to bind the essays into a book of drama analysis or make them available in an online collection for other students and English teachers to read. Answers will vary. Students should refer to Lesson 1.4 for proofreading strategies and publishing suggestions.

Chapter 4 • Writing Workshops **77**

Annotated Teacher's Edition, p. 77

Differentiating Instruction

To support students whose first language is not English, teachers must often differentiate instruction. Similarly, teachers may need to accommodate native English speakers as they strive for mastery. Both groups respond well to many of the same techniques, such as consistent modeling, extended repetition, and a slower pace. Research supports the specific methods shown below for helping English learners succeed. The charts on the following pages contain differentiating instruction for Chapters 1–12. For differentiating instruction for Chapters 13–16, visit www.grammarforwriting.com.

Develop Vocabulary

- Model correct pronunciation that students echo.

- Invite students to identify examples.

- Vary activities to increase exposure to new words.

- Encourage students to use new vocabulary in conversation.

Apply Knowledge

- Encourage students to make and use flash cards.

- Clarify complex grammatical concepts with real-world examples.

- Model out loud to demonstrate sensible and logical strategies.

- Use gestures, diagrams, and graphic organizers.

- Connect new ideas to previously mastered concepts.

- Guide students to anticipate and avoid errors.

Incorporate Other Strategies

- Say **Yes,** not **No,** to model and support understanding and correct usage for English learners and striving students. For example, "Yes, Juana, a conjunction joins sentences."

- Form pairs and small groups to increase students' comfort level when they respond aloud. Encourage them to discuss and complete tasks together.

- Invite students to use their broad experiences and knowledge to act as peer teachers. Have them write on the board, demonstrate or provide examples, explain a concept, or describe a strategy or process.

Chapter 1

Lesson	English Learners	Striving Learners
Lesson 1.1	Tell students that the prefix *pre-* means "before." Encourage students to share strategies they know or have used in this introductory stage.	Explain that gathering ideas *before* writing makes the process smoother. Practice *brainstorming*, *freewriting*, and *clustering* in small groups.
Lesson 1.2	Explain that *audience* comes from a Latin root for "to hear" and that a writer's audience is anyone who reads his or her work.	Pronounce and clarify the terms given in the lesson. Go over the drafting strategies, and help students identify each one in the writing model.
Lesson 1.3	Highlight words with the prefix *re-*, meaning "to do again": *revise, reshape, rewrite, reread.* Point out that these terms *reinforce* this part of the writing process.	Make a flow chart or checklist with students to summarize the writing process to this point. Help them recall the proper terms and list them in a sensible order.
Lesson 1.4	Go over the terms used in the editing process. Clarify the meaning of and symbol for common proofreading symbols.	Suggest that students edit in several passes, addressing only one or two types of corrections per pass. Encourage peer reviewers to work together.

Chapter Vocabulary

- prewriting
- writer's notebook
- brainstorming
- freewriting
- clustering
- mapping
- webbing
- *What If?* questions
- organizing
- outline
- word choice
- audience
- purpose
- drafting
- revise
- unity
- coherence
- sentence variety
- word choice
- edit
- proofread
- spelling
- capitalization
- punctuation
- sentence correctness
- usage
- publishing

Chapter Vocabulary

- unity
- main idea
- topic sentence
- elaboration
- facts
- statistics
- quotations
- definitions
- anecdotes
- examples
- reasons
- coherent
- chronological order
- spatial order
- order of importance
- logical order
- purpose
- sensory details
- mood
- narrative
- expository
- comparison/ contrast
- cause and effect
- persuasive
- evidence
- call to action
- essay
- introduction
- conclusion

Chapter 2

Lesson	English Learners	Striving Learners
Lesson 2.1	Create a word web around *unity* with its related forms *unit, unite, union,* and *unique.* Link these words to the Spanish words *unidad* and *unión.*	Read and discuss the Skills for Maintaining Unity together, linking them to the writing model. Help students understand how each term is used.
Lesson 2.2	Provide examples from print or digital sources to illustrate the nine types of details writers can use to elaborate or develop a main idea.	Have pairs work together on Exercise 3 to organize ideas and plan. Then have individuals write paragraphs alone.
Lesson 2.3	Invite pairs to discuss each of the five plans of order, using their own words (or languages). Clarify that one method is not better than another.	Focus on the chart of transitional words and expressions on page 28. Model for students how to create sentences with some of those transitions.
Lesson 2.4	Present related forms of the four purposes for writing: *descriptive* (to describe, tell about); *narrative* (to narrate, tell a story); *expository* (to expose, explain); and *persuasive* (to persuade, convince).	Have students write each of the four purposes for writing on the front of an index card. On the back, they can record its goals, key terms, or suggested organizational plan.
Lesson 2.5	Role-play an audition to model the parts of an essay. Ask a volunteer "actor" to explain what he or she will perform (introduction), give details as support (body), and close with a memorable remark (conclusion).	Provide a three-part graphic organizer students can use to note ideas for the introduction, body, and conclusion of an essay. Reiterate that the essay should support a claim.

Chapter 3

Lesson	English Learners	Striving Learners
Lesson 3.1	Pronounce *vary* and *very* to highlight their different vowel sounds. Link *vary* to related forms: *various, variety, varied, variable.*	Guide students to compare each varied sentence structure on page 37 with the original. Stress that the meaning of the sentence remained the same.
Lesson 3.2	Help students sort conjunctive adverbs by function: continuing/ changing direction, sequencing, emphasizing, comparing/contrasting, concluding.	Review sentences with simple subjects and simple verbs to lead into the combined sentences of this lesson.
Lesson 3.3	Pronounce the subordinating conjunctions on page 41, and have volunteers use them in sentences. Encourage pairs to discuss Exercises 5 and 6.	Identify the five relative pronouns that introduce adjective clauses: *that, which, who, whom, whose.*
Lesson 3.4	Have a volunteer read aloud the original sentences in each example. Analyze each combined sentence together.	Contrast sentences and phrases, pointing out that phrases add meaning but cannot stand alone because they lack both a subject and a verb.
Lesson 3.5	Concede that short sentences are easier to read, write, and understand, and demonstrate ways to express ideas in more advanced ways.	Present each set of choppy sentences on flash cards students can rearrange until they find an effective way to combine them.
Lesson 3.6	Define *wordiness* as using more words than needed. Go over each model together to clarify how it eliminates wordiness.	Assign Exercise 11 to pairs, asking students to take turns reading each sentence aloud and then work as a team to revise.

Chapter Vocabulary

- compound subject
- compound verb
- compound sentence
- coordinating conjunction
- correlative conjunction
- conjunctive adverb
- transitional expressions
- subordinate clause
- subordinating conjunction
- adjective clause
- adverb clause
- wordiness

Chapter Vocabulary

- personal narrative
- character
- setting
- chronological order
- sensory language
- persuasive essay
- argument
- claim
- thesis statement
- evidence
- logical appeals
- loaded words
- counterclaims (counter-arguments)
- emotional appeals
- transitions
- expository writing
- problem-solution essay
- editorial
- literary analysis
- research paper
- summarize
- synthesize
- works cited
- primary sources
- secondary sources
- documentation
- timed essay
- prompt

Chapter 4

Lesson	English Learners	Striving Learners
Lesson 4.1	Clarify that a *personal narrative* is *autobiographical*. It usually covers a single incident and includes details and the writer's reflections.	Have students create a Story Map like the one on page 56. It may benefit students to discuss their idea with a partner before writing.
Lesson 4.2	Define *loaded words, stereotype,* and *overgeneralize.* Clarify that, in writing, an *argument* is a claim supported by evidence, not a fight.	Offer several topics to students who have difficulty coming up with one on their own. Guide them to articulate a precise claim to anchor their essay.
Lesson 4.3	Present other forms of *critical: critic, criticize, criteria, criticism.* Discuss how critical reviews offer opinions supported by analysis of evidence.	Match each paragraph of the model with the Criteria for Movie Reviews. Have students use the table in Exercise 12 to develop their ideas.
Lesson 4.4	Clarify terms as needed. Point out that the writer does not solve the problem but supports the need for action.	Develop a graphic organizer for planning an essay: a box for the problem, a section for notes on evidence, and a box for a call to action.
Lesson 4.5	Discuss the term *playwright* (dramatist). Explain that the suffix *-wright* means "one who builds."	Compare and contrast analyzing drama with writing a critical review (Lesson 4.3). Highlight points that apply only to plays.
Lesson 4.6	Clarify that writing a research paper is usually done in stages over weeks. Help students plan sensible work schedules.	Discuss Strategies 3 and 4 to reinforce the value of using multiple sources and evaluating sources for reliability. Model online searching.
Lesson 4.7	Discuss the idiom *stick to the point.* Clarify that a timed essay must be organized and focused. Stress the value of prewriting.	Clarify that writing a timed essay still involves each step of the writing process: prewriting, drafting, revising, editing, and proofreading.

Chapter 5

Lesson	English Learners	Striving Learners
Lesson 5.1	Tell students that *collective* nouns are precise names for groups. Offer examples, i.e., *pride* of lions.	Focus on opposite groups of nouns to reinforce meaning: *abstract/concrete, common/ proper.*
Lesson 5.2	Explain that the prefix *in-* in *indefinite* means "not." By contrast, *demonstrative* pronouns show specificity.	Clarify that *interrogative* pronouns begin questions whose responses are usually nouns or pronouns. Link to *interrogate.*
Lesson 5.3	Explain that *action* verbs express physical or mental action. By contrast, *linking* verbs express states of being.	Have pairs work together on Exercise 5. Encourage them to look for *all* the verbs or verb phrases in each sentence.
Lesson 5.4	Not all languages use articles, and some use articles that show gender. Have students identify articles in a sample text.	Point out that all proper adjectives must be capitalized. Ask students to generate additional examples of proper adjectives.
Lesson 5.5	Offer simple sentences students can modify by adding an adverb. Model how the same adverb can appear in different positions.	Work through Exercise 10 with students to highlight each adverb and link it to the word it modifies.
Lesson 5.6	Explain that prepositions signal a relationship of time or space. Practice creating prepositional phrases.	Vary Exercise 14 by having students select a sensible preposition and one that creates an illogical sentence.
Lesson 5.7	Point out that conjunctions provide important signals of meaning. *Or* indicates a choice, while *yet* suggests a contrast.	Analyze *correlative* to show the prefix *co-* (together) and the root form *relate* to remind students that correlative conjunctions appear in pairs.
Lesson 5.8	Provide examples to show how part of speech depends on a word's usage.	Use Exercise 19 as a pre-test. Use its results to guide review as necessary.

Chapter Vocabulary

- nouns
- collective nouns
- compound nouns
- pronouns
- personal pronouns
- possessive pronouns
- indefinite pronouns
- demonstrative pronouns
- interrogative pronouns
- relative pronouns
- reflexive pronouns
- intensive pronouns
- verbs
- helping verbs
- adjectives
- indefinite articles
- definite articles
- predicate adjectives
- adverbs
- preposition
- compound prepositions
- conjunctions
- coordinating conjunctions
- correlative conjunctions
- subordinating conjunctions

Chapter Vocabulary

- sentence
- declarative sentence
- imperative sentence
- interrogative sentence
- exclamatory sentence
- sentence fragment
- subject
- predicate
- simple subject
- simple predicate
- inverted sentence
- run-on sentence
- fused sentence
- comma splice
- direct object
- transitive verb
- intransitive verb
- indirect object
- subject complement
- predicate nominative
- predicate adjective
- object complement

Chapter 6

Lesson	English Learners	Striving Learners
Lesson 6.1	Pronounce and define the four types of sentences and the purpose of each. Highlight the expected end mark.	Summarize that a complete sentence must have a subject and verb; express a thought; and begin with a capital letter and have an end mark.
Lesson 6.2	Compare and contrast a *simple/complete* subject and *simple/complete* predicate.	Model how a simple subject and simple predicate alone can form a sentence.
Lesson 6.3	Discuss how each sample fragment on page 119 is revised according to one of the three strategies described.	Model how to apply The Sentence Test to the fragments on page 119. Have students use it in Exercises 5 and 6.
Lesson 6.4	Provide additional examples of inverted sentences, understood subjects, and questions in which students must find the subject.	Alert students that some sentences in Exercise 7 may have compound subjects. Encourage them to underline complete subjects.
Lesson 6.5	Explain that the expression *to run on* means "to keep going."	Revise some of Exercise 9 with students before assigning the rest to pairs.
Lesson 6.6	Help students distinguish *transitive* (action) verbs from *intransitive* (linking) verbs, reminding them that only transitive verbs take objects.	Model using the Step by Step method to find direct and indirect objects.
Lesson 6.7	Review grammar terms as needed and emphasize that linking verbs do not take objects.	For Exercise 13, have students identify the verb and determine the nature of the subject complement.
Lesson 6.8	Reinforce that *object complements* appear only in sentences that use certain verbs. Read the verb list on page 129 together.	In Exercise 15, have students first circle each verb to determine whether it needs an object complement.

Chapter 7

Lesson	English Learners	Striving Learners
Lesson 7.1	Post a list of prepositions students can refer to as they identify phrases. Clearly enunciate key terms, and discuss the examples together.	Begin Exercise 1 together, asking identification questions for each sentence: *Where is the phrase? What is modified? How is it modified?*
Lesson 7.2	Distinguish *appositive* from *positive* (not negative) and from *opposite*. Contrast *essential* (necessary) with *nonessential* (helpful) appositives.	Explain that using an appositive lets writers combine two related sentences into one. Begin Exercise 2 together to model this strategy.
Lesson 7.3	Discuss examples on page 139, helping students distinguish the function of the highlighted word as it is used in the verb phrase and as a participle.	Begin a concept web with students for *verbals*. Focus first on *participles* and *participial phrases*; leave room to add *gerunds* and *infinitives* later.
Lesson 7.4	Emphasize that all gerunds end in *-ing,* but all words that end in *-ing* are not necessarily gerunds. Provide examples.	Add *gerunds* and *gerund phrases* to the *verbals* concept web. Begin Exercise 7 with students to model identifying these verbals.
Lesson 7.5	Relate *infinite* (never-ending) to *infinitive* in the sense that an infinitive is the most basic form of a verb, which can then have many forms and uses.	Analyze Sentence 1 in Exercise 9 together to differentiate the prepositional phrase *to a national park* from the infinitive phrase *to step in the oldest...*

Chapter Vocabulary

- prepositional phrase
- adjective phrase
- adverb phrase
- appositive
- appositive phrase
- essential appositive
- nonessential appositive
- verbal
- participle
- present participle
- past participle
- participial phrase
- gerund
- gerund phrase
- infinitive
- infinitive phrase

Chapter Vocabulary

- independent (main) clause
- compound sentence
- subordinate (dependent) clause
- adjective clause
- relative pronoun
- relative adverb
- essential clause
- nonessential clause
- adverb clause
- subordinating conjunctions
- elliptical adverb clause
- noun clause
- simple sentence
- compound sentence
- complex sentence
- compound-complex sentence
- parallel structure

Chapter 8

Lesson	English Learners	Striving Learners
Lesson 8.1	Pair antonyms *independent/dependent* and *main/subordinate.* Give examples of independent and dependent clauses for students to sort.	Link independent clauses to sentences and subordinate clauses to fragments. In Exercise 1, stress that subordinate clauses must be revised.
Lesson 8.2	Have students form adjective clauses beginning with relative pronouns and adverbs. Use the Editing Tip to model correct placement.	For essential clauses, read aloud the given examples without the clause to emphasize why the clause is crucial to convey meaning.
Lesson 8.3	Read only the subject and predicate from each example to highlight the need for the clarifying information each adverb clause provides.	In examples with elliptical adverb clauses, clarify that words in brackets should be understood by readers and need not be written.
Lesson 8.4	Do Exercise 9, sentence by sentence. First, have students locate the word that introduces a noun clause. Then help them determine meaning.	Assign Exercise 10 before Exercise 9. Guide students to employ a word from the list on page 157 to begin each noun clause.
Lesson 8.5	Point out similarities in and differences between *compound* and *complex* sentences. Explain that a *compound-complex* sentence is a hybrid of both.	Work through the first few sentences of Exercise 13 with students. Then have them complete the rest independently. Share and discuss revisions.
Lesson 8.6	Use the common meaning of *parallel* (corresponding) to make clear its grammatical meaning.	Explain why parallel structure makes content easier to readers to follow and remember.

Chapter 9

Lesson	English Learners	Striving Learners
Lesson 9.1	Compare and contrast *present/present participle* and *past/past participle*. Stress that participle forms require a helping verb.	Use the Editing Tip to help correct a common spoken and written error. Clarify the instructions for Exercise 2.
Lesson 9.2	Ask student groups to review the chart. Then have students identify the present form of verbs based on hearing their irregular past tense forms.	Prepare students for Exercise 3 by doing a similar task verbally. Permit students to consult the chart if needed.
Lesson 9.3	Have students identify irregular verbs with four forms (i.e., *know, knowing, knew, known*).	Provide verbal practice with irregular verb forms to prepare students to complete Exercises 5 and 6.
Lesson 9.4	Read the two verb charts aloud with students. Substitute different verbs to create more examples for each tense.	Focus on consistency of tense. Provide additional inconsistencies and revisions to model clear writing.
Lesson 9.5	Highlight that, in the *active* voice, the subject does the action and that, in the *passive* voice, the subject receives the action.	For Exercise 9, have students first identify each use of passive voice before they rewrite the sentences.
Lesson 9.6	Link *indicative mood* to *indicate* (signal or show) and *imperative mood* to *imperative sentences,* which command or request.	Clarify that verb forms in the *subjunctive mood* can be tricky. Highlight examples of indirectness and wishful thinking, i.e., *If I were king…*

Chapter Vocabulary

- verbs
- regular verbs
- principal parts
- present participle
- past participle
- irregular verbs
- verb tense
- simple tenses
- perfect tenses
- progressive form
- active voice
- passive voice
- indicative mood
- imperative mood
- subjunctive mood

Chapter Vocabulary

- first person
- second person
- third person
- number
- singular subject
- singular verb
- plural subject
- plural verb
- verb phrase
- intervening phrase or clause
- agreement
- indefinite pronoun
- compound subject
- collective nouns

Chapter 10

Lesson	English Learners	Striving Learners
Lesson 10.1	Clarify the grammatical traits of *person*: *first* person speaks; *second* person is spoken to; *third* person is spoken about. Provide examples.	Read aloud the chart with students. Have them replace *dream* and *wish* with other verbs in correct form. Model how to handle intervening clauses.
Lesson 10.2	Help students rank plural indefinite pronouns in relative number order: *few, one, both, several, many.* Repeat with singular indefinite pronouns.	Assign Exercise 4 to small groups to collect a variety of sentences for each phrase. Share and discuss, checking for agreement.
Lesson 10.3	Highlight the choice writers must make in the third rule of compound subject agreement. Provide more examples for student practice.	Have students identify the conjunction in each sentence in Exercise 6; then refer to the Step by Step box to verify the correct verb form.
Lesson 10.4	Clarify the anomaly of nouns that end in -*s* yet are singular. Have students refer to examples in the side column of page 195 as they do Exercise 10.	Model that, to check agreement in an inverted sentence, students should find the subject and verb and rearrange them in typical order.
Lesson 10.5	Highlight that, in the second and fourth rules, even when a work of art or organization's name ends in -*s*, its verb must be in singular form.	Do the first few sentences in Exercise 12 with students to model how to determine the correct verb form.

Chapter 11

Lesson	English Learners	Striving Learners
Lesson 11.1	Model separating compound sentence elements in the samples to verify correct pronoun use. Work through the Step by Step box with students.	Model applying the Step by Step test to the first few sentences of Exercise 1. Then assign the remainder to pairs.
Lesson 11.2	Have students recite singular and plural object pronouns. Help them construct simple sentences using object pronouns correctly.	Work through the Editing Tip with students. Refer them to a list of prepositions to help them avoid making that common error.
Lesson 11.3	Emphasize that the pronouns *who/he* are subject forms and *whom/him* are object forms.	Model how to apply the second Writing Hint before assigning Exercises 5 and 6.
Lesson 11.4	Review rules for subject and object pronouns to help students apply them to appositives with pronouns.	Review Lesson 7.2 on appositives. Model the first few sentences in Exercise 7; then assign the rest to pairs.
Lesson 11.5	Review *antecedent* as the noun or nouns that pronouns refer to. Highlight the antecedent in each sample sentence.	Revisit the singular indefinite pronouns on page 191 to help students choose the correct pronouns to use in Exercises 10 and 11.
Lesson 11.6	Help students visualize the scene of each sample sentence to aid them in recognizing potential confusion. Model think-alouds to clarify examples.	Present each unclear model in isolation. Have a volunteer read it aloud, asking classmates to recognize any confusion and suggest improvements.

Chapter Vocabulary

- subject pronoun
- predicate nominative
- object pronoun
- appositive
- incomplete construction
- antecedent
- gender
- number

Chapter Vocabulary

- degrees of comparison
- positive
- comparative
- superlative
- one- and two-syllable modifiers
- irregular modifiers
- double comparisons
- illogical comparisons
- unclear comparisons
- double negatives
- misplaced modifier
- dangling modifier

Chapter 12

Lesson	English Learners	Striving Learners
Lesson 12.1	Link *positive* to *good*, *comparative* to *better*, and *superlative* to *best*. Chant irregular degrees of comparison words for reinforcement.	Display various adjectives and adverbs for which students can form the degrees of comparison that follow the rules on page 223.
Lesson 12.2	Help students grasp the nuances between *less* and *fewer* by going over the Editing Tip together. Clarify the error of double comparisons.	For Exercises 4 and 5, have students read each sentence twice: first to get its overall meaning, then to ensure that the modifier is in the correct form.
Lesson 12.3	Clarify *illogical* as "not logical," and explain *unclear* comparisons can be misunderstood. Use think-aloud modeling to demonstrate these errors.	Discuss the common error of using double negatives by presenting incorrect examples of them. Have students identify both negatives.
Lesson 12.4	Define the prefix *mis-* as "wrongly." Work together on Exercise 9, helping students find and fix misplaced modifiers.	For each incorrect sentence in Exercise 9, have students explain why it needs fixing. Let partners work together to correct each sentence.
Lesson 12.5	Define *dangle* as "to hang loosely." Offer exaggerated examples to illustrate this often-humorous type of error, and show ways to correct it.	For each sentence in Exercise 11, help students visualize the scene the words describe. Model possible corrections.

For differentiating instruction for Chapters 13–16, visit www.grammarforwriting.com.

Grade 11

Grammar for Writing

Senior Series Consultant

Beverly Ann Chin
Professor of English
University of Montana
Missoula, MT

Series Consultant

Frederick J. Panzer, Sr.
English Dept. Chair, Emeritus
Christopher Columbus High School
Miami, FL

Series Consultant

Charlotte Rosenzweig, Ed. D.
English Dept. Chairperson
Long Beach High School
Long Beach, NY

Series Editor

Phyllis Goldenberg

Ⓢ Sadlier

Reviewers

John Manear
English Dept. Chair
Seton-La Salle High
  School
Pittsburgh, PA

Cary Fuller
English Teacher
Rye Country Day
  School
Rye, NY

Galen Rosenberg
English Dept.
  Coordinator
Los Altos High
  School
Los Altos, CA

Helen Gallagher
English Dept. Chair
Maine East High
  School
Park Ridge, IL

Rose F. Schmitt
Education
  Consultant
Melbourne, FL

Carolyn Waters
Language
  Arts/Reading 7–12
  Supervisor
Cobb County School
  District
Marietta, GA

Roxanne Hoblitt
English Dept. Chair
Belgrade High School
Belgrade, MT

Dr. Muriel Harris
Former Writing Lab
  Director
English Dept.
Purdue University
West Lafayette, IN

Thomas C. Anstett
English Dept. Chair
Lincoln-Way East
  High School
Frankfort, IL

Patricia Stack
English Teacher
South Park High
  School
South Park, PA

Mel Farberman
Former Assistant
  Principal
  Supervision–English
Cardozo High School
Bayside, NY

Wanda Porter
Former English Dept.
  Head
Kamehameha
  Secondary School
Honolulu, HI

Donna Fournier
English Dept. Chair
  and Teacher
Coyle Cassidy
  Memorial High
  School
Taunton, MA

**Katherine R.
Wilson**
Secondary English
  Coordinator, K–12
North Penn School
  District
Lansdale, PA

Student Writers

Michael Arcaro
Scarsdale, NY

Michael Berkowitz
New York, NY

Emily Broxterman
Overland Park, KS

Matisa Childs
Coral Gables, FL

Steve Gangemi
The Lawrenceville
School (a preparatory
school)
Lawrenceville, NJ

Adele Grundies
La Mesa, CA

Keane Kaneakua
Kaneohe, HI

Rudy Lewis
The Lawrenceville
School (a preparatory
school)
Lawrenceville, NJ

**Pia Lindstrom
Luedtke**
Pasadena, CA

Sara McCann
Gig Harbor, WA

Suzanne O'Kelley
Eugene, OR

Rusty Ryan
Cambridge, MA

Sara Wechter
Norwalk, CT

Alex Zane
Pottsville, PA

Acknowledgments

Every good faith effort has been made to locate the owners of copyrighted material to arrange permission to reprint selections. In several cases this has proved impossible.

Thanks to the following for permission to reprint copyrighted materials.

Excerpt from *The Complete Book of Running*, by James Fixx. Copyright © 1977 by James F. Fixx. Used by permission of Random House, Inc.

"Down with Curfews; Up with Children," by Nadine Strossen. From IntellectualCapital.com. Copyright © 1996 by Nadine Strossen. Reprinted by permission of the author.

"Hoot," by Ty Burr. Originally published in *The Boston Globe*, May 5, 2006.

"A Move to Save Coral Reefs." Originally published in *The New York Times*, June 5, 2006.

Excerpt from *Quiet Strength*, by Rosa L. Parks and Gregory J. Reed. Copyright © 1994 by Rosa L. Parks. Used by permission of Zondervan.

Excerpt from "Reform and the Triangle Shirtwaist Company Fire," by Hadley Davis. Copyright © 1998 by *The Concord Review*, 730 Boston Post Road, Suite 24, Sudbury, MA 01776. Reprinted by permission.

Excerpt from *Great Plays: Sophocles to Albee*, third edition, by Morton Bloomfield. Copyright © 1975. Reprinted with permission of Heinle, a division of Thomson Learning: www.thomsonrights.com.

Credits

Cover Art and Design
Quarasan, Inc.

Interior
Art Resource, NY/© 2012 Calder Foundation/Artist Rights Society (ARS), New York: 291 *background*. Corbis/Digital Stock Corporation: 8; Eric Fougere: 21. Neal Farris: 113 *left*. Getty Images/Blend Images: 113 *right*; Chad Baker/Ryan McVay: 203 *bottom*, 221; The Bridgeman Art Library: 21 *background*; Aaron Cobbett: 257 *background*; C Squared Studios: 203 *background*; George Doyle: 291 *left*; Glowimages: 36 *background*; Stuart Gregory: 203 *top*; Sean Justice: 277 *bottom*; Huy Lam: 239; James Squire: 277 *background*. iStockphoto.com/Csaba Fikker: 277 *face inset*; FreezingTime Photography: 149 *background*. Punchstock/Photodisc: 36, 52 top, 133, 169 *background*, 187, 257, 277 *center*; Rubberball: 93; Stockbyte: 52 *bottom*, 169. Used under license from Shutterstock.com/Heather Coleman: 149; Simone Conti: 221 *background*; Marten Czamanske: 52 *background*; Dusan Jankovic: 187 *background*; Slavoljub Pantelic: 133 *background*; Edyta Pawlowska: 8. Veer/CSA Images: 113 *background*.

Dear Student:

As a student, you are constantly being challenged to write correctly and effectively in a variety of subjects. From homework to standardized tests, more and more assignments require you to write in a clear, correct, and persuasive way.

This new *Enriched Edition* of *Grammar for Writing* has been prepared to help you master the writing and language skills you'll need to be an effective writer, and has been designed to ensure college and career readiness for all students.

The writing section of this book takes you through the writing process and contains **Writing Workshops** with instruction and practice in different types of writing, including the kinds of writing called for on standardized tests and the state assessments.

In the grammar section, **Test-Taking Tips** appear in lessons covering the grammar and usage skills most often assessed on tests, and **grammar and usage practice** in standardized-test formats is included as well.

Of course, there are many reasons to write effectively other than to score well on standardized tests and other assessments. People judge you by the way you write and speak. Your use of English is evaluated in the writing you do in school, on job and college applications, and in many different kinds of careers.

No textbook can make writing easy. Good writers work hard and revise their work often to find just the right words to move their audience. Consequently, in *Grammar for Writing,* you will find many exercises called **Write What You Think**. These exercises are designed to help guide you in developing clear, logical arguments to persuade people that your opinion is right. These exercises will sharpen your thinking as well as your writing skills.

No one has to prove that writing is important—it just *is*. But writing can always be improved, and the best way to improve it is to learn and practice the skills and strategies in this book. *Grammar for Writing* presents the rules of grammar as simply as possible; whether you are refreshing your memory or learning the concepts for the first time, you'll be able to understand the rules and *apply* them to your writing.

Grammar for Writing is designed to be used in a variety of ways. You should not, however, write in this hardcover edition. Instead, complete each exercise on a separate piece of paper. Pay careful attention to the directions and to any "Hints" that accompany them. They are meant to help you get the most out of the exercises.

Good Luck!
The Authors

CONTENTS

COMPOSITION

GRAMMAR

* Denotes lessons with skills most commonly assessed on standardized tests.

USAGE

* Denotes lessons with skills most commonly assessed on standardized tests.

* Denotes lessons with skills most commonly assessed on standardized tests.

STANDARDIZED TEST PRACTICE

> ***** Denotes lessons with skills most commonly assessed on standardized tests.

The Writing Process

Prewriting: Gathering Ideas

▸ **Prewriting** refers to all the thinking, planning, and organizing you do before you actually start writing.

To come up with topics to write about, as well as details that elaborate on those topics, try out one or more of the following prewriting strategies.

1. Writer's Notebook Keep a separate notebook or online journal in which you jot down experiences and thoughts about anything that interests you.

Your notebook will be like an album of souvenirs from various musings. You can include quotations, cartoons, poems, and magazine or newspaper articles. Try to jot down the reasons why these items captured your interest. Later on, you can look through your writer's notebook and expand them into writing assignments or essays. Use the following writer's notebook entry as a model.

C **CCSS**

Standards for this lesson focus on developing writing as needed by planning.

WRITING HINT

Some of the prewriting strategies covered in this lesson address the concept of narrowing a topic. Narrowing is a key to successful writing. How can you tell if a topic is too broad, too narrow, or just right?

Writing Model

Wed. 9/17
Gave my campaign speech for class president. Someone in the audience called out, "Are you an innovator, Annette?" Did that person or anyone else understand my 'peer justice' idea? Hope no one noticed my shoes. I almost (but didn't) tripped as I stepped off the platform because the laces were untied! I meant to sound as much a poet as a politician. How did it go? Well, next week's election will tell.

- If you can break down your topic into more than five subtopics, it may be too broad. Consider writing about one of the narrower subtopics.

- If you cannot break your topic down into more than two subtopics, it may be too narrow already. Think more broadly.

2. Brainstorming Focus on a single word or idea, and list everything that comes to mind.

If you're working with a partner or group, have one person act as a recorder. When you've completely run out of ideas, review what you've written, and check or circle those ideas that seem the most promising. Use the brainstorming list on the following page as a model.

> **Writing Model**
>
> ASSIGNMENT: *Choose an issue that you can campaign for in your run for class president. Write about how you can make a difference.*
> BRAINSTORMING NOTES:
> lack of selection in the cafeteria   school lunches
> the most successful junior prom   enthusiasm for yearbook
> potholes in the parking lot and frequent vandalism of student cars
> better communication between administration and students
> wider variety of language courses offered to juniors

3. Freewriting This strategy is similar to brainstorming but involves nonstop writing.

Focus on one word or topic, and don't stop writing for three to five minutes. If you can't think of a new word, keep writing that word until another finds its way into your mind and onto the page. Don't reread, and don't worry about the structure of your sentences or spelling at this point.

> **Writing Model**
>
> TOPIC: *How to win an election*
>
> *Talk with voters; don't walk around school with a sour or bored expression, even on a bad day. What about speeches—are they more effective if they're formal or informal in style, planned or spoken spontaneously? Campaign where voters gather—in the front hall before homeroom. Yes, that's not bad, campaigning. I could focus on the best places to campaign, or all the possible places—that's a big topic. I'll keep it to the best places only.*

4. Clustering (also called **Mapping** or **Webbing**) Create a cluster diagram to explore a topic, to break a large topic into smaller parts, or to gather details.

First, write your topic (or any word or phrase) in the middle of a piece of paper, and then circle it. Around the circled topic, write subtopics or related words and phrases. Circle each new word or phrase, and connect it to your original topic by drawing a line. Each new word or phrase may have subtopics, too. Keep going until you run out of thoughts. Refer to the example on the following page.

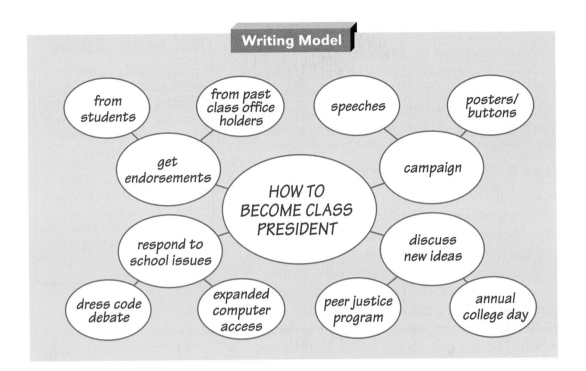

Writing Model

from students

from past class office holders

speeches

posters/ buttons

get endorsements

campaign

HOW TO BECOME CLASS PRESIDENT

respond to school issues

discuss new ideas

dress code debate

expanded computer access

peer justice program

annual college day

5. *What If?* Questions Write questions about subjects that interest you in order to explore a range of topics.

You might ask yourself *What If?* questions about a broad topic that you need to narrow down. For example, if a teacher assigns you the general topic "Issues at School," you might make a list of questions similar to the following:

For a discussion of outlining, audience, and purpose, see **Composition**, Lesson 1.2.

Writing Model

What if students were required to wear school uniforms?

What if the school cafeteria offered a vegetarian menu?

What if students acted as teachers and administrators for a day?

Try combining a few of the prewriting strategies. For example, a notebook entry or a *What if?* question might lead you to a topic for writing. You might brainstorm or freewrite to narrow down the topic or to think about related details; then you could organize your thoughts by clustering.

EXERCISE 1 Starting a Writer's Notebook

Start a writer's notebook or online journal. Create two entries—one for yesterday and one for today. Jot down notes about your experiences, thoughts, and observations for both days. For this assignment, you should write notes that you'd be willing to share with a writing group.

Encourage students to make a dedicated writer's notebook to keep throughout the school year.

EXERCISE 2 Exploring a Topic with Freewriting

After you've made entries in your writer's notebook for two days, choose one of the topics. Write a title for the topic on the top of a piece of paper. Then write nonstop for three minutes. **Hint:** If you have trouble getting started, write and repeat the phrase "I think" until you complete the sentence with an idea. Repeat the process whenever you become stuck. Remember, don't be concerned about your spelling, grammar, or sentence structure at this point. Students' topics will vary.

WRITING HINT

You'll come up with your most compelling writing when you're writing about something that sparks your interest or curiosity. As you think about topics to write about, ask yourself questions such as, "What do I want to know more about?"or "Why am I fascinated with this issue?"

EXERCISE 3 Thinking of Topic Ideas

For each of the following items, think of three or four topics to write about. Use at least three different prewriting strategies—the technique suggested in parentheses or one of your own choosing—to help you generate writing topics.
Students' topics will vary.

1. cultural traditions (brainstorming)

2. an event in history (*What if?* questions)

3. the Internet (clustering)

EXERCISE 4 Narrowing a Topic

Choose two of the broad, general topics below. For each topic, suggest three limited topics that you could cover in a three-page paper. Students' topics will vary.

TOO BROAD	Natural Disasters
LIMITED	Eyewitness account of 2010 earthquake in Haiti
	Damage that was caused by hurricane-force winds
	The effects of drought on farm families

1. Colleges

2. Sports

3. Driving

4. Endangered Species

5. Movies

Organizing the Ideas and Drafting

IIII➡ Now that you have gathered your ideas, think about the order in which you want to present them. Consider your purpose, and decide which order is most appropriate: chronological order, order of importance, or spatial order, for example.

IIII➡ Use your prewriting notes to create an **outline**. Your outline may include more details than the one at the right, or you may choose to write your outline in full sentences. Either way, your outline should help guide your writing.

IIII➡ Consider your **word choice**. Your word choice is determined by your audience as well as by your purpose for writing.

Your **audience** is the person or people who will read what you write. Ask yourself how much your audience might already know about your writing topic. For example, in an essay about basketball, an audience of players or fans will already know such technical terms as "slam dunk." You won't need to explain such terms. On the other hand, people unfamiliar with the game will not understand the technical terms. Your word choice will depend a great deal on your audience.

The **purpose** for your writing may be to describe, to inform, to tell a story, to persuade, to entertain, or any combination of these. Considering your purpose will help you make sound decisions about how much background and supporting details to include in your draft.

IIII➡ **Drafting** is the next step in the writing process. You will start by putting your thoughts on paper and into sentences and paragraphs.

DRAFTING STRATEGIES

1. **Write the Big Idea** Consider your writing purpose and audience as you draft a sentence that expresses the main idea of your paragraph or essay. Some writers use this as the first sentence in their paper. Even if it doesn't appear directly, it's useful to keep your main idea sentence in mind as you write.

2. **Grab Your Reader's Attention** Begin with a statement or question— something surprising or unique—to hook your reader's attention.

C CCSS

Standards for this lesson focus on developing writing and choosing an organization that is appropriate to purpose and audience.

Writing Model

Rough Outline:
The Alamo

I. *History Prior to Battle*

   A. *Mission of San Antonio de Valero (1718)*

   B. *Fortress for Texan Revolutionaries (1835)*

II. *Battle for the Alamo (1836)*

   A. *Mexican Forces*

   B. *Texan Forces*

III. *History After Battle*

   A. *Famous saying: "Remember the Alamo!"*

   B. *Alamo bought by Texas*

   C. *Area restored*

As you compose your draft, vary the structures and lengths of sentences. See Lesson 3.1 for suggestions on how to do this.

3. Stay Flexible In general, follow your organizational plan, but don't hesitate to make changes, adding or deleting details as appropriate. Now is not the time to fix mistakes; just get your ideas down on paper.

4. Write an Ending Bring your paper to a logical and graceful end by writing a concluding paragraph that restates your main idea. Then, add a call to action (in a persuasive paper) or an appropriate quotation, or perhaps end with your final thought on the subject.

Below is the writer's first draft based on the brief outline on page 13. The writer's purpose is to inform history classmates about the Alamo. Remember that when you're writing your first draft, you shouldn't interrupt your flow of ideas to stop and correct mistakes. Just keep writing sentences. You'll have plenty of time to improve and polish your writing during the next two steps of the writing process, revising and editing. Students will see a revised version of this draft in Lesson 1.3.

Writing Model

The Alamo was originally a chapel and trade school for Native Americans. It was built in 1718. It was named the Mission of San Antonio de Valero. The Alamo is famous because it is the site of a battle during Texas's independence. In 1836, a group of Texas revolutionaries vowed to fight to their deaths against Mexican troops. On March 6, 1836, the Mexicans jumped over the Alamo's fortress walls. All of the 189 Texas revolutionaries inside the Alamo died during the battle; Tennessee congressman Davy Crockett, commander of the troops William Travis, and James Bowie died there. Six weeks later, General Houston defeated the Mexican army at the battle of San Jacinto. Texas declared its independence from Mexico.

Does the writer use a hook to grab your attention?

What information appears in the draft that wasn't in the outline?

Does the writer include a logical ending?

Remember, drafting is just one part of the writing process.

EXERCISE 5 Drafting a Paper

Write a first draft using the prewriting notes you made in Exercise 4 on page 12. Consider your audience and purpose, and make a brief outline. Work with a partner to clearly summarize your topic, main ideas, and supporting details. When you're ready to start writing, follow the strategies suggested in this lesson.
Students' drafts will vary. Students will be asked to revise this draft on page 17 in Lesson 1.3, Exercise 7.

CCSS Writing 5; Language 6. (See pp. T14–T15.)

Revising

▶ When you **revise**, you shape your draft into its almost-final form.

When you revise a draft, you reshape and rewrite your material to make it clearer, more focused, and easier to understand. Revision may involve adding new content, deleting redundant thoughts or phrases, or changing the organization of your information.

Reread your paper four times—once for ideas and unity, once for organization and coherence, once for sentence variety, and once for word choice. Use the strategies that follow as a checklist to make sure your ideas and presentation are clear.

REVISING STRATEGIES

1. **Ideas and Unity** Does your paper adequately summarize your main ideas? Do you need to add or cut supporting details? Do you need more background information? Is everything relevant, or related, to your main idea(s), or have you wandered off track?

2. **Organization and Coherence** Do you grab the reader's attention with an interesting opening sentence? Is information presented in a logical order—that is, an order that makes sense to the reader? If not, change the order of paragraphs to present information differently. Would adding transition words help? Does the last sentence bring closure to the writing?

3. **Sentence Variety** Do your sentences read smoothly? (Try reading them aloud.) Have you varied sentence beginnings, lengths, and structures? Can you combine sentences with related ideas within a paragraph? Are ideas expressed clearly?

4. **Word Choice** Have you used words that are too general or vague? If so, replace them with more precise words. Have you used a cliché or an overworked word (such as *great*, *nice*, or *bad*)? If so, find fresh words to express your ideas. (You might want to use a thesaurus to find synonyms.) Does your writing sound stilted with too many difficult vocabulary words? Have you used appropriate vocabulary for your intended audience? Have you explained or defined any technical terms?

CCSS

Standards for this lesson focus on improving writing by revising and rewriting, focusing on changes appropriate to purpose and audience.

Enriching Your Vocabulary

The adjective *redundant* means "using more words than needed; wordy; unnecessary to the meaning." It comes from a Latin word, *redundare*, meaning "to overflow," and it has a connotation of overwhelming readers with unnecessary and irrelevant information.

Below is the writing piece on the Alamo from Lesson 1.2. Notice the revisions the writer has made to the first draft.

Writing Model

¶ If you visit the Alamo in San Antonio, Texas, today, you will find groups of tourists milling around this historic landmark, a modern-day symbol of heroism. The Alamo was originally a chapel and trade school for Native Americans. It was built in 1718. *and* ~~It was~~ named the Mission of San Antonio de Valero.

¶ The Alamo is famous because it is the site of a *great* battle during Texas's *the struggle for* independence *from Mexico*. In 1836, a group of Texas revolutionaries vowed to *endured a thirteen-day siege and* fight to their deaths against Mexican troops. On March 6, 1836, the *1,800* Mexicans ~~jumped over the Alamo's~~ *scaled the* fortress walls *of the Alamo* *led by General Santa Ana*. All of the 189 Texas revolutionaries inside the ~~Alamo~~ *fortress* died during the battle; *of the Alamo.* ~~Tennessee congressman Davy Crockett, commander of the troops William Travis, and James Bowie died there.~~ Among them were Tennessee congressman Davy Crockett, commander of the troops William Travis, and James Bowie. Six weeks later, General *Sam* Houston defeated the Mexican army ~~at the~~ *in a decisive* battle ~~of~~ *at* San Jacinto. *and* Texas declared its independence from Mexico.

¶ When people say, "Remember the Alamo!," they are referring to the heroism of the small band of brave fighters who sacrificed their lives for a cause they believed in—the independence of Texas from Mexico.

Side questions:
- Does the writer use a hook to grab your attention?
- What do you notice that is different from the first draft and this revision?
- Do you see any new ideas in this piece of writing?
- How did the writer's changes in word choice and sentence variety affect the quality of the writing?
- Does the writer create an ending?

▐▐▐▶ **Working with a writing partner** involves using revising strategies to give feedback to your classmates on their writing and getting the same from them on your works in progress.

EXERCISE 6 Revising an Editorial

On a separate piece of paper, work with a partner or small group, and use the four revising strategies (ideas and unity, organization and coherence, sentence variety, and word choice) to revise the following editorial that a student wrote for a school newspaper. The writer's purpose is to persuade; the audience is made up of students at the writer's high school. Feel free to rewrite, change details, add, or cut in order to maintain focus on the main idea. Consider adding transitions, combining sentences, and making other improvements.
Revised editorials will vary.

[1]We who live in smoggy cities such as Los Angeles, California, have too many days with a dirty fog. [2]It's all over our streets. [3]Where does smog come from? [4]A major source is fossil fuels. [5]Fossil fuel is the stuff that sends our cars through the beautiful California landscape. [6]April 22, 1970, was the first Earth Day. [7]Earth Day may seem like ancient history, but the message still matters. [8]I propose that we dedicate ourselves to finding new ways to decrease pollution problems. [9]Some of these problems include smog. [10]We must dedicate ourselves again to a clean environment every April 22. [11]In his final address, in 1963, President Kennedy looked forward to an America "which will build handsome and balanced cities for our future." [12]It's our turn to get cracking. [13]Maybe one of us will become a scientist or an engineer. [14]That person may be figuring out how to burn fuel cleanly. [15]That person may invent an engine that runs on air itself!

EXERCISE 7 Working with a Writing Partner

1. Revise the paper you drafted in Exercise 5. Use the revising strategies in this lesson to improve your draft.

2. Work with a partner to revise your paper. Allow your partner to read your paper without your input. Your partner should respond to your writing using the revising strategies on page 15 as a guide. Encourage your writing partner to make comments directly on your pages.

3. Review your writing partner's comments on your paper, and incorporate those that you feel will improve your writing. Don't be discouraged if you have to rewrite some passages.
Caution writing partners to be positive about the essays they read. Encourage them to suggest possible solutions to problems they find.

CCSS Writing 5; Language 1, 2, 6. (See pp. T14–T15.)

Editing and Proofreading

CCSS

Standards for this lesson focus on improving writing by editing and on showing a command of the conventions of standard English.

Enriching Your Vocabulary

The adjective *superficial*, derived from two words meaning "over" and "face," has several meanings—"of or on the surface" (a *superficial* burn); "concerned with only the obvious"; "shallow" (as used in the text); "merely apparent" (a *superficial* resemblance). *Superficial* often has a negative connotation, implying that someone's concern is merely on the surface and is not profound.

▐▶ When you **edit** or **proofread** (these terms refer to the same task), you search for any mechanical errors and correct them.

The old saying "Don't judge a book by its cover" may be relevant in some situations. No one likes to be judged on superficial qualities, but in writing, readers judge the clarity of a person's thought process, in part, by the way in which he or she presents ideas. So don't let easily corrected errors in spelling, punctuation, capitalization, and usage keep readers from appreciating your ideas, thoughts, and creativity. Your ability to use conventional standards of written English matters.

EDITING QUESTIONS

1. **Spelling** Are words spelled correctly? (Use a college dictionary or a spell-checker on a computer.) Have you used a correctly spelled word in an incorrect context (*they're* instead of *their*, for example, or *lie* instead of *lay*—mix-ups that a computer's spell-checker won't catch)? Are compound words spelled properly throughout—*earache, Middle Ages, self-consciousness*? Chapter 16: Spelling

2. **Capitalization** Do proper nouns and proper adjectives begin with capital letters? Are other words appropriately capitalized? Have you capitalized a word that's supposed to start with a lowercase letter? Chapter 15: Capitalization

3. **Punctuation** Are commas, colons, semicolons, quotation marks, and other punctuation marks used correctly? Is dialogue punctuated correctly? Chapter 13 and 14: Punctuation

4. **Sentence Correctness** Are there any fragments, run-ons, or misplaced or dangling modifiers? Chapter 6: Parts of a Sentence; Chapter 12: Using Modifiers

5. **Verbs** Do all verbs agree in number with their subjects? Are verb tenses consistent and verb forms correct? Chapter 9: Using Verbs; Chapter 10: Subject-Verb Agreement

6. **Pronouns** Do all pronouns agree with their antecedents? Are pronoun references clear? Chapter 11: Using Pronouns

7. **Usage** Do adjectives modify nouns and pronouns? Do adverbs modify verbs, adjectives, or other adverbs? Are comparisons clear and complete? Do comparisons use *-er/more* and *-est/most* forms correctly? Chapter 12: Using Modifiers; Lesson 5.4 Adjectives; Lesson 5.5 Adverbs

Use the proofreading symbols shown on the following page as you proofread your writing.

Proofreading Symbols		
CORRECTION	**SYMBOL**	**EXAMPLE**
Delete (remove).	ℰ	She sat sat down first.
Insert.	∧	I am so thirst. (y)
Transpose (switch).	⌐⌐	I said just, "Sure!"
Capitalize.	≡	Are you going to san francisco?
Make lowercase.	/	We sailed through the calm Harbor.
Start a new paragraph.	¶	¶She answered, "Certainly!"
Add space.	#	Paolo lives in Rio deJaneiro, Brazil. (#)
Close up space.	⌒	Martha has a head ache.

▐▶ Keep a **proofreading log**, a record of your spelling, punctuation, and capitalization mistakes.

The act of recording a mistake usually helps you to remember and avoid making that same mistake again. For insurance, keep your log in a separate notebook or online journal, and review it periodically.

▐▶ **Publishing** means sharing what you've written.

Writing a paper is something you do alone. But it is through publishing that you can share your ideas with classmates, friends, family, and even wider audiences. Your audience grows every time you let a family member read your writing or every time you read it aloud to a class. Think about publishing your writing in a school anthology or magazine. You can e-mail it to a pen pal, or you can enter it in a contest.

EXERCISE 8 Proofreading Paragraphs

Find and correct every error in the following paragraphs. Use the proofreading symbols from the chart above.

[1]Photography is a fascinating marriage of art and science. [2]Louis Jacques Mandé Daguerre, a paris opera set designer, invented the earliest Photograph in 1839. [3]That Photograph, named the daguerreotype, began with his work on opera sets.

Publishing Suggestions
WRITTEN WORDS
Magazine of student writing
School or local newspaper
Local or national poetry, story, or essay contest
Class anthology
Writing portfolio
Letter/e-mail/blog
SPOKEN WORDS
Speech
Podcast
Oral interpretation
Radio broadcast
Reader's theater
Interview
Debate
MULTIMEDIA
Web site
Book with illustrations
Video
Performance with music
Bulletin board or library display
Community literature festival

⁴He created illusions ~~threw~~ `through` mechanical tricks and the clever use of ~~lite~~ `light`.

⁵Unfortunately, this ~~brillyant~~ `brilliant` work was destroyed by fire in march 1839, forcing

Daguerre out of work.

⁶It was during this ~~idol~~ `idle` time. ⁷That Daguerre used his mechanical `h` know-how

when doing experiments in chemistry andphysics. ⁸He ~~magiclaly~~ `magically` created

photographs form silver-plated copper sheets treated with iodine vapors the

announcement of his discovery in august 1839—just five months after the

fire—astonished paris and the world. ⁹Heads of state and royalty rushed to have

~~they're~~ `their` portraits ¹⁰Done by Daguerre.

EXERCISE 9 Creating an Editing and Proofreading Exercise

Working Together

Create an editing/proofreading exercise for your classmates. Write one or two paragraphs that have at least ten mistakes (or more if you want) in spelling, punctuation, capitalization, or usage. Exchange paragraphs with classmates, and see if you can correct all of the errors. Answers will vary.

EXERCISE 10 Publishing Your Portfolio

Working Together

Look back at the papers in your writing portfolio, or folder, for this year or last year. For each paper in your portfolio, jot down some ideas on how you might share the portfolio with an audience. Brainstorm additional ideas with a writing group. Students' ideas will vary.

Writing Effective Paragraphs and Essays

Ideas and Unity

▮▶ A paragraph has **unity** (it is unified) when its sentences focus on a single main **idea**.

Focusing on one main idea as you draft a paragraph will provide a framework that you can later improve upon. Your first draft does not have to include every detail; nor does it require perfect sentence order or final word selection. You will make these changes when you revise and edit. But as you draft, try to keep a clear focus.

▮▶ A **topic sentence** states the main idea of a paragraph.

A topic sentence in the first or second sentence in a paragraph is like a headline or an announcement of the main idea. Readers will be able to relate supporting details to it. A topic sentence may also fall at the end of a paragraph, where it ties together and summarizes the ideas and details of the preceding sentences.

Not all paragraphs have topic sentences. A paragraph's main idea may be **implied** rather than stated directly, but the main idea must be clear to the reader.

▮▶ A paragraph that starts with a topic sentence may end with a **clincher sentence** that restates or summarizes the main idea. A clincher sentence is used to strongly restate the main point in the paragraph, to summarize information presented in the paragraph, or to create a transition to a new idea in the next paragraph.

WRiTiNG HiNT

Start a new paragraph whenever you:

1. introduce a new idea.
2. develop a subtopic related to the main idea and give supporting details.
3. write dialogue for a new speaker.
4. want to emphasize an idea.

Writing Model

Topic sentence

Two examples support topic sentence

Transition sentence supports the topic sentence

[1]Not all marathons are like the Boston Marathon; each has its own idiosyncrasies. [2]The mid-winter Atlantic City Marathon is a simple out-and-back course, flat as a billiard table and seemingly almost no challenge—except that it must be negotiated not once but three times. [3]The old New York City Marathon, before the inventive Fred Lebow and his fellow officials devised a course that snakes its way through the city's five boroughs, consisted of tedious repetitions of a villianously hilly roadway through Central Park. [4]Such marathons dull the spirit. [5]Boston is different. [6]Curiously, it is not the world's most prestigious race at that distance (the quadrennial Olympic marathon

Details support the topic sentence —

Clincher sentence strongly restates the main idea —

> is), nor its most difficult (the course is more downhill than up), nor even its most scenic (unless you have a liking for freight yards, trolley tracks, and uban sprawl). [7]Nevertheless, it is the single race that captures and summarizes most of what is excellent in marathoning.
>
> —James F. Fixx, *The Complete Book of Running*

SKILLS FOR MAINTAINING UNITY

1. Topic sentence Keep in mind that there's more than one way for a writer to write a topic sentence. For example, Fixx could have written the following topic sentence instead:

> The Boston Marathon may have its quirks, but it remains one of the most important races anywhere.

On the other hand, the following sentences are too weak to act as good topic sentences for the paragraph on the merits of the Boston Marathon.

> Running is inspiring. [too broad]
>
> The course of the Boston Marathon is mostly downhill. [too narrow]

2. Effective development of ideas The model paragraph sticks to the main idea. Every sentence adds a piece of important information that builds on what came before. Fixx doesn't clutter his paragraph with unnecessary sentences such as the following:

> Marathoners come from all over to participate in the Boston Marathon.

3. Clincher sentence Fixx's clincher sentence provides closure to the paragraph and adds impact. It also serves as a good transition to his next paragraph, which might focus on those things that are excellent in marathoning.

EXERCISE 1 Choosing a Topic Sentence

1. If you were going to write a paragraph on the changes in the New York City Marathon, which of the following two topic sentences would you use? Give reasons for your choice on a separate piece of paper.

   a. The course change inspired by Fred Lebow revitalized the New York City Marathon, making it one of the most important marathons in the United States today. Sentence *a* helps ask this question: "How did the changes improve the Marathon?" Sentence *b* focuses on Lebow rather than on the changes.

   b. Runners can thank Fred Lebow for changing the course of the New York City Marathon.

C cCSS Writing 2b, 10. (See pp. T14–T15.)

Elaborating with Supporting Details

▐▶ **Elaboration**, or **development**, means adding details to support a main idea.

When you present an idea, you keep the reader or listener interested by building supporting details for your main idea and by varying the types of details you give. Within a paragraph, you might include details such as **facts**, **statistics**, **quotations**, **definitions**, **anecdotes** or **incidents**, **examples**, **reasons**, and **comparisons**.

The writer of the following paragraph realized that the first draft did not contain enough specific details to support the topic sentence. Notice the details she added when she revised it.

Writing Model

[1]The December 21, 1913, issue of *The New York World* published something new: the crossword puzzle. [2]It was based on an English
called magic word squares   named Arthur Wynne
children's game. [3]A journalist created this puzzle, which included
a list of across and down   as they began to appear in every U.S. newspaper.
clues. [4]People enjoyed crossword puzzles that appeared. [5]Publishers
which immediately became national best-sellers.
began to print full-length books with crossword puzzles, and they

became popular.

When you start to revise your first draft, think about how to add details that will make your writing colorful. However, try to present new information in each sentence. Don't just say the same thing in different words.

EXERCISE 2 Improving Unity and Adding Details

Work with a partner or small group to revise the following paragraph. Cross out any words or sentences that weaken the paragraph's unity. Then, from the list on the next page, select the details that you think would improve the paragraph. Write the letter of the detail where you think it belongs in the paragraph. Then write your revised paragraph on a separate piece of paper. **Hint:** The details can be inserted as phrases and clauses.

Revisions will vary. Sample revisions given.

¹Every spring, Formosa termites enjoy the evening air of New Orleans, Louisiana.

²~~These insects came from Taiwan to the United States just fifty years ago.~~ ³Like all
Detail A

termites, they are wingless except during mating season. ⁴When they have wings,
^
Details B and C

they fly in swarms that make it difficult for people to see or even breathe. ⁵When just
^

one termite mates, reproduces, and settles into a deadwood habitat, trouble begins.
Detail D
⁶Park benches, stadium bleachers, stores, homes, and anything else made out of wood
^

can literally crumble from the damage done by the destructive Formosa termites.

Details

A. Termites with wings, called alates, seek mates and settle down.
B. New Orleans residents keep their lights off when swarms are spotted, because
   light attracts alates. Alates come indoors through the tiniest building cracks.
C. Fewer than one percent of these termites reproduce.
D. These termites are not harmful to humans, but they can damage anything made
   out of wood.

EXERCISE 3 Writing a Paragraph from Notes

Write a unified, well-developed paragraph about the Amazon River based
on the information on the note card below. You do not need to use all of
the information. Begin your paragraph with a topic sentence.
Students' paragraphs will vary.

> Flows from Peru through Brazil in South America for about 2,300 miles
>
> Located near the equator—hot all year long
>
> More than 100 inches (254 cm) of rainfall per year
>
> Surrounded by the rain forest—a warm, wet area with dense plant life
>
> Few human inhabitants in the rain forest because of climate—hot, humid
>
> People who live in the rain forest usually live in ports on the Amazon
>
> Rubber, wood, gold—natural resources of the Amazon basin,
> transported on the Amazon River
>
> Carries more water than the Nile, the Rhine, and the Mississippi combined
>
> River length nearly equals the distance between the East Coast and the
> West Coast of the United States

C **ccss** Writing 1, 2a, 2c, 10. (See pp. T14–T15.)

Organization and Coherence

▶ Each of your paragraphs should be **coherent**—that is, each one should be logically organized so that your reader can follow your thoughts easily. Your writing should flow naturally. Use the following three strategies for writing coherent paragraphs.

STRATEGIES FOR WRITING COHERENTLY

1. **Be clear.** Express your thoughts simply and directly. Eliminate wordiness, and avoid overly long and complicated sentences.

2. **Guide the reader.** Use signposts to show the reader what lies ahead and how ideas are related. Signposts can be transition words (see those on page 28). Others are pronouns and synonyms (words that mean almost the same thing) that refer to terms you've already used in your paragraph. Repeating key words or terms also improves coherence.

3. **Put your thoughts in order.** Arrange information so that "first things come first."

The following list includes five common and effective ways to organize paragraphs and essays. Unless you have a good reason not to do so, choose one of these organizing principles to guide your writing.

- **Chronological Order** Organize your essay in order of time, or chronologically, when you want to describe events in the order in which they occurred. Chronological organization works well for the following types of writing: narrative paragraphs about true or fictional events, expository paragraphs about historical events, and paragraphs that describe steps in a process.

- **Spatial Order** Organize your paragraph spatially when you want to describe a person, an animal, a place, or an object. Describe details in an orderly way: Move from left to right, top to bottom, near to far, or inside to outside.

- **Order of Importance** Organize your paragraph by level of importance when you are trying to persuade your audience. State the least important reasons and details first, and end with the most important ones—or the reverse. In news stories, you might notice that writers usually start with the most important detail in the lead sentence.

- **Logical Order** Organize your paragraph logically to give information in the order a reader needs to know it to understand your key points. Usually, logic determines which details you group together or where you provide background information or definitions of terms. For example, if you were writing about a cross-country trip, you might logically tell about your first stop, then your second, third, and so on.

- **Specific to General/General to Specific Order** Present details in a paragraph so that they either build toward and support a general idea or pare down a general idea to focus on a more specific, exact thought. Thus, if you were writing to persuade readers to protect wildlife, you might start with a specific example of an animal that had been hurt or killed due to careless humans: for example, a manatee that was badly injured by a speeding boat's propellors. You might use that specific detail to lead into a discussion of more general ways to protect wildlife.

The revisions in the following model show how one writer improved coherence in response to a writing partner's notes in the margin.

Writing Model

Use transition for emphasis.

[1]Owning a business is not just for adults. *In fact,* [2]Some teens run their own businesses successfully. [3]Teens might start a business in a field

Give examples.

such as pet care, house cleaning, lawn care, or another field in which they have skill or interest.

[4]Any beginning business owner will address certain questions.

Eliminate wordiness.

Combine sentences.

For example, he or she [5]~~Any beginning business owner~~ must ask, "What are my interests?" *and* [6]~~They must ask~~ "What is the potential for making a profit in this business?" [7]There are other things to think about, too. [8]Owners must

Give specific details. Add transition word.

check out government rules about business by using the library or *advertising and bookkeeping* *Finally,* going on the Internet. [9]They must think about ~~business details~~. [10]They need to think about whether they need any employees or equipment to run their businesses.

Some Common Transitional Words and Expressions

To show **time**		To show **examples**		To show **order of importance**		To **compare**	
after	first	for example	namely	above all	second	also	likewise
afterward	immediately	for instance	that is	finally	then	and	similarly
at last	later	in addition		first	last	as	too
before	soon	in other words		most important		like	
during	then						
finally	when	To **summarize**		To show **cause**		To **contrast**	
		all in all	finally	**and effect**		although	but
To show **position**		as a result	therefore	as a result	since	however	still
above	inside	in conclusion		because	so	in contrast	yet
across	into	in summary		consequently	so that	nevertheless	
among	off			if . . . then	therefore	on the other hand	
behind	outside	To **emphasize**		for that reason			
below	there	for this reason	again				
between	through	moreover	in fact				
in front of	under	most important					

EXERCISE 4 Revising Paragraphs for Organization and Coherence

Work with a partner or small group to improve the coherence of the following paragraphs. Try adding transitional words and expressions, reordering information, and combining sentences. Write your revised paragraphs on a separate piece of paper. Students' revised paragraphs will vary.

   [1]The words you speak may be your legacy on Earth. [2]This seemingly strange statement was supported by the findings of Johanna Nichols at a convention of the American Association for the Advancement of Science in 1998. [3]Johanna Nichols is an expert on Native American languages. [4]For a long time, it was believed that humans walked across the Bering Strait on a land bridge from Asia to Alaska about 11,500 years ago. [5]Humans slowly made their way southward. [6]It was also believed that one long migration occurred. [7]These settlers traveled south to warm regions, then back north when Earth warmed up again.

   [8]Nichols's research on the development of Native American languages indicates that there were three migrations before the last Ice Age and one migration (the Eskimo-Aleuts) afterward. [9]Nichols's research shows that the last migration took place around 5,000 years ago. [10]Nichols dates the first migrations as far back as 40,000 years ago. [11]The language you speak might tell where your ancestors lived. [12]The results of Johanna Nichols's research are based on calculations related to the amount of time it takes a language to develop.

EXERCISE 5 Writing a Coherent, Unified Paragraph

Choose one of the following assignments, and write a coherent, unified paragraph.
Students' paragraphs will vary.

1. Explain the basic rules of a game or sport for someone unfamiliar with it.

2. Think about a room or building you know well, such as a room in your home, the classroom, a movie theater, or a favorite store. Then write a detailed description of it.

3. Your school is considering placing on the local board of education a student representative who can cast a vote on behalf of the student body. Do you think this would be a good idea? Why or why not? Write a paragraph stating your opinion, and provide reasons and evidence to support that opinion.

EXERCISE 6 Writing a Paragraph from Notes

Write a coherent, unified paragraph based on the following note card. Include a topic sentence.

Willa Cather (1873–1947)—American novelist

Writer who emphasized strong, female characters well before the women's movement or feminism

Writing focused on immigrant characters involved in settling the American West

Raised in Red Cloud, Nebraska

One of few women to graduate from University of Nebraska in 1895

Worked as a journalist and a high school English teacher

Moved to New York City (1906), worked as a magazine editor

Publication of novel *O Pioneers!* (1913) brought acclaim

Two more well-received novels written in 5 years—*The Song of the Lark* (1915) and *My Ántonia* (1918)

Students' paragraphs will vary but should include a clear topic sentence. Students should stick to that topic and support it with related details or ideas from the card, and they should have a logical organization for these ideas. See teacher pages for assessment rubrics.

C **ccss** Writing 4. (See pp. T14–T15.)

Purpose

You write paragraphs and essays for a number of purposes. In this lesson, you'll study four of the main **purposes** for writing.

C ccss

Standards for this lesson focus on writing clear and coherent paragraphs with details and an organization that are appropriate to the task and purpose.

DESCRIPTIVE

When your purpose is to describe a person, a place, an object, or an animal, use the following suggestions.

- **Use sensory details** that appeal to the reader's sense of sight, hearing, smell, touch, and taste. Sensory details help create a **main impression** or **mood** in your writing.

- **Use spatial order** to present the sensory details from left to right, top to bottom, near to far, one direction to another—or in reverse.

Writing Model

Context: writer's location
Smell detail

Sight detail

Sound detail

Touch detail

Change of mood

¹As I stood in one corner of the garden, I could smell the lilac's perfume travel to me like the sweetness of the spring. ²I moved to the garden's center and began to weed a patch of wild daisies. ³Behind me, the hibiscus shrubs had just blossomed, each bloom looking like a show-off. ⁴Best of all, a meadowlark sat on the garden fence singing a song of new growth and joy. ⁵When I turned to survey this newcomer in full view, I stepped on a branch of flowering weeds whose thorny stems stung my legs. ⁶Needless to say, the pleasure of my morning in the garden suddenly evaporated.

NARRATIVE

When your purpose is to tell a story, either a fictional story or a true narrative, use the following suggestions.

- Use **specific details** to help make the reader feel like an eyewitness to the events.

- Use **chronological order** (time order) to relate the events in the order in which they occurred.

Writing Model

Quotation gives authenticity to setting

¹Monday night "the storm crosses offshore and the first-stage wind surge" passes over the *Satori*. ²The weather radio reports that ocean conditions will ease off briefly and then deteriorate again as the storm

Chronological organization

Specific details and description

Events create suspense

swings back toward the coast. ³By then, though, the *Satori* might be far enough south to escape the storm's full wrath. ⁴The boat wallows on through Monday night, the barometer rising slightly and the wind easing off to the northeast; but then late that night, like a bad fever, the storm comes on again. ⁵The wind climbs to fifty knots, and the seas rise up in huge dark mountains behind the boat. ⁶The crew take turns at the helm, clipped into a safety line, and occasionally take a breaking sea over the cockpit. ⁷The barometer crawls downward all night, and by dawn the conditions are worse than anything Stimson has ever seen in her life.

EXPOSITORY

There are several ways to explain and to inform: You can compare and contrast; you can discuss cause and effect; or you can define, classify, or analyze. The following suggestions will help you with expository writing.

- State your **main idea** as early and as clearly as possible.

- Use **facts**, **examples**, **quotations**, **statistics**, and **definitions** as supporting details to develop the main idea.

- Present details in a **logical order** so that they make sense to the reader. Transition words help your reader follow your train of thought (see page 28).

Types of Exposition

Comparison/Contrast The writer explores similarities and differences between two or more subjects.

Cause and Effect The writer examines reasons behind an occurrence (causes) and/or the results of an occurrence (effects).

Classification The writer gathers similar elements and details into a category to distinguish one category from another.

Definition The writer defines a term or concept and elaborates with supporting details (descriptions, comparisons, examples, or statistics).

Writing Model

Main idea stated

Statistic: distance, fact

Fact and definition of finding

Explanation of discovery

¹A group of entrepreneurs from Tampa, Florida, was searching the Mediterranean Sea for lost treasure. ²Using a robot equipped with a video camera, the searchers were able to view the sea's floor over a half-mile below the surface. ³The team's director, Greg Stemm, reported the discovery of clay storage jars, called amphoras, from an extremely old shipwreck. ⁴Stemm sent his video recording of the discovery to specialized archaeologists who tentatively identified the earthen jars as typical of the Carthaginian jars from around 400 B.C. ⁵Worth a fortune, these jars have been submerged for more than two thousand years.

Chapter 2 • Writing Effective Paragraphs and Essays **31**

PERSUASIVE

When your purpose is to convince readers to share your opinion or to encourage them to take action, use the following suggestions:

• Begin with a sentence that **grabs the reader's attention**.

• Include a **thesis statement,** or **claim,** that clearly expresses your point of view.

• Present valid **reasons** and relevant **evidence** to support your claim.

• Arrange the supporting details in **order of importance**—from most to least important, or the reverse.

• Include a **call to action**.

Writing Model

Attention grabber	[1]When was the last time you read a handwritten note from a friend that was perfectly legible and in good cursive letters? [2]Chances are this is a distant memory. [3]One of the most basic skills of elementary school—penmanship—is almost entirely overlooked, and elementary school students are getting to high school with virtually illegible handwriting. [4]This neglect by elementary schools
Claim	
Reason supports claim	must stop. [5]For starters, students should not be given a computer keyboard in place of pencil and paper.
Quotation supports reason	[6]"Handwriting is a motor skill," said a teacher in Glenford, Ohio. [7]"Practice is the only way to perfect any motor skill." [8]However, if this basic skill is not practiced regularly in elementary schools, this shift toward illegible handwriting
Call to action	will continue. [9]In short, elementary schools have a responsibility to instill the habits of good penmanship that will last a lifetime.

EXERCISE 7 Writing with Different Purposes

Write at least two different kinds of paragraphs. You may use the suggested topics below or choose topics of your own. Students' two paragraphs will vary. Check that each contains a topic sentence, sticks to and supports its main idea, and is logically organized. See teacher pages for assessment rubrics.

1. A **persuasive paragraph** about high school students leaving school before they graduate to take a job (make an argument for or against)

2. A **descriptive paragraph** about a special outdoor place

3. A **narrative paragraph** about a discovery, an adventure, or a journey

4. An **expository paragraph** giving information about your school, your community, a specific career, or a celebrity

Writing Essays

A well-written essay begins with an **introductory** paragraph, continues with several more paragraphs constituting the **body** of the essay, and ends with one or more **concluding** paragraphs. In other words, good essays have a definite beginning, middle, and end.

INTRODUCTION

An introductory paragraph has two key missions: to interest readers in reading further and to present them with the overall subject or idea of the essay.

 The **thesis statement** of an essay is the overall idea. It is also called a **claim** or a **controlling idea**.

The thesis statement in the introduction of an essay functions like the topic sentence in a paragraph. Sometimes, the thesis statement appears in an essay's very first sentence. On the other hand, as shown below, the writer may choose to first present readers with an interesting detail and then lead them to the more general thesis statement.

> Baggy pants, baseball caps worn backward, T-shirts two sizes too big—have you seen a third grader dressing like this recently? Because of wild swings in fashion trends, local school districts are now adopting strict dress codes or uniforms.

Here's what *not* to write:

> This paper that I'm about to write explains why . . .
> In this essay, I'll talk about . . .

BODY

Support and develop your thesis statement, or claim, by following your introduction with several more paragraphs that contain supporting details, anecdotes, and examples. Use these guidelines to help you draft the body of an essay.

1. Topic sentences Think of the body of your essay as a series of main ideas, each one expressed in the topic sentence of a separate paragraph. Each paragraph should contain specific details that support the topic sentence.

C cCSS

Standards for this lesson focus on writing clear and coherent essays with an organization that is appropriate to task, purpose, and audience, and writing over a short time period to develop the different parts of an essay.

Some Ways to Begin an Essay

- anecdote • vivid image
- example   • quotation
- question
- bit of dialogue
- startling statement of fact

2. **Organization** Decide how you're going to arrange your main ideas. You may choose one of the organizational methods described in Lesson 2.3. Try to begin with first things first—background information—and then move through your main ideas in the order your reader needs to know them. Creating an outline of an essay before you write (see Lesson 1.2) may help you organize the ideas for the body.

3. **Focus** Avoid repetition, and eliminate wordiness. Ask yourself, "What am I trying to say?"; then say it as clearly as you can.

Some Ways to End an Essay

- summary of main ideas
- comment on importance of topic
- thought-provoking question
- quotation
- prediction about the future
- call to action

CONCLUSION

The conclusion of your essay is your chance to wrap up your thoughts, information, or ideas. Try to sum up your main ideas and explain how they support your thesis statement (claim). Your essay will usually conclude with one or two sentences or possibly a full paragraph or more. In the margin, you'll find suggestions for concluding essays.

Here's what *not* to write:

> Well, that's everything I know about this subject. I wish I could tell you more, but that's all I have time for now.

WRITING HINT

Your conclusion may echo a thought or phrase from the introduction. This technique encourages readers to view your essay as a whole.

EXERCISE 8 Drafting an Introduction

You are writing an autobiographical, narrative essay about the time you gave a speech to introduce a friend who was running for class president. Here's what happened: You uttered one sentence of the introduction and forgot everything else you had planned to say. You reached into a pocket for your note cards but realized that you had left them at home. Draft an introduction to this autobiographical essay that will make your classmates want to read the whole story. Make up any details that you need. Students' introductions will vary.

EXERCISE 9 Writing Body Paragraphs Based on Notes

Review the notes below. Write one or more paragraphs for the body of a research paper about World War II. Give each paragraph a topic sentence, and support each topic sentence with facts. Your audience should be your high school social studies class.

Details of D-Day (background information)

Took place June 6, 1944

Allies crossed English Channel from Great Britain to attack Germans in Normandy (region of France)

Operations involved 11,000 planes, 600 warships, 1,500 tanks, and 175,000 soldiers

Entire operation was secret—surprise attack on Germans

Germans attacked Allies as soldiers stormed out of warships

Huge casualties—6,600 U.S. soldiers killed, wounded, or lost on beaches of Normandy

Due to the huge number of soldiers, enough troops survived the beach, and operation succeeded

---

Students' paragraphs will vary but should include a clear topic sentence, supporting details, and pertinent background information. See teacher pages for assessment rubrics.

EXERCISE 10 Drafting a Conclusion

Draft a concluding paragraph for a persuasive essay, or argument, about a proposed state law that would raise the eligibility age to drive to twenty. Make up any specific details that you need. In your conclusion, state your view of this proposed law and the key reasons behind that opinion. Students' conclusions will vary.

Writing Effective Sentences

Varying Sentence Beginnings, Structures, and Lengths

Now that you have experience with subordinate clauses, sentence structures, and other writing tools, you can express ideas in a variety of ways when you write paragraphs or longer papers.

▶ When you write paragraphs or longer papers, vary the sentence structures.

ORIGINAL	Jack London entertained gold prospectors in Canada's frozen wilderness by telling adventure stories.
PREPOSITIONAL PHRASE	**In Canada's frozen wilderness,** Jack London entertained gold prospectors by telling adventure stories.
PARTICIPIAL PHRASE	**Telling adventure stories,** Jack London entertained gold prospectors in Canada's frozen wilderness.
ADVERB CLAUSE	**While Jack London told adventure stories,** he entertained gold prospectors in Canada's frozen wilderness.
ADJECTIVE CLAUSE	Jack London, **who entertained gold prospectors in Canada's frozen wilderness,** told adventure stories.

Like professional writers, you can also experiment with a variety of sentence lengths to create smooth, flowing paragraphs. The following paragraph begins with two medium-length sentences and then follows with one short sentence and one long sentence.

[1]Renata had written dozens of adventure stories, but she dreamed of traveling to the Yukon like the famous novelist Jack London. [2]After researching the frigid wilderness of Canada, she made plans for her own real-life adventure. [3]Her first stop would be at an old gold miners' camp. [4]She would end her journey at the finish line of the famous annual dogsled race, the Iditarod, before returning home to Minnesota.

EXERCISE 1 Varying Sentence Beginnings

On a separate piece of paper, rewrite each of the following sentences to change its structure. You may reword the sentence if necessary or use other forms of words in the sentence. Just be sure to express the same idea. See Answer Key at www.grammarforwriting.com.

1. Jack London was born in San Francisco in January 1876 to parents known by the San Francisco public as eccentrics.

2. He went to work at age thirteen due to a family financial crisis.

Enriching Your Vocabulary

The adjective *perilous*, used on page 38, comes from the Latin noun *periculum*, meaning "a danger." Rock climbing can be particularly *perilous* in the winter, when snow covers loose rock.

3. A voyage to the Bering Sea on a ship trying to catch seals became his first of many world adventures.

4. Earning a living as a "vendor of brain" rather than as a laborer was the motto of Jack London.

5. One night in 1895, he wrote a 4,000-word essay for a newspaper contest, which brought him his first earnings as a writer.

6. He was self-taught and successfully passed exams that allowed him to graduate from high school when he was nineteen.

7. On the *Klondike*, Jack London sailed off for his first Yukon adventure after a brief college experience.

8. The perilous conditions in the Yukon weakened Jack London's health but provided a wealth of material for his most famous work, *The Call of the Wild*.

9. *The Call of the Wild* is a novel he finished in five weeks, and it became famous.

10. He got married, then he had two daughters, but he continued to travel.

EXERCISE 2 Writing a Paragraph with Varied Sentences

On a separate piece of paper, write a paragraph about Jack London's life. Use information from the research notes below. You don't have to use all the information. Try to vary sentence beginnings, lengths, and structures in the paragraph. **Remember:** Subordinate clauses allow you to connect related ideas in sentences. Students' paragraphs will vary. See teacher pages for assessment rubrics.

Traveled 2,000 miles on a raft down the Yukon River; then worked his way back to Oakland, California

"The White Silence"—first story about the Yukon: rejected

Short stories first published in 1899; begins to earn money

Marries, has two daughters, but continues to travel

In five weeks completes famous novel The Call of the Wild (1902)

Sea-Wolf (novel) makes him more famous and richer.

1904: Writes about Russo-Japanese War for Hearst newspaper from the war front

1905: Poor health, divorce, then remarriage to Charmain Kitteridge

More adventures—Hawaii

Moves to Glen Ellen, California; plans dream house called "Wolf House"

Fire destroys "Wolf House"; London dies in 1916—at age of 40

Combining Sentences: Using Conjunctions

▶ A sentence with a **compound subject** has two or more subjects sharing the same verb. The subjects are joined with a conjunction.
Both Anthony **and** Hannah wrote one-act plays.

▶ A sentence with a **compound verb** has two or more verbs sharing the same subject. Verbs can be combined with a conjunction.
The student **wrote** the poems **and published** them.

▶ A **compound sentence** combines two or more simple sentences into a single sentence.

ORIGINAL   Some enjoy writing poetry. Others prefer writing stories.
COMBINED   Some enjoy writing poetry, **while** others prefer writing stories.

ORIGINAL   Teachers and students named the anthology together. Only the students published and distributed the book.
COMBINED   Teachers and students titled the anthology together, **but** only the students published and distributed the book.

▶ Use these three strategies to combine sentences into a compound sentence.

1. Use a comma and a conjunction to combine the sentences.
ORIGINAL   Kita's story presents a slice of history. It also provides a mystery to keep readers entertained.
COMBINED   Kita's story **not only** presents a slice of history, **but** it **also** provides a mystery to keep readers entertained.

2. Use a semicolon alone to combine the sentences.
ORIGINAL   The main character lives in South Africa. During this time, Nelson Mandela becomes the first native South African president of the country.
COMBINED   The main character lives in South Africa; during this time, Nelson Mandela becomes the first native South African president of the country.

3. Use a semicolon followed by a conjunctive adverb to combine two sentences. A comma always follows the conjunctive adverb.
ORIGINAL   The heroine experiences segregation and prejudice. She survives and lives a long, prosperous life.
COMBINED   The heroine suffers segregation and prejudice; **nevertheless,** she survives and lives a long, prosperous life.

Coordinating Conjunctions
and   or
but   so
nor   yet

Some Correlative Conjunctions
either . . . or
neither . . . nor
not only . . . but also
both . . . and
just as . . . so (too)

Some Commonly Used Conjunctive Adverbs
accordingly   meanwhile
also   moreover
besides   nevertheless
consequently   otherwise
finally   similarly
furthermore   still
however   therefore
indeed   thus
instead   whereas

Some Transitional Expressions
as a result   on the other
at last   hand
for example   otherwise
for instance   such that
in fact   then
likewise

Exercise 3 Identifying Conjunctions

In the paragraph below, circle each conjunction. Underline each simple subject once and each verb twice.

¹Henry James (1843–1916) was born in the United States, but he spent most of his adult life in England. ²Brash, unsophisticated Americans and cultured Europeans are the main characters in his novels. ³Isabel Archer, one of his American characters, inherits a fortune and moves from New York to England in *The Portrait of a Lady* (1881). ⁴She falls for and marries the unscrupulous Gilbert Osmond; consequently, she loses her fortune to him. ⁵This and other novels by James are not typical love stories. ⁶Henry James's readers not only probe into but also understand characters' motives, actions, and beliefs. ⁷Because of this, James is respected as a founder of the modern psychological novel. ⁸James's *The Portrait of a Lady* and *Wings of a Dove* were made into movies in the 1990s; therefore, this proves their contemporary appeal. ⁹Curiously, Henry James's brother William was also a famous writer; however, William wrote books on philosophy and psychology. ¹⁰William James joked that Henry was the better psychologist; whereas, Henry considered William the greater writer.

Exercise 4 Revising a Report

Work with a partner or small group to revise the following passage on a separate piece of paper. Look for ways to combine subjects, verbs, or simple sentences into compound subjects, compound verbs, or compound sentences.

Revised passages will vary but should avoid repetition and use conjunctions correctly.

¹The first part of the word *psychology* has a Greek origin. ²The second part of the word *psychology* also has a Greek origin. ³*Psycho* means "breath or principles of life, spirit, and mind." ⁴*Logy* means "speech or discourse." ⁵These word parts mean that human behavior is based on reasons related to the mind. ⁶These word parts point to the mind's power over people's thoughts, feelings, and actions.

⁷The ancient Greek philosopher Aristotle had a theory about human behavior. ⁸The ancient Greek philosopher Aristotle wrote a book called *De Anima* about his theory. ⁹The ancient Greek philosopher Aristotle wrote his book in the fourth century B.C. ¹⁰*De Anima* states that human behavior is ruled by the heart. ¹¹Modern texts and ideas about human behavior have been influenced by this classic work.

Combining Sentences: Using Subordinate Clauses

When you combine sentences, you join ideas. By using a subordinate clause, you can combine related ideas from more than one sentence into a single sentence.

▐▐▐▶ You can combine two sentences by turning one sentence into an adjective clause.

Use the introductory words from the list on page 153, such as *who*, *which*, and *when*. **Remember:** An adjective clause usually follows the noun or pronoun it modifies, and commas set off a nonessential adjective clause from the rest of the sentence.

ORIGINAL   Rita Dove became the youngest poet laureate of the United States. She was born in 1955.

COMBINED   Rita Dove, **who was born in 1955,** became the youngest poet laureate of the United States.

ORIGINAL   Grandparents are important in Rita Dove's poetry. Her grandparents appear in *Thomas and Beulah*.

COMBINED   Rita Dove's grandparents, **who appear in** *Thomas and Beulah*, are important in her poetry.

COMBINED   Grandparents, **who are essential to Rita Dove's poetry,** appear in *Thomas and Beulah*.

▐▐▐▶ You can combine two sentences by turning one sentence into an adverb clause.

One way to combine sentences is by using a **subordinating conjunction** to create an adverb clause. Choose a subordinating conjunction that clearly expresses the relationship between the ideas. Note that adverb clauses may come at the beginning, middle, or end of a sentence.

ORIGINAL   Please don't throw that magazine away. It lists rules for a poetry contest.

COMBINED   Please don't throw that magazine away **because it lists rules for a poetry contest**.

ORIGINAL   I came in late. I still think I passed the test.

COMBINED   **Although I came in late,** I still think I passed the test.

P.S. When you write clauses, you don't need to identify which function they serve in a sentence, as long as each clause enhances the meaning and reads smoothly.

Some Subordinating Conjunctions

Cause-Effect Relationship
because   whereas
since

Time Relationship
after   when
as soon as   whenever
before   while
until

Resulting Relationship
in order that
so that

Conditional Relationship
although   if
even though   unless
provided that

Enriching Your Vocabulary

The root of *stagnated*, found on page 42, is a Latin noun, *stagnum*, meaning "a swamp, or a pool of standing water." Metaphorically, the word can be used for any lack of motion. Without a high school diploma, one might get stuck in a *stagnant* career.

EXERCISE 5 Combining Sentences with Adjective Clauses

Work with a partner to combine each pair of sentences into a single sentence by changing the second sentence into an adjective clause. An introductory word is suggested in parentheses. Write your responses on a separate piece of paper, and underline the adjective clause in your combined sentence. See Answer Key at www.grammarforwriting.com.

EXAMPLE   The stock market fascinates people. It fluctuates up or down. (when)
The stock market, <u>when it fluctuates up or down</u>, fascinates people.

1. The American workforce of the 1980s stagnated the economy. The workforce was considered too big and inefficient. (which)

2. In the next decade, the economy grew stronger. The workforce became smaller and more efficient. (when)

HiNT

Set off nonessential adjective and adverb clauses with commas.

3. Many economists advise people not to spend too much or too little when the economy changes. Economists study spending habits. (who)

4. Sudden changes in the economy often change a person's spending patterns. Sudden changes in the economy occur from time to time. (that)

5. People should know that economists warn against going into debt in both good and bad economies. People fuel the economy. (who)

6. Optimism may shrink margins of safety and allow credit card debts to grow out of control. People try to maintain margins of safety. (which)

EXERCISE 6 Combining Sentences with Adverb Clauses

Combine each pair of sentences into a single sentence with an adverb clause. Use the subordinating conjunction suggested in parentheses—or one of your choice. Write your responses on a separate piece of paper, and underline the adverb clause in each of your combined sentences. See Answer Key at www.grammarforwriting.com.

EXAMPLE   Virgil wrote often about Cupid. Cupid was a minor god. (although)
<u>Although Cupid was a minor god</u>, Virgil wrote about him often.

1. In Greek mythology, the leaves never fell from trees in autumn. Persephone made this happen. (until)

2. Odysseus finally finds his way home from the Trojan War. Many forces tried to stop him. (even though)

3. Greek gods and goddesses often helped humans. People respected and revered the gods and goddesses on Mt. Olympus. (as long as)

4. At times, the gods would punish people. People insulted a god. (if)

5. A person approached the gates of Hades. The three-headed guard dog, Cerberus, had to be confronted. (when)

6. The god Zeus threw thunderbolts. He wanted to display his strength or anger. (whenever)

Combining Sentences: Inserting Phrases

Combine short or choppy sentences by using phrases for smooth and seamless transitions. This will help you to express your ideas clearly.

➡ Combine related sentences by inserting a phrase from one sentence into another sentence.

When you combine sentences, you sometimes take a phrase from one sentence and simply put it into another. Other combinations require slight changes in word forms.

ORIGINAL   The grandfather was telling a story. He told a story about a coyote. The story was told to his grandchildren.

COMBINED   The grandfather was telling **his grandchildren** a story **about a coyote**. [indirect object; prepositional phrase]

ORIGINAL   The grandfather liked telling stories. He was Maria's favorite relative.

COMBINED   The grandfather, **Maria's favorite relative**, liked telling stories. [appositive phrase]

ORIGINAL   Maria was listening to the story. She realized that coyotes had always interested her.

COMBINED   **Listening to the story**, Maria realized that coyotes had always interested her. [participial phrase]

ORIGINAL   People recount their dreams. Dreams may be frightening or fascinating. Telling stories about dreams may help explain them.

COMBINED   **Recounting a frightening or fascinating dream** may help **explain the dream's meaning**. [gerund phrase; infinitive phrase]

ORIGINAL   Maria listened to the details in the story. The details helped her follow what was happening to the coyote.

COMBINED   Maria listened to the details in the story **to help her follow what was happening to the coyote**. [infinitive phrase]

Often there are different ways to combine the same sentences. Here's one more way the last group of sentences could be combined:

COMBINED   **Listening to the details in the story** helped Maria follow what was happening to the coyote. [gerund phrase with two prepositional phrases]

Working Together

EXERCISE 7 Combining Sentences by Inserting Phrases

Use phrases to combine the sentences in each numbered item. You may work with a partner or small group. Don't forget to add commas around nonessential appositive phrases. **Hint:** There is more than one way to combine most of these sentences. See Answer Key at www.grammarforwriting.com.

1. Rudolfo Anaya is a well-known American author. Pastura is his hometown. Pastura is a small New Mexican town.

2. *Bless Me, Ultima* is his first novel. He begins to show an interest in Mexican American folklore.

3. As a boy, Anaya liked Saturdays. On that day of the week he read in the Santa Rosa library. He stayed there until late in the day.

4. The young Anaya listened to *cuentos*. *Cuentos* are traditional Spanish stories. He became interested in writing.

5. A tradition of oral storytelling is part of Mexican-American culture. The imagination of a young Mexican-American writer, like Rudolfo Anaya, is sparked by this form of storytelling.

6. La Llorona is a crazy spirit. She is in some of Anaya's stories that are based on *cuentos*. She shouts and cries about lost loved ones.

7. Anaya also writes novels. These are about real-life, modern people. They live in New Mexico.

8. In 1992, *Albuquerque* was published. It is a novel. The novel is about a Hispanic boxer.

9. There are many readers of Anaya. They learn about Hispanic culture and the Southwest when they read his work.

10. He was interested in writing mysteries. Mysteries are a genre Anaya had not yet tried. He wrote and published one.

Working Together

EXERCISE 8 Writing a Paragraph

Students should combine sentences where possible by using phrases. You may have students exchange paragraphs with a partner and make suggestions for improving each other's paragraphs. Answers will vary.

Conduct a survey on your classmates' reading habits and preferences using the questions below. Feel free to create your own questions. As you survey three classmates, write a one-sentence response, based on each answer. Then, on another piece of paper, write the results of the survey in a paragraph.

1. How many books, on average, do you read in a month?

2. What kind of writing or literary genre (mystery, biography, novel, etc.) do you most enjoy reading?

3. What do you consider the ideal length for a book?

4. What are two qualities you look for in any book you read?

Eliminating Short, Choppy Sentences

⫸ You can express your ideas concisely and effectively by combining a series of short, choppy sentences into one flowing sentence. Combine sentences by inserting key words from one sentence into another sentence.

ORIGINAL   The bears lumbered near our campsite. The bears were grizzlies. The bears lumbered sluggishly.

COMBINED   The **grizzly** bears lumbered **sluggishly** near our campsite.

The combined sentence sounds a lot smoother because it avoids unnecessary repetition. Notice that the single words inserted into the sentence work as modifiers—adjectives and adverbs.

ORIGINAL   The eagle dived into the water. The eagle dived instantly. The water was icy.

COMBINED   **Instantly**, the eagle dived into the **icy** water.

Note: Sometimes the key words change form when you combine sentences (in the first example above, *grizzlies* becomes *grizzly*).

ORIGINAL   Members of Congress listened to debates and reports. The debates centered on ecology. The reports were made by congressional aides.

COMBINED   Members of Congress listened to **ecology** debates **and congressional aides'** reports.

ORIGINAL   People testified before Congress. Experts on ecology spoke about groundwater contamination. Congressional aides reported on voter concerns about their water.

COMBINED   **In testimony** before Congress, **ecology experts reported on** groundwater contamination, **while** congressional aides **cited** voter concerns about this **issue**.

STEP BY STEP

Combining Sentences

To combine a series of short sentences:

1. Find the sentence that gives readers the most information.

2. In the other sentences, look for single words that can be incorporated into the sentence identified in Step 1.

3. Insert the single words where they make sense. You may need to change the form of the words you're moving.

4. Test the combined sentence to see if it sounds natural and conveys the proper meaning.

EXERCISE 9 Combining Sentences

Combine the groups of sentences on the following page into single sentences. **Hint:** Omit some words and change the form of others to combine sentences successfully.

EXAMPLE   *Moby-Dick* is a novel by Herman Melville. *Moby-Dick* is a famous novel. Herman Melville was American.

Moby-Dick is a famous novel by the American Herman Melville.

See Answer Key at www.grammarforwriting.com.

1. "The Prologue" is a poem. "The Prologue" was written by Anne Bradstreet. Anne Bradstreet was the first woman author in the American colonies.

2. Henry James wrote about relationships among people. Henry James was a novelist. The people he wrote about were mostly British and American.

3. Washington Irving wrote about a headless horseman. The headless horseman appeared in a story called "The Legend of Sleepy Hollow." Washington Irving wrote "The Legend of Sleepy Hollow" in the early nineteenth century.

4. I heard a recording of Gwendolyn Brooks reading poems about love. Gwendolyn Brooks is an African American poet. Gwendolyn Brooks read poems from her Pulitzer Prize-winning collection, *Annie Allen*.

5. Did you ever read *Moby-Dick*? *Moby-Dick* is a famous novel about a whale. The book was written by Herman Melville. The book was written in 1851.

EXERCISE 10 Revising a Paragraph

Work with a partner to improve the following first paragraph of a story for the school literary magazine. Look for opportunities to combine sentences.

¹The Watson twins live on a street called Shadow Lane. ²Shadow Lane is usually a quiet street. ³It is a winding street. ⁴Tonight, the wind howls fiercely. ⁵The wind howls as fiercely as a pack of hungry wolves. ⁶The people on Shadow Lane usually turn out their lights by nine o'clock. ⁷But the people on Shadow Lane keep their lights burning brightly late into this night. ⁸The people on Shadow Lane have never before heard such a strange sound. ⁹The Watson twins and their parents keep their lights shining brightly in their house, too. ¹⁰The Watson twins are sixteen years old. ¹¹The Watsons live in the first house on the street. ¹²Tonight, the people of Shadow Lane will never forget the Watson twins. ¹³Tonight, the people of Shadow Lane will never forget the bizarre night sounds. ¹⁴The names of the Watson twins are Andrea and Clyde.

Extend this exercise by having students continue the story.

Eliminating Wordiness

In the writing that you do in school and on tests, it's essential to say what you mean as clearly as possible. Here are three ways to achieve clarity in your writing.

▶ **Take Out the Padding.** Don't try to "pad" your writing to make it longer.

ORIGINAL	Walt Whitman created a new type of poetic verse, which he called free verse, in which he rejected traditional poetic conventions of rhyme and meter and used instead the natural rhythms of spoken English, which, he claimed, has its own kinds of rhythm.
REVISED	Walt Whitman created a new type of verse—free verse—which uses the natural rhythms of spoken English.

▶ **Eliminate Unnecessary Repetition.** Repetition is effective when it's used to emphasize an important idea, as in Dr. Martin Luther King Jr.'s "I Have a Dream" speech. But unnecessary repetition is just another kind of padding.

ORIGINAL	The monetary unit of the nation of Japan is the yen, which is currently at this time worth on the order of approximately 82 yen to one American United States dollar.
REVISED	The monetary unit of Japan is the yen, which is currently worth approximately 82 yen to one United States dollar.

WRITING HINT

When you write the conclusion of an essay, it's a good idea to restate your main idea or main points. This kind of repetition is fine because it acts as a summary and brings your essay to a definite end.

▶ **Write in Your Own Voice.** Don't try to impress your audience with long, complicated sentences and difficult words that you think make you sound intelligent. Write in your own voice, and say what you mean as directly as you can.

ORIGINAL	*Candide*, a satire written by the French author Voltaire, is a fictional novel in which a whole lengthy series of disastrous events and proceedings befall the main character, for whom the novel is named, who is a youthful, naïve young hero named Candide.
REVISED	In the novel *Candide*, a satire by the French writer Voltaire, many disastrous events happen to the young, naïve hero, Candide.

EXERCISE 11 Revising Sentences

On a separate piece of paper, revise the following wordy sentences.
Answers will vary.

1. Irish immigration from Ireland to the United States increased during the Irish potato famine, which occurred in the 1840s, when the potato crops in Ireland failed, which caused many Irish people to die because they starved to death, and others left Ireland as a result of the potato famine.

2. "Casey at the Bat," a poem written by American writer Ernest Lawrence Thayer, is a narrative poem that tells the story of a baseball player named Casey, who, when he is the batter, lets the first two balls go by and then misses the third and strikes out without hitting the ball that he was pitched.

3. Blood is the liquid fluid that circulates and moves all through the body, through the heart, through the veins, and through the arteries and through the capillaries; the system by which blood moves and circulates throughout the body is called the circulatory system.

4. The American writer Henry David Thoreau published an essay that Thoreau titled "Civil Disobedience" after Thoreau was imprisoned in jail because he refused to pay his poll tax because he felt that his tax money would be spent in support of the Mexican War, which he opposed and was strongly against.

5. A person's fingerprint is a series of ridges and whorls on the skin surface of the underneath part of a person's fingers and thumbs, and the pattern of ridges and whorls is unique for each individual so that a person can be identified by examining the fingerprint carefully.

EXERCISE 12 Revising a Paragraph to Eliminate Wordiness

On a separate piece of paper, revise the following paragraph to eliminate wordiness. Make the writing as clear as possible, and make any other changes that you think will improve the paragraph. Revised paragraphs will vary.

[1]The Peace Corps is a federal government agency that was set up and created in 1961 when President John F. Kennedy was president of the United States. [2]President Kennedy founded and established the Peace Corps with a presidential executive order, and later that same year of 1961 Congress made it a permanent, everlasting agency under the aegis of the United States Department of State. [3]In 1981, the Peace Corps changed its status to that of an independent United States federal government agency. [4]Peace Corps volunteers volunteer for two-year periods to sojourn in a foreign land outside of the United States for the purpose of helping to improve the state of people's lives and living standards in developing nations. [5]Today more than 7,500 Peace Corps volunteers are being of assistance to individuals, businesses, and governments in more than 70 host nations worldwide in different parts of the world.

Revising and Editing Worksheet 1

Improve the following draft by revising for ideas, organization, word choice, and sentence variety. After revising, edit the draft for errors in spelling, capitalization, punctuation, and usage. Write your revised and edited version on a separate piece of paper. Compare your changes with those of a writing partner. Students' revisions will vary.

[1]The game of basketball was invented in America. [2]It was invented by a physical education teacher from Canada. [3]His name was James Naismith. [4]Basketball was devised in 1891 by Naismith. [5]Naismith was employed in the job of teaching a high-spirited group of young men in a gym class at the YMCA in Springfield, Massachusetts, he was instructed to create a new game that would keep the young men in his class busy indoors. [6]This was because the winter was too cold and windy in Springfield to be playing a sport outdoors. [7]Naismith tried to think up a game that would be easy to learn but would be challenging; it had to be one that could be played indoors by a large number of players and that would give a lot of exercise.

[8]Players used a soccer ball. [9]Players had to throw the ball into raised baskets, so he called the game "basketball." [10]It took Naismith only about an hour to make up the original rules for basketball. [11]There were thirteen of these rules. [12]Among them that a player cannot run with the ball. [13]The ball may be thrown in any direction with one or both hands. [14]But cannot be held with the arms or body.

[15]The original baskets that players threw the ball into were half-bushel peach baskets. [16]These baskets were nailed to the railing of the gym's balcony at either end of the court. [17]Whenever a goal was scored, a person standing on the balcony had to reach in and take the ball out of the basket.

[18]Basketball was immediately popular. [19]It spread to YMCAs throughout America and in many other countries. [20]Women's basketball was introduced at Smith College in 1892 and rapidly took off. [21]By 1905, there were private athletic clubs for basketball. [22]There were high school and college teams.

[23]Basketball was first played at the Olympic Games in Berlin, Germany, in 1936. [24]It was the very first time the Olympics included basketball. [25]James Naismith himself threw the opening jump ball at that first basketball game in the Olympics.

C **ccss** Language 1, 2. (See pp. T14–T15.)

Revising and Editing Worksheet 2

Improve the following draft by revising for ideas, organization, word choice, and sentence variety. After revising, edit the draft for errors in spelling, capitalization, punctuation, and usage. Write your revised and edited version on a separate piece of paper. Compare your changes with those of a writing partner. Students' revisions will vary.

[1]Immunization is the process that makes individuals become immune to a specific disease. [2]Usually by means of inoculation (which means the injection of a specially formulated serum or vaccine). [3]If you're immune, you can't get a disease. [4]Do you remember getting the shots you got as a child when you were little? [5]If you're like most childrens in the United States, you received a series of shots according to a schedule suggested by the American Academy of Pediatrics. [6]That's a professional organization for doctors who treat children. [7]When you were a newborn, the first vaccine you should have received was for hepatitis B. [8]During your first year, you were gave shots that vaccinated against diphtheria, tetanus, and whooping cough in a series of three shots. [9]Vaccines are also given to young children and kids against the diseases of measles, mumps, rubella (which is also called German measles), and to protect them against getting chicken pox and also polio.

[10]Vaccines contain parts or all of a bacteria or virus that are uniquely treated so that they don't infect you and make you sick with the disease. [11]What they do is to cause the body to trigger the body's immune system. [12]Which manufactures and creates antibodies or white blood cells that ward off the real disease if the person is ever exposed to it. [13]Say, for instance, you got your measles-mumps-rubella shot on schedule at 12–15 months and again at either 4–6 years or 11–12 years. [14]If you did and then you come in contact with the honest-to-goodness measles virus, you won't get the disease, your immunization will protect you.

[15]The process of inoculation against diseases go back to ancient times in India, Persia, and China. [16]It wasn't until 1796 that an English doctor named Dr. Edward Jenner (1749–1823) introduces the idea of vaccination to Western civilization. [17]The branch of science based on Jenner's work is called immunology—the science of making someone immune to infections.

C **CCSS** Language 1, 2. (See pp. T14–T15.)

Chapter 3

Composition

Revising and Editing Worksheet 3

Improve the following draft by revising for ideas, organization, word choice, and sentence variety. After revising, edit the draft for errors in spelling, capitalization, punctuation, and usage. Write your revised and edited version on a separate piece of paper. Compare your changes with those of a writing partner.

Students' revisions will vary.

[1]We cook in it and we look through it and we use it for drinking, and we take it very much exceedingly for granted. [2]Did you ever for a second realize that glass is one of the oldest manufactured man-made products made by human beings? [3]Dating back to prehistoric times approximately about 5,000 years ago.

[4]Before they began manufacturing glass, humans carved natural, transparent materials found in nature such as obsidian (a kind of dark volcanic glass) and a transparent form of quartz called rock crystal, which has no color. [5]Glass objects (mostly glass beads but vases also) was produced in ancient Egypt about 2,000 B.C. [6]Ancient Romans had many different kinds and varieties of glass, stained glass appeared in the tenth century A.D.

[7]Here's how glass is made. [8]Glass is made up mainly of liquid sand which various materials have been added to, including reused waste glass, sodium carbonate which lowers the melting point of sand, limestone which makes the glass impervious to water. [9]Chemicals are added to create colored glass. [10]Selenium sulfide makes glass red. [11]Copper oxide is added for a blue color. [12]All of the ingredients is put into a furnace, heated at very high temperatures (more higher than 2000°F) to melt the raw materials, then the liquid glass is slowly cooled or poured into molds.

[13]Glassblowing began in Syria somewhere during the period approximately around 27 B.C. to 14 A.D. [14]A glob of molten glass is put on one end of a long, thin tube by a glassblower, through which they blow a bubble of glass. [15]They shape the glass bubbles with tools into the desired shape. [16]The same process is used today. [17]Glass artists shape molten glass by hand into highly prized art objects. [18]Such as large bowls and sculptures. [19]Many people collect art glass, you can see beautiful examples in craft shows and museums around the world as well as ancient glass objects, such as pieces of Roman and Egyptian glass.

Writing Workshops

Narrative Writing: Personal Narrative

When you write a **personal narrative**, you tell a true autobiographical story that happened in a limited time. You strive to make it interesting, and you reflect on how you felt about the incident then and now.

The following passage is an excerpt from *Quiet Strength: The Faith, the Hope, and the Heart of a Woman Who Changed a Nation* by Rosa Parks. In the book, Parks, an African American woman, recalls the day she refused to give up her seat on a city bus, an event that prompted one of the hallmarks of the civil rights movement: the Montgomery bus boycott.

from **Quiet Strength: The Faith, the Hope, and the Heart of a Woman Who Changed a Nation**
by Rosa Parks with Gregory J. Reed

[1]The custom for getting on the bus for black persons in Montgomery in 1955 was to pay at the front door, get off the bus, and re-enter through the back door to find a seat. [2]On the buses, if white persons got on, the colored would move back if the white section was filled. [3]Black people could not sit in the same row with white people. [4]They could not even sit across the aisle from each other. [5]Some customs were humiliating, and this one was intolerable since we were the majority of the ridership.

[6]On Thursday evening, December 1, I was riding the bus home from work. [7]A white man got on, and the driver looked our way and said, "Let me have those seats." [8]It did not seem proper, particularly for a woman to give her seat to a man. [9]All the passengers paid ten cents, just as he did. [10]When more whites boarded the bus, the driver, J.P. Blake, ordered the blacks in the fifth row, the first row of the colored section (the row I was sitting in), to move to the rear. [11]Bus drivers then had police powers, under both municipal and state laws, to enforce racial segregation. [12]However, we were sitting in the section designated for colored.

[13]At first none of us moved.

[14]"Y'all better make it light on yourselves and let me have those seats," Blake said.

[15]Then three of the blacks in my row got up, but I stayed in my seat and slid closer to the window.

Provides background information and establishes setting

Reveals feelings

Describes details in chronological (time) order

Quotes dialogue

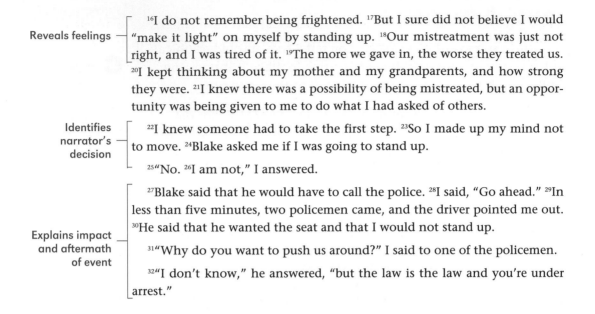

Reveals feelings

¹⁶I do not remember being frightened. ¹⁷But I sure did not believe I would "make it light" on myself by standing up. ¹⁸Our mistreatment was just not right, and I was tired of it. ¹⁹The more we gave in, the worse they treated us. ²⁰I kept thinking about my mother and my grandparents, and how strong they were. ²¹I knew there was a possibility of being mistreated, but an opportunity was being given to me to do what I had asked of others.

Identifies narrator's decision

²²I knew someone had to take the first step. ²³So I made up my mind not to move. ²⁴Blake asked me if I was going to stand up.

²⁵"No. ²⁶I am not," I answered.

Explains impact and aftermath of event

²⁷Blake said that he would have to call the police. ²⁸I said, "Go ahead." ²⁹In less than five minutes, two policemen came, and the driver pointed me out. ³⁰He said that he wanted the seat and that I would not stand up.

³¹"Why do you want to push us around?" I said to one of the policemen.

³²"I don't know," he answered, "but the law is the law and you're under arrest."

Critical Thinking   After you read the personal narrative, answer the questions below. Use the following questions to lead a class discussion.

1. What is the main issue addressed in this narrative? Using time order, summarize what happens to Ms. Parks in this narrative.

2. How do the direct quotes affect your response to this event in Ms. Parks's life?

3. This narrative provides a glimpse into what Ms. Parks was thinking and feeling. Whom was she thinking of when she decided not to give up her seat? Why do you think she chose to share this information?

4. Reread sentences 21–23. Why does Ms. Parks decide to stay in her seat, even though she knew "there was a possibility of being mistreated"?

5. With a partner, discuss an incident from another text in which someone did the right thing, even though it was unpopular.

Writing Strategies   The purpose of a personal narrative is to explain or relate a series of events. Because a personal narrative not only recounts an incident but also reflects on the incident's meaning, use writing strategies that serve these dual purposes.

1. **Select an incident.** An incident is a mini-story. It has a **plot** (the series of events), **characters**, and a **setting** (when and where the incident occurred). Because you are the narrator—the person telling the story—you should narrate the incident from the **first-person point of view** using first-person pronouns (*I, me, mine, we, us, ours*).

2. **Set the scene.** Engage the reader by introducing the situation you will describe, as well as the significance of the event—that is, how and why the event is important and meaningful to you. Establish yourself as the narrator, and introduce the other characters and the setting.

3. **Sequence events to create a coherent whole.** A complete event sequence is made up of individual events that occur over a period of time. If you write in **chronological order**, you'll start at the beginning and relate the events in the order they occurred until you've recounted the entire incident. You may also use reverse chronological order to recount an incident from its conclusion back to its beginning.

> **WRITING HINT**
>
> Envision the incident in your mind as if it were a movie filmed through a camera lens. As the camera pans the incident, select the sensory details that stand out for you.

4. **Include dialogue.** Words are powerful, especially exact words that are spoken, so include some direct quotes. If you don't remember the exact words from the event you are narrating, take a guess at who said what. Rosa Parks includes dialogue between herself and the bus driver and later between herself and one of the police officers.

5. **Add vivid descriptions and sensory language.** Use precise words and phrases to vividly describe the incident as you experienced it. Note what you saw, heard, smelled, tasted, or touched. Too many sensory details, however, may slow the pace of the action, so choose only the most relevant ones.

6. **Reflect on the experience.** Think back on how you felt while the incident was unfolding. How do you feel about it in retrospect? Remember to include your reflections—or thoughts and feelings about the incident—throughout the narrative. End with a conclusion that reflects on your experiences and sums up your insights about the incident.

EXERCISE 1 Get Started

Use one or two of the prewriting techniques (writer's notebook, freewriting, brainstorming, clustering, and so on) from Lesson 1.1 to generate some incidents you can write about. Like Rosa Parks, you might focus on a decision you once made. You could also concentrate on an incident that changed you or on something extraordinary that happened to you. The incident or decision can be serious or funny. Think of the incident as if it were a story with a plot, characters, a setting, and a point of view.
Answers will vary.

EXERCISE 2 Plan Your Personal Narrative

Create a story map similar to the one below to sort out the relationships among elements in your personal narrative and your feelings or insights about them. Include as many details in your story map as you can.
Answers will vary. Encourage students to err on the side of too many details at this stage of writing.

Story Map	
a. What is the **setting?**	
b. Identify the **characters** and describe them.	
c. Identify the **conflict** or event in your narrative.	
d. Why was the event important to you?	

Exercise 3 Draft Your Personal Narrative

As you draft, remember that your audience is your classmates. Your purpose may be to tell an entertaining story or an important one. Note that in addition to the story itself, Rosa Parks shares her feelings about the incident throughout her narrative. Answers will vary.

- **Make your point clearly.** A personal narrative goes beyond simply describing an incident; you have to reflect on and explain the significance the incident had for you. If you spent a day volunteering at a soup kitchen, for example, you might write about how you felt looking at the people in line. What did you learn about them and about yourself through your experience?

- **Include essential events and telling details.** Sometimes, one piece of dialogue or one telltale action reveals the whole point of your narrative. Look for these kinds of telling quotes or moments and use them to illustrate the point of your narrative. Let them unfold naturally so readers sense their meaning as an integral part of the incident.

Exercise 4 Revise Your Personal Narrative

Read your paper aloud to yourself and then to a partner. First, make sure the events are organized logically (use either chronological order or order of importance). Listen for active verbs, sensory details, and dialogue. Make any changes to improve the narrative flow. Then reread the essay to see if it is coherent and unified. Eliminate wordiness and replace general nouns or verbs with precise ones. When you're satisfied with your draft, share it with a small writers' group. Ask the members of the group for their comments, questions, and suggestions, and then decide if you want to revise further. Answers will vary. Students should refer to Lesson 1.3 for more revising strategies.

Exercise 5 Edit and Publish

Edit your revised paper for errors in grammar, usage, punctuation, capitalization, and spelling. Exchange papers with a partner to see if you've missed any mistakes. Answers will vary. Students should refer to Mechanics, Chapters 13–16, for additional proofreading skills.

Share your personal narrative with friends and family, especially anyone who might have had a similar experience or who was directly involved in yours. If you enjoyed this assignment, continue to write about incidents that mean something to you as chapters in an ongoing memoir. You might also consider presenting this personal narrative as a gift to a friend or relative.

C **ccss** Reading Informational Text 1, 4; Writing 1a–e, 4, 5, 10; Language 1, 2, 4c.
(See pp. T14–T15.)

Persuasive Writing

C **ccss**

Standards for this lesson focus on writing coherent arguments that include a precise claim (supported by logically sequenced reasons and relevant evidence) and that effectively address counterclaims.

How do you hold readers' interest, win them over to your viewpoint, and convince them to act on an issue—all at the same time? You write a **persuasive essay** with clear **arguments** that are well supported by strong reasons and relevant evidence. As you read the following essay about curfews, pay attention to the author's argument and her evidence to support it.

Down with Curfews; Up with Children
by Nadine Strossen

Attention grabber —

¹In San Diego, the American Civil Liberties Union (ACLU) is now representing a group of clients who face criminal prosecution because they engage in the following activities: working in a Rescue Mission soup kitchen; volunteering for "Safe Rides," a program providing teenagers with rides home from weekend parties; acting in plays; and participating in study groups. ²The dregs of society, eh?

Loaded words make claim clear

³Why do our clients face arrest for these perfectly lawful—indeed, laudable—activities? ⁴Because they are teenagers who live in San Diego, which has been aggressively enforcing a curfew law that bars anyone under eighteen from all public places after 10 P.M. ⁵Moreover, many other cities, all across the country, have recently adopted similar policies, putting all teens under virtual house arrest.

States claim of curfew supporters

⁶Politicians across the spectrum have applauded these martial law-type measures. ⁷In his 1996 "State of the State" address, California Governor Pete Wilson denounced the ACLU's lawsuit against the San Diego curfew, saying, "If anyone ought to be sued, it's the ACLU—for defying common sense."

Logical appeal with evidence: businesses and police oppose curfew

⁸Our teenage clients and their parents might not agree with the governor—and they would not be alone. ⁹The many businesses harmed by the loss of young patrons, and the police officers who would rather pursue real criminals—of all ages—than turn innocent young people into criminals, undoubtedly would join the ACLU in "defying" common sense.

Direct quote by police captain endorses ACLU claim

¹⁰Significantly, the decision to aggressively enforce San Diego's strict curfew was made by the city council, not police officials. ¹¹As one police captain reported to the department's assistant chief, "Field officials tend to see this program as a politically inspired boondoggle that has no real relevance to crime problems on their beats."

Statistical evidence on teenage crime

¹²San Diego's arrest statistics bear out the police officers' view that enforcing the teen curfew is a waste of their time. ¹³Since the strict enforcement began, the number of juvenile arrests for violent crimes decreased almost four times as much during noncurfew hours as it did during curfew hours. ¹⁴Likewise,

the number of juveniles who were victims of violent crime decreased almost twice as much during noncurfew hours as during curfew hours.

Emotional appeal supported by evidence

[15]Most crimes committed by and against minors occur between 3 and 6 P.M. [16]And, tragically, most violence against young people takes place in their own homes. [17]Under the "logic" of the curfew advocates, should we therefore banish our nation's youth from their own homes? [18]Or hold them hostage there during the midafternoon? . . .

Use of loaded term—"Big Brother"—supported by concept of constitutional rights

[19]When Big Brother acts like Big Daddy, by imposing a curfew on all children, he violates the constitutional rights of parents and children alike. [20]A federal judge in Washington, D.C., so ruled at the end of October. [21]He struck down the District's 1995 curfew law, which the ACLU challenged on behalf of a group of young people, their parents and grandparents, and a movie theater. [22]Unfortunately, though, the unconstitutionality of the recent rash of curfew laws is far from settled. [23]The D.C. government promptly appealed the ACLU's victory; other lower courts have split on the issue—for example, a federal judge in San Diego upheld its draconian curfew last summer; and the U.S. Supreme Court has never resolved the issue.

Call to action against teenage curfews

[24]We have to hope that when the Supreme Court does face this important issue, it will follow the sound approach of the Washington, D.C., ruling. [25]Along with so many of the faddish policies that are touted as "anticrime," "pro-children," and "pro-family," curfew laws are, in fact, just the opposite. [26]If we really want to do something for young people and their families—as well as for public safety—maybe we should impose strict curfews on all politicians, to stop them from enacting ineffective and dangerous measures.

Critical Thinking   After you read the persuasive essay, answer the questions below. Use the following questions to lead a class discussion.

1. Which details in the first and second paragraphs make the writer's claim clear?

2. To what audience do you think this writer is addressing her essay? Cite details in the essay that make you think this.

3. List two reasons—with specific examples of evidence—that support the writer's claim.

4. How does the writer counter the opposing claims of those in favor of teenage curfews in San Diego? Cite examples from the essay.

5. The next to last paragraph begins with this statement: "When Big Brother acts like Big Daddy. . . ." How do the terms "Big Brother" and "Big Daddy" influence how you feel about Nadine Strossen's argument against teenage curfews?

6. Read the last paragraph aloud. In what way does this paragraph affect your opinion on the subject of curfews for teenagers? What kind of action would you consider taking after reading this essay?

Build Your Vocabulary. Which of these words from the essay can you define: *laudable* (sentence 3), *boondoggle* (sentence 11), *draconian* (sentence 23), *touted* (sentence 25)? Look up the words you don't know in the dictionary, and use the phonetic symbols to pronounce the words correctly. Add these words to your vocabulary notebook.

Writing Strategies   The purpose of writing a persuasive essay is to convince your reader to support your opinion. As you write, include a variety of the following strategies to strengthen your argument.

1. **Introduce a precise claim.** Your opinion is the heart of your argument— a concise summary of your entire essay. Clearly state your opinion at the beginning of your essay in a well-developed **claim,** or **thesis statement**. Make your claim thorough but succinct—no more than a sentence or two. Later in your argument, you will distinguish your claim from alternate or opposing claims.

2. **Develop your claim with reasons and evidence.** Develop a logically organized argument by supporting your claim with valid reasons, or statements that explain why you hold your opinion. Include at least two convincing reasons to support your claim, and support your reasons with relevant evidence. Include transitions to clarify your reasoning and to make your organization clear. Some forms of evidence are listed below; use those that are most appropriate and convincing for your audience and purpose.

   - State **facts** or **statistics** from reliable reference sources.

   - Include **expert opinions** in the form of quotations. (Make sure to identify the expert and use an exact quote.)

   - Drop in **examples** and **anecdotes** (including some drawn from personal experience or observation).

3. **Support reasons with emotional appeals.** Emotional appeals strengthen your argument *only* when accompanied by evidence-supported reasons, which are **logical appeals**. Emotional appeals used alone may offend readers, make them lose interest

---

WRITING HINT

As you write your essay, carefully consider your word choice, style, and tone.

1. Identify your audience, including their knowledge level of your subject. Use language that will both persuade and appeal to them.

2. Establish and maintain a formal style. Use standard English and appropriate word choice to show that you are knowledgeable and reliable.

3. Use an objective tone. Presenting your claim fairly and respectfully will strengthen your argument and show that you have considered multiple perspectives on your subject.

in your ideas, or raise suspicions about the validity of your reasoning. Use emotional appeals carefully.

Loaded words may carry either positive or negative connotations. For example, the word *dregs* often has a negative connotation, which communicates a negative emotion. When Nadine Strossen writes about teenagers as "the *dregs* of society, eh?" (sentence 2), she is heightening readers' awareness of negative feelings toward teenagers with this loaded word. Indeed, she hopes her readers will reject the negativity inherent in the word *dregs* and come around to her viewpoint, which she feels is more positive toward teenagers.

4. **Avoid fallacies of thinking.** These are unproved assumptions communicated when writers **stereotype** (present a fixed idea about all members of a group) and **overgeneralize** (present a conclusion applied to everyone). The words *everyone* or *most* often introduce these kinds of fallacies.

OVERGENERALIZATION *Everyone* knows that rock music is simplistic. [overgeneralization about the qualities of rock music]

STEREOTYPING *Most* writers are mere dreamers, not doers. [stereotyping the personalities of all people who write]

5. **Address counterclaims.** In your persuasive essay, be sure to acknowledge opposing viewpoints, or **counterclaims (counterarguments)**. Give valid reasons—along with relevant evidence—to disprove these counterclaims.

6. **Conclude with a call to action.** End your essay with a concluding statement that follows logically from your reasons and evidence. Persuasive writers often conclude by urging readers to take constructive action, such as writing letters, donating money, voting in an election, or volunteering. A **call to action** effectively reinforces your claim.

Exercise 6 Choose a Topic

Work with a small group to brainstorm topics for a persuasive essay. Use these hints. Answers will vary. Suggest that students use the prewriting suggestions in Lesson 1.1.

• The topic must be debatable, not just a matter of personal opinion. It should be an issue or question that people disagree about.

• You must have a strong opinion about the topic you choose. Keep in mind, however, that some topics are inappropriate for school assignments. Check with your teacher if you suspect that your topic may be inappropriate.

EXERCISE 7 State Your Claim

The chart below shows how one writer developed a precise claim for a persuasive essay. With your writing group, complete the chart with other possible claims that are clear and knowledgeable on the topics listed.

Answers will vary.

Developing a Claim

Subject of Essay	Precise Claim
Physical Fitness	High school physical education departments should help students develop and maintain individual fitness programs.
Student Government	
Teen Volunteers	
Your Topic	

Now, add the topic for your persuasive essay to the chart and develop a clear, precise claim.

EXERCISE 8 Support Your Claim

Before you write, think about your audience and choose the reasons, evidence, and emotional appeals that will persuade the members of this audience to embrace your point of view. Write down as many arguments as you can think of to support your claim. Answers will vary.

• Choose the two or three strongest arguments.

• Jot down the reasons, evidence, and emotional appeals that support each argument. These notes can serve as a rough outline as you start Exercise 9.

EXERCISE 9 Draft Your Essay

As you write your draft, support your claim with the reasons and relevant evidence you outlined in Exercise 8. Keep the following in mind.

Answers will vary. Students should refer to Lesson 1.2 for drafting strategies.

- Provide background information that you think your intended audience will need to understand your subject and to follow your argument.

- Mention your sources and be specific in the evidence you present. Thorough research will make your argument more convincing.

- As you write, consider your audience and purpose. Keep your argument focused.

EXERCISE 10 Revise, Proofread, and Publish

Revise your writing carefully to eliminate unnecessary words and sentences. Tighten your argument by omitting anything that doesn't directly support your main point. To influence readers' emotions, selectively include loaded words and emotional appeals in your essay. After revising, proofread for errors in spelling, capitalization, punctuation, and usage. Share your essay with a writing group, or use the following publishing suggestions.

- Send your persuasive essay to the editor of a school or local newspaper as an editorial or a letter to the editor.

- If you've written on issues that affect government, send your essay to a government representative from your community or state.

- Send your persuasive essay to a local television or radio program with a letter asking the producer to consider addressing the issue on the air.

- Use the claim in your essay as the starting point for a team debate among classmates.

Answers will vary. Students should refer to Lesson 1.4 for proofreading strategies and publishing suggestions.

CCSS Reading Informational Text 1; Writing 1a–c, 1e, 4, 5, 6, 10; Language 1, 2, 4c. (See pp. T14–T15.)

Persuasive Writing: Critical Review

CCSS

Standards for this lesson focus on writing coherent arguments to analyze topics or texts, introducing a precise claim supported by logically sequenced and valid reasons, as well as relevant and sufficient evidence.

When you watch a movie, read a book, or look at a painting or sculpture, you have a reaction to it—either positive or negative. If you write about your reaction and analyze why that work of art makes you feel that way, your essay—or **critical review**—becomes a form of **persuasive writing**. Sometimes, a critical review may summarize the plot and give an opinion about the overall work. But a critical review goes beyond a plot summary and a stated opinion: You must make a precise **claim** about the work and support it with valid **reasons** and relevant **evidence**. The evidence you cite may encompass **comparisons** with other works of the same genre or **emotional appeals** based on your personal reaction.

Below is one person's review about a movie. Think critically about the author's opinion as you read.

"Hoot" delivers message of empowerment to kids
by Ty Burr

Grabs reader's attention

[1]"Hoot," the new film adapted from Carl Hiaasen's 2002 young-adult novel, isn't the most elegantly made movie. [2]Writer-director Wil Shriner comes from TV—he made a lot of "Frasier" episodes—and it shows. [3]Close one eye and you could mistake the film for an After School Special.

Claim and identification of the movie's themes

[4]So what? [5]"Hoot" tells kids they can make a difference in this world, and that's worth a hundred "Ice Age 2"s. [6]Of the several different messages knocking around in the movie—overdevelopment is bad, nature is good, don't stand on a golf course during peak drive-time—the most effective is the simplest: You have more power than you think.

Introduces the movie's plot

[7]After six relocations in eight years, 13-year-old Roy Eberhardt (Logan Lerman) is once again the new kid in town, instantly preyed on by the bullies who ride the bus with him to Florida's Coconut Cove Middle School. [8]As Roy is getting thrashed one day, he glimpses a barefoot boy (Cody Linley) running at blinding speed alongside the bus, and his curiosity grows into an obsession.

Analyzes the characters

[9]Someone, meanwhile, keeps vandalizing the wooded construction site where a Mother Paula's Pancake House franchise is about to be erected, and it's driving site foreman Curly (Tim Blake Nelson) crazy. [10]Kind but dimwitted town cop Dave Delinko (Luke Wilson) tries to catch the culprit but has his cruiser windows spray-painted black when he falls asleep on night watch. [11]In his high-rise office in the city, Mother Paula regional manager Chuck Muckle (Clark Gregg) fumes and shouts.

Analyzes the characters

¹²They're all helpless against the barefoot boy, who turns out to be a military school runaway nicknamed Mullet Fingers (because, uh, he can catch mullets with his fingers). ¹³He, in turn is cared for by his stepsister Beatrice (Brie Larson), a fearsome middle school soccer jock who keeps Roy and other nosy parkers at bay. ¹⁴The movie hints just enough about the miserable home life of these two for us to be glad we don't know more.

States the movie's theme

¹⁵Why do these kids care about a parcel of dirt? ¹⁶Because the holes in the ground are filled with burrowing owls and their young—endangered species that Muckle would just as soon bulldoze. ¹⁷The movie takes a longer view as well, wondering how much building is too much in a fragile ecosystem like Florida (or, it's implied, your own town). ¹⁸Says Mullet Fingers, "As long as I've been growing up here, I've been watching this place disappear."

Compares film to the novel on which it is based

¹⁹He's the Edward Abbey-style nature boy of the film, in touch with the manatees and dedicated to monkey-wrenching the Man. ²⁰Roy is a more lawfully minded kid and his ethical dilemma is the film's. ²¹I see by my daughter's book report that Hiaasen's novel delved more deeply into these issues, but they're present in the movie and well worth chewing over when the lights come up.

Relates movie to previous works from the same studio

²²"Hoot" comes from Walden Media, the small "family values" studio that has been turning thoughtful young-adult books like *Holes* and *Because of Winn-Dixie* into solid little movies (and that successfully rolled the dice on *The Chronicles of Narnia* last year). ²³The movie balances cardboard comic bad-guys with believable teenagers, has the courage to avoid romance, and unlike most Hollywood films suggests parents can be helpful and loving as well as clueless. ²⁴(Parrothead alert: Jimmy Buffett coproduced the film, sings on the soundtrack, and has a role as Roy's *very* laid-back science teacher.)

Makes a comparison between this movie and others

Identifies a weakness

Concludes by re-stating the movie's strongest point

²⁵The one thing "Hoot" gets wrong is the title. Burrowing owls grumble, chatter, scream, and say "coo-coo," but they don't hoot, and as far as I can tell that's a great horned owl dubbed onto the soundtrack. ²⁶But the film nails the sound of a young person getting empowered, which is all that matters.

Critical Thinking   After you read the critical review, answer the questions below.
Use the following questions to lead a class discussion.

1. Based on the first two paragraphs of the review, what does the author think the movie's strengths are? What does he think the movie's weaknesses are?

2. What evidence does the author give to justify his statement that "the movie balances cardboard comic bad-guys with believable teenagers"?

3. Reread sentence 19. Edward Abbey was a famous writer who loved nature and the environment. Do you think the author of the review supports his assertion that Mullet Fingers is an environmentalist? Explain your answer.

4. In his conclusion, the author identifies a weakness and restates one of the movie's strengths. Do you think that this technique improves or detracts from the critical review? Explain your answer.

Build Your Vocabulary. Which of these words from the essay can you define: *preyed* (sentence 7), *obsession* (sentence 8), *franchise* (sentence 9), *culprit* (sentence 10), *mullets* (sentence 12), *delved* (sentence 21)? Look up the words you don't know in a dictionary, and use the phonetic symbols to pronounce the words correctly. Add these words to your vocabulary notebook.

Writing Strategies The purpose of a critical review is to present your opinion of a movie, live performance, book, or other work of art and to persuade your readers that your opinion is correct. Here are some strategies that you can use to persuade readers.

1. **Choose a subject, and identify your audience.**
   Choose a film, book, or artwork you know well and about which you have strong feelings—positive or negative. Then think about your readers. How much do you need to explain to them about the work you are reviewing? For example, if your readers have never seen the movie or read the book you are reviewing, you may wish to give a brief plot summary. If you are writing about a very famous movie, play, or book, a plot summary may be unnecessary.

2. **Introduce a precise claim.** Make your opinion of the work clear by stating it in a precise claim. Your claim should be thorough, but concise—no more than a sentence or two. Your claim usually belongs in the first paragraph of your critical review.

3. **Develop your claim with reasons and evidence.**
   As in any persuasive writing, develop and support your claim with valid reasons and relevant evidence. For example, if you claim that the major weakness of a film or play is the acting, cite specific examples as evidence and explain how it affects the overall work.

4. **Organize your essay, and use transitions.** In writing a critical review, you can present your opinion at the beginning and support it with reasons and evidence, or you can build your case throughout the review and offer your opinion as the overall conclusion.

Criteria for Movie Reviews

- What kind of movie are you reviewing— adventure, drama, science fiction, romance, comedy, children's feature?

- What element of the film—writing, acting, cinematography, special effects—captivates you the most?

- How do the technical aspects of the film— cinematography, color, special effects, music, lighting—contribute to the overall point of the movie?

- Do the actors succeed in their roles?

- Is the script well written?

- Does the story progress coherently from scene to scene?

Whichever organization you choose, use transition words and phrases to create coherence and help readers understand how your claims, reasons, and evidence relate to each another.

5. **End with a conclusion.** Depending on the organization of your review, your conclusion may summarize your opinion of the work or explain how your claim follows logically from your reasons and evidence.

EXERCISE 11 Choose a Subject

In a small group, list the books you've read, movies you've watched, or plays you've seen in the last month. Choose one for the subject of your review, and consider other works in the same category to use as comparisons. Answers will vary.

- Group the works by genre—that is, adventure, drama, comedy, science fiction, and so on.

- Name the characters and author, or the actors and director, involved in each book, movie, or play.

- Discuss the plot of the work and any outstanding features, such as special effects, a remarkable setting, or effective dialect.

EXERCISE 12 Explore the Subject and Develop Your Opinion

Go over the information you listed in your group in Exercise 11. If you are reviewing a movie, think about your subject in terms of the Criteria for Movie Reviews on page 66 in this lesson. The aspects for judging books, movies, and plays listed in the chart below may help you evaluate various elements of the work that you can mention in your review. Answers will vary.

Movie	Book	Play
location of film	setting	sets
theme	theme	theme
dialogue	writing style	script
casting/acting	characters	casting/acting
directing	movement of plot	stage direction
technical aspects (special effects/music score/etc.)	attention to detail	atmosphere of theater

Exercise 13 State Your Opinion and Organize Ideas

For the work you've chosen to review, summarize your opinion in one or two sentences. You may want to test out your opinion on your writing group. Then list the reasons for your opinion. Organize those reasons—and the evidence supporting each one—in a way that strengthens your argument and makes it persuasive. Draw details from your notes from Exercise 12 to bolster your opinion. Answers will vary. Tell students to make sure their opinions are supported by reasons.

Exercise 14 Draft Your Critical Review

Think of your review in three parts: the introduction, the body, and the conclusion. Remember that a critical review is much more than an opinion and plot summary. Answers will vary. Drafts should reflect a coherent structure.

• **Introduction** Grab your reader's attention with an appeal to his or her emotions, a strong claim, or a striking comparison.

• **Body** In the midsection of your review, specify the reasons for your claim. Cite evidence from the work itself, and detail your own emotional reaction to it.

• **Conclusion** Restate your claim in an interesting way. Summarize your argument from both the introduction and the body of the review.

Exercise 15 Revise and Edit Your Review

Allow at least a few hours between drafting and revising. Make sure your claim is precise. Check the order in which you present reasons and evidence. Would a different order be more persuasive? Did you provide enough evidence to successfully persuade your readers? Have a partner read your review and point out paragraphs that succeed and others that could use more work. Finally, edit your critical review for mistakes in grammar, usage, punctuation, capitalization, and spelling. Answers will vary.

Exercise 16 Publish Your Review

Share your review with your writing group. Then discuss where movie or book reviews by teens are published. Consider sending your review to a school or community newspaper—or even to a local radio station. Check Web sites where teens exchange critical reviews. Publish your review at a site where you can get feedback from students in other schools around the nation.

Expository Writing: Problem-Solution Essay

Sometimes in an essay, you identify a **problem** and offer one or more possible **solutions**. Here's an editorial about two kinds of coral that have been identified as "threatened."

A Move to Save Coral Reefs

Editorial from *The New York Times,* June 5, 2006

[1]Anyone who has given thought to the pitifully fragile state of the oceans' coral reefs should have been heartened by the recent classification of two kinds of coral as threatened under the Endangered Species Act. [2]The inclusion of the elkhorn and staghorn, two species of Caribbean coral, was a welcome first for the list, prompted by a task force on coral reefs established by President Bill Clinton and continued by the Bush administration.

[3]The prominence given to the two spiky formations may help to educate the public about creatures that many people do not understand. [4]Coral colonies consist of billions of tiny organisms and can take centuries to grow just a few feet. [5]But now whole stretches are being killed off at alarming rates around the world by bad human behavior. [6]That includes the dumping of untreated sewage or industrial runoff into the ocean. [7]Coral that is constantly broken by irresponsible snorkelers, divers, poachers, or fishing boats takes decades to recover, if it ever can. [8]Human dependency on fossil fuels contributes to global warming and rising ocean temperatures.

[9]Coral reefs, wildly colored when healthy, can go chalk white when they are sick and dying, usually the result of stress from sustained higher temperatures in the sea or exposure to ultraviolet rays of the sun. [10]Last fall, record amounts of bleaching occurred in the Caribbean, killing at least 8 percent of the elkhorn coral colonies off the Virgin Islands.

[11]Coral reefs cover a very small part of the ocean, less than 1 percent. [12]But they contribute mightily to the sustenance of ecosystems needed in the oceans, attracting and supporting diverse sea life. [13]When reef systems die—as happened off the Seychelles islands, where sea temperatures were elevated for several years—varieties of fish become extinct. [14]Coral reefs also provide natural barriers to severe weather, like storm surges from hurricanes. [15]And they process and recycle carbon dioxide from the atmosphere.

CCSS

Standards for this lesson focus on writing informative/explanatory texts that convey complex information by identifying a problem and using facts and details to propose a solution.

Identifies problem and a recent attempt at a solution

Lists reasons that the problem exists

Further analysis of the problem, including a statistic

Explanation of the seriousness of the problem

Expository Writing:
Problem-Solution Essay

Uses conclusion
to reinforce initial
solution and make
a call to action

[16]The official recognition that coral deserves to be protected is a step in the right direction and may buy some time. [17]But more action is needed, and quickly, if the underwater wonders that support so much life are to survive intact.

Critical Thinking   After you read the problem-solution essay, answer the questions below. Use the following questions to lead a class discussion.

1. With a partner, reread the essay. Identify which paragraph introduces the problem. Identify the paragraphs in which the problem is analyzed. Identify where in the essay the author identifies a solution.

2. How does the author analyze the problem? How does he or she use statistics and examples to clarify and strengthen the ideas?

3. Reread paragraphs 4–5. How does the author analyze the problem?

4. How does the author conclude the essay?

Build Your Vocabulary.   Which of these words from the essay can you define based on what you already know or on context clues: *pitifully* (sentence 1), *prominence* (sentence 3), *organisms* (sentence 4), *snorkelers* (sentence 7), *sustenance* (sentence 12), *ecosystems* (sentence 12)? Look up the words you don't know in a dictionary, and add these words to your vocabulary notebook.

Writing Strategies   The purpose of a problem-solution essay is to identify a problem and to explain a possible solution to the problem. To make a strong case in a problem-solution essay, you must gather information, present details in a logical order, and express your ideas clearly. Use the following strategies:

1. **Identify a problem.** Leaf through your writer's notebook, and see if you have written about a problem that you feel should be solved. Try brainstorming (page 9) problems that arise in science, medicine, or politics. Consider freewriting (page 10) about a local, national, or international issue that you and your readers feel strongly about. Your problem can be one that already has a working solution or one for which you can propose an original solution.

2. **Gather information.** Research the solutions to the problem you've chosen to write about. How have others suggested handling the problem?

3. **Build your case.** Come up with reasons why the solution is effective. Explain the solution using evidence: facts, statistics, quotations, expert opinions, anecdotes, or examples.

4. **Make an outline.** After you've gathered evidence to support your solution, organize this material into an outline to help you figure out the strongest and most logical way to explain that evidence. If appropriate, you may wish to include a step-by-step proposal to implement your solution.

5. **Address any anticipated resistance.** Many social problems— homelessness, substance abuse, elevated dropout rates, for example—are difficult to solve because there are at least two sides to the issue. In your problem-solution essay, be sure to acknowledge the arguments of those opposed to your solution, and point out why your solution is workable.

6. **Connect ideas.** In writing your essay, make sure that one idea flows seamlessly into the next by connecting ideas with the proper transition words. Highlight similar ideas with words such as *similarly*, *likewise*, *also*, and *too*. As you shift from one thought to a contrasting one, guide readers with transitions such as *however*, *yet*, *but*, and *on the other hand*. To show that one point results from another, insert transitions such as *if . . . then*, *when*, *as a result of*, and *because*.

EXERCISE 17 Choose a Topic

Use one or all of the following suggestions to come up with a topic for your problem-solution essay. Your audience will be your classmates and teachers.
Answers will vary. Students should refer to Lesson 1.1 for prewriting strategies.

• **It's personal.** Interview friends and classmates, or leaf through the advice column in a school or local newspaper to identify a personal problem that teens typically experience.

• **It's academic.** Do a survey of your peers to come up with specific school problems that need to be solved. From the responses, choose a problem that interests you.

• **It's political.** Read newspapers and magazines, listen to radio shows, or watch television programs dealing with current events. To find out about community problems, attend a meeting of a local political or volunteer organization, or call the offices of these groups. Choose a political issue that you care about.

EXERCISE 18 Gather and Organize Information

Brainstorm several possible solutions to the problem you've chosen to write about. Then gather evidence, such as facts, statistics, quotations, expert opinions, examples, and anecdotes. Some of your evidence may derive from online or printed sources, such as newspapers; other evidence (including anecdotes or quotations) may come from interviews or discussions. Take notes or summarize the evidence supporting each solution. This will help you decide which solution would work best and which evidence supports the reasons for that solution.

Answers will vary. Research may reveal weaknesses in students' topics. Encourage students to adjust their topics based on new information.

EXERCISE 19 Organize and Draft Your Essay

Use the following instructions to organize and draft your problem-solution essay. Concentrate on getting your ideas down in your draft. Answers will vary.

1. **Identify and define the problem.** Introduce the topic of your essay by first identifying and defining the problem that you will address. Consider introducing the topic with an interesting quotation, statistic, or observation.

2. **Develop the topic thoroughly.** Think about the people in your audience (classmates and teachers) and what they might or might not know about your topic. Select the most important and relevant facts, definitions, concrete details, quotations, or other information and examples related to your topic. Be careful not to include minor or unnecessary details.

3. **Use transitions and precise language.** Use transitions to link the different sections of your essay and help your readers understand the relationships among complex ideas and concepts. Include precise language, such as specialized vocabulary terms and relevant analogies, to help your audience better understand the issue.

4. **Maintain a formal style and objective tone.** In your essay, use standard English and an objective tone to show your audience that you are authoritative and reliable and to help your readers stay focused on the topic.

5. **Present your proposed solution.** State your solution clearly. Use relevant evidence to explain why the solution solves the problem. Provide facts, statistics, quotations, expert opinions, anecdotes, and examples. Tell why it's better—for example, more workable, less costly, or more comprehensive—than the alternatives.

6. **Conclude your case.** In the conclusion, briefly restate your solution, adding a powerful quotation or question, if appropriate, that provokes your readers to seriously think through the ideas in your essay.

EXERCISE 20 Revise Your Essay

Ask yourself the following revision questions to help you improve your essay.

Have I stated the problem clearly and analyzed it clearly? Have I presented a solution that readers can understand? Did I include enough compelling evidence? Have I restated my solution with enough emphasis in the conclusion? Have I eliminated wordiness and inserted transitions to connect one idea to the next? Answers will vary. Students should refer to Lesson 1.3 for more revising strategies.

EXERCISE 21 Edit and Publish Your Essay

Edit your essay to check for mistakes in grammar, usage, punctuation, capitalization, mechanics, and spelling. Then ask a partner to check it for mistakes. Answers will vary. Students should refer to Lesson 1.4 for proofreading strategies and publishing suggestions.

• Read your essay aloud to classmates. When you're finished, ask them to summarize the problem you targeted and your solution. Allow time for listeners to ask questions about your solution.

• If another student tackles the same or a similar topic, create student teams to debate the problem. Related essays may be used to develop arguments for either side of the debate.

ⓒ CCSS Reading Literature 1; Reading Informational Text 1, 6; Writing 4, 5, 6, 9a, 10; Language 1, 2, 4, 4a, 6.
(See pp. T14–T15.)

Writing About Literature: Analyzing Drama

ⓒ CCSS

Standards for this lesson focus on analyzing literary texts students have read and writing a brief essay that analyzes one element in a drama, drawing evidence from the text to support the analysis.

Enriching Your Vocabulary

The noun *credence* comes from the Latin verb *credere*, which means "to believe in," or "to put faith in." It's easy to misinterpret a conflict if you give *credence* to rumors about it.

When you write about a play, you take into account a number of factors, such as your overall response to the work, the power of the writing, the strength of the plot, and how each theatrical element interacts with the others. Here are three ways to structure an essay about a work of drama:

1. In a **personal response** essay, you communicate your feelings about what the play means to you.

2. In an **evaluation**, you focus on the strengths and weaknesses of the play. You answer this question: How good is the play?

3. In a **literary analysis**, you analyze the play by examining each element separately—writing, character development, plot, staging, and theme. Then you explain how each element contributes to the play and how the elements interact to create an overall effect.

The following excerpt is from a longer literary analysis of Sophocles's *Antigone*. The writer, Eliot Bloomfield, discusses which of the main characters (Antigone or Creon) is the true tragic hero—and why.

Sophocles' *Antigone*
by Eliot Bloomfield

Title and playwright
Main conflict

. . . [1]*Antigone* by Sophocles is based on an incident taken from the history of the royal family of Thebes. [2]The tragedy arises from the conflict of two loyalties—loyalty to God (or the gods) and loyalty to the state. [3]Antigone

Statement about characters and theme

represents the first and Creon the second. [4]Caught between these two forces is Haemon, Creon's son and Antigone's fiancé. [5]He is torn between filial piety and love for his bride-to-be. [6]The tragedy could have been written around him, but that was not the way Sophocles chose. [7]Rather, [Sophocles] turned his back on Haemon's problem to take up the larger intellectual tragic problems.

[8]Actually, there is a real question in *Antigone* as to who is the tragic hero. [9]That it must be either Antigone or Creon is clear from the play itself, and the

Analysis of title

title should lend credence to those who favor Antigone. [10]But it is most likely that the title was used by Sophocles merely to indicate the general subject matter. [11]A stronger case can be made for the theory that *Antigone* is

Notion of tragic hero stems from pride.

Creon's tragedy. [12]It is [Creon's] tragic fault of pride (*hubris*) or obstinacy which brings upon him his doom in the deaths of his son and wife. [13]The chorus points this out clearly throughout the play and especially at the end. . . .

[14]Creon pitted himself against the gods, who demand that honor be paid to the dead, and in his presumption, he was brought low. [15]The Greeks looked

Ideas about loyalty in Greek society — with particular horror at those who refused to allow the dead to be buried properly. [16]Such a deed would still arouse indignation today, but to the Greeks it would be the violation of a religious duty and a true sacrilege. [17]It meant

Explains central conflict — that the shade (or soul) of the unburied would not be allowed to enter Hades, the abode of the dead.

Writer advances controversial interpretation of the play. — [18]Although Antigone, in our opinion, is not the tragic hero of this play, she does more than serve as a mere foil and as opposition to Creon. [19]She is a majestic and moving figure in her own right. [20]Inflexible and perhaps somewhat arrogant, she nevertheless moves us in her dignity and in her defense of a higher morality than the expedient and the immediate. [21]She is not in love with death, as her grief over her unmarried state shows, but she is willing to die for what she knows is right. [22]She serves as an eternal symbol and warning for all men.

Supports thesis, or claim, with idea from Aristotle's Poetics — [23]Aristotle in his *Poetics* held that the playgoer, witnessing a great tragedy, undergoes a purgation of soul (catharsis) as he pities the characters and feels terror for their (and his) human lot. [24]Much ink has been spilled trying to explain exactly what catharsis is, and the subject cannot be dealt with here. [25]But the experience should become clear to those who enter into the spirit of this great drama, whose relevance to moral and political issues of our own time is strikingly clear.

Critical Thinking After you read the literary analysis, answer the questions below. Use the following questions to lead a class discussion.

1. What specific information does the writer convey about the plot, characters, setting, and theme of *Antigone*?

2. Find two statements in the essay that identify the essay's main idea.

3. How would you describe the style (e.g., formal, informal, academic, friendly) and tone of this essay?

4. Do you think Eliot Bloomfield makes a strong case for his claim? Explain your response.

Build Your Vocabulary. How does context help you understand these terms: *filial piety* (sentence 5), *tragic hero* (sentence 8), *sacrilege* (sentence 16), *foil* (sentence 18), *purgation of soul* (sentence 23)? Underline any other words that are unfamiliar to you. Look up each word in a dictionary, and add those words to your vocabulary notebook.

Writing Strategies In an **analysis** of a play, you evaluate each element separately. You consider how individual aspects contribute to the play and how the aspects work together to create an overall effect. Use the following strategies to develop and write an analysis of a play.

1. **Identify title and playwright.** In the first paragraph, identify the work and the author that you're writing about.

2. **Explain briefly what the play is about.** Write a very short plot summary. You should include the central theme or conflict that drives the action of the play.

3. **Present a thesis statement, or claim.** Your claim expresses your main idea about the play. It may focus on one or more of these elements: **characters**, **plot**, **theme**, and **setting**. Narrow your claim to just one aspect of the play for a three-page essay.

4. **Support what you say.** Find lines in the play that support your claim and explain why you feel they are relevant. Try to find three quotations or events that support your claim.

5. **Watch your tone.** The tone of your essay should be formal and serious. Avoid contractions, sentence fragments, and slang words.

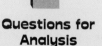

Questions for Analysis

- **Characters** Are they complex or simple? What motivates them?

- **Conflict, Resolution, and Suspense** What effect does the structure—the division of scenes and acts— have on the action of the play?

- **Theme** What is the overall meaning of the play?

- **Setting and Stage Directions** How do they influence the interpretation of the plot?

6. **Use the present tense.** When you refer to characters or events in the plot, use present tense verbs. For example, Bloomfield uses the present tense in sentence 13 ("The chorus *points* this out clearly . . .").

EXERCISE 22 Prewriting: Choose a Play

With a writing group, list plays you have read for school or have seen on stage. Go through the list, and share your initial reactions to these plays. If one play resonates strongly with your own experience, talk about why that play moves you. Answers will vary.

EXERCISE 23 Prewriting: Develop a Claim

If possible, reread your play to reconsider the effect of stage directions, to understand the structure, or to identify the theme. Then choose the literary or dramatic element that stands out most for you, and develop your claim with that element in mind. Be careful to limit your topic. Consider narrowing your topic to one character, one scene, or one brief dialogue.
Answers will vary. Students should refer to Lesson 1.1 for prewriting strategies.

EXERCISE 24 Organize and Draft Your Essay

Start writing anywhere in the essay, focusing on two or three of your most important points. Don't concentrate on writing perfect sentences. Just get your ideas down in sentence and paragraph form so you'll have something to revise. Feel free to add new ideas as you write. You can sort out ideas, reorganize, and add or delete words, phrases, and sentences later.

Answers will vary. Students should refer to Lesson 1.2 for drafting strategies.

EXERCISE 25 Revise and Title Your Essay

Let the draft sit for awhile. After you reread your essay, develop a title that leads the reader to your claim or simply states the name of the play. Then use the four-step revising strategy suggested in Lesson 1.3. Read for ideas and unity, organization and coherence, sentence variety, and appropriate word choice for your purpose and audience. As you and your writing partners revise your draft, ask questions such as those that follow.

Is the essay coherent, well organized, and easy to follow? Are the general statements clear and concise? Do you cite specific lines from the play to back up each point you make in the essay? Does every point you make in the essay bolster your claim? Is everything unified (directly related to the claim)?

Answers will vary.

EXERCISE 26 Edit and Publish Your Essay

Double-check each quotation for accuracy, including punctuation. When you are satisfied that you have corrected all errors in grammar, usage, punctuation, capitalization, and spelling, exchange papers with a partner to check for any errors you may have missed.

• If you and several of your classmates write about the same play—or plays in the same genre or historical period—form groups to read your classmates' essays, and then comment on them. After one of you reads an analysis to the group out loud, elicit questions and disagreements from your audience.

• You may wish to bind the essays into a book of drama analysis or make them available in an online collection for other students and English teachers to read. Answers will vary. Students should refer to Lesson 1.4 for proofreading strategies and publishing suggestions.

C CCSS Writing 4, 5, 6, 7, 8, 9, 10; Language 1, 2. (See pp. T14–T15.)

Expository Writing: Research Paper

A **research paper** is based on a thorough investigation of a limited topic. You may be asked to write a research paper in any of your classes, not just in English class. The purpose of a research paper may be to answer a specific question or solve a particular problem. Consider the following types of research papers:

1. The most common type of research paper **summarizes** or **explains** information you have gathered from several different sources. Your writing **synthesizes** (puts together to form a new whole) what other writers have reported.

2. Another type of research paper adds your own **evaluation**, or opinion, about your topic. For example, in a problem-solution paper based on research, you might focus on a community problem and evaluate the effectiveness of several proposed solutions.

3. A third type of research paper distills and summarizes your own **original research**. In social studies, you might draw conclusions and present findings based on surveys, questionnaires, or interviews you conduct. A science research paper might report your observations and experiments. For this kind of paper, you explain the idea or theory that you begin with and the carefully controlled experiments you conduct to test that theory. As part of an original research paper, you also include a **survey of the literature**, citing published articles related to your investigation.

Many research papers combine an evaluation with a summary or an explanation. In this case, you usually evaluate the research of others and then report your own research or interpretation of the evidence.

Depending on the type of research paper you are being asked to write, as well as the amount of information you find on a given topic, you may need to broaden or narrow the focus of your research as you write.

The following excerpt is from an original student research paper printed in *The Concord Review*. In the paper, the student summarizes and explains a historical incident. Then she evaluates related events, ideas, and legislation that followed it. The paper includes **parenthetical references** to its sources and ends with a **Works Cited** list, both of which are covered later in this lesson.

Keep in mind that MLA (Modern Language Association) style has guidelines for research paper format. Research papers should have one-half-inch margins on all sides, and the first word of every paragraph should be indented one-half inch from the left margin.

4-line heading:
Name/Teacher/
Class/Due Date

Title, centered

Brief description
and evaluation
of historical
incident

Claim:
Commission
created to protect
workers

Research sources
cited in
parentheses

Margins set to
one-half inch

Primary source
further explains
incident and
supports claim.

Hadley Davis
Dr. Alan Proctor
Social Studies
16 Nov. 2012

Reform and the Triangle Shirtwaist Company Fire

[1]On March 25, 1911, a terrible tragedy struck New York City, a horrifying fire, claiming scores of lives at the Triangle Shirtwaist Company. [2]But the 146 people who perished in the fire did not die in vain. [3]Their deaths sparked a new flame in New York City. [4]The pleas of the working class for better factory conditions, long ignored, were finally heard after the Triangle deaths. [5]For those deaths stimulated a guilty concern over the state of factory safety, a concern which called for action, for change. [6]And so out of the ashes of the Triangle victims, a Factory Investigating Commission was built, a commission which over a period of four years examined thousands of industrial establishments, listened to hundreds of witnesses, held public hearings, and finally pushed through the legislation needed to reorganize the New York City labor and fire departments, and to insure safer factories for the working class (Stein 209).

[7]When Frances Perkins, a member of the Factory Investigating Commission, dubbed the workshops and factories of the clothing industry virtual "fire and death traps," she was not exaggerating (Foner 367). [8]And the fire which began in Washington Square at 4:40 on Saturday afternoon, March 25, 1911, inside the Asch Building—where the Triangle Shirtwaist Company and its 500 employees occupied the eighth, ninth, and tenth floors—was her testimony.

[9]The cause of the fire was unknown, but suddenly people on the eighth floor of the Triangle Company began to cry "fire," and, according to one survivor, flames seemed simply "to push up from under" tables (Stein 34–35). [10]The eighth floor of the factory (like all the floors in Triangle) was overcrowded, and the sewing-machine tables were crammed so closely together that there was little aisle space in which to move ("Waist" 5). [11]Furthermore, scraps of the flimsy fabric and paper patterns used to make the shirtwaists lay scattered everywhere and caught fire quickly, only aiding the spread of the flames (Schoener 172). [12]Those on the eighth floor who were able to make an escape rushed to the stairway or pushed their way into one of the two narrow passenger elevators. [13]But within minutes, the entire floor became a "mass of fire" (Stein 36–42). [14]The girls were met at the stairs by the blaze. [15]The elevator ceased to function.

[16]The elevator never even reached the ninth floor, the biggest "fire and death trap" (Foner 367). [17]The ninth floor was the last to learn of the fire. [18]On the tenth, where the offices were located, a phone call of warning

Running head:
one-half inch from
top of paper

was received, and employees climbed onto the roof and managed to escape (Stein 43, 46). [19]However, on the ninth, the most crowded floor, fire simply instantaneously appeared. [20]Many jumped on machine tables (Llewellyn 24). [21]Others, their dresses on fire, ran to the windows, preferring to jump rather than be burned to death ("Waist" 4). [22]Some were caught so unaware that, later, firemen found "skeletons bending over sewing machines" and fifty-eight girls frozen dead in the dressing room (Schoener 171; Foner 359). [23]The people on nine who had the time to escape were, nevertheless, just as trapped: The door to the ninth floor was locked (to keep the girls from stealing cloth during the day); the passenger elevators never came; and the one fire escape that the building possessed quickly collapsed ("Waist" 2; Foner 359). [24]Desperate and with nowhere to turn, more Triangle workers [dived] off window ledges. . . .

Reliable source:
New York Times
verifies
information.

[25]According to the *New York Times*, "The firemen had trouble bringing their apparatus into position because of the bodies which strewed the pavement and sidewalks" ("Waist" 1). [26]The bodies, said fireman Frank Rubino, "were hitting us all around" (Stein 17). [27]But there was little help the firemen could offer the falling girls. [28]Their ladders were not tall enough to reach the three top floors of the building, and the life nets they had were of no use (Stein 17). [29]This was because, Battalion Chief Edward J. Worth explained, the girls came down with such force that they "went right through life nets, pavement, and all" (Stein 17). [30]The firemen could only drag the dead bodies away and later use pulleys to remove one blackened body after another from the building's remains ("Waist" 2). [31]The *New York Times* reported the morning after the fire that "two girls, charred beyond all hope of identification, were found in the smoking ruins with their arms clasped around each other's necks" ("Waist" 3).

Explains impact
of fire

[32]It was this, the drama of the tragedy, which was powerful and poignant enough to reach the public of New York and make it stop to consider the city's factories—that they were unsafe, that they were fire traps. . . .

Summary and
evaluation of
pre-fire strike

[33]On November 24, 1909, 1,800 waistmakers, including the workers of the Triangle Shirtwaist Company, went on strike as members of the Garment Workers' Union. [34]However, the shirtmakers' demands—unlocked doors and sufficient fire escapes among them—were never met (Wertheimer 309). [35]Rather, Triangle management responded by locking out its 500 strikers and by advertising for replacements (Foner 324). [36]"If the union had won," explained 1909 Triangle Shirtwaist Company striker Rose Safran,

Indented
quotation

we would have been safe. [37]Two of our demands were for adequate fire escapes and for open doors from the factories to the street. [38]But the bosses defeated us and we didn't get the open doors or the better fire escapes. [39]So our friends are dead. (Stein 168)

Davis 3

Details of public response to fire

⁴⁰At the public funeral for the Triangle victims, the garment workers marched under one banner: "We Demand Fire Protection" (Stein 154). ⁴¹This time, they would be heard: Numerous citizens, ranging from businessmen to suffragists, from priests to East Side workers, met and spoke in the weeks and months following the conflagration (Stein 135). ⁴²Through these people, the conscience of the city emerged. ⁴³They aired a sense of public guilt and genuine concern over conditions in factories, conditions which they realized no one had previously taken enough responsibility for (Stein 135). . . .

Topic sentence with supporting details about effect of fire on the workers and lawmakers

⁴⁴The commission took its job seriously. ⁴⁵Within the first year of its work alone, it inspected 1,836 industrial establishments in New York and heard a total of 222 witnesses (Stein 209). ⁴⁶Throughout this process, it held hearings before the New York legislature and proposed new laws or amendments (*Laws 1911* 1269). ⁴⁷The legislature in turn enacted remedial legislation. ⁴⁸The four-year term of the commission is, in fact, commonly acknowledged as "the golden era in remedial factory legislation" (Stein 210). ⁴⁹The labor laws passed between 1911 and 1919 correspond to the commission's findings—when the commission discovered a problem, change ensued. . . .

⁵⁰In 1912, legislation was enacted requiring the installation of an automatic sprinkler system in factory buildings over seven stories high with more than 200 people employed above the seventh floor (*Laws 1912* 661). ⁵¹Fire Chief John Kenlon had previously reported to the Commission that although an automatic sprinkler system would have cost the Asch Building $5,000, it was his belief that no life would have been lost in the Triangle Shirtwaist Company fire had one been installed (Stein 209). ⁵²Similarly, it was agreed that the fact that there had been no fire drills at Triangle caused panic when fire broke out ("Waist" 2). ⁵³And undoubtedly, at Triangle, where fire swept through the building without warning, a fire alarm would have insured an earlier detection of fire—and an earlier escape. ⁵⁴Consequently, an addition to the labor law called for both a fire drill at least every three months as well as the installation of a fire-alarm signal system in any factory building over two stories high that employed twenty-five persons above the ground floor (*Laws 1913* 363). ⁵⁵Also, during the Triangle fire, scraps of fabric and paper cuttings, which lay in heaps and covered the floor and tables, fed the spread of the blaze (Schoener 72). ⁵⁶Hence, a new law ordered that all waste in factories (e.g., cuttings) must be deposited into fireproof receptacles and that no such waste be allowed to accumulate on the floor (*Laws 1912* 658). ⁵⁷Thirty bodies were discovered in the shirtwaist company's open elevator shafts after the conflagration,

Davis 4

and so the New York legislature in July 1911 dictated that all elevator shafts in all city buildings must be enclosed ("Waist" 1; *Laws 1911* 1820). . . .

[58]During their strike in 1909, the workers at the Triangle Shirtwaist Company probably sang this popular and optimistic Garment Workers' Union song:

Popular union song lyrics illustrate workers' spirit and resolve.

[59]Hail! [60]The waistmakers of nineteen nine . . .
Breaking the power of those who reign,
Pointing the way, smashing the chain.

[61]We showed the world that women could fight.
[62]And we rose and won with women's might. (Foner 345)

Conclusion summarizes impact of fire.

[63]Their strike in 1909 was not successful, but the Triangle waistmakers still "won." [64]By 1914, the law, not factory owners, reigned in the garment industry and in the manufacturing buildings of New York. [65]Although they had died for their cause, the victims of the Triangle Shirtwaist Company fire had pointed the way toward a safer future for the working class.

This Works Cited list uses MLA (Modern Language Association) style to cite sources. See page 86 for more information on how to cite sources.

Davis 5

Works Cited

Newspaper article

"141 Men and Girls Die in Waist Factory Fire." *New York Times* 26 Mar. 1911. PBS American Experience. Web. 17 Oct 2012.

Book by one author

Foner, Phillip S. *Women and the American Labor Movement.* New York: The Free Press, 1979. Print.

Printed laws of the State of New York

Laws of the State of New York. Albany: New York State, Chapter 561 of 1911 (p. 1269); Chapter 693 of 1911 (1820); Chapter 332 of 1912 (661); Chapter 329 of 1912 (658); Chapter 203 of 1913 (363). Print.

Llewellyn, Chris. *Fragment from the Fire.* New York: Penguin Books, 1977. Print.

Scholarly work compiled by editor

Schoener, Allon, ed. *Portal to America: The Lower East Side, 1870–1925.* New York: Holt, Rinehart and Winston, 1967. Print.

Stein, Leon. *The Triangle Fire.* Ithaca: ILR Press/Cornell UP, 2011. *Google Books.* Web. 19 Oct. 2012.

Wertheimer, Barbara Mayer. *We Were There: The Story of Working Women in America.* New York: Pantheon Books, 1977. Print.

Writing Strategies The purpose of a research paper is to provide in-depth information on a limited topic. The following specific strategies apply to all three types of research papers.

1. **Choose and limit a topic.** First of all, choose a topic you would like to know more about. Look through your writer's notebook for ideas or ask *What If?* questions. Also make sure you choose a topic for which you can find sufficient sources—about five listings in a library index. On the other hand, narrow your topic when there are so many sources that you hardly know where to focus. One way to do this is to name a large topic and list as many smaller topics related to it as you can in order to come up with a limited topic for your paper. Use the following cluster map as an example.

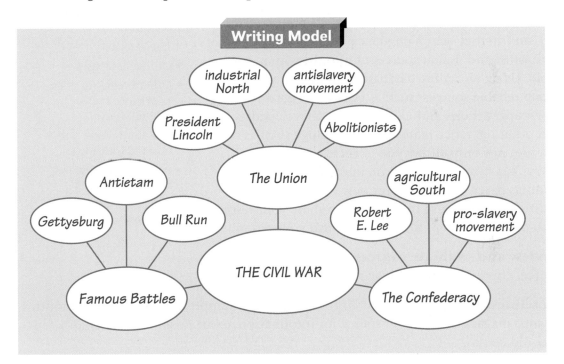

Writing Model

industrial North

antislavery movement

President Lincoln

Abolitionists

Antietam

The Union

agricultural South

Gettysburg

Bull Run

Robert E. Lee

pro-slavery movement

THE CIVIL WAR

Famous Battles

The Confederacy

2. **Make a schedule.** Budget your time to keep your focus, and pace yourself through each of the following steps in writing a research paper: (1) choosing and limiting a topic; (2) finding and evaluating sources; (3) taking notes; (4) drafting a claim and title; (5) developing an outline; (6) writing a first draft; (7) documenting sources; (8) revising; (9) proofreading; and (10) preparing the final manuscript.

For a six- to eight-week assignment, most steps take one to three days; allow about a week and a half for taking notes, writing a first draft, and revising.

3. Look for several sources. Make sure you include both **primary** and **secondary sources**.

A **primary source** is an original text or document, such as a literary work, a diary, a letter, a speech, an interview, or a historical document.

A **secondary source** presents the writer's comments on a primary source. Reference books, biographies, literary criticism, and history and science textbooks are secondary sources.

You can use a computer to gather relevant information from primary and secondary sources. For example, entering the term "Triangle Shirtwaist Company Fire" into an Internet search engine can help you find both print and digital sources of information on the topic. Using an online database is another way to locate reliable sources, such as relevant magazine and newspaper articles and excerpts from encyclopedias and other reference materials. Technology such as the Internet not only allows you to access information easily, but it can also help you update your research findings based on feedback or new information. In addition, you can use the Internet to share your research with others and to produce and publish your report.

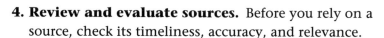

Some Sources to Explore

- Periodicals (newspapers, magazines, journals)
- Books
- Reference books (encyclopedias, specialized books such as an atlas)
- Government publications
- Publications by nonprofit organizations
- The Internet
- Online databases
- Other media (movies, television, radio, CD-ROMs)
- Museums, zoos, and other institutions
- Published interviews and surveys
- Original interviews you conduct

4. Review and evaluate sources. Before you rely on a source, check its timeliness, accuracy, and relevance.

Timeliness Look for up-to-date information. For example, an article in last month's *Atlantic* magazine is a better source for information about juvenile crime than a ten-year-old book.

Accuracy Evaluate your sources for accuracy, and don't believe everything you read. For example, an Internet source from a government or university database is more reliable and unbiased than an individual's home page. You can trust major newspapers (*The San Francisco Chronicle* or *The New York Times*) more than a tabloid.

Relevance Look for information directly related to your limited topic. Stay focused, and make sure the information you gather is appropriate for your purpose and audience.

5. **Track sources and cross-reference notes.** Record essential publishing information for each source either in an electronic document or on a **source card**. Each card or entry should include all the bibliographical information you'll need for your Works Cited list. This includes author, title, publisher, date, and place of publication as well as any other pertinent information. Assign each source card or entry a number. Then, when you take notes, just indicate the source number on your notes, and you won't need to rewrite all the source data.

SAMPLE SOURCE CARD

> 1
>
> Stein, Leon. *The Triangle Fire*. Ithaca: ILR Press/Cornell UP, 2011. *Google Books*. Web. 19 Oct. 2012.

6. **Take notes.** You may quote a source directly (using quotation marks) or use your own words. Be sure to include the page number of each note you take on your note card or entry.

When you **summarize**, you state only the most important ideas in your own words.

When you **paraphrase**, you spell out every idea in the same order as in the original, using your own words.

SAMPLE NOTE CARD

> 1
>
> Fire in top three floors of Asch building, corner of Washington & Greene streets, New York City, March 25, 1911 (p. 7)
>
> Worst fire in history of New York City (p. 8)

7. **Map ideas in outline form.** Sort your notes according to main ideas. Based on the information, create an organizational pattern that shows at least three main ideas, in order, with at least two supporting points for each one.

8. **Draft a claim.** Your **claim**, or statement of your controlling idea, comes at the end of the introduction. It tells your readers the main point you're going to make in the rest of the paper.

DRAFT   After the Triangle Shirtwaist Company fire, a commission was appointed.

REVISED   After the Triangle Shirtwaist Company fire, a commission investigated factory conditions and proposed laws to ensure worker safety.

9. **Acknowledge sources.** Always credit sources whenever you directly quote a phrase, sentence, or passage; or whenever you summarize or paraphrase someone else's original idea.

The research paper model on pages 79–82 follows The Modern Language Association (MLA) style for citing sources.

- Use **parenthetical citations** wherever you make reference to a source in your paper. Each citation should include the author and page number of your source.

- Give complete information about each source at the end of the paper in a **Works Cited** list.

For specific rules about citations and bibliographical references, consult the *MLA Handbook for Writers of Research Papers*, 7th edition. Some instructors prefer that students use footnotes or endnotes rather than parenthetical citations. Follow your instructor's guidelines or those in the *MLA Handbook*.

10. **Do not plagiarize.** Using someone else's words or ideas without giving credit constitutes **plagiarism**, which is a serious offense. Plagiarism has prompted lawsuits, job firings, and expulsions from colleges and universities. Borrowing or buying a research paper written by someone else is also plagiarism. Teachers can tell when the writing in a paper isn't your own.

EXERCISE 27 Prewriting: Choose a Limited Topic

Your teacher may specify a general subject (for example, how the life of a famous American writer or artist influenced his or her work), or you may be free to choose your own topic. Keep in mind the number of pages you have to write when you choose, and limit your topic. If you can choose your own topic, start by listing subjects that interest you, such as politics, space, or endangered animals. Look through your writer's journal to come up with ideas. Then write down questions you have about each listed item. Freewriting about a specific topic may also help you limit your topic.

Answers will vary. Students should refer to Lesson 1.1 for prewriting strategies.

EXERCISE 28 Prewriting: Gather Information

Write a **direction statement** or question about what you are planning to research. For example, "I am going to write about how the effects of war influenced the writing of Ernest Hemingway." Use strategies 3–6 on pages 84–85 to begin your research. As you find sources and examine them, keep the following ideas in mind: Answers will vary.

Purpose Your purpose is to give information. You need to provide background information and define technical terms but also look for new and interesting facts. Try to present information that sheds new light on a topic. Don't just repeat facts that readers already know.

Audience Make sure the depth and complexity of your sources, evidence, and word choice are appropriate for your audience.

EXERCISE 29 Prewriting: Develop an Outline

After you've prepared notes from a number of sources, organize your notes by main ideas. Do you have enough ideas and strong enough evidence to back up your ideas? Answers will vary.

Too few main ideas Make sure you have at least three or four main ideas. Try dividing a broad main idea into two. If you have fewer than three ideas, consider doing more research.

Too little supporting evidence If you need more evidence to support your ideas, continue researching.

Too much irrelevant information Look through your notes, and select only the strongest, most relevant information for your purpose and audience. Organize your information from most to least important or least to most important.

**Plan for
Research Paper**

Title page or heading

Introduction
Attention grabber
Claim

Body
Main idea 1
    Support
Main idea 2
    Support
Main idea 3
    Support

Conclusion
Summary of Claim
Works Cited Page

EXERCISE 30 Write a First Draft with Documentation

Start drafting long before your paper is due so that you will have plenty of time
to revise. Apply skills 8–10 from page 86. If necessary, research further to fill in
any holes you find as you draft. Keep the following advice in mind, too.
Answers will vary. Students should refer to Lesson 1.2 for drafting strategies.

Title As you draft, think about a title for your research paper.

Quotations Quotations show that you have done your
research, but only insert quotations that add something
special—a particular tone, a poignant observation, a clever
turn of phrase. Your paper should mostly be written in your
own words.

> Refer to **Mechanics**,
> Lessons 14.4 and 14.5
> for the rules for
> punctuating quotations.

Documentation Include your parenthetical citations and complete citations
as you draft.

Introduction and conclusion Many writers write these parts last, after
they see what they've written in the body of the paper.

EXERCISE 31 Revise Your Draft

If you follow a schedule, you should allow yourself more than a week to revise.
Read through your draft many times, focusing on one aspect of your paper for
each reading. Consider one reading for ideas and unity, one for organization
and coherence, one for sentence variety, and one for word choice. Check to see
that you have arranged your ideas in the most logical order. Look for places to
add transitions within a paragraph as well as at the beginning of a paragraph.
Do the best revising job you can, and then ask for input from writing partners.
Answers will vary. Students should refer to Lesson 1.3 for additional revising strategies.

EXERCISE 32 Edit and Proofread Your Paper

At this point, check carefully for the accuracy and punctuation of all the
quotations that you have included. Check the style of parenthetical citations
and of your Works Cited list. Make sure that you have provided publishing
information in the right order and punctuated exactly as required.
Answers will vary. Students should refer to Lesson 1.4 for editing/proofreading strategies.

EXERCISE 33 Prepare the Final Copy and Publish

Do your best to make your paper error free so that your ideas shine through
clearly. Double-space your entire paper, including the Works Cited page. Read
the final paper again before you turn it in. If you find any last-minute mistakes in
grammar, usage, punctuation, capitalization, or spelling, correct them. Consider
using the Internet to publish your paper on a class blog or in another online format.
Answers will vary.

Writing a Timed Essay

Essay questions on standardized tests measure your ability to generate ideas relevant to a specific topic and to present those ideas clearly and logically in an appealing style while following the conventions of standard written English. You are expected to do all of this within a limited amount of time.

On a standardized test, you will find essay topics, also called "prompts," that present an issue or question and ask you to develop a thoughtful written response.

Although you will be given a limited amount of time to plan and write your essay, you will be expected to develop your ideas thoroughly. The goal of a timed essay is to produce in a short time frame a clear essay that is logically organized and maintains a formal style.

Most standardized tests allot 25–30 minutes for timed writing. During that time, you should organize your ideas in an outline or cluster diagram, write your essay, and use any remaining time to revise what you wrote. Edit your finished essay, and check your use of capitalization, punctuation, and spelling.

The writing prompt below is similar to one you might find on a standardized test. After the prompt, you will find one writer's essay in response to it.

Consider the following issue. Then write an essay as directed.

> Psychologists have determined that people are inherently social and that companionship and teamwork are beneficial to an individual's personal and professional development. Yet, after voluntarily isolating himself from society for two years, Henry David Thoreau wrote, "I never found the companion that was so companionable as solitude."
>
> **Assignment:** When is solitude beneficial? Consider a work of literary nonfiction, such as Thoreau's *Walden* or an essay that you have read that deals with this issue. Write an essay in which you determine two or more central ideas of the text, briefly summarize them, and analyze their development over the course of the text, including how they build on one another to make a point.

In his essay, "Society and Solitude," Ralph Waldo Emerson writes about the advantages and disadvantages of solitude and society, advocating a healthy balance of both. Emerson claims that geniuses require solitude but also that new ideas should always be shared.

First, Emerson explains that solitude has its merits, but they come at a cost. Citing Dante and Columbus as examples of individuals who realized

Lesson 4.7
Composition

CCSS

Standards for this lesson focus on analyzing literary nonfiction texts and drawing textual evidence as support for a clear, well-organized, formal essay.

Most standardized test essays are scored from 6 (highest) to 1 (lowest).

Introduces the topic in a claim

Develops the topic with concrete details	their potential in isolation, Emerson claims that solitude is necessary for the development of innovative minds. Yet, he also warns that isolation hinders a person's ability to communicate with others, and he questions the usefulness of innovation that cannot be shared with society.
Uses transitions to clarify the relationship between ideas	Second, the essay explores the necessity of social relationships. Emerson states that everyone has parents and is therefore born into a set of social circumstances that cannot be ignored. On the other hand, he expresses concern that a society's shared values and beliefs might suppress the thoughts of the individual. For example, Emerson writes about an educated man from a rural area who claimed that he judged his own ideas more harshly when discussing them with men from the university just because his background was different from theirs.
Uses specific vocabulary for a complex topic	Last, Emerson synthesizes both of his central ideas regarding solitude and society to argue that people should participate moderately in both. He writes, "People are to be taken in very small doses," but he also claims, "Society we must have." This balance forms the basis of Emerson's argument. The best ideas should be nurtured in solitude, but they also must be shared with others.
Provides a conclusion that supports the information presented	In conclusion, Emerson believes that solitude is beneficial, but society is too. Similarly, total isolation is just as disadvantageous as relying on popular opinion instead of thinking for oneself. A person must spend time alone *and* with others for innovation to flourish.

Critical Thinking   After you read the essay on pages 89–90, answer the following questions.

1. In the essay's introduction, how does the writer address the topic discussed in the prompt? Review the thesis statement, or claim, and determine how it relates to the prompt.

2. What text evidence does the writer include throughout the essay? Briefly outline supporting details, such as quotations, facts, and examples.

3. Using the scoring suggestion on page 89, how would you score this essay? What suggestions, if any, might you make to improve it?

Writing Strategies   Use the following strategies as you write a timed essay.

1. Read the prompt carefully. Make sure you understand exactly what you are being asked to do. For example, is the purpose to inform or to persuade? Then, identify (underline or circle) key ideas as you read the prompt a second time.

2. **Prewrite: Narrow your focus.** Remember that you will have only a limited amount of time and space in which to write your essay. Know your word and time limit, and plan accordingly. You will not be able to write everything you know about a topic, so limit your response to a manageable focus.

3. **Prewrite: Gather and organize ideas.** You might use an outline or a cluster diagram to generate ideas. Spend no more than two or three minutes jotting down ideas, key words, and supporting details. Number the ideas in the sequence you plan to use them.

4. **Write the main idea in a claim.** Remember that this sentence usually appears early on in your essay and should announce your opinion.

5. **Start writing and stick to the point.** Begin with an introductory paragraph that includes your thesis statement and grabs the reader's attention. Use details that support your ideas in the clearest, most logical way possible. Use topic sentences and transitions to organize your writing. End with a brief concluding paragraph that restates your main idea, poses a new question, or adds a final thought.

6. **Consider word choice and sentence variety.** Clarity is your goal, so avoid vague words and confusing sentences. Strive for vocabulary and sentence variety that fit your writing purpose.

7. **Proofread your essay.** Save two or three minutes to proofread your essay and neatly correct any errors in spelling, punctuation, or usage.

EXERCISE 34 Read the Prompt Carefully

Choose one of the prompts below, and refer to that prompt as you complete Exercises 35–38. (You might set a time limit of 25–30 minutes.)

(A) Consider the following issue. Then write an essay as directed.

Some critics argue that too many cultural references can alienate some readers, but in "Take the Tortillas Out of Your Poetry," Rudolfo Anaya claims that authentic cultural references are critical to a writer's perspective.

Assignment: Consider a literary nonfiction text, such as an essay or autobiography, that you have read that is written from a distinct cultural viewpoint. Write an essay that determines the author's purpose and analyzes how the rhetoric, style, and content add to the power and beauty of the text.

(B) Consider the following issue. Then write an essay as directed.

A common expression claims that a house is only as strong as its foundation. Likewise, a nation's foundational documents must be firm but also flexible so they can remain relevant as the nation grows and develops.

Assignment: Select two foundational U.S. documents from the seventeenth, eighteenth, or nineteenth centuries, such as the Declaration of Independence and the U.S Constitution. Write an essay in which you analyze these foundational documents and compare how their themes, purposes, and rhetorical features have withstood the test of time.

Allow students to access to the text(s) they are writing about to encourage close reading and analysis.

EXERCISE 35 Prewrite: Focus, Gather, and Organize Ideas

Consider your topic, and list the text evidence you will use as support, such as relevant facts, concrete details, quotations, and other examples from the texts you chose to analyze. You might use a graphic organizer or an outline. Number your ideas in the sequence you plan to use them.

EXERCISE 36 Prewrite: Claim

Write your main idea in a claim. Decide where you will use this sentence in your essay.

EXERCISE 37 Write Your Essay

Begin with an introductory paragraph that grabs the reader's attention and includes your thesis statement. Say everything as clearly and logically as you can, and develop your essay with relevant examples to support your main idea. Use topic sentences and transitions to organize your ideas. Remember to choose effective words and sentences that accomplish your writing purpose. End with a concluding paragraph that restates your main idea, poses a new question, or adds a final thought.

EXERCISE 38 Revise and Proofread Your Essay

Save two or three minutes to reread your writing. Make sure the sentences flow smoothly and are clear and succinct. Neatly cross out anything that strays from your main idea. Correct any errors in spelling, punctuation, capitalization, and usage.

Parts of Speech

CHAPTER 5

Grammar

STUDENT WRITING
Research Paper

In War and in Peace
by Michael Berkowitz
high school student, New York, New York

Direct students to
www.grammarforwriting.com
for chapter-specific
portfolio projects.

The sun rose slowly over Mount Vernon on December 12, 1799, revealing a cold and wintry day. Aside from periods of rain, sleet, and snow, it seemed like a normal day. Indeed, no one could have foreseen that this day would lead to the death of a great American hero.

Undaunted by the bad weather, Lieutenant General George Washington, who had been retired from the presidency for nearly two years, set out on his daily horseback ride around his five-hundred-acre Virginia estate, Mount Vernon. The harsh weather beat down on Washington, but he continued to ride. After five hours in the cold, he returned to his house and sat down to dinner without even changing his damp clothes. His close friend and secretary Tobias Lear later commented that chunks of snow rested in Washington's hair while he ate (Thane 407).

It continued to snow through the next day. Washington began to develop a cold and a sore throat from being out the day before, so he did not go on his usual rounds. At night, Washington and Lear sat down in the parlor to read. When Washington left the room to go to bed, Lear advised him to take some medicine to get rid of his cold. Washington turned to Lear and replied, "You know I never take anything for a cold. Let it go as it came" (Irving 4: 394).

Between two and three o'clock on the morning of the fourteenth, Washington woke his wife to tell her that he was very ill. He was breathing with great difficulty as he instructed her not to notify anyone until dawn.

Thus, it was not until Mount Vernon was fully awake that its inhabitants learned of Washington's condition. Three doctors were sent for. The first, Dr. James Craik, had been Washington's friend and doctor since Washington was a young man. The other two doctors, Dr. Brown and Dr. Dick, were called at Craik's request (Thane 409). Washington was diagnosed with a throat infection known as "inflammatory quinsy." After a number of futile attempts at bleeding him, the doctors realized they could do nothing to help Washington. Craik took a seat by the fireplace in Washington's room, and there he sat in despair for the rest of the day.

Finally, Washington, barely able to speak, told the three doctors, "I feel myself going; you had better not take any more trouble about me" (Thane 410). Hours later, the first President of the United States died at the age of sixty-seven. . . .

Works Cited

Thane, Elswyth. *Potomac Squire*. New York: Duell, Sloan and Pearce, 1963. Print.

Irving, Washington. *The Life of George Washington*. 5 vols. New York: Cooperative Publication Society, Inc., 1859. Print.

Reprinted by permission of *The Concord Review*.

Allow time for
students to discuss
the student
writing. Suggest
that they identify
its strengths and
propose possible
improvements.
Use the model
to introduce the
concepts in the
chapter.

The first paragraphs of Michael Berkowitz's research paper are an account of George Washington's final days. This episode is an effective beginning for a thorough research paper on Washington's life as soldier and peacemaker.

In this chapter, you'll take a close look at the different kinds of work that words do—that is, you will learn about the parts of speech. As you do the writing exercises in this chapter, you'll apply what you learn to your own writing.

Nouns

Whatever you name that you experience through your senses, thoughts, and feelings is a noun.

⬛➤ **Nouns** are words that name persons, places, things, or ideas.

PERSONS   stepfather, Michael Jordan, acquaintance, Sally Ride, scientist

PLACES   avenue, peninsula, Houston, New Mexico, White House

THINGS   jeans, backpack, software, couch, television, music

IDEAS   calmness, freedom, friendship, self-confidence, pleasure

⬛➤ Nouns that name ideas are called **abstract nouns**. You use abstract nouns when writing or speaking about feelings, characteristics, or qualities. By contrast, **concrete nouns** name things that you can see, hear, smell, taste, or touch.

ABSTRACT   love, innocence, knowledge, endurance

CONCRETE   rain, finger, soil, computer, garage, parakeet

⬛➤ **Proper nouns** name *particular* persons, places, things, ideas, or events. Always capitalize proper nouns. Some proper nouns contain two or more words. **Common nouns** refer to general, not particular, persons, places, things, ideas, or events. Therefore, they are not capitalized.

COMMON   river, holiday, street, official, battle, ceiling

PROPER   Mississippi River, Earth Day, Richard the Lion-Hearted

> **WRITING HINT**
>
> Use nouns that are as specific as possible.
>   *mansion* *sandy bluff*
> The ~~house~~ on the ~~hill~~
>   *Gulf of Mexico*
> overlooked the ~~water.~~

⬛➤ **Collective nouns** name a group of people, animals, or things. Can you think of one or more collective nouns that name groups to which you belong?

COLLECTIVE   swarm, accumulation, couple, flock, student council

⬛➤ **Compound nouns** consist of two or more words. Use a dictionary to find out if a compound word is hyphenated, written as one word, or written as two or more words.

COMPOUND   stepson, DVD player, Declaration of Independence,
           air conditioner, great-uncle

⬛➤ A **noun phrase** is a group of words that acts like a noun in a sentence. Like other phrases, a noun phrase does not form a complete sentence.

EXERCISE 1 Identifying Nouns

Underline all the nouns in the following passage from a travel journal. Look for common nouns, proper nouns, abstract nouns, concrete nouns, compound nouns, and collective nouns. **Hint:** Pronouns such as *I, you*, and *we* do not count as nouns.

¹Our drive from Albuquerque, New Mexico, through the Jémez Reservation stunned me. ²From the bus I photographed dramatic landscapes in the high desert. ³Passing a village, I took pictures of dried red peppers, called *ristras*, which hung in strings outside each adobe home.

⁴We continued into the mountains outside Santa Fe. ⁵My spirits soared when I spotted an elk. ⁶Of course, I took a few snapshots. ⁷Most amazing of all, though, was our visit to Bandelier National Monument. ⁸There we viewed the ruins of prehistoric cliff dwellings and ceremonial sites that belonged to the Pueblo Indians. ⁹The homes are carved into the rock of Frijoles Canyon, overlooking beautifully forested land crisscrossed by freshwater streams. ¹⁰My favorite photograph shows my friend Jesse climbing the last of many steep ladders up to the *kiva*, a sacred cave reserved for ceremonies.

¹¹Our guide explained that this area holds important keys to the past. ¹²The Pueblo Indians did not have a written language, but they did leave behind petroglyphs—drawings etched into rock—and artifacts that reveal much about the beliefs and traditions of these ancient people of the Southwest.

EXERCISE 2 Adding Nouns to Sentences

Fill in the blanks in each sentence with the kinds of nouns indicated in parentheses. Choose specific nouns to create vivid, clear sentences.
Sample answers shown.

1. The place I would like most to visit is (proper noun) ___Acadia National Park___, located near (proper noun) ___Ellsworth, Maine___.

2. At my favorite spot, the (concrete noun) ___ocean___ and the (concrete noun) ___landscape___ are unforgettable.

3. When I listen to my favorite (common noun) ___music___, I am overcome with feelings of (abstract noun)___happiness___.

4. The reporter wrote an in-depth (common noun) ___piece___ about a candidate for (proper noun) ___the U.S. Senate___.

5. The sailor bravely steered his (concrete noun) ___ship___ through a raging (common noun) ___storm___.

Pronouns

It may seem necessary to repeat nouns in order to communicate ideas. But pronouns break the monotony of repeated nouns and act like a breath of fresh air.

Pronouns are words that take the place of a noun or another pronoun.

Most pronouns clearly refer to a noun or a noun phrase in the same sentence or in a preceding sentence. The word or phrase the pronoun replaces is known as its **antecedent**. The arrows in the following sentences point to the antecedents of the **personal pronouns** and their **possessive forms**—the most common pronouns you use.

Aretha played a jazz medley on the trumpet for **her** classmates. **It** captured **their** interest. **She** knew **it** would because **she** believed that the appreciation of jazz could be communicated through **her** performance.

Indefinite pronouns express an amount or refer to an unspecified person or thing.

Some lingered outside the theater.
Nobody heard a word the actor said.

Demonstrative pronouns point to specific people or things.

This is exactly what the audience wants.
That was a moving performance.

Interrogative pronouns begin a question.

When will the play begin? **Who** has the lead? **Where** is it set?

Relative pronouns introduce adjective clauses. (See Lesson 8.2 for more on adjective clauses.)

The author **whose** books have won awards visited our school.
The topic **that** the author covered fascinated us.

Reflexive pronouns end in -*self* or -*selves* and refer to an earlier noun or pronoun in the sentence. These are called **intensive pronouns** when they are used to add emphasis.

Manuel helped **himself** to a concert program. [reflexive]
I **myself** could never perform on stage. [intensive]

Personal Pronouns

I	you	her
me	he	it
we	him	they
us	she	them

Possessive Pronouns

my	your	his
mine	yours	its
our	her	their
ours	hers	theirs

Some Indefinite Pronouns

all	another
any	anybody
anyone	anything
both	each
either	everybody
everyone	everything
few	many
most	neither
nobody	none
no one	one
several	some
somebody	someone

Demonstrative Pronouns

this	these
that	those

Some Interrogative Pronouns

Who?	Which?
What?	Whom?
When?	Whose?
Where?	

Relative Pronouns

that	whom
which	whose
who	where

Reflexive and Intensive Pronouns

myself	yourself
himself	herself
itself	ourselves
yourselves	themselves

EXERCISE 3 Identifying Pronouns

Underline all the pronouns in this paragraph, including possessive pronouns that come before nouns.

¹Paul Simon became a rock musician in the 1960s, along with <u>his</u> friend Art Garfunkel. ²Together <u>they</u> performed as Simon and Garfunkel. ³Since then, Paul Simon's musical journey has continued. ⁴<u>He</u> wrote the songs for the movie *The Graduate*. ⁵<u>Few</u> can forget songs like "The Sound of Silence." ⁶To challenge <u>himself</u> further, Paul Simon began to perform on <u>his</u> own in the 1970s. ⁷By the mid-1980s <u>he</u> again became an innovator, creating the album *Graceland* with Ladysmith Black Mambazo, a popular South African group. ⁸Brazilian drummers worked with Simon on <u>his</u> next album, *The Rhythm of the Saints*. ⁹<u>Who</u> could guess <u>that</u> in the 1990s Paul Simon would team up with the Caribbean-born, Nobel Prize-winning poet, Derek Walcott? ¹⁰<u>They</u> co-wrote the musical *The Capeman* for the Broadway stage. ¹¹<u>It</u> starred Marc Anthony, a famous singer. ¹²<u>This</u> last endeavor shows <u>that</u> people continue to challenge <u>themselves</u>, even <u>those</u> as famous as Paul Simon.

EXERCISE 4 Writing with Pronouns

Work with a partner to create an interview with a performer or musician. Write at least five questions. Then develop answers the performer might give as responses. Try to use each kind of pronoun from page 97 at least once. Underline all the pronouns in your sentences.   Students' interview questions will vary. You might ask students to imagine they are on TV conducting their interviews.

Write What You Think

For more on writing persuasively, see **Composition**, Lesson 4.2.

Politicians and other activists have often called for censorship of the lyrics of certain popular music to protect young listeners from negative influences. Do you think a law should be passed that permits the censorship of music of any kind? Write a letter to a member of Congress protesting or supporting the censorship of lyrics in popular music. State your opinion clearly and support it with reasons, facts, and examples. Be sure to revise and edit your writing.   Answers will vary. Give students full credit if they have stated an opinion and attempted to support their opinions. They should also have written grammatically complete sentences that begin with a capital letter and end with an appropriate end punctuation mark.

Verbs

▐▐▐▶ **Verbs** are words that express an action or a state of being. Every complete sentence has at least one verb.

▐▐▐▶ **Action verbs** come in two varieties. You can observe some action verbs: *rebound, echo, squirm*. Others express emotions: *envy, despise, cherish*.
Luis **hit** a double, while Johnny **dashed** for home plate. The fans **hoped** their team **scored**.

Verbs change form to indicate time. (For more about verb tenses, see Lesson 9.4.)
The audience **applauded**. The audience **applauds**. The audience **has been applauding.**

Some action verbs (**V**) take direct objects (**DO**). (For more about direct objects, see Lesson 6.6.)
V   DO
The pitcher **threw** the **ball**.

▐▐▐▶ **Linking verbs** join—or link—the subject of a sentence with a word that identifies or describes it. (See Lesson 6.2 for more about subjects and predicates.)
From an airplane, a highway **seems** narrow.

Some verbs can be both linking and action verbs—but not at the same time. They are used as linking verbs only when they precede a word that identifies or describes the subject.

LINKING VERB   I **feel** much better.   She **remains** a good friend.
ACTION VERB   I **feel** the bumps.   She **remains** in her seat.

▐▐▐▶ A **verb phrase** contains a main verb plus one or more **helping** (or **auxiliary**) **verbs** (**HV**). *Not* (*n't* in a contraction) is never part of the verb phrase.
HV   V
Couldn't David **meet** us at the movies?
          HV   V
She **must have been** shopping for hours.

Linking Verbs: Some Forms of *To Be*

am	is
are	should be
being	was
can be	were
have been	will be
would have been	

Some Other Linking Verbs

appear	become
feel	grow
look	remain
seem	smell
sound	stay
taste	turn

Some Helping Verbs

be (is, am, are, was, were, been, being)
have (has, had)
do (does, did)

can	shall
could	should
may	will
might	would
must	

WRITING HINT

To communicate ideas with precision and appeal, use strong verbs rather than a form of the verb *to be*.

His preference **is** comedies. [to be]
He **prefers** comedies. [strong verb]

EXERCISE 5 Identifying Verbs

Underline every verb and verb phrase in the sentences on the following page. **Hint:** Three sentences have two verbs or verb phrases and one sentence has three verbs or verb phrases.

1. In 1857, Samuel Clemens <u>became</u> a Mississippi River pilot in New Orleans and <u>changed</u> his name to Mark Twain.

2. The name *Mark Twain* literally <u>means</u> "a river depth of two fathoms."

3. Mark Twain first <u>worked</u> as a journalist in Nevada and California; he later <u>turned</u> to other forms of writing.

4. Readers <u>enjoyed</u> his humorous essays and tall tales.

5. Twain <u>chose</u> respectability over adventure when he <u>settled</u> in Hartford, Connecticut, and <u>married</u> in 1870.

6. Twain <u>drew</u> on his Western experiences for the anecdotes he <u>used</u> in his popular book *Roughing It*.

7. Using his own childhood memories, Twain <u>began to write</u> the adventures of Tom Sawyer and Huckleberry Finn.

8. The novels *The Adventures of Tom Sawyer* and *The Adventures of Huckleberry Finn* <u>were published</u> in 1876 and 1884, respectively.

9. Everyday speech and realistic American settings <u>remain</u> a hallmark of Twain's greatest novels.

10. Investments in failed business ventures <u>caused</u> Twain's depression later in his life.

EXERCISE 6 Revising a Paragraph

Strengthen the following paragraph by adding vivid verbs and precise nouns. You can make up details and add, drop, or combine sentences.
Students' revisions will vary.

   [1]A student got an assignment to write a short story. [2]She was confused. [3]She needed help. [4]A friend helped her. [5]The friend talked about real-life stories. [6]The girl's preference was a news story that might appear in the newspaper. [7]The girl and her friend exchanged ideas about a news story. [8]They decided it would be about a woman who was volunteering her time to help out at a soup kitchen. [9]While the woman was helping at the soup kitchen, she had an accident. [10]The woman could no longer volunteer at the soup kitchen or work at her job. [11]Soon, many of the people she had helped at the soup kitchen started visiting her at home. [12]Some of them even brought her food. [13]She realized how much she meant to these people.

Adjectives

Adjectives help readers picture things accurately and precisely.

IIII➤ **Adjectives** are modifiers. They give information about the nouns and pronouns they modify.

WHAT KIND?	**slippery** ice, **sophisticated** remark, **brilliant** color, **silent** room
HOW MANY?	**two** months, **several** poems
HOW MUCH?	**more** cake, **less** milk
WHICH ONE?	**worst** movie, **last** train, **that** concert, **third** apartment

A noun may be modified by two or more adjectives.

The **tall**, **majestic** skyscraper loomed before us.

The weather was not only **dry**, but **hot**.

IIII➤ The adjectives *a* and *an* are called **indefinite articles** because they refer to any one member of a group. The adjective *the* is known as the **definite article** because it points out a particular noun.

INDEFINITE   You can write **a** humorous poem.

DEFINITE   **The** humorous poem you wrote made me howl with laughter.

IIII➤ **Proper adjectives**, which are derived from proper nouns, always begin with a capital letter.

| **Southern** accent | **Korean** paintings |
| **Mexican** pyramids | **Franklin** stove |

IIII➤ Adjectives usually come right before the nouns they modify, but **predicate adjectives** follow a linking verb to modify the subject of a sentence.

The bus trip was **difficult**.

The sky appears **blue** and **clear**.

IIII➤ When a noun or a possessive pronoun modifies another noun, it functions as an adjective.

epic poem	**baseball** bat
office building	**kitchen** sink
his mitt	**their** wedding

C **CCSS**

Standards for this lesson focus on applying the conventions of standard English, including correctly using hyphens.

WRITING **HINT**

For more vivid writing, try combining two adjectives, or two words that function as adjectives, to create one specific modifier—a compound adjective. Many compound adjectives are hyphenated.

The mayor retained **decision-making** authority.

A **self-appointed** leader helped the committee solve its problem.

EXERCISE 7 Identifying Adjectives

Underline the adjectives in the following paragraphs, including proper adjectives, articles, and possessive pronouns.

¹With more than four thousand soldiers under his command, the Spanish explorer Francisco Vásquez de Coronado headed north in 1540 from what is now Mexico. ²He was hoping to find the immense wealth of the legendary Seven Cities of Cibola, also known as the Seven Cities of Gold. ³He never found the imaginary cities, but he did explore areas of the southwestern United States. ⁴To escape the dry climate of Arizona, Coronado and his troops marched northeast into New Mexico. ⁵Here he saw the magnificent Rocky Mountains in the distance from his winter campsite. ⁶When his troops later crossed into present-day Texas, they experienced a dramatic change in scenery. ⁷The landscape became barren and flat. ⁸Grass-covered plains stretched to the horizon. ⁹Coronado and his troops never found the mythical cities of gold they were searching for. ¹⁰When they reached what is now south-central Kansas, they turned back. ¹¹Their long adventure took two difficult years. ¹²Coronado retired to a quiet, uneventful life in Mexico City, richer in knowledge of the North American continent than in gold.

EXERCISE 8 Revising Sentences to Add Information

Revise the sentences below to give the reader more information and to create more interesting sentences. Underline all the adjectives in your revised sentences. Revised sentences will vary.

EXAMPLE   The dessert was on the table.

The tasty chocolate cake tempted us from the dining room table.

1. We fished in the pond.

2. The boys ran around the track.

3. Dad slept on the couch.

4. The family drove to the city.

5. Juan swam in the ocean.

6. I read the book on the train.

7. She met friends for dinner.

8. They walked on the beach.

EXERCISE 9 Writing with Adjectives

Ask a classmate to describe an activity that interests him or her. Listen carefully, take notes, and ask questions. Then write a brief paragraph about what you learned. Include clear descriptions of the activity as well as the reasons your classmate gives for enjoying that activity. Use adjectives to expand sentences, making them colorful and sharp. Students' paragraphs will vary.

Adverbs

To describe an action completely and clearly, you sometimes use a modifier called an adverb.

▶ Adverbs modify, or tell more about, verbs, adjectives, and other adverbs.

MODIFIES VERB	The athlete ran **quickly**.
MODIFIES ADJECTIVE	They swam in a **pleasantly** cool lake.
MODIFIES ADVERB	Who can sit **most** quietly?

Many adverbs may come either before or after the verbs they modify.
Briskly, the horse rounded the bend. The horse rounded the bend **briskly**. The horse **briskly** rounded the bend.

Many adverbs end with the suffix -ly (*slowly, modestly, thoughtfully*, for example). However, many common adverbs do not end in -ly (*today, much, already*).

▶ Intensifiers are adverbs that answer the question *to what extent?*
The game was the **least** interesting of all.
We ate **too** much food.

Some Common Adverbs That Do Not End in *-ly*

almost	not (n't)
already	seldom
also	still
always	then
fast	there
here	today
just	tomorrow
late	too
more	well
much	yesterday
never	yet

Some Common Intensifiers

less	rather
least	really
more	so
most	somewhat
nearly	too
only	truly
quite	very
exceptionally	
extraordinarily	

EXERCISE 10 Identifying Adverbs

Underline the adverbs in each sentence. Draw an arrow to the word the adverb modifies. **Hint:** Four sentences contain more than one adverb.

1. Arizona State University effectively runs an academic "boot camp."

2. It substantially increases the number of minority, college-bound math majors.

3. Sixteen-year-olds develop their math skills quite successfully here.

4. They work cooperatively to solve one hundred math problems nightly.

5. The students study intensely, but they work happily together.

6. Initially, this program helped only thirty-two minority students.

7. The academic "boot camp" has progressed significantly, becoming part of the university's Institute for Strengthening Underrepresented Minority Students in Mathematics and Science.

STEP BY STEP

Adjective or Adverb?
1. Decide which word you need to modify.
   He speaks (*soft, softly*).
2. If you need to modify a noun or pronoun, use an adjective.
3. If you need to modify a verb, adjective, or another adverb, use an adverb.
   He speaks **softly**.

8. Dr. Joaquin Bustoz, a founder of the institute, who is from a minority background himself, generously gives of his time.

9. He hopes some of his students will eventually become teachers, too.

10. Imagine spending a summer day doing ten hours of math that absorbs your attention completely.

EXERCISE 11 Choosing the Correct Modifier

When you talk with friends, you may mix up adjectives and adverbs. In more formal settings—in school and in business—you need to choose modifiers that correctly fit your sentences. Underline the modifier in the parentheses that correctly completes each sentence.

1. It takes an (extreme, extremely) (creative, creatively) person to develop a new invention.

2. Alexander Graham Bell worked (extraordinary, extraordinarily) hard to perfect his (high, highly) successful invention, the telephone.

3. Marie Curie won a second Nobel Prize in 1911 for her (exceptional, exceptionally) work with (dangerous, dangerously) (radioactive, radioactively) elements.

4. Pi Sheng created one of the first (entire, entirely) (mechanical, mechanically) printing presses in China in 1040.

5. Samuel Morse's first (complete, completely) (accurate, accurately) telegraph message was sent from Baltimore to Washington, D.C., in 1844.

6. Nineteenth-century French physician René Laennec invented the stethoscope, a (strange, strangely), foot-long device, to listen to his patients' chest sounds and to diagnose (previous, previously) undetermined heart ailments.

7. Thomas Edison, an (ingenious, ingeniously) inventor, registered more than one thousand patents for such (brilliant, brilliantly) imaginative products as the light bulb, the phonograph, and the movie projector.

8. Basketball fans owe a (deep, deeply) debt of gratitude to James Naismith, who invented the game in 1891 by (clever, cleverly) using two peach baskets and a soccer ball.

EXERCISE 12 Writing with Adverbs

Picture the way something moves. Imagine a bird in flight, a skater gliding on ice, a basketball player dunking the ball, or a friend walking. Write a paragraph in which you describe in detail the motion you envision. Use adverbs and adjectives to create a vivid, accurate description. Students' paragraphs will vary. Make sure students have included an adequate number of adverbs and adjectives to paint a picture for the reader.

Prepositions

Prepositional phrases add color and depth to writing, amplifying the thoughts in a sentence.

▶ **Prepositions** connect a noun or pronoun to another word in the sentence to form a **prepositional phrase**. (For more about prepositional phrases, see Lesson 7.1.)

> **beneath** the carpet
>
> **toward** a greater understanding

Some prepositions are **compound** (made up of more than one word).

> **in spite of** them
>
> **according to** the Constitution

▶ Words that are prepositions in one sentence may be adverbs in another sentence. Look to see if a word starts a prepositional phrase. If it does not, it is an *adverb*.

ADVERBS	Get **inside** quickly.
	Set the food **down** on the table.
PREPOSITIONS	The treasure is **inside** the cave.
	The mouse ran **down** the clock.

EXERCISE 13 Identifying Prepositions

The following passage is the famous first sentence from *A Tale of Two Cities* written by Charles Dickens. Underline every preposition.

It was the best of times, it was the worst of times, it was the age of wisdom, it was the age of foolishness, it was the epoch of belief, it was the epoch of incredulity, it was the season of Light, it was the season of Darkness, it was the spring of hope, it was the winter of despair, we had everything before us, we had nothing before us, we were all going direct to Heaven, we were all going direct the other way—in short, the period was so far like the present period, that some of its noisiest authorities insisted on its being received, for good or for evil, in the superlative degree of comparison only.

Some Commonly Used Prepositions

about	during	out
after	except	outside
along	for	over
around	from	since
at	in	through
before	inside	to
below	into	toward
beneath	like	under
beside	near	until
between	of	up
beyond	off	upon
by	on	
down	onto	
but (meaning "except")		
with/without		

Some Common Compound Prepositions

according to	along with
apart from	aside from
as to	due to
because of	in front of
in place of	in spite of
instead of	out of
in addition to	

WRITING HINT

In the past, students were taught never to end a sentence with a preposition. British Prime Minister Winston Churchill is said to have challenged this rule by saying: "This is the sort of [English] up with which I will not put." Today, ending a sentence with a preposition is usually acceptable.
What are you looking **for**?
Here's the pen I spoke **about**.

EXERCISE 14 Selecting Prepositions

Complete each sentence with one or more prepositions. Your selection will determine the meaning of the sentence. Choose carefully so that the sentences make sense.

1. A telescope can detect stars ___in___ the Milky Way.

2. The astronauts conducted experiments ___during___ their later orbits.

3. The campers chose dried beef and rice ___instead of or in addition to___ a sandwich.

4. The experience ___of___ weightlessness was new ___to___ them.

5. ___After___ touchdown, an official walked ___through___ the spacecraft.

6. The cat leapt ___onto___ the counter, where frozen fish was defrosting.

7. The fighter pilots reported some problems ___during___ the test run.

8. The mascot entertained ___between___ innings.

9. Luisa's poodle came in first ___at___ the dog show.

10. The Invisible Man could disappear ___into___ thin air.

EXERCISE 15 Revising Sentences

Expand the sentences below by adding prepositional phrases. Make up all the details you need to make interesting sentences. Underline all the prepositions in your sentences. Revised sentences will vary.

EXAMPLE   Howard drove his car.
           In spite of the snow, Howard drove his car over the mountain to school.

1. The parking lot was full.

2. The lot had potholes.

3. All parking spots are full.

4. All parking spots are empty.

5. The bus stopped.

6. My car needs repair.

7. I take the bus.

8. The bus arrives late.

EXERCISE 16 Writing with Prepositions

Write a brief paragraph in which you explain how you do something. You might write about getting dressed in the morning, making muffins, or scoring a goal in soccer. Try to use some prepositional phrases in your paragraph. When you've finished writing, read your paragraph aloud to yourself. If some sentences sound too monotonous and singsongy, try removing one or more of the prepositional phrases. Students' paragraphs will vary. Suggest that students add some humor to this paragraph.

CCSS Writing 1, 10; Speaking and Listening 6; Language 1. (See pp. T14–T15.)

Lesson 5.7

Grammar

Conjunctions and Interjections

➠ **Conjunctions** join words or groups of words.

Coordinating conjunctions join words or groups of words that are equal in importance.

> Thunder, lightning, **and** hail hit the area. The thunder **and** lightning finally stopped, **but** the hail kept falling.

Correlative conjunctions are always used in pairs.

> **Either** it's raining **or** snowing. **Both** you **and** I are going dancing.
> **Neither** Lakisha **nor** Abdul took first prize.
> **Just as** thunder rumbles, **so** (too) lightning eventually strikes.

Place correlative conjunctions correctly when you write. The words or phrases joined by a correlative conjunction should play the same role in the sentence. For example, the conjunction might join two subjects or two clauses.

INCORRECT	**Either** people love frog legs **or** hate them.
CORRECT	People **either** love frog legs **or** hate them.
CORRECT	**Either** people love frog legs **or** they hate them.

INCORRECT	**Either** the girls went to the mall **or** to the grocery store.
CORRECT	**Either** the girls went to the mall **or** they went to the grocery store.
CORRECT	The girls went **either** to the mall **or** to the grocery store.

Subordinating conjunctions connect adverb clauses to main clauses. (For more about adverb clauses, see Lesson 8.3.)

> The author smiled **because** a reader asked for her autograph.
> We studied together **so that** we could all pass the test.
> The team needs more practice **since** the game is tomorrow.

➠ **Interjections** express mild or strong emotion.

Interjections have no grammatical connection to the rest of the sentence. They are set off by a comma or an exclamation point.

> **Darn!** I forgot my book again.
> **No way!** I certainly will not resign.
> She exclaimed, "**Wow!** What a parade!"

Coordinating Conjunctions

and	but	or
nor	yet	

Some Correlative Conjunctions

both . . . and
either . . . or
neither . . . nor
not only . . . but also
whether . . . or
just as . . . so (too)

Some Common Subordinating Conjunctions

after	in order that
although	provided that
as far as	since
as long as	so that
as soon as	unless
as though	until
because	when
before	where
if	whereas
while	

Some Common Interjections

aha	ouch
cool	ugh

TEST-TAKING TIP

Check to see if correlative conjunctions are used correctly on standardized-test questions. Sometimes an error will result from improper combinations of them. See item 2 on page 312.

EXERCISE 17 Identifying Conjunctions and Interjections

Underline all the conjunctions and interjections in the sentences below.
Hint: Only two sentences contain an interjection.

1. <u>Both</u> artist Georgia O'Keeffe <u>and</u> the photographer Alfred Stieglitz contributed significantly to American culture.

2. Stieglitz made his reputation <u>not only</u> as a gallery owner <u>but also</u> as a photographer.

3. After art school O'Keeffe's work was ignored, <u>but</u> she later became an important painter.

4. <u>When</u> he first saw her work, Stieglitz exclaimed, "<u>At last!</u> A woman on paper!"

5. <u>Just</u> as many artists loved big cities, <u>so</u> O'Keeffe loved deserts.

6. O'Keeffe painted flowers, <u>yet</u> her work wasn't sentimental.

7. <u>Whether</u> you see them at a museum <u>or</u> find them in a gallery, the paintings and photographs are remarkable.

8. Many people say "<u>Wow!</u>" <u>when</u> they see an O'Keeffe painting.

9. <u>Not only</u> did O'Keeffe paint, <u>but</u> she <u>also</u> posed for Stieglitz.

10. <u>Neither</u> Stieglitz <u>nor</u> O'Keeffe could've predicted their success.

EXERCISE 18 Writing with Interjections

Work with a partner to write a conversation of at least ten lines of dialogue between two friends. Have the characters discuss movies they love or hate. Include an interjection in each line. Then read the dialogue aloud with your partner. Add, remove, or rewrite interjections to end up with a dialogue that sounds natural. Students' dialogues will vary.

Write What You Think

Write a paragraph that expresses your thoughts on the following statement. Support your opinion with facts and examples.

> Private foundations and public donations should be the sole supports of fine art and public television and radio in this country. The federal government should end all financial support of those institutions.

After revising, edit your paragraph to be certain that you have used prepositions and interjections correctly. Suggest that students research information to support their opinions. Answers will vary. Give students full credit if they have stated an opinion and attempted to support that opinion. They should also have written grammatically complete sentences that begin with a capital letter and end with an appropriate end punctuation mark.

C **CCSS** Language 1. (See pp. T14–T15.)

Lesson 5.8

Grammar

Determining a Word's Part of Speech

||||➤ A word's part of speech is determined by how the word is used in the sentence. For example, the word *down* can be used as a noun, a verb, an adjective, or an adverb.

NOUN   The football coach explained a first **down**.

VERB   The runner **downed** a quart of water after the race.

ADJECTIVE   The **down** side is that we don't get a raise.

ADVERB   When the tree fell **down**, it damaged my car.

EXERCISE 19 Identifying Parts of Speech

Identify the part of speech of each underlined word as it is used in the sentence. Use these abbreviations.

N = noun	ADJ = adjective	CONJ = conjunction
P = pronoun	ADV = adverb	INT = interjection
V = verb	PREP = preposition	

___ADJ___ 1. W. E. B. Du Bois was an <u>American</u> civil rights leader and author.

___V___ 2. Born and raised in Massachusetts, he <u>graduated</u> from Harvard.

___CONJ___ 3. Du Bois championed both economic <u>and</u> political equality for African Americans.

___PREP___ 4. He cofounded the National Association for the Advancement <u>of</u> Colored People (NAACP) in 1909.

___PREP___ 5. He edited the NAACP magazine, *Crisis*, <u>until</u> 1934.

___ADV___ 6. Du Bois <u>tirelessly</u> worked to help all oppressed people.

___ADJ___ 7. Du Bois encouraged the development of <u>African American</u> literature and art.

___ADV___ 8. He <u>strongly</u> advocated the power of African American–owned businesses.

___N___ 9. Du Bois's international <u>concerns</u> prompted the first Pan African Congress.

___P___ 10. <u>Several</u> of the delegates became leaders of African nations.

Chapter 5

Grammar

C **CCSS** Language 1, 2. (See pp. T14–T15.)

Revising and Editing Worksheet

Improve the following draft by revising for ideas, organization, word choice, and sentence variety. After revising, edit the draft for errors in spelling, capitalization, punctuation, and usage. Write your revised and edited version on a separate piece of paper. Compare your changes with those of a writing partner.
Students' revisions will vary.

[1]Sitting Bull, a famous native american, deeply understood the Sioux spirit world.

[2]Sitting Bull communicated his thoughts and experiences clearly. [3]His father, the warrior and mystic Returns Again, first called his son "Slow," because of the babys quiet, contemplative nature. [4]Years later, Returns Again renamed his son Sitting Bull. [5]Sitting Bull was fourteen years old when his father renamed him. [6]The name was "Tatanka Yotanka" or "Sitting Bull."

[7]As a teenager, young Sitting Bull himself had dreamlike states. [8]In one dreamlike state Sitting Bull heard an animal. [9]Sitting Bull heard an animal calling from a high perch on a rocky butte. [10]Sitting Bull went to the spot. [11]Sitting Bull found an eagle. [12]From that moment, Sitting Bull believed he was going to lead his people.

[13]By 1868, Sitting Bull was considered a leader among the Hunkpapas, a band of Lakota Sioux. [14]Other Sioux leaders signed the treaty of Fort Laramie that required them to live on a reservation in southern south dakota. [15]Sitting Bull could have signed the treaty. [16]Sitting Bull refused to give up any ancestral lands.

[17]Sitting Bull's people suffered. [18]Their suffering was long. [19]After many years of fleeing from the U.S. Army, Sitting Bull and his people finally surrendered. [20]His surrender saved his people from starvation in Canada. [21]Sitting Bull traveled with Buffalo Bill Cody and Annie Oakley in the Wild West Show run by Buffalo Bill Cody and Annie Oakley. [22]Sitting Bull also continued to speak up for his people. [23]Sitting Bull lived until 1890.

C CCSS Language 1. (See pp. T14–T15.)

Chapter 5
REVIEW

Grammar

Chapter Review

EXERCISE A Identifying Parts of Speech

In the space provided, identify the part of speech of the underlined word in each of the following sentences about some of the first ten presidents of the United States. Use these abbreviations.

N = noun	ADJ = adjective	CONJ = conjunction
P = pronoun	ADV = adverb	INT = interjection
V = verb	PREP = preposition	

____ADJ____ 1. George Washington was trained as a <u>land</u> surveyor.

____N____ 2. George Washington was the <u>commander in chief</u> of the Continental Army troops.

____ADV____ 3. Washington, of course, <u>eventually</u> was elected president.

____CONJ____ 4. Thomas Jefferson <u>not only</u> became president <u>but also</u> helped plan the capital city, Washington, D.C.

____N____ 5. The War of 1812 occurred during the <u>presidency</u> of James Madison.

____PREP____ 6. James Monroe learned about politics and law <u>from</u> Thomas Jefferson.

____ADJ____ 7. Andrew Jackson was the first <u>presidential</u> nominee from Tennessee.

____ADV____ 8. Martin Van Buren was one of the <u>most</u> unpopular presidents.

____P____ 9. <u>Who</u> can forget the name "Tippecanoe," a battle between the Native American leader Tecumseh and the future ninth U.S. president, William Henry Harrison?

____V____ 10. John Tyler <u>is remembered</u> as the vice president who became president after Harrison's death.

EXERCISE B Revising a Business Letter

On a separate piece of paper, revise the following draft of a business letter. Make sure to clarify any confusing or awkward phrasing. Feel free to replace words, add new details, combine sentences, and delete words or entire sentences.

Students' revisions will vary.

Dear Ms. Jabbar:

[1]When the New York Yankees won the World Series, it was a big deal in my neighborhood. [2]Because of that, I wanted to see if you had any special

souvenirs from the postseason that I might be able to get. ³I was interested in such things as pennants, coffee mugs, caps, and other things like that that I could put on display in my room.

⁴I wanted to get things to remind me of all the big moments. ⁵Souvenirs of this kind bring back happy memories to me.

⁶When you send me information about the memorabilia you are offering from the postseason, please include information about how I can order this memorabilia. ⁷I want to see this information as soon as possible. ⁸Rush it to me in the mail. ⁹You can also send it on the fax. ¹⁰My fax number is (718) 555-9280.

¹¹I would like to thank you very much in advance for sending me this information so I can place my order right away.

Sincerely,
Marisa Fielder

Exercise C Revising a Personal Narrative

On a separate piece of paper, revise the following draft of a personal narrative. Feel free to make any changes that will make these paragraphs stronger and more interesting. Replace words, add specific details, add direct quotes, combine sentences, and cut words or sentences. Students' revisions will vary.

¹There was snow everywhere. ²I had never seen so much snow. ³The snow was white. ⁴The snow sparkled like diamonds under the blue sky.

⁵This was my first time on a ski slope. ⁶I had never gone skiing before. ⁷I was excited. ⁸I was nervous. ⁹My friends had gone skiing before. ¹⁰I was the only beginning skier in our Teen Tours group.

¹¹Sam used ski poles to begin moving across the slope. ¹²He began by putting ski poles in the snow. ¹³Sam pushed off using the poles he was using. ¹⁴Sam motioned to me to copy what he was doing. ¹⁵Sam liked to say "way to go." ¹⁶That's what Sam said to me. ¹⁷I copied Sam. ¹⁸I began to move quickly across the mountain slope. ¹⁹I was moving too quickly.

²⁰I couldn't turn. ²¹I was heading for a tree. ²²Sam yelled for me to fall backward into the snow. ²³Cherise yelled the same words. ²⁴I followed the advice of Sam and Cherise. ²⁵I avoided the tree. ²⁶With the help of Sam and Cherise, I got up. ²⁷I brushed off the snow. ²⁸I tried again. ²⁹Each time I tried, I got a little bit better. ³⁰By the end of the day, I could ski down the beginner slope without falling once.

Parts of a Sentence

STUDENT WRITING
Narrative Essay

The Earthquake
by Keane Kaneakua
high school student, Kaneohe, Hawaii

Direct students to www.grammarforwriting.com for chapter-specific portfolio projects.

All was well in the city of Kaneohe. It was a cool Saturday morning and the first day of 1984's Christmas vacation. There was an uncommon stillness in the air. All of a sudden, a rumbling under the earth broke the stillness. The rumbling grew immense in a very short amount of time. No one knew what was going on for a few seconds, and then there were screams of fright: "Earthquake!"

The shaking lasted for about five minutes, yet the shaking during those five minutes was enough to level houses and buildings. Then the real chaos of trying to find family and friends and of trying to put lives back together began.

The estimated cost of the damages was about $5,000,000,000. It would take years to put Oahu back together. People scrounged around looking for lost pieces of their lives as if they were putting together a puzzle. Lost family members, pets, and friends were just a few of the major losses resulting from the earthquake.

For ten years, Oahu has shown the physical scars of the earthquake that mentally and physically shook the island. For generations to come, no one will forget the wrath of 1984.

> Keane Kaneakua's narrative writing relates the events of a natural disaster in the order in which they occurred. His transition words throughout the essay help guide his readers, and the varied sentence lengths help keep his style lively and interesting.
>
> Reread Keane's essay, and notice that his sentences vary in structure. As you work on sentences in this chapter, think about how you can manipulate them to communicate your ideas in an interesting way.

Allow time for students to discuss the student writing. Suggest that they identify its strengths and propose possible improvements. Use the model to introduce the concepts in the chapter.

Using Complete Sentences

||||➡ A **sentence** is a grammatically complete group of words that expresses a thought.

Don't judge whether a sentence is grammatically correct by its length. A short sentence may be as complete as a long one.

> Did the Trinity River flood?
>
> This afternoon, after two hours of nonstop rain, the Trinity River rose above its banks and flooded Trinity Road.

What makes both of these sentences grammatically correct? First, they begin with a capital letter and end with a punctuation mark—a period, a question mark, or an exclamation point. In addition, all complete sentences do the following two things: (1) name the person, animal, thing, or state of being that the sentence is about and (2) tell what that person, animal, thing, or state of being does or is.

||||➡ A sentence has one of four purposes.

Purpose of Sentence	End Punctuation	Examples
Declarative sentences make a statement.	period	It rained the day the president visited.
Imperative sentences issue a command or request.	period or exclamation point	Line up in front of the entrance. No talking!
Interrogative sentences ask a question.	question mark	Did you notice the First Lady's red, white, and blue suit?
Exclamatory sentences express a strong feeling.	exclamation point	Wow! His speech really impressed me!

A group of words may begin with a capital letter and conclude with end punctuation, but those words may not express a complete thought.

||||➡ A **sentence fragment** is a group of words that is not grammatically complete. Avoid sentence fragments when you write.

FRAGMENT Because the president talked about education. [This doesn't tell *what* happened.]

SENTENCE Students listened because the president talked about education.

FRAGMENT Spoke out on issues concerning education. [This doesn't identify *who* the speaker is.]

SENTENCE The president, who spoke out on issues concerning education, received a standing ovation.

WRITING HINT

Occasionally, fragments can be used in informal writing for effect. When you write what people say, in dialogue, or when you write an advertisement, you might use fragments to imitate everyday speech or to create memorable phrases.

Not now.

Okay by me.

Best by far.

EXERCISE 1 Identifying Sentence Fragments

Write *S* on the line before each numbered item if the group of words is a complete sentence. Write *F* if the group of words is a fragment. Correct the fragments on a separate piece of paper.
See Answer Key at www.grammarforwriting.com.

___S___ 1. What makes space voyages to Mars fascinating to scientists is the planet's glow.

___F___ 2. The president proposing a manned space mission to Mars.

___F___ 3. Which was on the twentieth anniversary of the *Apollo 11* moon landing.

___S___ 4. The $500 million cost delayed the proposal.

___F___ 5. However low the costs for new methods of space exploration.

___S___ 6. A trip now might only cost $55 million.

___F___ 7. This trip, which the public seems interested in recently.

___F___ 8. Showing microscopic signs of ancient life there, a meteorite discovered on Antarctica.

___F___ 9. Better to send astronauts or a robot into space experts debate?

___F___10. To use the International Space Station to explore Mars.

EXERCISE 2 Writing Complete Sentences

With a partner or a small group, come up with five questions you might ask a NASA official or an astronaut about U.S. space exploration. Then write the answers the NASA official or astronaut might give. Try to use each of the four kinds of sentences in your interview. Remember to use capital letters and end punctuation correctly.

Write What You Think

Write a paragraph in response to the statement below. Support your opinion with facts, reasons, and examples. After revising, edit your writing to make sure you eliminate all sentence fragments.

> Billions of tax dollars have been spent on space exploration since NASA was launched more than five decades ago. That money would have been better spent to remedy social ills here on Earth, such as poverty, inadequate health care, crime, and unequal access to a good education.

Answers will vary. Give students full credit if they have stated an opinion and attempted to support their opinions. They should also have written grammatically complete sentences that begin with a capital letter and end with an appropriate end punctuation mark.

Subject and Predicate

Every sentence has two essential parts: a **subject** and a **predicate**. The subject names the person, place, thing, or idea the sentence is about. The predicate tells what the subject does or is.

SUBJECT	PREDICATE
The restaurant called Café Aroma	attracts many students.
My classmates Jerry and Elaine	drink coffee all afternoon.

▐▶ The **simple subject** is the key word or words in the subject. A simple subject may contain a proper noun, which may be made up of more than one word. The complete subject is made up of the simple subject and all of its modifiers (such as adjectives and prepositional phrases).

▐▶ The **simple predicate** is always the verb or verb phrase that tells something about the subject. The complete predicate contains the verb and all of its modifiers (such as adverbs and prepositional phrases), objects, and complements.

You'll review objects and complements in Lessons 6.6 and 6.8.

In the sentences below, all simple subjects and simple predicates are **boldfaced**. Notice that a sentence can begin with either the subject or the predicate.

> **EDITING TIP**
>
> Don't get confused by contractions. A contraction may contain both the simple subject and part of the verb in a sentence. **You've eaten** the whole cake!
>
> The subject is **you**, and the verb is *have eaten*.

COMPLETE SUBJECT	COMPLETE PREDICATE
The **River Restaurant**	**will open** this Monday.
I	**can set** a table blindfolded.
A **cloud** of steam	**rose** off the baked lasagna.
These plastic **plates** and **cups**	**may be placed** in a microwave.

COMPLETE PREDICATE	COMPLETE SUBJECT
Here **steam**	fresh **broccoli** and **carrots**.
In the kitchen **hums**	the **sound** of busy cooks and waiters.

EXERCISE 3 Identifying Subjects and Verbs

Underline the subject (the simple subject) once and the verb (the simple predicate) twice in each sentence of this press release. **Hint:** There is more than one subject or verb in several sentences.

¹The Carson City International Food Festival will take place on the last weekend in September. ²Full meals and delicious snacks will tempt passersby from dawn to dusk. ³All day long will the scents of delicious

foods <u>fill</u> the air. ⁴<u>Visitors</u> and food <u>critics</u> <u>will sample</u> and <u>savor</u> shrimp-filled spring rolls from Vietnam. ⁵<u>Luigi Salerno</u> and his <u>son</u> <u>will serve</u> pizza and pasta. ⁶<u>Café Abyssinia</u> <u>will</u> also <u>show</u> customers how to eat with sheets of traditional Ethiopian bread.

⁷The <u>Barbecue Bistro</u> and the <u>China Coast</u> <u>will</u> each <u>provide</u> hungry festival guests with highly unusual dishes. ⁸If spice and variety are the keys to great cooking, the <u>Barbecue Bistro</u> <u>will win</u> the "spice" category hands down. ⁹<u>Variety</u>, that other essential ingredient of great cooking, <u>will be</u> on grand display at the China Coast. ¹⁰In fact, <u>visitors</u> <u>will smack</u> their lips with every bite of delicious food from booths at this tantalizing festival coming soon to our city.

EXERCISE 4 Writing Complete Sentences

On a separate piece of paper, write the directions for following the recipe for the Barbecue Bistro's Barn Chili in complete sentences. You may write the recipe as a numbered list or in paragraph form. Use capital letters and end punctuation correctly in your sentences. Students' recipes will vary.

Barbecue Bistro's Barn Chili

large pot with lid

1 pound pinto beans—soak overnight in water, cook in pot on top of stove until tender

onions (2), bell pepper (1), tomatoes (4)—chop 1 pound ground beef (lean)—brown in large skillet

add Barbecue Bistro's Special Spice Mix to beef

vegetables—add to beef, 15 minutes

skillet contents into bean pot

simmer—30 minutes

salt and pepper to taste

(optional) top servings with sour cream, shredded cheese

C **CCSS** Language 1. (See pp. T14–T15.)

Lesson 6.3
Grammar

Correcting Sentence Fragments

You may form complete sentences from sentence fragments by using these three strategies:

1. Attach it. Join the fragment to a complete sentence before or after it.

FRAGMENT   Did you ever visit Mt. Rushmore. While on vacation?

REVISED   Did you ever visit Mt. Rushmore while on vacation?

2. Add some words. Add the missing subject, verb, or whatever other words are necessary to make the group of words grammatically complete.

FRAGMENT   Western legends were chosen. The original figures on Mt. Rushmore.

REVISED   Western legends were chosen as the original figures on Mt. Rushmore.

3. Drop some words. Drop the subordinating conjunction that creates a sentence fragment.

FRAGMENT   As though nature also sculpted Mt. Rushmore.

REVISED   Nature also sculpted Mt. Rushmore.

STEP BY STEP

The Sentence Test

To determine whether a group of words forms a complete sentence, ask these three questions:

1. Does it have a subject?
2. Does it have a verb?
3. Does it express a complete thought?

If you can't answer *yes* to all three questions, you have a fragment. Correct it.

EXERCISE 5 Correcting Sentence Fragments

On a separate piece of paper, edit each numbered item to eliminate all sentence fragments. Use the three strategies above to form complete sentences. Edited sentences will vary. Sample answers given.

1. Back in 1885, A lawyer named Charles E. Rushmore named the peak of a rock dome in South Dakota.

2. He believed / That the peaks of that dome would someday be carved as human heads.

3. The idea was developed by Doane Robinson, a South Dakotan.

4. ~~When~~ the state hired an Idaho sculptor named Borglum, known for working on a large scale.

5. At first Borglum was hired by others To sculpt Robert E. Lee on Stone Mountain, Georgia.

6. Carving Mt. Rushmore was A more interesting project for Borglum.

7. Borglum's letter of 1925 suggested Portraying American presidents rather than Western legends.

8. ~~Because~~ materials had to be hauled up the mountain by horse or on foot for more than fourteen years.

9. Fortunately, ~~since~~ lack of access protects the carvings from vandals.

10. From 1941 until the present, people ~~marveling~~ at the $990,000 New World wonder.
      ^{have marveled}

Exercise 6 Editing for Fragments

Improve the paragraph below. If the numbered line is not a sentence, add, omit, or change words and punctuation. Be sure to add capital letters and end punctuation marks where necessary. Make sure every sentence expresses a complete thought. Edited paragraphs will vary. Sample answers are given.

¹One of the most controversial but popular monuments erected in the United States_ ²The 1980 Vietnam Veterans Memorial in Washington, D.C. ³Maya Lin,
   ^{is}

an architecture student from Yale, submitted design plans in a contest_ ⁴~~That a~~
                                                                    ^{and her}

~~student's~~ design was chosen over others by a panel of experts! ⁵At the

monument, people reading the names of those who died or disappeared in the
            ^{can}

Vietnam War. ⁶All the names ~~on~~ two black granite walls, each 200 feet long.
            ^{have been carved into}

⁷There, beside the two walls_ ⁸Stands a realistic sculpture of soldiers from this

tragic conflict. ⁹In Montgomery, Alabama, another Maya Lin sculpture_ ¹⁰~~To~~

~~honor~~ the memory of both Dr. Martin Luther King Jr. and others who died in
^{honors}

the civil rights. ¹¹~~The~~ monument that Lin designed. ¹²It is a circular

black granite table. ¹³Forty names engraved on the table_ ¹⁴~~Which~~ are names
                   ^{The}   ^{that are}

of people killed during the civil rights movement. ¹⁵Water flows_ ¹⁶From the

center of the table. ¹⁷~~Water~~ also ~~on~~ a wall behind the table. ¹⁸Engraved on the
                  ^{It} ^{cascades down}

wall_ the words that Dr. King quoted from the Bible: ". . . until justice rolls
   ^{are}

like water and righteousness like a mighty stream." ¹⁹~~Which~~ creates a very
                                                ^{The monument}

powerful impact.

Finding the Subject

Every sentence has a subject and a verb that together make a complete thought. You'll need to identify the subject so that you'll know the correct verb form to match it. Chapter 10 focuses on subject-verb agreement.

As you look for subjects, keep the following tips in mind:

▸ In an **inverted sentence**, the verb (v) comes before the subject (s).

>   v   s
> Beneath the lake's surface **swam** a **school** of tropical fish.

>   v   s   s
> In the gallery **hung paintings** and **photographs** of marine life.

▸ The words *here* and *there* are never the subject of a sentence. In a sentence beginning with *here* or *there*, look for the subject after the verb.

>   v   s
> Here **sprouts** a single **blade** of grass.

>   v   s   s
> There **will be wildflowers** and cultivated **roses** in the community garden.

In the first example, the word *here* acts as an adverb that modifies the verb *sprouts* by indicating "where." In the next sentence, the word *there* is used as an expletive, which is a word that has no role in the grammar of the sentence except, in this case, to start it.

▸ The subject of a sentence is never part of a prepositional phrase.

>   s
> The **lack** of rain created a drought in the state. [The prepositional phrase *of rain* modifies the subject *lack*.]

▸ To find the subject of a question, turn the question into a statement.

>   s
> Are **you** the person with the windowbox? [*You* are the person with the windowbox.]

▸ In a command or request (an imperative sentence), the subject is understood to be *you* (the person being spoken to).

> s
> **[You]** Turn off the garden hose.

>   s
> Casey, **[you]** tell Joey how to arrange the flowers.

In the second imperative sentence above, the name *Casey* is a direct address but is not the subject.

EXERCISE 7 Finding the Subject

Underline the subject(s) in each of the sentences below. If the subject is understood to be *you*, write *You* at the end of the sentence.

1. In 1955, <u>Dr. Martin Luther King Jr.</u> gained national attention when he staged a bus boycott in Montgomery, Alabama.
2. The <u>bus companies</u> allowed African Americans to sit only at the back.
3. <u>Most</u> of the people who rode buses in Montgomery were African American.
4. <u>Dr. King</u> and his <u>neighbors</u> decided not to ride the bus.
5. When the African Americans walked to work, bus <u>companies</u> and other <u>businesses</u> suffered.
6. How many days did the <u>boycott</u> last?
7. There were <u>groups</u> of African Americans who formed carpools or stayed home.
8. The nonviolent <u>tactics</u> of the protesters were successful.
9. In December 1956, the <u>U.S. Supreme Court</u> ruled that segregation on buses was unconstitutional.
10. Read an account of the boycott in your history textbook.   You

EXERCISE 8 Identifying Subjects

Underline the subject(s) in each sentence of this school flyer. If the subject is understood to be *you*, write *You* at the beginning of the sentence.

¹Do <u>you</u> think science is no more than memorizing facts from a textbook or doing a few mildly interesting classroom experiments? ²(You) Join the troop of students already signed up to create fascinating projects for the science fair. ³One <u>group</u> of students is planning to build its own greenhouse to grow healthy, organic foods. ⁴Does the <u>idea</u> of inventing your own classroom robot sound more appealing? ⁵(You) Discover the amazing projects you can design using nothing more than your imagination. ⁶There are only a few <u>rules</u> to follow in order to submit a project for the fair. ⁷In the front hall of the main building <u>you</u> will find the forms and cards to be filled out. ⁸Along with our science faculty, two <u>professors</u> from the city university will judge the entries. ⁹The winning <u>projects</u> will represent our school in a citywide science fair. ¹⁰Judging from our students' inventive minds, <u>we</u> expect the science fair to generate tremendous interest.

Correcting Run-on Sentences

▐▶ A **run-on sentence** is made up of two or more sentences that are incorrectly run together as a single sentence.

One of these five strategies may help you correct a run-on sentence.

1. Separate them. Add end punctuation and a capital letter to separate the sentences.

RUN-ON   New York City celebrated its 100th anniversary in 1998 before January 1, 1898, New York consisted only of the island of Manhattan.

CORRECTED   New York City celebrated its 100th anniversary in 1998. Before January 1, 1898, New York consisted only of the island of Manhattan.

2. Use a conjunction. Use a coordinating or correlative conjunction preceded by a comma.

RUN-ON   Brooklyn did not necessarily want to become part of New York City Manhattan wanted its neighbor within its boundaries.

CORRECTED   Brooklyn did not necessarily want to become part of New York City, **but** Manhattan wanted its neighbor within its boundaries.

3. Try a semicolon. Use a semicolon to separate two sentences.

RUN-ON   The students have to park on the street the parking lot is full.

CORRECTED   The students have to park on the street; the parking lot is full.

4. Add a conjunctive adverb. Use a semicolon together with a conjunctive adverb or transitional expression. (See the lists on page 39.) Be sure to put a comma after the conjunctive adverb.

RUN-ON   In the 1940s, fans in Brooklyn cheered for the Dodgers people in Manhattan supported the Yankees.

CORRECTED   In the 1940s, fans in Brooklyn cheered for the Dodgers; **on the other hand,** people in Manhattan supported the Yankees.

5. Create a clause. Turn one of the sentences into a subordinate clause.

RUN-ON   Comic strips made Fiorello LaGuardia a popular mayor in the 1930s he read comics over the radio to the children of New York.

CORRECTED   **By reading comic strips over the radio to the children of New York,** Fiorello LaGuardia became a popular mayor in the 1930s.

EDITING TIP

A **fused sentence** is a run-on sentence with no punctuation. A **comma splice** is a run-on sentence with only a comma separating the sentences.

New York City had a total of forty-three newspapers in 1898 *but* only twenty-three were written in English.

WRITING HINT

Vary sentence lengths. Short sentences, one after the other, sound as bad as run-on sentences.

CHOPPY
The subway car stopped. The subway car jolted. A tunnel was dark. The train raced through it.

SMOOTH
The subway car stopped; then it jolted forward as the train raced through a dark tunnel.

See **Grammar**, Lessons 8.1–8.4, for more information on subordinate clauses.

EXERCISE 9 Correcting Run-on Sentences

On a separate piece of paper, rewrite each run-on sentence as one or more well-written sentences. Use a variety of strategies.
See Answer Key at www.grammarforwriting.com.

1. Giovanni da Verrazano and Henry Hudson explored the waterways around New York in 1524 and 1609, Verrazano sailed for the French and Hudson for the Dutch.

2. In 1623, European settlers traveled to New York with the Dutch West India Company they farmed on the lower end of the island of Manhattan.

3. Many newcomers from England came to New York they were invited by the Dutch West India Company.

4. New York, called New Amsterdam by the Dutch, came under English control in 1664, Dutch influence on the island of Manhattan remained strong.

5. The colors of the Dutch flag are the colors of today's New York City flag, the Dutch word for *farm*—*Bowery*—is the name of a section in Manhattan.

6. New York City became the first capital for the nation George Washington worshiped in Manhattan's St. Paul's Chapel.

7. By the 1870s, William M. ("Boss") Tweed firmly controlled politics in New York his power came from political corruption.

8. *The New York Times* exposed political scandals in 1871, corrupt Boss Tweed spent the next seven years in and out of jail, where he died in 1878.

EXERCISE 10 Editing a Report

With a partner or in a small group, correct all of the run-on sentences and fragments in this report. Use a variety of strategies, and write your changes on a separate piece of paper.

    ¹Walt Whitman ~~is~~ a famous nineteenth-century American poet, ~~he~~ is also a beloved citizen of New York City. ²~~That he was~~ born on Long Island. ³Eventually ~~Whitman~~ became the editor of the *Daily Eagle*, a Brooklyn newspaper; poetry also interested him. ⁴Because he advocated an antislavery position. ⁵Whitman lost his job with the newspaper ~~he~~ began to work on a group of unusual poems. ⁶Whitman published *Leaves of Grass* himself in 1847; however, the book it did not receive an enthusiastic reception from the reading public. ⁷He wrote a preface anointing himself as the voice of the common people. ⁸Today, no one would disagree; most people would consider him a major voice of the American experience in the years surrounding the Civil War and beyond. ⁹He wrote about individual pleasures in life he also ~~wrote~~ about President Lincoln after his assassination and about different regions of the United States. ¹⁰He may have begun his life as a common man, Walt Whitman became an uncommonly keen observer of our country through his work.

Added words shown: he; and then; however, the book; and; not only; but; Although

Direct and Indirect Objects

In this lesson, you'll review two kinds of objects: direct objects and indirect objects. Both of these appear in the predicate of a sentence.

▶ A **direct object** (DO) is a noun or pronoun that receives the action of an action verb. A direct object answers the question *whom* or *what* following the verb.

> **DO**
> A complete revolution of the Earth around the sun takes a **year**.
> [*Year* answers the question *takes what*.]

> **DO**
> Mr. Arnold asked **us** how we celebrate the New Year. [*Us* answers the question *asked whom*.]

Not all verbs take objects. When you consider action verbs and linking verbs (see Lesson 5.3), only action verbs take objects. An action verb that takes an object is a **transitive verb**. A verb that doesn't take an object is an **intransitive verb**.

▶ An **indirect object** (IO) is a noun or pronoun that answers the question *to whom* or *for whom* or *to what* or *for what* following an action verb.

Sentences may have direct objects without indirect objects, but they never have an indirect object without a direct object. Also, the indirect object always appears before the direct object.

> **IO**   **DO**
> Babette will hand the **teacher** the **report** on Wednesday.
> [Will hand—*to whom?*—the teacher. *Teacher* is the indirect object; *report* is the direct object.]

> **IO**   **IO**   **DO**
> The reporter gave **John** and **me** a **tour** of the newspaper.
> [Gave—*to whom?*—John and me. Gave—*what?*—a tour. *John* and *me* are the indirect objects; *tour* is the direct object.]

Two sentences may express the same meaning, but one may contain an indirect object while the other contains a prepositional phrase. Neither direct nor indirect objects ever appear in prepositional phrases.

> **IO**   **IO**   **DO**   **DO**
> Give **Eli** and **me** a **notebook** and a **pen**.
> **DO**   **DO**
> Give a **notebook** and a **pen** to Eli and me.
> [To *Eli and me* is a prepositional phrase.]

STEP BY STEP

Finding Direct and Indirect Objects

To find a direct object:

1. Find the action verb.
2. Ask the question *whom* or *what* after the action verb.

To find an indirect object:

1. Find the action verb.
2. Find the direct object.
3. Ask the question *to* or *for whom* or *to* or *for what* after the action verb.

EXERCISE 11 Identifying Direct and Indirect Objects

For each sentence from the following product advertisements, write *IO* over an indirect object and *DO* over a direct object. **Hint:** Some direct objects or indirect objects in these sentences may be compound.

1. Wipe & Swipe washes away every speck of dirt.
                                  DO

2. Give yourself the gift of gab with Talk Back software.
      IO   DO

3. Students love the ease of ABC Computers.
                DO

4. A swarm of bees can't make honey as sweet as we make Taste O'Honey.
                          DO   DO

5. You can take us for a ride on your new Olympic exercycle.
              DO

6. We'll show you the money if you show us a dead Eterno battery.
        IO   DO   IO   DO

7. It takes only three minutes for Red Alert Security Systems to respond to our
                DO

   home alarm.

8. Face Pure gel makes your complexion sparkle.
                      DO

9. Visit us just one time, and you'll discover a paradise on Earth.
      DO   DO

10. Gather one and all for after-school fun and food at Ben's Border Cafe.
        DO   DO

EXERCISE 12 Writing with Direct and Indirect Objects

With a partner or in a small group, write a paragraph-length advertisement that might be read on the radio. The product or service may be real or made up. Write *DO* over each direct object and *IO* over each indirect object in your paragraph. **Remember:** Don't confuse objects of prepositions in prepositional phrases with indirect objects. Write your advertisement on a separate piece of paper and compare your work with that of other groups of classmates.

Students' advertisements will vary. Direct and indirect objects should be marked correctly.

Write What You Think

Write a paragraph in response to the statement below. Support your opinion with facts and examples. Be sure to revise and edit your writing.

> The Federal Trade Commission should fine advertisers who make false claims about their products. The fine should equal three times the annual sales of the product to discourage this kind of unscrupulous business practice.

Answers will vary. Give students full credit if they have stated an opinion and attempted to support their opinions. They should also have written grammatically complete sentences that begin with a capital letter and end with an appropriate end punctuation mark.

Predicate Nominatives and Predicate Adjectives

Sometimes, a sentence is incomplete even though it includes a subject (S) and a verb (V).

    S   V   S   S   V   S   V
That music sounds. You and I will be. The singer in the band is.

▓▶ A **linking verb** needs a **subject complement**—a noun (N) or an adjective (ADJ)—in order to express a complete thought. The verbs *sounds*, *be*, and *is* are some linking verbs.

                 ADJ   N
That music sounds **loud**.   You and I will be **friends**.

Subject complements fall into one of two categories—**predicate nominatives** or **predicate adjectives**.

▓▶ A **predicate nominative** (PN) is a noun or pronoun that follows a linking verb (LV) and renames or identifies the subject of the sentence.

        S   LV PN
The lead singer in the band is **José Luis**. [*José Luis* is a proper noun that renames the subject *singer*.]

        S   LV PN
The salesperson who can help you is **she**. [*She* is a pronoun that identifies the subject *salesperson*.]

▓▶ A **predicate adjective** (PA) is an adjective that follows a linking verb and modifies or describes the subject.

        S   S   LV   PA
The fiddler and the accordion player seem **upbeat**. [The adjective *upbeat* modifies the subjects *fiddler* and *accordion player*.]

       S   LV   PA   PA
Will the CD become **warped** or **scratched**? [The adjectives *warped* and *scratched* modify the subject *CD*.]

EXERCISE 13 Identifying Subject Complements

Underline every predicate nominative and predicate adjective in the sentences below. In the space provided, write *PN* for predicate nominative or *PA* for predicate adjective.

   _PN_   1. One of the most respected people in the music world is Quincy Jones.

EDITING TIP

In formal speech and writing, a pronoun used as a subject complement takes the subjective case. However, in informal usage, most people consider the object case acceptable. For example, the correct answer to the question, "Who's there?" is: "It is *I*." [*I* is a subjective case pronoun.] But in friendly conversations, people commonly answer, "It's *me*." [*Me* is an objective case pronoun.]

TEST-TAKING TIP

On a standardized test you might be asked to decide whether a pronoun following a linking verb is the correct one. Remember: When used as a predicate nominative, a pronoun renames the subject and must reflect the subjective, or nominative, case. See the Example on page 308.

_____PA_____ 2. To this day, he seems <u>excited</u> about the subject of rock music.

_____PN_____ 3. Early in his career, Quincy Jones was a <u>musician</u>.

_____PA_____ 4. As an African American on band tours, he often looked <u>angry</u> when confronted with prejudice and segregation.

_____PN_____ 5. In the 1950s, the most celebrated people in pop music were <u>African Americans</u> and <u>Elvis</u>.

_____PN_____ 6. Jones became the first African American record <u>producer</u>.

_____PA_____ 7. His work as a producer seemed <u>strange</u> but <u>exciting</u> to him.

_____PA_____ 8. In the early 1960s, it seemed <u>improbable</u> that any foreign band would top Americans on the charts.

_____PN_____ 9. Quincy Jones was a <u>fan</u> of the Beatles and the Rolling Stones before their first American tours.

_____PN_____ 10. For Quincy Jones, rock music remains the quintessential <u>expression</u> of human feelings.

EXERCISE 14 Writing with Predicate Nominatives and Predicate Adjectives

With a partner or in a small group, use the sentences below to help you write with subject complements. If a complement you write is a predicate nominative, write *PN* above it. If the complement you write is a predicate adjective, write *PA* above it. Answers will vary. Sample answers given.

¹Music you listen to too often may grow ____PA monotonous____. ²Do you want to solve this problem? ³Here is our ____PN suggestion____. ⁴Exchange CDs among your group of friends. ⁵Different CDs may sound ____PA refreshing____. ⁶Used CDs are often ____PA undamaged____. ⁷Now your music tastes will look ____PA expansive____. ⁸Your music collection will become ____PA dynamic____ and ____PA broad____. ⁹Sharing music will now be ____PA routine____ and ____PA customary____.

Write What You Think

Write a paragraph in response to the statement below. Support your opinion with facts, reasons, and examples. Be sure to revise and edit your writing.

Some contemporary music lyrics call on listeners to commit crimes, brutalize women, and use obscenities. CDs that advocate such antisocial behavior and violent acts should be censored or banned.

Answers will vary. Give students full credit if they have stated an opinion and attempted to support their opinions. They should also have written grammatically complete sentences that begin with a capital letter and end with appropriate punctuation.

Object Complements

Certain kinds of action verbs require more than just a direct object to make a sentence complete.

▶ An **object complement** (OC) is a noun, pronoun, or adjective that completes the meaning of a direct object.

<pre>
      S   V   DO   OC
</pre>
The mole made the burrow **deep**. [*Deep* is an object complement that describes *burrow*, the direct object.]

Only sentences with the verbs *make* and *consider* (along with their synonyms) take object complements.

<pre>
      S   V   DO   OC
</pre>
We appointed Mirna **editor** of the school paper. [*Editor* is an object complement that completes the meaning of the direct object, *Mirna*.]

Some Synonyms for Make and Consider

appoint	judge
call	name
choose	paint
cut	sweep
elect	think
find	

EXERCISE 15 Identifying Object Complements

Underline each object complement in the paragraph below. Draw an arrow from the object complement to the direct object it identifies or describes. **Hint:** Two sentences do not contain object complements. **Remember:** Object complements only appear in sentences that use the verbs *make*, *consider*, or their synonyms. Don't consider phrases or clauses to be object complements.

¹Seen from a distance, some bird watchers consider the white ibis a snow goose. ²Flocks of white ibises find fish abundant in shallow water. ³The many marshes of Texas make an appealing habitat for these birds. ⁴Recently, some glossy ibises from the Atlantic Ocean or Eastern Gulf Coast made Texas their home, also. ⁵Did you know that ancient Egyptians thought ibises sacred? ⁶The word *Ibis* names a divine being in the Egyptian language. ⁷Why do others consider these birds special? ⁸For many, these creatures have been made into images both exotic and beautiful. ⁹Spot a flock of ibises anywhere, and you'll make the dazzling memory yours forever.

C **CCSS** Language 1, 2. (See pp. T14–T15.)

Revising and Editing Worksheet

Improve the following draft by revising for ideas, organization, word choice, and sentence variety. After revising, edit the draft for errors in spelling, capitalization, punctuation, and usage. Write your revised and edited version on a separate piece of paper. Compare your changes with those of a writing partner.

Students' revisions will vary. Sample revisions are given.

¹If members of the International World Calendar Association (IWCA) had their ~~weigh~~ way. ²Every date in the year would fall on the same day of the month. ³The New Year would be celebrated on Sunday, January 1. *Each year,* ~~each year~~

⁴To this day, the Chinese Calendar ~~does not consider January 1 New Year's Day~~. ⁵The Jewish Calendar ~~does not consider January 1 New Year's Day,~~ and the Indian Calendar does not consider January 1 to be New Year's Day. ⁶There are other reasons to consider, too. ⁷The American colonies celebrated New Year's Day in March until 1752. ⁸To the colonists, who were farmers, ~~March seemed the best time of year for celebration. ⁹The colonists were farmers.~~ ¹⁰Planting time seemed to be the best time of the year for a celebration of the New Year.

¹¹There are 365 days, 5 hours, 48 minutes, and 46 seconds in a year. ¹²How do you divide ¹³this amount of time evenly? ¹⁴What determines the length of a week or month? ¹⁵Julius caesar, the emperor of Rome, developed a new calendar and ¹⁶~~Julius caesar was dictator of Rome; Julius caesar~~ corrected earlier Roman calendars. ¹⁷The Julian calendar has twelve months; consequently, ¹⁸Our calendar has twelve months, too. Although ¹⁹Both calendars mark the New Year on January 1, ²⁰~~But~~ the Julian Calendar doesn't add up because it gives every fourth year an extra day. In addition, ~~and~~ this original calendar needs 445 days in a year to correct earlier errors in counting the time it takes earth to revolve around the sun.

²¹The calendar we use that ²²It is named after Pope Gregory XIII. ²³The ~~calender is~~ a Gregorian calendar, ~~it was~~ invented by astronomers, and it dropped ten days between ~~from~~ October 5 and ~~to~~ October 15 in 1582 in order ²⁴To fix an error from earlier calendars.

²⁵After 1582, the Gregorian Calendar was adopted in Europe.

Chapter Review

EXERCISE A Identifying Subjects and Verbs

In each sentence, underline the subject (simple subject) once and the verb twice. If the subject is understood to be *you*, write *You* following the sentence.

1. As a junior, you or a friend may become interested in driving a car.

2. On streets and roads, heed the sign that says, "Student Driver."   You

3. Teenagers in suburbs long to get out on their own in a car.

4. City dwellers, though, enjoy the benefits of public transportation.

5. Nevertheless, students should be trained in the rules of the road.

EXERCISE B Identifying Complements

Underline the direct and indirect objects, the subject complements, and the object complements in the sentences below. Above each, write *DO* (direct object), *IO* (indirect object), *OC* (object complement), *PA* (predicate adjective), or *PN* (predicate nominative).

1. The work of William Shakespeare remains a *(PN)* mystery for many readers.

2. An English teacher once showed *(IO)* them a movie *(DO)* version of *Romeo and Juliet*.

3. The film of this play seemed *(PA)* understandable and *(PA)* dramatic.

4. The drama coach gave the *(IO)* class *(DO)* instructions on how to read the poetry of Shakespeare, one sentence at a time.

5. Without movie versions, our class considered these *(DO)* plays *(OC)* boring at first.

6. "Movies gave *(IO)* Vicky and *(IO)* me a new *(DO)* insight into Shakespeare," Winston confessed.

EXERCISE C Writing Complete Sentences

On a separate piece of paper, edit the following sentence fragments and run-on sentences so they make one or two complete sentences. You may change, add, or omit words and punctuation. See Answer Key at www.grammarforwriting.com.

1. Grand Canyon National Park covering more than a million acres in northwestern Arizona.

2. In December 1947 President Harry S. Truman dedicated Everglades National Park in southern Florida, its highest elevation is 8 feet above sea level.

3. Yosemite National Park, which is located in east-central California in the Sierra Nevada Mountains. It was declared a national park in 1890.

4. Yosemite, famous for its series of high waterfalls and for its steep Yosemite Valley.

5. You have probably seen the stunning black and white photographs by Ansel Adams, he lived and worked in Yosemite for more than fifty years.

6. Bryce Canyon National Park in southwestern Utah, renowned for its fantastic eroded limestone rock spires known as hoodoos.

7. Close to Bryce in southwestern Utah, Zion National Park, containing Zion Canyon, which Mormon settlers named about 1860.

8. The Petrified Forest National Park in east-central Arizona, with petrified tree trunks dating back about 225 million years to the Triassic Period. When dinosaurs roamed the Earth.

Exercise D Revising and Editing Paragraphs

Revise and edit the following paragraph to eliminate wordiness, sentence fragments, and run-on sentences. Make any other changes you think will improve the writing. Revised paragraphs will vary.

¹I believe that books are superior entertainment to movies, Wilson completely disagrees with me. ²Since he likes movies. ³I read a book about the slave revolt on the ship *Amistad*. ⁴I saw a movie by Steven Spielberg about the slave revolt on the ship *Amistad*. ⁵Although I liked the book slightly more than the movie because of its greater wealth of details. ⁶Wilson read a book version of *Star Wars*. ⁷The movie, he argued, was far superior to any written version of this science fiction tale. ⁸The special effects of *Star Wars* can't be translated easily with words alone, they dazzle the viewer. ⁹That is Wilson's argument. ¹⁰With which I agree, at least about *Star Wars*. ¹¹Someday I will write a detailed novel, someday Wilson will direct the movie. ¹²We will let professional critics decide which version is better.

Write What You Think

Write one or two paragraphs in response to the statement below. Support your opinion with facts, reasons, and examples. Be sure to revise and edit your writing.

Only books with lots of action make good movies. Filmmakers should make action-packed movies rather than intellectual or true-life stories.

Answers will vary. Give students full credit if they have stated an opinion and attempted to support their opinions. They should also have written grammatically complete sentences that begin with a capital letter and end with an appropriate end punctuation mark.

Phrases

STUDENT WRITING
Narrative Essay

Sunday Soccer Clinic
by Rudy Lewis and Steve Gangemi
high school students, Lawrenceville, New Jersey

Direct students to www.grammarforwriting.com for chapter-specific portfolio projects.

Soccer is the most popular sport on earth, and Sunday is the most uneventful day in Lawrenceville. Combine these two and you get Sunday Soccer, arguably the most inspirational and valuable community-service project on campus. When we first laced on our cleats and headed to the field on a warm autumn day, we were unaware of the impact we were about to have on the lives of forty Trenton children. The first day was full of surprises. The ragtag team of children arrived clothed in anything from dresses and sandals to jeans and boots. Many of the children were unfamiliar with the game of soccer. Few could kick the ball well, and no one knew the rules. Each player was determined to win, and everyone wanted to be a star, but no one realized that the only way to win was through teamwork. As the weeks passed, the skills of the children rapidly improved, and they began to function as a team. By the end of the session, they had a real grasp of the game. But their learning experience went beyond the field. They learned skills which they were able to apply to their lives at home.

Cooperation and communication are key to any group effort. Although it was a valuable experience for the children, it was equally rewarding for us coaches. Sunday Soccer was more than just fulfilling the volunteer requirement; it was also an experience that allowed us to partake in the players' growth, not only as soccer players, but also as individuals. Because we knew that the athletic facilities the children were offered at Lawrenceville would have been otherwise unavailable to them, it was a great pleasure for us to allow them this experience. We also learned just how lucky we are to have the amenities and opportunities that we as students here have. Overall, it was a truly rewarding experience for both the volunteers and the children.

> The autobiographical incident above is effective because the authors tell the reader not only what happened but also why those events were significant to them. The reader understands what impact the Sunday Soccer Clinic had on both the children and the coaches.
>
> The essay above is also effective because the authors use phrases to describe and to explain, as well as to combine sentences. As you work on the exercises in this chapter, you will learn to use phrases to improve your own writing.

Allow time for students to discuss the student writing. Suggest that they identify its strengths and propose possible improvements. Use the model to introduce the concepts in the chapter.

C CCSS Language 1. (See pp. T14–T15.)

Lesson 7.1
Grammar

Adjective and Adverb Phrases

⫸ A **prepositional phrase** always begins with a preposition and ends with an object (a noun or pronoun).

The modifiers between the preposition and its object(s) are part of the prepositional phrase. The prepositional phrase may have a compound object, two or more objects joined by a conjunction such as *and* or *or*.

PREP	OBJ	ADJ OBJ		PREP OBJ	OBJ
beside the umbrella and red blanket				for him and me	

In the sentence below, each of the three prepositional phrases adds information to the sentence by modifying another word in the sentence.

The students **in the last row** moved **to the first row of the auditorium**.

⫸ An **adjective phrase** is a prepositional phrase that modifies a noun or pronoun in a sentence and answers the questions *Which one?* or *What kind?*

The whale **with the huge blowhole** is a female.

⫸ An **adverb phrase** is a prepositional phrase that modifies a verb, an adjective, or another adverb, and it answers the questions *When? How? Where?* or *To what extent?*

The seagull flew **against the wind**.

Please grill the salmon **for ten minutes**.

Some words function as both prepositions and adverbs, depending on how they are used in a sentence. In the first sentence below, the word *under* is used as a preposition. In the second sentence, the word *under* stands alone and acts as an adverb. **Remember:** Prepositions never stand alone.

PREP
Did the surfboard go **under** the wave?

ADV
Did the diver go **under**?

WRITING HINT

Do you "stand *in* line" or "stand *on* line"? It depends on the region of the United States where you live.

For most prepositions, however, certain choices are more appropriate than others.

write *in* pencil/write *with* pencil

dance *with* the music/dance *to* the music

reach *to* the stars/reach *for* the stars

EDITING TIP

It's never wrong to use a comma after one introductory prepositional phrase, and you *should* use a comma after two or more. However, don't use a comma when an introductory prepositional phrase immediately precedes a verb.

INCORRECT
In the front closet, is the old TV set.

CORRECT
In the front closet is the old TV set.

Exercise 1 Identifying Adjective and Adverb Phrases

Underline each prepositional phrase in the sentences below, and draw an arrow to the word each phrase modifies. Label the phrase *ADJ* for adjective phrase and *ADV* for adverb phrase.

See **Grammar**, Lesson 5.6, for a list of prepositions.

1. The waters of the Gulf Stream begin in Florida. ADJ; ADV

2. The Gulf Stream is unusually warm for ocean water. ADJ

3. The width of the Gulf Stream is about fifty miles. ADJ; ADV

4. Within the Atlantic Ocean, it flows like a river toward Europe and Africa. ADV; ADV; ADV

5. The current flows north from Florida toward Maine. ADV; ADV

6. The Gulf Stream sweeps through the wide Sargasso Sea, located around the Bermuda Islands. ADV; ADV

7. The Sargasso Sea is strewn with seaweed floating on its surface. ADV; ADV

8. The seaweed in the Sargasso Sea is called sargassum. ADJ

9. Sargassum is found in warm seas and has special branches with berry-like air sacs. ADV; ADJ

10. When Christopher Columbus crossed the Sargasso Sea, he believed he was near land. ADV

11. However, sargassum in the Gulf Stream does not usually float near land. ADJ; ADV

12. Early navigators feared becoming entangled in the seaweed. ADV

13. Jean Rhys wrote *Wide Sargasso Sea* after moving to England from the West Indies. ADV; ADV

14. This novel is based on the English classic *Jane Eyre*. ADV

15. Both novels have been made into movies. ADV

Appositives and Appositive Phrases

Imagine that a friend tells you about someone who participated in a national track competition. The friend might communicate one piece of information about that person, then add another detail.

> Lara competed in a national track competition. Lara is the new student in our math class.

Here's a way to combine these ideas into one sentence.

> Lara, the new student in our math class, competed in a national track competition.

▶ An **appositive** is a noun or pronoun that identifies or explains the noun or pronoun that precedes or follows it. An **appositive phrase** is made up of an appositive and all of its modifiers.

In the combined sentence above, the phrase *the new student in our math class* is an appositive phrase. The noun *student* is an appositive that identifies *Lara*.

Essential appositives provide information essential to understanding the sentence.

Do not use commas to set off essential appositives.

> My cousin **Jason** broke the school record in the long jump.
> The California track clubs **the Jaguars and the Coasters** shared first place.

Nonessential appositives provide extra information that is not essential to understanding the sentence.

Use commas to set off nonessential appositives.

> Olga, **the youngest competitor,** took third place in the 100-meter dash.
> Denver, **a city at a high altitude,** hosted a national junior track event.

EXERCISE 2 Combining Sentences with Appositives

On a separate piece of paper, combine these sentences using appositives or appositive phrases. **Remember:** Use commas to set off nonessential appositives. See Answer Key at www.grammarforwriting.com.

EXAMPLE   Carl Lewis was a multitalented track star. Carl Lewis competed in various events.

Carl Lewis, a multitalented track star, competed in various events.

1. Carl Lewis won many gold medals in Olympic track events. Carl Lewis was an extraordinary runner.

2. His younger sister also competed as a long jumper. His sister is Carol.

3. He was born in Birmingham, Alabama, in 1961. Birmingham is an industrial city.

4. At his college, he came to national attention. Carl Lewis attended the University of Houston.

5. He earned three medals at the 1983 World Championships in Helsinki. All his medals were gold.

6. In 1984, Carl Lewis broke the record held by Jesse Owens. Jesse Owens was the previous greatest runner in U.S. history.

7. Carl Lewis's Olympic record has not yet been surpassed. He holds the Olympic record of four consecutive gold medals in the long jump.

8. He earned his four gold medals in three solo events and in the relay. The relay is a four-man race.

9. In his last competition, he won another gold medal. His final competition was the 1996 Atlanta Olympics.

10. The gold medalist was thirty-five years old then. Thirty-five is an advanced age for an Olympian.

Exercise 3 Writing Sentences with Appositives

On a separate piece of paper, write five sentences about a hobby or interest you have, such as playing a sport, painting, gardening, caring for a pet, or playing a musical instrument. Write from your own experience as either a participant or an observer. Try to provide details, either essential or nonessential, as appositives or appositive phrases. After you finish writing, underline any appositives or appositive phrases you included. Students' sentences will vary.

CONNECTING
Writing & Grammar

Write What You Think

On a separate piece of paper, write a few paragraphs in response to the following statement:

> The Olympic Games should be abolished because the competition places a premium on winning at all costs.

Support your opinion with facts and examples. Be sure to revise and edit your writing.

Answers will vary. Give students full credit if they have stated an opinion and attempted to support their opinions. Look for grammatically complete sentences that begin with a capital letter and end with an appropriate end punctuation mark.

C CCSS Language 1. (See pp. T14–T15.)

Lesson 7.3

Grammar

Participles and Participial Phrases

A **verbal** is a verb form that functions as another part of speech. There are three kinds of verbals: participles, infinitives, and gerunds.

▶ A **participle** is a verb form that acts as an adjective by modifying a noun or a pronoun.

You can use a **present participle**, which ends in *-ing*, or a **past participle**, which usually ends in either *-d* or *-ed*. Irregular verbs have irregular participles. [See the list of common irregular verbs in Lessons 9.2 and 9.3.]

Don't confuse a participle with a verb phrase. A verb phrase is formed by placing a helping verb before a participle. It functions as a verb in a sentence. A participle standing alone acts as an adjective in a sentence.

VERB PHRASE	The fire **is burning** slowly.
PARTICIPLE	The **burning** building is collapsing.
VERB PHRASE	The class **has collected** donations for uniforms.
PARTICIPLE	José has the **collected** works of Shakespeare.

▶ A **participial phrase** is made up of a participle and all of its modifiers. The whole phrase acts as an adjective.

Cheering loudly, we greeted the singer. [modifies *we*]
One teenager held a photograph **signed by the singer herself**. [modifies *photograph*]

P.S. Participles and participial phrases sound more complicated than they are in reality. You use participles and participial phrases naturally when you're talking.

> See **Usage**, Lessons 12.4 and 12.5, for more about misplaced or dangling modifiers in a sentence.

> **WRITING HINT**
>
> Place a participial phrase close to the word it modifies. Otherwise, you may say something you don't mean.
>
> **ORIGINAL**
> I found a picture of the Grand Canyon **surfing the Internet**.
>
> **REVISED**
> **Surfing the Internet**, I found a picture of the Grand Canyon.

EXERCISE 4 Identifying Participles and Participial Phrases

Underline the participles and participial phrases in each sentence. Draw an arrow to the noun or pronoun it modifies. **Hint:** A sentence may contain more than one participle or participial phrase. Be sure to underline prepositional phrases that are part of the participial phrase.

EXAMPLE   Tom saw two murals by Marc Chagall hanging in the Metropolitan Opera House.

1. Marc Chagall painted scenes based on Jewish culture.

2. The talented Chagall first took painting lessons in Vitebsk, Russia.

3. He moved to St. Petersburg, a city filled with artists.

4. He moved to Paris, known as the art center of Europe.

5. In Paris, he missed his intriguing girlfriend, Bella.

6. During a visit home in 1914, the renowned Chagall was prevented from returning to Paris with his bride, Bella, by the outbreak of World War I.

7. Heading the new department of fine arts, Chagall stayed in Vitebsk after the Russian Revolution of 1917.

8. A frustrated Chagall and his wife, Bella, left Russia for good in 1922.

9. An admiring world audience hailed Chagall's paintings depicting dreamlike scenes of life in Vitebsk.

10. Floating animals and people often appear upside down in his paintings.

Working Together

EXERCISE 5 Writing with Participial Phrases

On a separate piece of paper, create complete sentences that contain each of the participial phrases below. Place the participial phrase as close as possible to the word it modifies. Share your sentences with your writing group to check that you have not used the phrases as verbs. Students' sentences will vary.

1. shocked by the news

2. satisfying everyone

3. diving for the ground ball

4. fascinated by the movie

5. established long ago

6. cleaning his room

7. stopped in traffic

8. changing trains

EXERCISE 6 Writing with Participles

Rewrite the art review below by combining sentences and using participles to streamline the narrative. Students' paragraphs will vary.

[1]The paintings of artist Elena Gonzales were exhibited this week. [2]They were exhibited at the Windswept Gallery. [3]They were stunning. [4]Many of the canvases feature the ocean and the shore. [5]People are playing in the water. [6]They are playing on the sand. [7]Details are striking in the paintings. [8]She shows every wave, rock, or object on the Maine beach where she lives. [9]The artist paints driftwood. [10]The artist pays careful attention to every detail. [11]*Drifting Driftwood* is her favorite painting. [12]That painting earned first place in an art show last year. [13]This reviewer appreciated them. [14]Anyone who loves the sea will treasure these paintings. [15]Directions to the gallery are simple. [16]The gallery has a bright red awning. [17]It is located between Second and Third Streets off Main.

Gerunds and Gerund Phrases

Gerunds, like participles, are verb forms. But participles act as adjectives, and gerunds act as nouns in a sentence.

▸ A **gerund**, ending in *-ing*, is a verb form that acts as a noun.

Whatever a noun can do, a gerund can do, too.

> **Mining** is an occupation. [subject]
> Bob's occupation was **mining**. [predicate nominative]
> Who has attempted **mining** for gold? [direct object]
> Have you given **mining** a try as a possible career? [indirect object]
> Nancy likes to read about **mining**. [object of a preposition]

▸ A **gerund phrase** is made up of a gerund and all of its modifiers and complements. The entire phrase functions as a noun. **Remember:** Complements, such as direct and indirect objects, are words that complete the meaning of a verb.

> **Being a forty-niner** was an important role in California history. [subject]
> **Panning for gold** seldom brought the forty-niners real wealth. [subject]
> Photographers enjoyed **taking pictures of forty-niners**. [direct object]
> Forty-niners ended a day by **weighing their gold nuggets**. [object of a preposition]

EDITING TIP

Nouns and pronouns that modify a gerund are possessive.

INCORRECT
The **chalks** screeching disturbed the class.

REVISED
The **chalk's** screeching disturbed the class.

INCORRECT
We applauded **him** singing.

REVISED
We applauded **his** singing.

Enriching Your Vocabulary

The word *intriguing*, as used in Exercise 8, has the same Latin root as *intricate*. The root, *intricare*, means "to entangle, or embarrass." Thus, an *intriguing* personality is one that incites curiosity and fascination.

EXERCISE 7 Identifying Gerunds and Gerund Phrases

Underline every gerund and gerund phrase in the sentences below. A gerund phrase may contain one or more prepositional phrases. Count these as part of the gerund phrase. **Remember:** Not every *-ing* word is a gerund; it must function as a noun in the sentence to be considered a gerund.

1. Sonya enjoyed studying photographs at the Oakland Museum one day.
2. Looking at the exhibition of gold miners was both fascinating and surprising.
3. Taking photographs of forty-niners became part of the gold rush experience.
4. One forty-niner, James Woolsey, is pictured holding a huge gold nugget.
5. By paying three or four dollars, Woolsey had his picture taken.
6. The Oakland Museum encouraged reading about the photographs by placing captions beside them.

7. By <u>posing for these photographs</u>, the forty-niners gave themselves dignity.

8. <u>Documenting the presence of Asian miners in California</u> is an 1851 photograph by Isaac Wallace Baker.

9. William Shew promoted <u>photographing miners</u> with their gold in front of the steamers that waited to take them home.

10. By <u>observing photographs of Spanish-Californian miners</u>, Sonya understood her ancestors' past.

Exercise 8 Writing Sentences with Gerunds and Gerund Phrases

On a separate piece of paper, write questions and answers for an interview about future career plans. First, have one partner or a small group write questions about the future careers and activities students might pursue after graduation. Then, have the other partner or small group answer these questions in complete sentences. Include a gerund or gerund phrase in the sentence that represents each question and/or its accompanying answer (see sample below).

Q: Would working in advertising interest you?

A: As a person with artistic ability, I'd consider working in advertising a very intriguing career. Answers will vary.

Write What You Think

On a separate piece of paper, write a few paragraphs in response to the statement below. Support your opinion with facts, reasons, and examples. Be sure to revise and edit your writing.

Scientists believe that the rise in asthma in young people today is caused by the rise in air pollution from automobiles. The automobile industry should take responsibility for this pollution and should pay to clean up the air.

Answers will vary. Give students full credit if they have stated an opinion and attempted to support their opinions. Look for grammatically complete sentences that begin with a capital letter and end with an appropriate end punctuation mark.

Infinitives and Infinitive Phrases

||||▶ An **infinitive** is a verb form that is almost always preceded by the word *to*. An infinitive can play several parts in a sentence. It can be a noun, an adjective, or an adverb.

> My uncle likes **to dig** for fossils. [infinitive as noun]
> He was the first person **to see** the ancient footprint. [infinitive as adjective]
> What was it like **to roam** the ancient Earth [infinitive as adverb]

The word *to* is the *sign*, or *marker*, that begins an infinitive. But don't confuse the infinitive marker *to* with the preposition *to*. **Remember:** An infinitive *to* is always followed by a verb.

> INFINITIVE   They began **to dig**.
> PREPOSITION   Please give this **to her**.

||||▶ An **infinitive phrase** is made up of an infinitive and all of its modifiers and complements.

Like participial phrases and gerund phrases, infinitive phrases may contain one or more prepositional phrases.

> She began **to sketch the ancient footprint in the rock**.
> **To become an archaeologist** takes long study and training.
> They asked him **to write an article about his discovery**.

Infinitives sometimes appear without the word *to*. In these cases, the word *to* is understood.

> The student helped **[to] organize** the notes.

P.S. To use infinitives and infinitive phrases properly, you don't have to worry about whether they are functioning as nouns, adjectives, or adverbs. You use them in everyday speech.

WRITING *HiNT*

Placing a modifier between *to* and the verb is called a split infinitive.

SPLIT INFINITIVE
The player tried **to** quickly **dunk** the ball.

Avoid split infinitives unless by doing so, the result is awkward or sounds unnatural.

EXERCISE 9 Identifying Infinitives and Infinitive Phrases

Underline the infinitives and infinitive phrases in these sentences. Remember that an infinitive phrase includes the infinitive and all of its modifiers (including prepositional phrases) and complements. **Hint:** Not every phrase beginning with *to* is an infinitive.

1. Tourists flock to a national park in South Africa <u>to step in the oldest known human footprints on Earth.</u>

2. These prints are believed <u>to have been made over 100,000 years ago.</u>

3. How were they able <u>to survive so long</u>?

4. Soon after the prints were made, sand blew in <u>to cover them</u>.

5. Afterward, the prints turned to stone, which allowed them <u>to endure</u>.

6. These fossils are beginning <u>to wear away</u> because too many people have stepped in them.

7. <u>To preserve these fossils</u>, the South African government has taken action.

8. The original footprint stone was taken to a museum, and a mold was made <u>to replace the original</u>.

9. Archaeologists were able <u>to determine</u> that the ancient footprint belonged to a female who was five foot three inches tall.

10. Soon archaeologists hope <u>to uncover more ancient prints</u> that show who else walked with her.

EXERCISE 10 Writing Sentences with Infinitives and Infinitive Phrases

On a separate piece of paper, write five sentences from a speech that the ancient person mentioned in Exercise 9 might address to a modern-day audience. What would she say about her experience of being immortalized in rock? What would she say about the modern world she witnesses? What would she say about any hopes or dreams she has for her descendants? In each sentence, try to include at least one infinitive or infinitive phrase. Underline the infinitives and the full infinitive phrases you write. Here's one way to start:

I can't begin <u>to express my amazement</u> at the speed of modern life.
Students' sentences will vary.

Write What You Think

On a separate piece of paper, write a message you would like to leave in a time capsule for people of the future. Write your message in paragraph form. Use the instructions below to help you formulate your ideas. Be sure to revise and edit your writing.

1. Describe some of the thoughts and feelings that motivated people during your lifetime.

2. Describe some important events or discoveries during your lifetime.

3. Explain your own hopes and dreams for humanity.

Students' paragraphs will vary. Look for grammatically complete sentences that begin with a capital letter and end with an appropriate end punctuation mark.

C CCSS Language 1, 2. (See pp. T14–T15.)

Chapter 7

Grammar

Revising and Editing Worksheet 1

Improve the following draft by revising for ideas, organization, word choice, and sentence variety. After revising, edit the draft for errors in spelling, capitalization, punctuation, and usage. Write your revised and edited version on a separate piece of paper. Compare your changes with those of a writing partner.
Students' revisions will vary.

[1]A Navajo artist from New Mexico and Arizona. [2]Carl Gorman was also a World War II hero. [3]He helped create a code. [4]Using the Navajo language. [5]The Navajo language is little-known. [6]This code was so successful that Gorman did not speak about it publicly. [7]Until 1969. [8]He honored the governments request for his silence. [9]After 1969, though, he lectured about successfully inventing the code in the Pacific front. [10]He lectured throughout the country.

[11]The Japanese hoped to break the code. [12]But breaking this code. [13]Demanded more than mere knowledge of Navajo. [14]Apart from 50,000 Navajos, fewer than thirty people understood Navajo when World War II broke out. [15]Navajo is a language without an alphabet. [16]Through cooperation with other Navajo soldiers. [17]Navajo words took on new English meanings. [18]These words were in this code. [19]For example, the Navajo word, *jay-sho*. [20]*Jay-sho* means buzzard. [21]*Jay-sho* translated as "bomber" in this code. [22]It was in this code. [23]Without question, the Japanese was at a disadvantage. [24]Because they couldn't figure out what their enemy was planning to do. [25]They did not understand this amazing way information was safely exchanged. [26]The information was exchanged among Americans.

[27]Carl Gorman was born on the Navajo reservation in Chinle, Arizona. [28]Using Navajo was not permitted in a mission school. [29]He attended a mission school. [30]It became a difficult experience for Gorman. [31]Gorman insisted during his school experience. [32]On speaking his native language despite rules prohibiting it. [33]This was a beloved language to him.

C CCSS Language 1, 2. (See pp. T14–T15.)

Revising and Editing Worksheet 2

Improve the following draft by revising for ideas, organization, word choice, and sentence variety. After revising, edit the draft for errors in spelling, capitalization, punctuation, and usage. Write your revised and edited version on a separate piece of paper. Compare your changes with those of a writing partner. Students' revisions will vary.

[1]Between 1840 and 1870, more than a quarter of a million people. [2]Traveled in wagon trains on overland trails. [3]They traveled across the continental United States. [4]A new life out West was what they looked for. [5]Establishing a new life proved to be a difficult task. [6]They hoped to eventually claim free land in Oregon or California. [7]Travelers braved bad weather. [8]They braved treacherous crossings. [9]The weather was harsh. [10]The crossings were over Rivers and Mountains. [11]Iowa is a Midwestern state. [12]The 2,400 mile trip from Iowa to the West Coast is long. [13]It marks one of the

greatest migrations of modern times.

[14]Travelers wrote diaries and journal entries. [15]This allowed them to record the details of this trip, and the trip was amazing. [16]Woman took part in recording the events they experienced that happened along the way. [17]They were from every state in the union. [18]Women would travel the overland trails. [19]It wasn't easy. [20]It wasn't easy for anyone. [21]It was especially difficult for women with small children.

[22]Lydia Rudd was one of the many migrants. [23]Lydia Rudd wrote a diary. [24]It was written during her trip to Oregon. [25]In 1852. [26]Her husbands' name was Harry. [27]She and her husband hoped to acquire free land threw the Donation Act. [28]The Donation act allowed for land. [29]Men and women signed up for land through the Donation Act. [30]Lydia looked forward. [31]To land carrying her name alone.

Chapter Review

EXERCISE A Matching Definitions

Match the term in Column 1 with its definition in Column 2. Write the letter of the definition in the space provided.

_____ e _____ 1. gerund   a. the *-ing* verb form that functions as an adjective

_____ c _____ 2. preposition   b. a verb form that is almost always preceded by the word *to*

_____ b _____ 3. infinitive   c. a word used to show the relationship between two words in a sentence, such as *in*, *with*, or *over*.

_____ a _____ 4. participle   d. a noun or pronoun that identifies or explains the noun or pronoun preceding or following it

_____ d _____ 5. appositive   e. the *-ing* verb form that functions as a noun

EXERCISE B Identifying Phrases

Identify each underlined phrase by writing one of these abbreviations at the end of the line. **Remember:** A prepositional phrase may be a part of another kind of phrase. Label the main phrases, not the prepositional phrases within other phrases.

PREP = prepositional phrase   INF = infinitive phrase
PART = participial phrase   APP = appositive phrase
GER = gerund phrase

1. She hoped <u>to learn about the poet and doctor William Carlos Williams.</u> INF

2. <u>Coming from an English and Cuban background</u> influenced this American poet. GER

3. Some people questioned the poetry <u>written by a doctor after office hours.</u> PART

4. His personal writing style gave rise to a new way of thinking <u>about American poetry.</u> PREP

5. One famous poem, "This Is Just to Say," is written as a late-night note from Dr. Williams <u>to his wife.</u> PREP

6. This note describes nothing more than some plums <u>enjoyed as a late-night snack.</u> PART

7. <u>In its short 28 words,</u> "This Is Just to Say" touches on his marriage. PREP

8. The shattered glass, <u>glittering in an alleyway,</u> is the subject of "Between Walls." PART

9. This observation, <u>made by Dr. Williams</u> at work, demonstrates the poetry of everyday life. PART

10. Dr. Williams finds poetry in daily observations or in his relationship with Flossie, <u>his wife of many years</u>. APP

EXERCISE C Using Phrases

On a separate piece of paper, use each of the phrases below to write a complete sentence. In your sentences, underline each phrase and identify it as a prepositional phrase (PREP), an appositive phrase (APP), a participial phrase (PART), a gerund phrase (GER), or an infinitive phrase (INF). **Hint:** Do not use any phrase as part of a verb phrase. See Answer Key at www.grammarforwriting.com.

1. In most American cities and towns

2. My favorite singer

3. Bought more than a hundred years ago

4. Doing her research on the Internet

5. To write a clever, suspenseful mystery story

6. Expecting the worst

7. Painting the kitchen

8. Studying hard for her physics test

9. To pack his grandmother's dishes

10. Without any experience or training

11. To help them find their lost dog

12. A baseball legend

13. To apply to several small, liberal arts colleges

14. Winning every race

15. Except my Aunt Cele, Uncle Ralph, and their two children

16. Burrowing under the fence

17. Transferring to a new school in the middle of the school year

18. Waiting for the school bus

19. To meet new friends

20. Reading in a car or on a subway

Write What You Think

Write a few paragraphs in response to the following statement. Support your position with facts, reasons, and examples. Be sure to revise and edit your writing.

> In some countries ruled by dictators, poetry and other forms of creative expression are censored or banned. In the United States, freedom of expression is a basic right and must be safeguarded.

Answers will vary. Give students full credit if they have stated a position and attempted to support their position with facts, reasons, and examples. Look for grammatically complete sentences that begin with a capital letter and end with an appropriate end punctuation mark.

Clauses

STUDENT WRITING
Persuasive Essay

New Sports Policy a Boon for Athletes
by Rusty Ryan
high school student, Cambridge, Massachusetts

The sports department's new policy of organizing nonvarsity sports according to a player's ability, instead of by age, represents a significant improvement over the former system. As of this season, freshmen are permitted to play on JV [Junior Varsity] teams in soccer and field hockey, and juniors and sophomores can also play on third teams, which were formerly reserved for freshmen. By strengthening the JV program, the new policy has the potential to improve the performances of both JV and varsity teams.

In past years, many students have complained about the "dead end" nature of JV teams. Players who wished to improve their skills and make varsity teams in future years often found themselves at odds with students who merely wanted to fulfill their sports requirement with a minimum of effort. The wide disparity of talent on JV teams prevented ambitious players from improving and frustrated less talented players who often received little playing time.

Under the new system, competitive players, both freshmen and upperclassmen alike, will be able to develop their skills without being held back by less serious athletes. JV teams will be more successful, and varsity teams will benefit because players moving up from JV will have had the experience of playing in a competitive environment.

The system will also provide a more enjoyable environment for less serious players. Although some upperclassmen were disappointed to be cut from JV and have quit the program entirely, those who chose to play on third teams will likely enjoy both the greater playing time and the more relaxed pace. Once the system has been in place for a few years, it will be less of a shock for upperclassmen to be cut from JV, and more will elect to continue playing. Another benefit of the new system is its potential to ease the isolation many freshmen feel from the rest of the school.

> The opinion statement of Rusty Ryan's persuasive essay appears in the last sentence of the first paragraph. He supports his statement with background information, with reasons that support his opinion, and even with a response to opposing viewpoints.
>
> One of the reasons that Rusty's essay is effective is that he uses clauses to connect sentences and to give variety to his writing. In this chapter, you'll practice using clauses to express ideas clearly and to vary your own sentences.

Allow time for students to discuss the student writing. Suggest that they identify its strengths and propose possible improvements. Use the model to introduce the concepts in the chapter.

Independent Clauses and Subordinate Clauses

▐▐▐▶ An **independent** (or **main**) **clause** has a subject (s) and a verb (v) and expresses a complete thought.

Like a complete sentence, an independent clause within a sentence can stand alone. That's why it's *independent*!

              S   V
Long ago, immigrants came to America from Europe.

                   V   S   S   S
In the steerage section traveled parents, children, and others.

A **compound sentence** contains two or more independent clauses joined by a conjunction and no subordinate clauses.

    INDEPENDENT CLAUSE   INDEPENDENT CLAUSE
One family traveled from Russia, **and** another came from Italy.

▐▐▐▶ A **subordinate** (or **dependent**) **clause** has a subject and a verb but doesn't express a complete thought.

       S   V   S   V
because they hoped for a better life   who barely had a penny

Subordinate clauses may appear at the beginning, middle, or end of a sentence.

A subordinate clause is a sentence fragment. It can't stand alone. It must be inserted into or attached to an independent clause.

People **who had money** traveled first class. [The subordinate clause is inserted into the independent clause.]

Immigrants endured difficult journeys **because they hoped for a better life**. [The subordinate clause is attached to the independent clause.]

> **EDITING TIP**
>
> Place the major idea of a sentence in an independent clause. Do not bury a major idea in a subordinate clause.
>
> **ORIGINAL**
> Workers, who hoped for good jobs in America, had skills.
>
> **CORRECTED**
> Workers who had skills hoped for good jobs in America.

EXERCISE 1 Identifying Clauses

On the blank before each numbered item, write *I* for an independent clause or *S* for a subordinate clause. On a separate piece of paper, revise every subordinate clause to make it a complete sentence.
Students' revisions to subordinate clauses will vary. Sample revisions are given.

   I   1. Ellis Island greeted immigrants between 1892 and 1954.

   S   2. Whoever entered the United States by the Atlantic Ocean. braved rough seas and ⌃ uncertain weather.

   I   3. New York City's population exploded from 60,000 to over 3 million. City schools were filled with children

   S   4. Who came from Italy, Russia, Ireland, and Greece, among other ⌃ countries.

, schools had to adjust to students who couldn't speak English.

___S___ 5. Since many immigrants settled in the Northeast, especially in cities.
        overwhelmed city services. ∧

___S___ 6. Crowded urban neighborhoods with many immigrants.
   Many   ∧

___S___ 7. ~~Although they~~ came because of religious or political persecution.

___S___ 8. Even though the immigrant life was tough. hundreds of thousands made the
                                           difficult journey.

EXERCISE 2 Editing Paragraphs

Review the following paragraphs, correcting all fragments. **Remember:** You may place a subordinate clause at the beginning, middle, or end of a sentence. You may also change a subordinate clause into an independent clause.

Edited paragraphs will vary.

¹The trip many poorer immigrants made in steerage was difficult. ²Even though the journey may have proved worthwhile over time. ³Who kept journals about their trip. ⁴People included details about the hardships. ⁵The ship voyage from a port in Europe to Ellis Island usually took up to two weeks. ⁶Although some ships could make it in six days. ⁷Because the ship's food was often inedible or against the religious practices of some travelers. ⁸Many immigrants ate the little food they could bring on board. ⁹Which got stale during the journey.

¹⁰Many feared shipwrecks or accidents. ¹¹When bad weather made the water rough. ¹²Morris Raphael Cohen wrote about his fear of an accident. ¹³He wrote about the crowded conditions in steerage. ¹⁴Who left Europe because of prejudice. ¹⁵Against Jewish people. ¹⁶Whatever happened mattered less when the Statue of Liberty was spotted. ¹⁷This symbolized freedom. ¹⁸The written memories of immigrants from the turn of the twentieth century reveal. ¹⁹Who among us has a great wealth of spirit. ²⁰How the human spirit can triumph.

EXERCISE 3 Writing a Family Narrative

Refer to **Composition,** Lesson 4.1, to find strategies for writing a family narrative.

On a separate piece of paper, write a few paragraphs about when and from where your family first came to America. You may need to interview your relatives to gather information. If you don't know these facts, use your imagination to picture your ancestors and what might have motivated them to leave their homeland and travel to a foreign land. If you're a Native American, write a few paragraphs about the early history of your people in the United States.

Students' narratives will vary. Give students full credit if they have stated an opinion and attempted to support their opinions. They should also have written grammatically correct sentences that begin with a capital letter and end with an appropriate end punctuation mark.

Adjective Clauses

In this chapter, you'll review three kinds of subordinate clauses: adjective clauses, adverb clauses, and noun clauses.

▐▐▶ An **adjective clause** is a subordinate clause that functions as an adjective. It modifies a noun or pronoun.

> The trumpet player, **who wears a tuxedo**, stands in front.
> The trumpet **that she bought** sounds magnificent.

Adjective clauses usually follow the word they modify. They usually begin with an introductory word called a **relative pronoun** or a **relative adverb**. Refer to the list in the side column.

Sometimes, these introductory words are omitted. The sentences below make sense with or without the bracketed words.

> Where is the music [**that**] **I bought**?
> Rafael is the guitarist [**whom**] **you will accompany on the trumpet**.

Like appositives [see Lesson 7.2], adjective clauses provide information that is either essential to the meaning of a sentence or not essential. An **essential clause** delivers the main message of a sentence. A **nonessential clause** adds extra information but does not contain the main message of the sentence.

When the clause is essential, it must not be set off with commas.

ESSENTIAL   This is the hall **where the orchestra performs**.
NONESSENTIAL   This hall, **where the orchestra performs**, will be remodeled next year.

P.S. You learned about essential and nonessential clauses when you studied appositives in Lesson 7.2. The same rules about commas apply to adjective clauses. In other textbooks, you may see the term *nonrestrictive* used for *nonessential* and *restrictive* used for *essential*. These terms are synonyms.

EXERCISE 4 Identifying Adjective Clauses

Underline the adjective clauses in the sentences below.

1. Yo-Yo Ma, who is a world-famous cellist, was born in Paris.

2. The two cellos that he plays were made in Italy and Austria.

3. Julliard, where Yo-Yo Ma studied, is a world-class music school.

Some Words That Introduce Adjective Clauses

Relative Pronouns

that	who
what	whoever
where	whom
which	whose

Relative Adverbs

where	why
when	

EDITING TIP

Place the adjective clause right next to the word it modifies.

INCORRECT
The book is a bestseller that I'm reading now.

CORRECT
The book that I'm reading now is a bestseller.

TEST-TAKING TIP

Keep in mind that an adjective clause may begin with *whose* but never *who's*. On a standardized test, you may be asked to correct such an error. Remember that *who's* is a contraction for *who is*. See the Example on page 312.

4. He performs for young audiences <u>who respond enthusiastically</u>.

5. The pianist Emanuel Ax is a musician <u>whom Yo-Yo Ma admires</u>.

6. A program, <u>which Yo-Yo Ma and Emanuel Ax developed</u>, presents family concerts at Carnegie Hall.

7. The city of Hong Kong, <u>which was about to rejoin China</u>, was the site of Yo-Yo Ma's solo performance in 1997.

8. Some music <u>that Yo-Yo Ma has studied</u> comes from China and Africa.

9. Nashville, <u>where country music is king</u>, has hosted Yo-Yo Ma in concert.

10. Music is the universal language <u>that allows everyone to communicate</u>.

EXERCISE 5 Identifying Sentences with Adjective Clauses

Read the following paragraph one student wrote about his favorite instrument. Underline the adjective clauses.

¹At the age of ten, people <u>whom I admired</u> wanted me to play the piano. ²My parents could not find a piano <u>that would fit in our apartment</u>. ³In fact, the piano, <u>which had been my instrument of choice</u>, didn't turn out to be my favorite. ⁴My favorite instrument, <u>which is in my pocket right now</u>, is the harmonica. ⁵The place <u>where I first heard the harmonica</u> was in my own living room. ⁶CDs of the blues, <u>which my parents like to play</u>, captured my interest. ⁷John Mayall, <u>who is a well-known musician from the 1960s and 1970s</u>, became my favorite harmonica player. ⁸Then I listened to folk music <u>that featured the harmonica</u>. ⁹Bob Dylan, <u>who became popular in the 1960s</u>, played a terrific harmonica along with a guitar. ¹⁰Now I look for harmonica solos and harmonica players <u>that sound as good as Dylan</u>.

EXERCISE 6 Writing from Experience

On a separate piece of paper, write five sentences about instruments, musicians, and kinds of music that interest you. When you have finished writing, underline any adjective clauses you have included in your paragraph. Then, exchange papers with a classmate to see if you've underlined all the adjective clauses. **Remember**: Use commas to set off nonessential adjective clauses from the rest of a sentence. Students' sentences will vary.

Adverb Clauses

⫸ An **adverb clause** is a subordinate clause that functions as an adverb. It modifies a verb, adjective, or another adverb.

Unless it rains, young plants cannot grow. [modifies the verb *can grow*]

The animals seemed nervous **whenever rolling thunder began.** [modifies the adjective *nervous*]

The rain fell sooner **than we had expected.** [modifies the adverb *sooner*]

An introductory adverb clause is always followed by a comma. You'll find a list of introductory words and phrases for adverb clauses in the side column. When these words or phrases begin an adverb clause, they're referred to as **subordinating conjunctions**.

When words are omitted from an adverb clause, the clause is called an **elliptical adverb clause**. You can see the missing words in brackets below.

Yesterday's rain fell harder **than today's** [**did**].

The farmers are more concerned about rainfall **than the merchants are** [**concerned about rainfall**].

We won't worry **as long as you don't** [**worry**].

Have you ever known anyone **as lucky as Felice** [**is**]?

Subordinating Conjunctions

after	so that
although	than
as . . . as	though
as long as	unless
as soon as	until
as though	when
because	whenever
before	where
even though	whereas
if	wherever
in order that	whether
provided that	while
since	

TEST-TAKING TIP

You may be asked on a standardized test to recognize an error in which a subordinating conjunction such as *unless, because, although,* or *so* does not accurately reflect the meaning of a sentence. See item 12 on page 310.

EXERCISE 7 Identifying Adverb Clauses

Underline the adverb clauses in the following sentences.

1. Where farms now thrive, a desert once covered the Great Plains.

2. Sand covered this region before it was inhabited.

3. Until the Dust Bowl of the 1930s, the Great Plains attracted thousands of settlers.

4. Though conditions were poor, farmers continued to grow crops.

5. A series of droughts struck the Plains region as the Great Depression tightened its grip on the nation.

6. <u>Since the grasslands had been cleared for crops,</u> loose, dry soil was swept away with the fierce winds.

7. <u>While the Great Depression made life difficult,</u> the Dust Bowl destroyed lives.

8. A curtain of dust blew all the way to the East Coast, <u>although the worst of the damage was in the Plains.</u>

9. Easterners ignored the Dust Bowl <u>until black dust clouds struck them, too.</u>

10. <u>After rain put an end to the Dust Bowl in 1935,</u> floods became the problem.

Working Together

EXERCISE 8 Writing a Paragraph with Adverb Clauses

On a separate piece of paper, work with a partner to write a paragraph from the following notes about the Dust Bowl days of the 1930s. When you've finished writing, exchange paragraphs with other student pairs and underline the adverb clauses you find. Students' paragraphs will vary.

Observations at the Watson Farm on the Great Plains in Oklahoma

The farm used to produce a surplus of crops.

Sand dunes now surround the Watson farm.

Cattle cannot find grass easily.

Bean crops don't grow an inch all summer.

Big black cloud of dust races across the plains in Oklahoma.

Neighbors warn one another about the approaching storm.

Sand found covering the crops and grazing lands after the storm.

Family experiences coughing fits from the sandstorm.

Frustration is overwhelming when clouds appear, but no rain falls.

U.S. Congress decides to help those struggling on the plains.

Noun Clauses

▐▶ A **noun clause** is a subordinate clause that functions as a noun.

A noun clause can do anything a noun can do. It can act as a subject, a direct object, a predicate nominative, an indirect object, or the object of a preposition. A noun clause may appear at the beginning, middle, or end of a sentence. As in adjective and adverb clauses, certain words usually introduce a noun clause. You'll find some of those introductory words listed in the side column. As in other clauses, you may find modifiers and complements within a noun clause.

> **Whoever was stealing the precious stones** had many accomplices. [subject]
> Detectives believed they would never know **what happened to the diamonds**. [direct object]
> The anonymous midnight phone call was **what tipped off the police**. [predicate nominative]
> The lawyer instructed Betty to testify truthfully about **whether she knew the suspect**. [object of a preposition]

P.S. As you write, you don't have to identify how noun clauses function in sentences. Think of them as just another tool to express ideas and vary sentence structure.

Sometimes, the introductory word of a noun clause is omitted because it is understood. The sentences below make sense if you read them with or without the bracketed word.

> The prosecutor hopes [**that**] **the jury will convict the suspect**.
> The defense lawyer knows [**that**] **he has a strong case**.

Some Words That Introduce Noun Clauses

how	which
if	whichever
that	who
what	whoever
whatever	whom
when	whose
where	why
whether	

EDITING TIP

Only omit the introductory word in a noun clause if it doesn't cause misunderstanding.

UNCLEAR
Tom didn't believe **Jerry would leave town**.

CLEAR
Tom didn't believe **that Jerry would leave town**.

UNCLEAR
Mom didn't say **you called**.

CLEAR
Mom didn't say **that you called**.

EXERCISE 9 Identifying Noun Clauses

Read these paragraphs from a report about free verse in American poetry. Underline all the noun clauses. **Hint:** There are more than ten noun clauses.

¹Twentieth-century American poetry is distinguished by <u>what is called free verse</u>. ²<u>Whoever wrote the first unrhymed poem</u> broke new literary ground. ³Free-verse sound patterns reflect <u>what the ideas of a poem are</u>. ⁴In other words, rhyme and meter are not <u>what determine how a poem sounds</u>. ⁵Robert Frost was a famous American poet who was opposed to

free verse. ⁶He felt that writing in free verse was like playing tennis without a net.

⁷Robert Lowell, in his *Life Studies*, writes what he feels without using formal patterns of rhyme. ⁸His statement on free verse is clear: "The law says that I am completely free." ⁹In his free verse, Lowell examines how experience affects him by using a conversational tone. ¹⁰This doesn't mean that he rejects rhyme and meter outright. ¹¹What he questions is why a poet would give up either kind of writing. ¹²Both serve a purpose, depending on who the poet is and what he or she wants to express.

EXERCISE 10 Writing Sentences with Noun Clauses

Review the list of words that introduce noun clauses on page 157. Then fill in the blanks below with noun clauses. Exchange papers with a partner to check that you have written a noun clause, not an adjective clause or an adverb clause.
Students' sentences will vary. Sample answers are given.

1. I know _____ which is the right train _____.

2. Sam worries _____ that he won't get into college _____.

3. Jared will be happy with _____ whatever he gets for his birthday _____.

4. Has anyone checked _____ whose boots those are _____?

5. Do you really care _____ how the job gets done _____?

6. The most important question is _____ where the dog has gone _____.

7. _____ How to find a job _____ is something to think about.

8. Natalie wondered _____ why the birds stopped singing _____.

9. Waldo learned _____ which chess players were unbeatable _____.

10. Kramer swung at _____ whatever ball was pitched _____.

EXERCISE 11 Create Your Own Exercise

With a partner, make up ten sentences that include noun clauses. Your sentences may be about any topic. Exchange sentences with another student pair and see if you can identify all of their noun clauses.
Students' exercises will vary.

Four Types of Sentence Structures

To express yourself well, you need to write with a variety of sentence structures. By understanding different sentence structures, you can vary the way you communicate information.

⟱ A **simple sentence** has one independent clause and no subordinate clauses. However, it may have a compound subject (S) or verb (V).

   S   V
She breathed.

     S   S   V
Shoshona and Raymond took in a deep breath of cold, fresh air.

⟱ A **compound sentence** has two (or more) independent clauses and no subordinate clauses.

   S V   S   V
She took in one long breath, yet she still didn't feel completely at ease.

⟱ A **complex sentence** has one independent clause and at least one subordinate clause.

       S   V   S   V
If your chest expands too much, you may not be breathing correctly. [introductory subordinate clause]

    S   S   V   V
A teacher, who knows breathing exercises, can help a person relax. [a subordinate clause within an independent clause]

⟱ A **compound-complex sentence** has two or more independent clauses and at least one subordinate clause.

      S   V   S   V
Three sisters took yoga so that they could learn relaxation techniques,

         S   V
but their brother was not interested. [a subordinate clause between two independent clauses.]

> **WRITING HINT**
>
> Besides varying sentence structure, good writers vary the number of sentences in each paragraph. Most paragraphs should not include more than five sentences; some have only one. A one-sentence paragraph tends to stand out and add emphasis.

EXERCISE 12 Identifying Sentence Structure

Identify the sentence structure of each sentence in the paragraph below. In the blank before each numbered sentence, write *S* for simple, *Cd* for compound, *Cx* for complex, or *Cd-Cx* for compound-complex.

_____Cx_____ ¹Yoga, which was developed by Hindus in India, is a system of exercises for mental and physical control. _____S_____ ²For the millions of people who participate in yoga classes, breathing properly is essential.

_____Cd-Cx_____ [3]Yoga masters believe that oxygen provides the body with energy, so they have developed exercises to increase oxygen intake. _____Cd_____ [4]Anyone can benefit from simple yoga breathing techniques, but only healthy people should try the more intense exercises.

_____Cx_____ [5]By learning proper breathing techniques, people improve their health, increase their life span, and even lose weight, yoga experts believe.

_____S_____ [6]To breathe correctly, a person must take in air through the nostrils, not the mouth. _____Cx_____ [7]Because the hair, or cilia, within the nostrils acts as a filter, yoga experts feel sure that this is a healthier way to breathe.

_____Cd-Cx_____ [8]If you inhale correctly, your stomach will expand, and your chest will fill with air. _____Cd-Cx_____ [9]When you breathe out, your chest should withdraw slightly, and your stomach should draw back toward your spine.

EXERCISE 13 Writing with a Variety of Sentence Structures

On a separate piece of paper, expand each item into a sentence with the structure indicated in parentheses—*Cd* for compound, *Cx* for complex, *Cd-Cx* for compound-complex. Students' sentences will vary.

> EXAMPLE   (Cd) Arthur touches his toes.
> *Arthur can touch his toes, and he can stand on his head.*

1. (Cx) Betina does fifteen push-ups in a row.

2. (Cd) Troy cycles daily.

3. (Cd-Cx) We skate for forty minutes.

4. (Cx) She gave us a lesson on the history of surfing.

5. (Cd) Dancing is good exercise.

6. (Cx) How many laps did he do?

7. (Cx) Walking increases your heart rate.

8. (Cd-Cx) Exercise is important for mental health.

9. (Cd) Juanita practices karate five times a week.

10. (Cd-Cx) I want to learn to dance.

Effective Sentences: Parallel Structure

||||➤ When you express two or more closely related ideas in a sentence, each should follow a similar structure.

Parallel grammatical structure in a sentence signals that items are similar or closely related.

NONPARALLEL	Food at the ballpark is greasy, doesn't taste very good, and I spend a lot of money on it.
PARALLEL	Food at the ballpark is greasy, tasteless, and expensive.

Parallel structure applies to clauses and phrases as well as words. When you write a series of clauses in one sentence, the structure of the clauses should be parallel.

NONPARALLEL	Kansas City suffered in the Depression, when the drought came, and after the beginning of the war.
PARALLEL	Kansas City suffered when the Depression hit, when the drought came, and when the war began. [Each item in this series is an adverb clause.]
PARALLEL	Over the river, through the woods, and under the fence, the fox ran from the hounds. [Each item in this series is a prepositional phrase.]

TEST-TAKING TiP

A standardized-test item contains an error if a series of words, phrases, or clauses is not composed of parallel grammatical structures. See item 9 on page 314.

EXERCISE 14 Identifying Parallel Structure in Sentences

On a separate piece of paper, rewrite the sentences below so that they contain correct parallel structure.
See Answer Key at www.grammarforwriting.com.

1. Cross-country travel in 1870 was exhausting, not very comfortable, and cost a lot of money.

2. Stagecoaches were the fastest, you could rely on them, and they were the safest way to travel.

3. No one expected a woman to drive a stagecoach because taking a physical job was not what most women did, because women were more likely to be homemakers, and no woman had ever applied for the job.

4. You may have heard of an unusual woman who lived in the 1870s, using the name "Charley," and a stagecoach was driven by her.

5. Charley kept her identity hidden by cutting her hair short, by scruffy men's clothes, and acting like the other drivers.

6. Charley was known among stagecoach drivers to be honest with money, working reliably, and she was always polite to passengers.

7. After her death, the stagecoach company, her co-workers, and whoever was one of her passengers were amazed to find out she was a woman.

8. Like the stagecoach drivers, Pony Express riders worked long hours, didn't eat very many meals, and sleeping was hard to do, too.

9. The Pony Express was a mail service lasting for only eighteen months and that the transcontinental railroad put out of business.

10. For a Pony Express rider, getting a letter from the East to the West required many horses changed, knowing how to avoid danger, and being able to sleep in the saddle.

EXERCISE 15 Writing Sentences with Parallel Structure

On a separate piece of paper, write five sentences with parallel structure that express two closely related ideas. For subject matter, write on the subject of travel, using the following questions to help you with ideas.

Students' sentences should contain parallel structures.

1. What form of travel do you like best?

2. What are some of the most memorable trips you have taken, either to places close by or far away?

3. Where would you like to travel to if you could? Why?

4. How do you think traveling gives us insights into our own lives?

5. How do other people's customs and ways of life make us examine our own?

CONNECTING
Writing & Grammar

Write What You Think

Write several paragraphs in response to the following position. Support your opinion with facts and examples. After revising, edit your paragraphs. Make sure to check for parallel structure.

> Refer to **Composition**, Lesson 4.2, to find strategies for persuasive writing.

In the mid-1800s, the transcontinental railroad put the Pony Express and the stagecoaches out of business. Likewise, cars and trucks have almost put the railroads out of business. However, cars and trucks have had a negative impact on air pollution and energy conservation. Americans should revitalize the railroad system and do away with car and truck transportation.

Students' paragraphs will vary. Give students full credit if they have stated an opinion and attempted to support their opinions. They should also have written grammatically correct sentences that begin with a capital letter and end with an appropriate end punctuation mark.

C CCSS Language 1, 2. (See pp. T14–T15.)

Chapter 8

Grammar

Revising and Editing Worksheet 1

Improve the following draft by revising for ideas, organization, word choice, and sentence variety. After revising, edit the draft for errors in spelling, capitalization, punctuation, and usage. Write your revised and edited version on a separate piece of paper. Compare your changes with those of a writing partner.

[1]When Hurricane Katrina crashed into New Orleans. [2]In August 2005. [3]It not only brought devastation to a historic port city. [4]It also delivered a blow to the center of Cajun and Creole cultures in the United States.

[5]Creoles are descendants of early French and Spanish settlers. [6]Creole dominates the famous cuisine people love to eat in New Orleans. [7]You won't know the pleasure of Creole culture until you try gumbo. [8]Gumbo is a rich and flavorful fish soup that is a signature Creole dish. [9]Hot sausage and peppers in gumbo from the Spanish influence. [10]Green peppers and okra show an African influence. [11]The word *gumbo* actually comes from *gombo*. [12]*Gombo* is the word for "okra" in the African language of Bantu.

[13]Visitors to New Orleans have also enjoyed the wonderful music of the city. [14]New Orleans, which is sometimes called the Big Easy. [15]It is the home of jazz. [16]New Orleans celebrates it's native son. [17]That native son is Louis Armstrong. [18]He was a great trumpet player. [19]New Orleans is also the home of Cajun music. [20]The Cajun music is Zydeco. [21]Zydeco has a rich, complex sound. [22]Zydeco incorporates French, North American, and Caribbean sounds. [23]People love that sound. [24]Visitors to New Orleans have praised it. [25]The culture in New Orleans earns more praise than its location or its business.

Students' revisions will vary but should feature complete sentences and correct spelling, capitalization, punctuation, and usage. Check that students have varied sentence structures, beginnings, and lengths.

CCSS Language 1, 2. (See pp. T14–T15.)

Revising and Editing Worksheet 2

Improve the following draft by revising for ideas, organization, word choice, and sentence variety. After revising, edit the draft for errors in spelling, capitalization, punctuation, and usage. Write your revised and edited version on a separate piece of paper. Compare your changes with those of a writing partner.

[1]No one, because this was the night before their departure from the weeklong train ride, slept. [2]When Roselle looked out her window, she saw nothing moved or made a sound. [3]Whatever project Sam attempted lost his concentration. [4]So he looked out the window along with Roselle. [5]Suddenly, a jolt disturbed the otherwise smooth ride of the sleek train. [6]Flashing before their eyes Sam and Roselle, who were cousins. [7]They envisioned their family get-togethers in Michigan. [8]Hoping they would again see their parents, brothers, and sisters.

[9]Originally, the idea of the first student field trip. [10]To Mars thrilled Roselle and Sam. [11]Whoever had signed up for the trip had high hopes. [12]They had high hopes of one day earning a living as an astronaut or space scientist. [13]It wasn't that Roselle had now changed her mind, but the length of the trip and the unexpected occurrences had worn her out. [14]Without much sleep, as if it were filled with cotton, her brain barely worked. [15]Nothing making sense.

[16]Sam had taken a good catnap earlier in the day. [17]Sam took a catnap as the train traveled through the Martian fire desert. [18]So Sam was rested! [19]Never mind that his cousin kept shaking him to look at the fascinated landscape. [20]She entitled "a flamescape." [21]He took Roselle by the arm. [22]They walked to the back of the train car. [23]The locked compartment that held the emergency escape map and for the protection of special breathing tanks had popped open in the thunderous jolt. [24]Sam and Roselle were born leaders. [25]They decided to lead their tour group on foot. [26]The brand new Martian Motel on Red Mars Lake. [27]Where they were to be the first occupants from Earth.

Students' revisions will vary but should feature complete sentences and correct spelling, capitalization, punctuation, and usage. Check that students have varied sentence structures, beginnings, and lengths.

C **CCSS** Language 1, 3. (See pp. T14–T15.)

Chapter 8
REVIEW

Grammar

Chapter Review

Exercise A Identifying Types of Clauses

On the blank before each numbered item, identify the underlined clause in each sentence by writing *ADJ* for an adjective clause, *ADV* for an adverb clause, or *N* for a noun clause.

ADV 1. People don't notice whether it's winter or summer <u>when they're happy</u>. —Anton Chekhov

ADV 2. I only regret <u>that I have but one life to lose for my country</u>. —Nathan Hale

ADJ 3. I have a dream that my four little children will one day live in a nation <u>where they will not be judged by the color of their skin but by the content of their character</u>. —Martin Luther King Jr.

ADJ 4. The man <u>who usually makes no mistakes</u> does not usually make anything. —Edward John Phelps

N 5. I know not <u>what course others may take</u>; but as for me, give me liberty, or give me death! —Patrick Henry

ADJ 6. No matter where its seed falls, it makes a tree <u>which struggles to reach the sky</u>. —Betty Smith

ADV 7. Nothing is ever done in this world <u>until men are prepared to kill one another</u> if it is not done. —George Bernard Shaw

N 8. Ask not <u>what your country can do for you</u>; ask what you can do for your country. —John F. Kennedy

ADJ 9. I had a dream <u>which was not a dream at all</u>. —Lord Byron

ADV 10. <u>When a man assumes a public trust</u>, he should consider himself a public property. —Thomas Jefferson

Exercise B Identifying Sentence Structure

Underline every subordinate clause in the sentences below. Then, in the blank before each numbered item, identify the sentence structure by writing *S* for simple, *Cd* for compound, *Cx* for complex, and *Cd-Cx* for compound-complex.

Cx 1. <u>While reading American poetry</u>, you absorb American history and culture.

S 2. Edward Taylor's poetry was in the "wilderness baroque" style and was full of word play and puns.

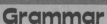
___Cx___ 3. The seventeenth-century poet Anne Bradstreet, <u>who was married to the governor of Massachusetts</u>, was one of the few women to publish poetry in colonial America.

___Cd-Cx___ 4. Phillis Wheatley, <u>who arrived on American shores in 1761</u>, was sold into slavery, and still she became a world-famous poet.

___Cx___ 5. <u>As a supporter of the antislavery movement</u>, African American poet Frances Harper lectured against slavery.

___Cd___ 6. The powerful songs of slaves were not sung for entertainment; instead, they played a crucial role in work and in social and religious gatherings.

___Cd___ 7. People enjoy the haunting tales of Edgar Allan Poe, but few know his poetry.

___Cx___ 8. *Song of Myself* was published numerous times <u>before the poet Walt Whitman felt that it was complete.</u>

___Cx___ 9. Over one thousand handwritten copies of poems were found in Emily Dickinson's home <u>after she died in 1886.</u>

___Cx___ 10. Speeches by Native American leaders, such as Chief Joseph, have <u>as much power and intensity as the greatest poetry.</u>

EXERCISE C Editing Sentences to Create Parallel Structure

On a separate piece of paper, rewrite each sentence so that items in a series are parallel in structure. See Answer Key at www.grammarforwriting.com.

1. We arrived at the concert an hour early, hoping to buy someone's extra tickets and that we might catch a glimpse of the band.

2. Noah said that he had three things he wanted to accomplish this weekend: finishing his research paper, to cut the lawn, and he wanted to fix the flat tire on his bicycle.

3. The drama critics for the local newspaper complained that the play's lighting was poor and having a weak sound system.

4. Be sure to turn off your cell phone while you are watching a movie or play and also during the time that you are in an airplane or if you are in a hospital.

5. Driving safely on an interstate highway requires that you stay alert, left one car length between your car and the car in front of you for every 10 mph, and obeying the speed limit.

6. The person who recommended this Mexican restaurant is my cousin's friend and someone who is a retired chef and she knows a lot about Mexican food.

Cumulative Review

EXERCISE A Identifying Parts of Speech

Read the sayings and fortunes below. In the blank before each numbered item, identify the part of speech of the underlined word in each sentence. Use these abbreviations.

N = noun   ADJ = adjective   CONJ = conjunction
PRON = pronoun   ADV = adverb   INTER = interjection
V = verb   PREP = preposition

___PRON___ 1. Today will be <u>yours</u> for the asking.

___INTER___ 2. <u>Alas</u>, you are the apple of my eye.

___N___ 3. Do you know that <u>beauty</u> is in the eye of the beholder?

___ADV___ 4. It is <u>equally</u> good to give as it is to receive.

___PREP___ 5. You must choose one thing or another, one <u>at</u> a time.

___ADJ___ 6. Success is like a <u>beautiful</u> sunrise, for it comes and goes.

___ADV___ 7. The days and nights pass all <u>too</u> quickly when you are content.

___N___ 8. <u>Success</u> occurs for those who believe in it.

___V___ 9. In the still of the night <u>rises</u> the storm.

___CONJ___ 10. To choose <u>or</u> not to choose is always a question to ponder.

EXERCISE B Writing Complete Sentences

Revise and edit the following paragraph to eliminate wordiness and correct sentence fragments and run-on sentences. Make any other changes that you think will improve the paragraph. Write your revised paragraph on a separate piece of paper. **Hint:** Not every sentence needs revision. Students' revisions will vary.

[1]Whenever British soldiers sang the song "Yankee Doodle." [2]They insulted American patriots. [3]Ironically, the song became an anthem for George Washington's revolutionary army. [4]In one line of the song, a feather in a soldier's cap is calling "macaroni," an Italian pasta, considering "macaroni" was a derogatory term used in the eighteenth century to ridicule people who attempted to look and act as sophisticated as people from Europe. [5]The British thought of the Americans as uncultured people. [6]The British never thought of the Americans as capable. [7]The Americans would never triumph. [8]Over Britain. [9]Under the command of George Washington, the colonial army proving the British wrong. [10]When the British surrendered, the American military band struck up the tune of "Yankee Doodle." [11]The American military band enjoyed a last laugh about this song.

CUMULATIVE REVIEW

EXERCISE C Identifying Phrases

On the blank before each numbered item, identify each underlined phrase by writing one of these abbreviations in the space provided.

PREP = prepositional phrase   INF = infinitive phrase
PART = participial phrase   APP = appositive phrase
GER = gerund phrase

___GER___ 1. You may not enjoy <u>focusing on mental fitness</u>.

___APP___ 2. Coach Star, <u>the author of *Get Strong, Get Smart,*</u> believes in mental preparation for sports.

___INF___ 3. <u>To believe that you can win</u>, you must think positively.

___PREP___ 4. If you go <u>into a game</u> without mental preparation, the game is harder to win.

___PART___ 5. Many athletes, <u>upset by a loss</u>, have to work on attitude.

___GER___ 6. <u>Envisioning good results</u> is one way to prepare mentally for a sport.

EXERCISE D Identifying Clauses

Underline every subordinate clause in the sentences below. Then identify each clause by writing *ADJ* for an adjective clause, *ADV* for an adverb clause, or *N* for a noun clause in the space before each sentence.

___ADJ___ [1]The United States Treasury released a silver dollar <u>that commemorates African American soldiers from the American Revolution</u>.

___ADJ___ [2]Crispus Attucks, <u>who was the first patriot to die at British hands</u>, is on one side of the coin. ___ADV___ [3]<u>Because African American families suffered losses</u>, a family appears on the flip side. ___ADJ___ [4]A man <u>who spied for George Washington</u>, James Armistead, was African American. ___ADV___ [5]<u>Wherever the 1st Rhode Island regiment went</u>, African Americans joined in. ___ADJ___ [6]Virginians <u>who died at Valley Forge</u> fought alongside African American patriots. ___N___ [7]<u>That African Americans fought in the Revolution</u> is a little-known fact. ___ADV___ [8]Historians note <u>that more than 5,000 African Americans fought against the British</u>.

Using Verbs

STUDENT WRITING
Narrative Essay

Direct students to
www.grammarforwriting.com
for chapter-specific
portfolio projects.

'Grounds' Brews a Delicious, Earful Experience
by Sara McCann
high school student, Gig Harbor, Washington

Plenty of pastries, exceptional espresso, and wailing harmonicas—all of these things comprise live jazz nights at Grounds for Coffee, a hip joint in Tacoma.

As I parked my car next to the Pantages Theatre, I was a little apprehensive about going through with this experience. I didn't know what to expect from live jazz . . .

As I approached the brick building, the aroma of coffee beans hung in the air. Through the large windows, I could see more than forty people lounging in couches, waiting in line, or sitting around tables talking intensely. It didn't look too scary yet.

Upon opening the door, my senses were overcome with joy. My nose was filled with the smell of pies and other desserts as well as the alluring scent of espresso. My ears were filled with dancing notes from the harmonicas and guitars coming from the room in the far end of the building.

I saw colorful posters clinging to the muted flamingo pink painted wall. I saw people of all ages, from eight to eighty-five, talking to one another, as well as all types of people sitting together. The barriers of diversity were overcome. It was nothing less than amazing.

I made my way to the coffee bar to order drinks. Espresso syrup flavors lined the walls, and the workers behind the counter looked eager to take my order. I took a seat at a table located in the middle of the building. At one end were couches and pillows, and at the other end of the building was the sitting room that has been turned into "jazz room" every Friday and Saturday night.

I sat for awhile, sipping my vanilla latte and listening to the conversations around me. This was perhaps as entertaining as anything else I saw or heard. The talk ranged from the weather to the subconscious state of mind. The thing that I found most interesting was that anybody could just sit down at any random table and be welcomed without introductions. That doesn't happen every day.

When I finished the foam at the bottom of my latte, I decided to join the crowd of people enjoying the music in the adjoining room. I was surprised to see that the people playing music were two men in their twenties who were very talented.

The wailing and moaning I expected to be exposed to turned out to be melodious notes floating and jumping up and down the scale. One man was playing a mean harmonica, while the other was strumming blues chords that made my heart ache. Their style was great, and their music was excellent—lively jazz with a twist of the blues.

Allow time for
students to discuss
the student
writing. Suggest
that they identify
its strengths and
propose possible
improvements.
Use the model
to introduce the
concepts in the
chapter.

I've never really listened to jazz, but after that night, I decided I just might broaden my horizons a bit.

Sara McCann's narrative essay tells about an experience at a unique coffee shop. Sara includes many sensory details that help the atmosphere come alive.

As you reread the essay, notice how Sara uses mostly past tense verbs. Using verb tenses accurately helps your reader understand the progression of your thoughts. The exercises in this chapter will give you practice using verb tenses correctly.

Regular Verbs

▐▐▐▶ All verbs have four basic forms, or **principal parts**. They are the present, the present participle, the past, and the past participle.

▐▐▐▶ Regular verbs add -*d* or -*ed* to the present tense to form the past and past participle.

Principal Parts of Verbs			
PRESENT	PRESENT PARTICIPLE (Use with *am, is, are, was, were.*)	PAST	PAST PARTICIPLE (Use with *has, had, have.*)
discover study guess	(is) discovering (is) studying (is) guessing	discovered studied guessed	(had) discovered (had) studied (had) guessed

The **present participle** of regular verbs ends in -*ing*. It works with the verb *to be* (*am, is, are, was,* or *were*) to make a verb phrase.

　　She **is looking** for proof. 　　He **was searching** for bones.

The **past participle** of regular verbs ends in -*d* or -*ed*. It works with the helping verb *have* (*has, have,* or *had*) to make a verb phrase.

　　They **have asked** permission. 　　You **have** also **received** help.

When you add -*ing* and -*ed* to the present form of a verb, you must apply the spelling rules about dropping the final -*e*, changing the -*y* to *i*, and doubling consonants: *cope, coping, coped; marry, marrying, married; mop, mopping, mopped.* (For more about spelling rules, see Lesson 16.2.)

The past and past participle forms of some verbs may be spelled with two alternative endings: -*ed* or -*t*.

　　I **have dreamed** that before. 　　You **burned** the toast.
　　She **dreamt** about a train ride. 　　The fire **had burnt** through the night.

P.S. Don't get too worried about the labels for all the verb forms. It's their correct use that is important in writing.

> **EDITING** *TIP*
>
> When the verbs *use* and *suppose* appear before an infinitive, add the ending -*d*, even though it may be silent in conversation.
> 　　*used*
> I ~~use~~ to play the piano.
> 　　*supposed*
> Are you ~~suppose~~ to go to the concert?

EXERCISE 1 Using the Principal Parts of Regular Verbs

To complete each sentence, write in the blank the correct past form or past participle form of the verb in parentheses.

EXAMPLE   Parts of the fossil (resemble) _resembled_ both a bird and a dinosaur.

1. Many paleontologists (study) —studied— and (collect) —collected— fossils as children.

2. Recently, paleontologists (unearth) —unearthed— interesting evidence.

3. The evidence (indicate) —indicated— an evolutionary link between birds and dinosaurs.

4. An ancient bird claw (look) —looked— like the claw of a dinosaur.

5. One fossil (remind) —reminded— paleontologists of a turkey.

6. A debate has (continue) —continued— about the link between birds and dinosaurs.

7. Birds may have (descend) —descended— from dinosaurs, or dinosaurs may have (develop) —developed— from birds.

8. This question has (puzzle) —puzzled— paleontologists for decades.

9. They (use) —used— to look for evolutionary evidence of dinosaurs in birds.

10. Recently, however, paleontologists have (concentrate) —concentrated— on evidence of birds in dinosaurs.

EXERCISE 2 Revising a Journal Entry

Revise this paragraph so that it describes an event that happened in the past. Use the past form and past participle form of the italicized verbs.

[1]I _enjoy_ {enjoyed} visiting Madagascar, a small island off the coast of east Africa. [2]With other paleontologists, I _work_ {worked} at a dig where we _hope_ {hoped} to find fossils of ancient birds and dinosaurs. [3]One paleontologist _uncovers_ {uncovered} a rare specimen in a previous dig. [4]She _locates_ {located} a fossil of a feathered meat-eater. [5]Strangely, the fossil _dates_ {dated} to a time after the mass extinction of dinosaurs. [6]The paleontologist _ships_ {shipped} the rock containing the fossil back to the United States. [7]Our dig _creates_ {created} great interest in these ancient feathered creatures. [8]We _discover_ {discovered} a tail similar to one on a dinosaur called a theropod and also a forearm like one on a bird. [9]Paleontologists _spot_ {spotted} similar discoveries in the United States.

Irregular Verbs 1

Not every past verb form or past participle ends in *-d* or *-ed*. Verbs that vary from the standard pattern are called **irregular verbs**.

▶ Use the principal parts of these common irregular verbs correctly when you write and speak. The first verb on this chart is also the most irregular English verb—*be*. *Be* has singular and plural forms in both the present and past tenses. Notice that the word *be* by itself is not one of its principal parts. Students will encounter many irregular verbs in their own writing that are not listed on this chart.

Principal Parts of Common Irregular Verbs			
PRESENT	**PRESENT PARTICIPLE** (Use with *am, is, are, was, were.*)	**PAST**	**PAST PARTICIPLE** (Use with *has, had, have.*)
[be] is, are	(is) being	was, were	(had) been
become	(is) becoming	became	(had) become
begin	(is) beginning	began	(had) begun
bite	(is) biting	bit	(had) bitten
blow	(is) blowing	blew	(had) blown
break	(is) breaking	broke	(had) broken
bring	(is) bringing	brought	(had) brought
build	(is) building	built	(had) built
burst	(is) bursting	burst	(had) burst
buy	(is) buying	bought	(had) bought
catch	(is) catching	caught	(had) caught
choose	(is) choosing	chose	(had) chosen
come	(is) coming	came	(had) come
cost	(is) costing	cost	(had) cost
do	(is) doing	did	(had) done
draw	(is) drawing	drew	(had) drawn
drink	(is) drinking	drank	(had) drunk
drive	(is) driving	drove	(had) driven
eat	(is) eating	ate	(had) eaten
fall	(is) falling	fell	(had) fallen
feel	(is) feeling	felt	(had) felt
find	(is) finding	found	(had) found
fly	(is) flying	flew	(had) flown
forget	(is) forgetting	forgot	(had) forgotten; (had) forgot
freeze	(is) freezing	froze	(had) frozen
get	(is) getting	got	(had) gotten; (had) got
give	(is) giving	gave	(had) given
go	(is) going	went	(had) gone
grow	(is) growing	grew	(had) grown

Enriching Your Vocabulary

The adjective *indulgent*, as used in Exercise 3, comes from the Latin word *indulgens*, which means "lenient." You would be considered *indulgent* if you listened to unceasing complaints from a friend.

P.S. You can always use a dictionary to check a verb form. A dictionary entry word appears in the present form, but if a verb is irregular, its past, past participle, and present participle forms are listed after the pronunciation.

fly \ flī \ **flew, flown, flying**

EXERCISE 3 Using Irregular Verbs

To complete each sentence, fill in the blank with the correct past form or past participle form of the verb that appears in parentheses.

EXAMPLE   (forget) She had ___*forgotten*___ to lock the door. *or* forgot

1. (give) This author ___gave___ away signed copies of her new novel.

2. (break) The speed skater had ___broken___ the record by a split second.

3. (buy) Had he ___bought___ the skis before the sale?

4. (feel) Yesterday ___felt___ like spring.

5. (build) The indulgent parents have ___built___ a tree house in the woods.

6. (bring) The tourist ___brought___ oranges home from Florida.

7. (grow) The farmer ___grew___ organic vegetables.

8. (catch) The shortstop ___caught___ the ball for the double play.

9. (be) What ___were___ the words to the school song?

10. (go) We ___went___ to the amusement park last summer.

EXERCISE 4 Editing a Paragraph

Cross out each incorrect past form verb, and write the correct past form verb above it. Make any other changes you think will improve the article.

¹One state high school ~~gotted~~ *got* a special state award last week. ²The governor had ~~chose~~ *chosen* a school that developed a community involvement program. ³This program ~~brung~~ *brought* happiness to senior citizens. ⁴Because of this program, recipients have ~~ate~~ *eaten* hot, nutritious meals. ⁵Although volunteer chefs had cooked the meals, students with licenses had ~~drove~~ *driven* them to people's homes. ⁶One student participant in the program said, "I ~~feeled~~ *felt* my work was important. ⁷I always ~~catched~~ *caught* a glimpse of a broad smile on Ms. Tan's face when I ~~brung~~ *brought* her each meal." ⁸Another student noted, "I had ~~forgotted~~ *forgotten* how great volunteer work is. ⁹With this experience, I ~~felted~~ *felt* like a positive part of my community." ¹⁰Since the governor has ~~gived~~ *given* the award to Silver Creek High School, other schools have ~~became~~ *become* interested in developing community-based programs of their own.

C CCSS Language 1. (See pp. T14–T15.)

Lesson 9.3

Usage

Irregular Verbs 2

In addition to the twenty-nine irregular verbs from the previous lesson, here are another thirty-seven commonly used irregular verbs.

⫸ Use the principal parts of these common irregular verbs correctly when you write and speak. Students will encounter many irregular verbs in their own writing that are not listed on this chart.

Principal Parts of Common Irregular Verbs			
PRESENT	**PRESENT PARTICIPLE** (Use with *am, is, are, was, were.*)	**PAST**	**PAST PARTICIPLE** (Use with *has, had, have.*)
hold	(is) holding	held	(had) held
hurt	(is) hurting	hurt	(had) hurt
keep	(is) keeping	kept	(had) kept
know	(is) knowing	knew	(had) known
lay [to put or place]	(is) laying	laid	(had) laid
lead	(is) leading	led	(had) led
lend	(is) lending	lent	(had) lent
lie [to rest or recline]	(is) lying	lay	(had) lain
lose	(is) losing	lost	(had) lost
make	(is) making	made	(had) made
meet	(is) meeting	met	(had) met
put	(is) putting	put	(had) put
ride	(is) riding	rode	(had) ridden
ring [to make a sound]	(is) ringing	rang	(had) rung
rise [to stand up]	(is) rising	rose	(had) risen
run	(is) running	ran	(had) run
say	(is) saying	said	(had) said
see	(is) seeing	saw	(had) seen
sell	(is) selling	sold	(had) sold
send	(is) sending	sent	(had) sent
set [to put]	(is) setting	set	(had) set
show	(is) showing	showed	(had) shown
shrink	(is) shrinking	shrank; shrunk	(had) shrunk; shrunken
sing	(is) singing	sang	(had) sung
sink	(is) sinking	sank; sunk	(had) sunk
sit [to rest oneself on a chair]	(is) sitting	sat	(had) sat
speak	(is) speaking	spoke	(had) spoken
stand	(is) standing	stood	(had) stood
steal	(is) stealing	stole	(had) stolen
swim	(is) swimming	swam	(had) swum
swing	(is) swinging	swung	(had) swung
take	(is) taking	took	(had) taken
tell	(is) telling	told	(had) told
throw	(is) throwing	threw	(had) thrown
wear	(is) wearing	wore	(had) worn
win	(is) winning	won	(had) won
write	(is) writing	wrote	(had) written

WRITING *HINT*

Here's a memory trick to help you distinguish *lay*, *raise*, and *set* from *lie*, *rise*, and *sit*. Remember that the first three take direct objects.

YOU CAN:
lay an egg if you are a chicken.

set an egg down on a counter.

raise an egg over your head before you throw it.

BUT YOU CANNOT:
lie an egg,

sit an egg, or

rise an egg.

EXERCISE 5 Using Irregular Verbs

Complete each sentence by writing the correct past form or past participle form of the verb in parentheses.

1. (rise) The first scene opened just after the moon had —— risen ——.

2. (meet) Didi —— met —— Sam, the detective.

3. (take, speak) In the first scene, Sam —— took —— notes and Didi —— spoke ——.

4. (win) Didi thought she had —— won —— Sam over.

5. (lay) When Sam left, Didi —— laid —— a canvas on a closet shelf.

6. (write) But first, Didi read a note she had —— written —— to her husband Al.

7. (lie) Al had —— lain —— down for a nap before Sam arrived.

8. (sing, run) When Al heard a loud voice that —— sang —— off key, he —— ran —— downstairs.

9. (throw, say, lose) Didi —— threw —— some towels over the canvas and —— said —— she had —— lost —— a painting.

10. (tell, lead) We wondered if Didi had ever —— told —— Al about Sam, who —— led —— the investigation.

11. (put) In Act 2, Sam —— put —— Al under suspicion.

12. (sit, steal) Then Al —— sat —— down to talk with Didi and discovered she had —— stolen —— the painting.

13. (sink, shrink) Al's heart —— sank —— and his world —— shrank or shrunk —— instantly.

14. (make) Sam had —— made —— remarks Didi didn't appreciate.

15. (show) Sam had —— shown —— his ignorance about art.

16. (see) Didi —— saw —— a chance to test Sam's abilities.

17. (steal, speak) That's why she had —— stolen —— her own artwork and —— spoken —— to Sam.

18. (rise) Sam —— rose —— to the occasion and solved the case.

EXERCISE 6 Writing Sentences with Irregular Verbs

For each of the following verbs, write a sentence that uses the past form or past participle form of each one: Sentences will vary.

lie (to rest or recline), *lose, make, ring* (to make a sound), *say, set, shrink, swim*

Verb Tense

IIII➡ A **verb tense** expresses the time an action is performed.

Every English verb has three **simple tenses** (present, past, and future) and three **perfect tenses** (present perfect, past perfect, and future perfect).

The Six Verb Tenses		
TENSE	**WHAT IT SHOWS**	**EXAMPLE**
Present	action happening in the present; action that happens repeatedly	We **dance** in pairs. We **dance** all night.
Past	action completed in the past	We **danced**.
Future	action that will happen in the future	We **shall dance**. We **will dance**.
Present perfect	action completed recently or in indefinite past	I **have danced.**
Past perfect	action that happened before another action	I **had** already **danced** the foxtrot.
Future perfect	action that will happen before a future action or time	By nine o'clock, I **will have danced**.

Each tense also has a **progressive form**, which is made up of a helping verb and the present participle (the -*ing* form). The progressive forms show ongoing action.

The Progressive Forms for the Six Tenses	
PROGRESSIVE FORM	**EXAMPLE**
Present progressive	**(am, is, are) dancing**
Past progressive	**(was, were) dancing**
Future progressive	**will (shall) be dancing**
Present perfect progressive	**(has, have) been dancing**
Past perfect progressive	**had been dancing**
Future perfect progressive	**will have been dancing; shall have been dancing**

IIII➡ Don't switch verb tenses needlessly. Keep tenses consistent whenever possible.

INCONSISTENT   The referee **blows** a whistle, and we **stopped** the game.
CONSISTENT   The referee **blew** a whistle, and we **stopped** the game.

Sometimes, the meaning of a sentence requires a shift in verb tense. Use the verb tense that makes sense, based on what you're trying to communicate.

I **ordered** a sweater that **will arrive** tomorrow.

EDITING TIP

Use present tense verbs (the **literary present tense**) when you write about an author's writing.

In *Walden*, Henry David Thoreau **writes** about his two-year residence at Walden Pond. He **lives** by himself, and for these two years, he **views** the life of society as an outsider. He **comes** to the famous conclusion that people "lead lives of quiet desperation."

TEST-TAKING TIP

You may be asked on a standardized test to correct an error by making verbs consistent in tense if they are meant to express the same time. See items 3 and 6 on page 313.

EXERCISE 7 Using Verb Tenses

Replace the italicized verbs either to show actions completed in the past or to show ongoing action, depending on the context.

¹Last summer, we ~~take~~ [took] a vacation in New England. ²The first stop ~~is~~ [was] Boston, Massachusetts. ³On the way into the city, we ~~stop~~ [stopped] at Walden Pond. ⁴The famous writer Ralph Waldo Emerson ~~owns~~ [owned] the land. ⁵His friend Henry David Thoreau ~~builds~~ [built] a cabin on the land and ~~moves~~ [moved] in on July 4, 1845. ⁶He ~~wants~~ [wanted] to live a simple life with as few possessions as possible. ⁷He ~~hopes~~ [hoped] to turn back the clock to simpler times. ⁸Industrialization and its effects on New England life ~~worry~~ [worried] him greatly. ⁹Because of this, he ~~keeps~~ [kept] a journal of his experiment in living. ¹⁰The ideas of Henry David Thoreau ~~affect~~ [have affected] many people since the 1854 publication of his journal *Walden*.

EXERCISE 8 Making Verb Tenses Consistent

On a separate piece of paper, edit any of the following sentences in which you find unnecessary shifts in verb tenses. **Hint:** Most of the sentences that do need editing can be fixed in more than one way.

1. If the temperature drops too low, we ~~wore~~ [will wear] heavy coats and hats.

2. They judged the speed-skating contest only when the finishing times ~~will have been~~ [were] confirmed.

3. I will be competing in the race only after I ~~sharpened~~ [sharpen] the blades on my skates.

4. When Mary ~~had already gone~~ [goes] to the starting line, the race will begin.

5. Mary has been training in the hopes that she ~~had made~~ [will make] the Olympic team.

6. The cloud has passed, and the sun ~~will be~~ [is] shining.

7. I lace up and tighten my skates as I ~~have prepared~~ [prepare] for the race.

8. I would have placed second, but I ~~will have been falling~~ [fell].

9. Mary is crossing the finish line that she ~~will have~~ planned to cross tomorrow.

10. If we ~~had been starting~~ [start] training today, we will be in good shape for the race this fall.

Using the Active Voice

▐▶ When a verb is in the **active voice**, the subject of the sentence performs an action. When a verb is in the **passive voice**, the subject receives an action. The passive voice always uses some form of the helping verb *be*.

ACTIVE   The outfielder **made** a spectacular play.

PASSIVE   A spectacular play **was made** by the outfielder.

ACTIVE   The runner **spiked** the second baseman.

PASSIVE   The second baseman **was spiked** by the runner.

ACTIVE   The relief pitcher **dazzled** the opposing team.

PASSIVE   The opposing team **was dazzled** by the relief pitcher.

▐▶ Use the active voice when you write because it is stronger and more direct. The passive voice is acceptable when you don't know the performer of an action or when you want to emphasize the action, not the performer.

The best players **were fielded** in the All-Star Game.
[The performer of the action is unknown.]

A glittering trophy **was presented** to the most valuable player.
[The object of the action is stressed instead of the performer.]

WRITING HINT

Technical and scientific writers often use the passive voice because the emphasis is placed on the object of the study rather than on the performer.

The experiment **was designed** to test the ability of a cancer vaccine to attack only cancer cells—not healthy cells. The vaccine **was given** to people with advanced lung cancer in hopes that it would reverse the progress of the disease. [Emphasis throughout is on the experiment itself, not on those who performed it.]

EXERCISE 9 Using the Active Voice

On a separate piece of paper, rewrite the sentences below using the active voice. If the passive voice is acceptable, explain why.

EXAMPLE   An Oscar was presented to Gregory Peck for his performance as Atticus Finch.

Gregory Peck received an Oscar for his performance as Atticus Finch.

See Answer Key at www.grammarforwriting.com.

1. The poem at President John F. Kennedy's 1961 inauguration was read by Robert Frost.

2. A poem for the 1997 inauguration of President Bill Clinton was recited by Miller Williams.

3. Poems have been read by their authors at various presidential inaugurations.

4. A new surgical procedure was tested by a team of doctors.

5. A cure for brain cancer was developed by researchers at UCLA.

6. Coverage of the experimental procedure was denied by the HMO.

7. Herbal treatments are recommended by some health professionals.

8. Some infectious diseases are cured by antibiotics.

9. Major diseases as well as simple aches or pains can be treated by practitioners of holistic medicine.

10. Herbal tea is drunk by many people as a remedy for anxiety.

11. A survey was done by Landmark Healthcare, Inc., to find out how many people used alternative medicine in the year 1998.

12. It was shown by the survey that health care is growing in popularity.

13. Some type of alternative medicine was used by forty-two percent of the adults surveyed in the study.

14. Herbal therapy, chiropractic care, and massage therapy were turned to most often by the people surveyed.

15. In general, alternative medicine is not usually employed by the people surveyed as a replacement for traditional care.

Exercise 10 Writing with the Passive and Active Voice

On a separate piece of paper, write a paragraph about a hobby or interest you enjoy, such as music, movies, or sports. Most of the sentences in your paragraph should be written in the active voice, but one or two may be in the passive voice. Identify the voice of each of your verbs by marking *A* for active voice or *P* for passive voice above each one.

Answers will vary. See teacher pages for assessment rubrics.

Write What You Think

On a separate piece of paper, write a paragraph in response to the following statement. State your opinion clearly, and support it with reasons and examples. Revise for the correct use of the active and passive voices; then edit for spelling, capitalization, punctuation, and usage.

Refer to **Composition,** Lesson 4.2, to find strategies for writing persuasively.

> Most doctors trained in traditional medicine are quick to prescribe drugs— some with serious side effects—for any medical complaint, but they discount the beneficial effects of holistic health care. Medical students should all be trained in such alternative health care methods as acupuncture, therapeutic massage, nutrition, and herbal remedies as well as traditional medicine.

Answers will vary. Give students full credit if they have stated an opinion and attempted to support their opinions. Look for grammatically complete sentences that begin with a capital letter and end with an appropriate end punctuation mark.

CCSS Writing 10; Language 1. (See pp. T14–T15.)

Lesson 9.6
Usage

Mood

Mood expresses attitude in a sentence and affects the verb forms you use. The three moods you use all the time without even thinking about it are the indicative, the imperative, and the subjunctive.

▶ A verb is in the **indicative mood** when the sentence makes a statement or asks a question.

> The cowboy herds the cattle.
> Did he forget that calf in the field?

▶ A verb is in the **imperative mood** when the sentence makes a direct command or makes a direct request.

> Herd the cattle by noon.
> Please bring that calf to the corral.

The subject of an imperative sentence is omitted but is understood to be *you*.

Mood is something you don't need to worry about because you use mood instinctively and correctly. The only mood that causes writers trouble is the subjunctive mood. If you follow the rules listed below, you'll use the right mood all the time.

▶ A verb is in the **subjunctive mood** when the sentence expresses an indirect command, an indirect suggestion, an indirect statement of necessity, or a condition or a wish that is contrary to fact.

In a *that* clause expressing a requirement, necessity, or wish, the subjunctive calls for the use of the infinitive form of a verb without the word *to*. Use this form whether the subject is singular or plural.

INDIRECT COMMAND	My brother insisted **that** she **follow** him.
INDIRECT SUGGESTION	The rancher urged **that** he **learn** about young calves.
INDIRECT STATEMENT OF NECESSITY	It was necessary **that** she **wear** protective gear.

In a wish or a contrary-to-fact clause beginning with the word *if*, the subjunctive calls for using *were* instead of *was* whether the subject is singular or plural.

> One cowboy wished he **were** the owner of his own ranch.
> If the ranch **were** in Texas, they wouldn't worry about snow.

WRITING HINT

Sometimes, the subjunctive mood sounds awkward in a sentence, even though it's grammatically correct. In such cases, rewrite the sentence using an infinitive.

AWKWARD
It was necessary that Kathy attend the workshop.

SMOOTH
It was necessary for Kathy to attend the workshop.

EDITING TIP

When you're writing about a wish or something contrary to fact, make sure you use the verb form *were* rather than *was*.

were
If I ~~was~~ rich, I'd buy a huge ranch in Montana.

The verb forms for the subjunctive mood are the same as those for the indicative mood with three exceptions:

1. In the third person singular, the -*s* is omitted:
   I recommend that Blair **seek** additional tutoring. [not *seeks*]

2. In the present subjunctive mood, the verb form for *be* is always *be*:
   We suggest that the news anchor **be** present on camera during the report. [not *is*]

3. In the past subjunctive mood, the verb form for *be* is always *were*:
   If I **were** able to play an instrument, I'd be in a band. [not *was*]

EXERCISE 11 Using the Subjunctive Mood

In each sentence, fill in the blank with the correct subjunctive form of the verb in parentheses. Rewrite any awkward sentences on a separate piece of paper.

1. (be) If I ——— were ——— a doctor, I would specialize in skin problems.

2. (study) The teacher suggested that Mara ——— study ——— harder.

3. (be) Alex wished he ——— were ——— in the band.

   The coach urged everyone to practice hard.
4. (practice) The coach urged that everyone ——— practice ——— hard.

5. (be) If we ——— were ——— professional athletes, we would be role models.

   It was necessary for Elena to work after school.
6. (work) It was necessary that Elena ——— work ——— after school.

7. (be) My mother wished that she ——— were ——— a professional dancer.

8. (memorize) The teacher insisted that Melanie ——— memorize ——— the poem.

9. (be) "If I ——— were ——— you, I would tell the truth," Sam said.

10. (take) Alicia demanded that her boyfriend ——— take ——— her to the prom.

EXERCISE 12 Writing Sentences in the Subjunctive Mood

On a separate piece of paper, write sentences about places you would like to travel to, about how you would get there, about how long it would take, and about what you would like to do or see in those places. Write sentences in the subjunctive mood as much as possible. Then exchange papers with classmates or other student pairs to identify the verb's mood in each sentence and the correct verb form. Students should use the subjunctive mood correctly in their sentences.

C CCSS Language 1, 2. (See pp. T14–T15.)

Chapter 9

Usage

Revising and Editing Worksheet 1

Improve the following draft by revising for ideas, organization, word choice, and sentence variety. After revising, edit the draft for errors in spelling, capitalization, punctuation, and usage. Write your revised and edited version on a separate piece of paper. Compare your changes with those of a writing partner.

Students' revisions will vary. Sample revisions are given.

[1]Do you think that time ~~went~~ *goes* by more quickly for you now than it ~~does~~ *did* when you ~~was~~ *were* five years old? [2]The feeling that "time flies" is often ~~been~~ considered to be a psychological or emotional response. [3]The human response to time ~~lays~~ *lies* in the brain.

[4]Recent studies ^*have* shown that changes in a person's sense of time relate to changes in a person's central nervous system. [5]People in different age groups were ~~suppose~~ *supposed* to estimate a time period of three minutes. [6]People who most often estimated the time ~~correct~~ *correctly* were in ~~there~~ *their* twenties. [7]People in ~~there~~ *their* sixties had estimated ^*that* three minutes ~~were~~ *was* closer to three minutes and forty seconds. [8]The perception of the passage of time ~~lie~~ *lay* somewhere between these amounts for people in their thirties and forties.

[9]Researchers think the brain contains a special clock. ~~[10]Researchers think the clock kept~~ *that keeps* track of time. [11]Imagine that every day you ~~had been rided~~ *ride* a bus to school. ~~[12]The bus stopped~~ *which stops* at a red light. ~~[13]The light always had remained red~~ for one full minute. [14]If the light ~~was~~ *were* to ~~remains~~ *remain* red for two minutes one day, the driver would probably be ready to ~~moves~~ *move* a foot off the brake after one minute ~~is passing~~ *had passed*.

[15]Dopamine is a chemical produced in the brain. ~~[16]The human brain clock has been regulated by dopamine.~~ *that regulates the human clock.* [17]Studies ~~would~~ have ~~been~~ shown that by adding dopamine, the brain clock ~~runned~~ *runs* faster. *and that* [18]By removing dopamine, the brain clock ~~is ran~~ *runs* more slowly. [19]Why ~~does~~ *do* musicians and athletes have good hand-eye coordination, and why do some people struggle with this? [20]The brain clock may hold answers to these and other questions.

Chapter 9

Usage

ⓒ CCSS Language 1, 2. (See pp. T14–T15.)

Revising and Editing Worksheet 2

Improve the following draft by revising for ideas, organization, word choice, and sentence variety. After revising, edit the draft for errors in spelling, capitalization, punctuation, and usage. Write your revised and edited version on a separate piece of paper. Compare your changes with those of a writing partner.

Students' revisions will vary. Sample revisions are given.

¹In Bozeman, Montana, John Baden, a retired college professor and writer, was

concerned about social issues. ²He ~~suggests~~ *suggested* to other Montana writers that they

meet. ³Bozeman ~~are~~ *is* located in Gallatin County. ⁴Gallatin County needs help,

and John Baden ~~feeled~~ *felt* that writers might be part of a solution. ⁵The county

~~would~~ had been ~~struggled~~ *struggling* with a poor economy. ⁶In addition, people with

~~different~~ *differing* interests ~~was use to locking~~ *locked* horns like the cattle on the Montana range.

⁷It was necessary that writers ~~were~~ *be* involved with important issues affecting

the county, such as land development. ⁸But how could writers influence land

use? ⁹More than once in the past, public opinion has been influenced by a

writer's words, and Baden hopes his writers ~~might could~~ *will* do the same. ¹⁰So he

and other writers in the state ~~meeted~~ *met* in a workshop that has ~~became~~ *become* a privately

funded, popular project in Montana.

¹¹Writing by the Gallatin members ~~appear~~ *appears* in various newspapers throughout

the West. ¹²Their words ~~has~~ *have* helped residents of Montana confront issues they

have ~~been~~ disagreed on, including the environment.

¹³Lately, a new issue has ~~been~~ given the Gallatin writers an unexpectedly

worthy subject: the modern cowboy. ¹⁴The modern cowboy is a person who ~~live~~ *lives*

in Montana but who ~~is working~~ *works* on a computer. ¹⁵The modern cowboy is

someone who doesn't ~~worked~~ *work* the land in a state noted for its ranchers,

foresters, and miners.

C **CCSS** Language 1. (See pp. T14–T15.)

Chapter **9**
REVIEW

Chapter Review

EXERCISE A Using Verb Tenses

Change the italicized verb to the verb tense specified in parentheses. You may look back at the charts on page 177. Write your answers on a separate piece of paper.

1. I *set* the table for Thanksgiving dinner. (past perfect) had set

2. Brad *stirred* the pumpkin soup. (past perfect progressive) had been stirring

3. Suzy *throws* some flour onto the breadboard. (past) threw

4. The bread dough *rises* for about an hour. (future perfect progressive)
   will have been rising

5. The guests *arrive* on time. (present perfect) have arrived

6. The host *serves* dinner exactly at 6 P.M. (future) will serve

7. We *hang* our coats in the closet. (present perfect progressive) have been hanging

8. The meal *ends* by dark. (future perfect) will have ended

9. One guest *told* hilarious jokes after dinner. (past progressive) was telling

10. No one *forgot* this delicious meal. (future) will forget

EXERCISE B Using the Active Voice

On a separate piece of paper, rewrite the sentences below to use the active voice whenever possible. If the passive voice is acceptable, explain why.
See Answer Key at www.grammarforwriting.com.

1. Experiments were conducted by a team of researchers.

2. The poem was recited by Margo after the break.

3. The sailboat was propelled by the strong wind.

4. The dam was built by beavers.

5. The Nobel Prize for Literature was won by Polish poets twice in the last forty years.

6. The gold medal was earned by the world's fastest runner.

7. The shutter in my camera was repaired by the photo technician.

8. The play's set was created by an award-winning scenic designer.

9. A lifesaving drug was developed by the pharmaceutical company.

10. A calendar featuring illustrations of cats was produced by the animal shelter.

EXERCISE C Revising a Paragraph

On a separate piece of paper, revise the paragraph below. Use the active voice whenever possible. Decide whether the paragraph should be past or present tense, and make verb tenses consistent. Students' revisions will vary. Sample revisions are given.

¹Tornadoes are also ~~knowed~~ known as twisters. ²Tornadoes often ~~had caused~~ cause damage when they touch down~~;~~, ~~especially~~ if people ~~were~~ are in the path of one~~.~~, ³They would be wise to dive into a ditch or hide under something heavy. ⁴~~It is suggested that~~ a person ~~hides~~ should hide from falling debris inside a house. ⁵After a tornado warning, people are ~~suppose~~ supposed to go into enclosed rooms without windows for protection. ⁶But where will a tornado ~~striked~~ strike? ⁷Tornadoes ~~would have struck~~ can strike anywhere and everywhere. ⁸Weather conditions, though, ~~had made~~ make areas of the Midwest and the South the most likely candidates for tornadoes. ⁹A tornado ~~formed~~ forms when a warm front hits a cold front during a thunderstorm. ¹⁰This crazy mix of cold and warm fronts ~~shall tilt~~ tilts the layers of air, creating the trademark funnel of a tornado. ¹¹Fortunately, scientists have learned how to predict many tornadoes so they can warn people to seek protection.

EXERCISE D Using the Subjunctive Mood

Write a verb in the subjunctive mood for each sentence below.

1. If I _____were_____ you, I'd return the money.

2. She suggested that the group _____remain_____ quiet during rehearsal.

3. It is necessary that Bill _____finish_____ his dinner.

4. I wish the movie _____were_____ more interesting.

5. If it _____were_____ sunny, we could eat outdoors.

6. The police officer demanded that the thief _____stop_____ running.

7. I require that Roger _____go_____ with us to the beach.

8. The engineer suggested that the astronaut _____put on_____ his space suit.

9. If Beth _____weren't_____ so busy, she would phone her Aunt Kate.

10. If I _____were_____ a carpenter, I would make you a shelf.

Subject-Verb Agreement

STUDENT WRITING
Expository Essay

Twin Titans
by Sara Wechter
high school student, Norwalk, Connecticut

To someone sitting at the top of the bleachers at a Norwalk High School girls' basketball game, it is easy to see why senior Heather Hanson and junior Ayanna Brown have been nicknamed the "twin titans." Standing at 6'3" each, they have been a major backbone in the undefeated 1999 season of girls' basketball. Heather and Ayanna grace the court with a confident air; but off the court, they are anything but cocky.

Both girls say that teamwork is a major component of the game, and one of the major reasons the team has done so well this year (compared to last season's 19–6 record) is that the talent is so spread out. There are many great players on the team who score consistently. Ayanna has an impressive game point average of 15.6, while Heather manages to contribute an average of 10 points per game.

With talent like this, one has to wonder where basketball can take them. Realistically, basketball should be used as a stepping stone to other opportunities, such as college. Heather and Ayanna have big plans for their futures, including a college education and steady careers. Heather has been accepted to Dartmouth, but she has not yet settled on a major. Will she join the WNBA? We will have to wait and see because college is her first priority.

With the talent, hard work, and encouragement of Coach English, these girls have the potential to achieve anything.

Sara Wechter's expository essay about two remarkable athletes is effective because it begins with an attention grabber, offers statistics about the two athletes' success, and tells about their future plans.

Several of Sara Wechter's sentences have two subjects, since she writes about two players. In such cases, subject-verb agreement can be especially tricky. You will learn more about subject-verb agreement as you do the lessons and exercises in this chapter.

Allow time for students to discuss the student writing. Suggest that they identify its strengths and propose possible improvements. Use the model to introduce the concepts in the chapter.

Person, Number, and Intervening Phrases

The subject of a sentence may be in the **first**, **second**, or **third person**, and it may be **singular** or **plural** in number. *I* and *we* are first person; *you* is second person; *he*, *she*, *it*, and *they* are third person.

▶ A third-person **singular subject** takes a **singular verb**. A third-person **plural subject** takes a **plural verb**.

The following chart shows how present tense verbs change when the subject is third-person singular.

Subject-Verb Agreement in the Present Tense		
PERSON	**SINGULAR SUBJECT**	**PLURAL SUBJECT**
1st	I dream and wish.	We dream and wish.
2nd	You dream and wish.	You dream and wish.
3rd	He dreams and wishes. Ann dreams and wishes.	They dream and wish. The boys dream and wish.

The verb *be* has three forms to match person and number in the present tense. (See the side column.)

▶ In a **verb phrase**, the helping verb (HV) must agree with the subject.

   HV   S   V   S HV V
Have they sung that song?   She **has** read the novel.

When a negative construction follows the subject, use the number that agrees with the subject.

   S   V
Math, not social studies or English, **remains** her best subject.

   S   V
Raif, but not Saul or Keith, **completes** the crossword puzzle in the newspaper.

▶ Sometimes, a prepositional phrase or a clause comes between the subject and verb; this is referred to as an **intervening phrase** or **clause**.

Make sure the verb agrees with the subject of the sentence, not with the object of a preposition or the subject of a clause.

   S   V
The **room** for the student council members **contains** a new computer.

   S   V
The **jobs** that the newspaper advertises **require** sales experience.

Present Tense Forms of *Be*

Singular
I **am** here.
You **are** here.
He **is** here.

Plural
We **are** here.
You **are** here.
They **are** here.

EDITING TIP

Use *don't* (*do not*) with third-person plural subjects and *doesn't* (*does not*) with third-person singular subjects.

The girls **don't** swim this afternoon.

They **don't** require a signed pass.

Ralph **doesn't** have the assignment.

She **doesn't** support that opinion.

STEP BY STEP

Subject-Verb Agreement in the Present Tense

1. Find the subject of the sentence. **Remember:** The subject of a sentence never appears in a prepositional phrase or clause.
2. Decide whether the subject is singular or plural.
3. Choose the verb form that agrees in number with the subject.

EXERCISE 1 Choosing the Correct Verb

Underline the subject of each sentence and the verb in parentheses that agrees with the subject. **Hint:** Watch out for intervening clauses or phrases.

1. <u>Students</u> (<u>volunteer</u>, volunteers) to teach minicourses after school.

2. One <u>student</u> (prepare, <u>prepares</u>) a course called Geometry in Art.

3. Eleventh-grade <u>teachers</u> from the same school (<u>supervise</u>, supervises) each instructor.

4. One <u>course</u> (teach, <u>teaches</u>) the history of political speeches.

5. A poetry <u>course</u> (present, <u>presents</u>) English sonnets and Japanese haiku.

6. One student <u>instructor</u> (challenge, <u>challenges</u>) all the math teachers.

7. A <u>course</u> that focuses on wellness (meet, <u>meets</u>) on Mondays.

8. <u>Ms. Shyre</u>, the principal, (hope, <u>hopes</u>) to visit each miniclass.

9. One <u>problem</u> for these classes (<u>is</u>, are) lack of room.

10. (Have, Has) new <u>programs</u> ever begun without a few problems?

EXERCISE 2 Proofreading a Paragraph

For each mistake in subject-verb agreement in the following paragraphs, cross out the incorrect verb and write the correct verb above it.

¹How ~~does~~ [do] publishers decide which books to publish? ²They hire experts in marketing who research the interests of readers and then report their findings to the editors of publishing companies.

³~~Doesn't~~ [Don't] authors influence what gets published? ⁴For example, Aneela French, not John Alep or Elena Cayge, ~~hire~~ [hires] a literary agent to contact publishers about a book she wrote on sailing. ⁵John Alep ~~don't~~ [doesn't] have an agent, so he participates in publishing contests advertised in magazines. ⁶Elena Cayge, who has written five unpublished books, ~~send~~ [sends] a manuscript for a children's book directly to a publisher for consideration. ⁷An editorial board of readers and marketing experts ~~decide~~ [decides] whether or not a manuscript, with merits as well as shortcomings, ~~become~~ [becomes] a published book.

Agreement with Indefinite Pronouns

An **indefinite pronoun** expresses an amount or refers to an unspecified person or thing. Some indefinite pronouns are always singular; others are always plural.

▐▐▶ In the present tense, use a singular verb when the subject is a singular indefinite pronoun. Use a plural verb when the subject is a plural indefinite pronoun.

SINGULAR **Each** of the scientists **performs** experiments.

PLURAL **Several** of the experiment results **help** doctors treat illnesses.

SINGULAR **Either** of the laboratories **contains** lasers.

▐▐▶ Depending on how they're used in a sentence, the following indefinite pronouns may take a singular or a plural verb: *all, any, some, most, none.*

SINGULAR **Most** of the hospital **remains** open on weekends.
Some of this cake **belongs** to the nurses.
Is any of the medicine ready to be picked up?
All of the blood **is** donated by students.

PLURAL **Most** of the patients **complete** an information form.
Some of our doctors **work** the midnight shift.
Any of the diseases on this floor **are** contagious.
All of the rooms **are** clean.

Always Singular

anybody	neither
anyone	nobody
each	no one
either	one
everybody	somebody
everyone	someone

Always Plural

both	many
few	several

EDITING TIP

The pronoun *none* is especially tricky. Use a singular verb only when you can think of the subject as "none of it." Use a plural verb when you can substitute "none of them."

None of the test **is** easy. [None of *it* is easy.]

None of your answers **are** right. [None of *them* are right.]

EXERCISE 3 Choosing the Correct Verb

Underline the subject of each sentence and the verb in parentheses that agrees in number with the subject.

1. Many (participate, participates) in volunteer programs throughout high school.

2. Several of my classmates (belong, belongs) to Youth Engaged in Service, or YES.

3. All of the communities (benefit, benefits) from YES's programs.

4. One of the schools (ask, asks) the entire freshman class to participate.

5. In YES, everybody who volunteers (choose, chooses) a charity to help.

6. YES provides grants, and everyone on YES teams (work, works) to match them.

7. One of the group's favorite charities (is, are) literacy promotion.

8. Everybody (is, are) encouraged to join the YES network.

9. All in the YES network (start, starts) with a phone call to Washington.

10. Most of the volunteers (reap, reaps) the rewards of helping others.

Working Together

EXERCISE 4 Writing Complete Sentences

Working in pairs or small groups, write a complete sentence on a separate piece of paper for each numbered item. Use the group of words as the subject of the sentence. Use present tense verbs, and check your sentences for correct subject-verb agreement. Read your sentences aloud for extra practice listening for subject-verb agreement. Students' sentences will vary.

1. Everyone I know

2. Few of the students

3. None in this group

4. Most of my time

5. Several of us wandering through

6. All of the tutors

7. Nobody over there

8. Neither of these papers

9. Any of the group members

10. Both of the textbooks

EXERCISE 5 Proofreading a Paragraph

Proofread the paragraph below. Correct any errors you find in subject-verb agreement. **Hint:** One of the sentences contains no errors; two sentences have more than one error.

¹One of the many feelings student volunteers gain ~~are~~ *is* a sense of self-worth. ²How ~~do~~ *does* this feeling come about in teens who volunteer for community service? ³Well, many of them ~~says~~ *say* that raising money to help others ~~make~~ *makes* them feel that they are giving to rather than taking from their community. ⁴Based on student comments, everybody in such a volunteer group ~~feel~~ *feels* gratified by his or her efforts. ⁵There ~~is~~ *are* local organizations as well as national ones to help teens organize volunteer groups. ⁶Volunteers decide how to raise money for a charity or group. ⁷In time, everybody on the team ~~raise~~ *raises* money or ~~assist~~ *assists* the charity directly. ⁸These methods ~~serves~~ *serve* a community and the individual volunteers well. ⁹Volunteers often ~~says~~ *say* that they feel a new sense of connection to their communities.

Agreement with Compound Subjects

When two or more subjects share the same verb, a sentence has a **compound subject**. There are particular rules that apply to compound subjects and verb forms in the present tense.

▥▥▶ When two or more singular subjects are joined by *and*, they take a plural verb.

> Arizona, New Mexico, Utah, **and** Colorado **meet** at an area known as the Four Corners.

▥▥▶ When two or more singular subjects are joined by *or* or *nor*, they take a singular verb.

> Neither Iowa **nor** Nebraska **borders** an ocean.
> Either Interstate 70 **or** 80 **spans** the United States.

▥▥▶ When a singular subject and a plural subject are joined by *or* or *nor*, the verb agrees with the subject closer to it.

> Corn **or** soybeans **grow** on most Iowa farms.
> **Is** barley **or** oats grown in Iowa, too?
> Neither the White Mountains **nor** Lake Winnipesaukee **disappoints** a visitor to New Hampshire.
> **Are** water skis **or** a surfboard easier to use in the ocean?

EDITING TIP

A singular subject followed by *as well as* or *together with* takes a singular verb form; the subject is not compound.

Hawaii as well as Alaska ~~are~~ *is* not part of the mainland United States.

Salt together with garlic ~~season~~ *seasons* the meat.

STEP BY STEP

Agreement with Compound Subjects

1. Identify the compound subjects. **Remember:** The subject of a sentence never appears in a prepositional phrase.
2. Find the conjunction that connects the subjects: *and, or,* or *nor*.
3. When *or* or *nor* connects the subjects, use a singular verb only if the subject nearer the verb is third-person singular.

EXERCISE 6 Choosing the Correct Verb

Underline the subject of each sentence and the verb in parentheses that agrees with the subject. **Hint:** Not every sentence has a compound subject.

1. Vermont and New Hampshire (lie, lies) on the Massachusetts border.

2. Both the Atlantic and the Pacific (border, borders) the United States.

3. Neither the bus nor the trains (stop, stops) at every small town.

4. (Is, Are) buttes or a mesa visible from the banks of the Rio Grande?

5. The children or their guide (has, have) wandered off the trail.

6. Pikes Peak together with the Continental Divide (stun, stuns) me on every visit to Colorado.

7. San Francisco or the northern counties (is, are) where we'll visit.

8. The <u>Delaware River</u> as well as the Hudson River (form, <u>forms</u>) a state border.

9. Neither <u>Kansas</u> nor the two <u>Dakotas</u> (<u>produce</u>, produces) as much cattle as Texas.

10. Either my <u>brother</u> or my <u>parents</u> (<u>want</u>, wants) to tour NASA.

EXERCISE 7 Writing a Description

In one paragraph on a separate piece of paper, describe a place that means something special to you. It could be a waterfall, a beach, a library, a shop, a park, a stadium, even a city street—any place that you cherish. Describe how the place makes you feel. What makes it special to you? How does the place look, smell, and sound? Try to include compound subjects and at least one indefinite pronoun in your paragraph. When you're done, ask a classmate to look over your work to check it for subject-verb agreement.
Students' paragraphs will vary. Refer to the teacher pages for assessment rubrics.

EXERCISE 8 Writing a Paragraph

Based on the following notes, write a paragraph for a report about the structure of the U.S. government. Use present tense verbs. Then, get together in a small group to read your paragraphs aloud and to check one another's sentences for correct subject-verb agreement. Students' paragraphs will vary.

Executive, Legislative, Judicial: 3 branches of U.S. government

Congress = legislative branch of federal government

Elected positions in Congress: 2 senators for each state in Senate, differing numbers of representatives for each state in House of Representatives

All federal courts and the Supreme Court = Judicial branch

President and vice president of United States = Elected officials in executive branch

Make laws: legislative branch

Carry out laws: executive branch

Check fairness, decide punishment for breaking laws: judicial branch

Checks and balances—the three branches of government work together

Constitution and the Bill of Rights: documents allow for development of new laws by legislative branch; these documents check actions and behavior of people and groups by judicial branch

---

Agreement with Subjects Following Verbs and with Collective Nouns

▸ A verb (V) must agree with the subject (S) even when the subject follows the verb.

     V   S
Where **are** those **articles** about jogging from *Runners* magazine?

        V   S
Across the sky **scoot** the billowing **clouds**.

▸ A verb agrees with the subject, *not* with the predicate nominative.

    S   V   PN
Tonight's **topic is vacations**.

    S   V   PN
Vacations in Italy **seem** an **answer** to my prayers.

▸ **Collective nouns**, like those listed in the side column, name a group of people or things.

Use a singular verb when you think of a collective noun as one unit. Use a plural noun when you think of a collective noun as lots of separate individuals.

    The **committee votes** tomorrow. [*Committee* refers to a single unit and takes a singular verb.]
    The **press** usually **ask** a variety of questions. [*Press* refers to multiple members in the group and takes a plural verb.]

▸ Some nouns ending in *-s* function as singular subjects and take a singular verb. Some function as plural subjects and take a plural verb. A few may be either singular or plural, depending on the context and meaning.

Some nouns that end in *-s* are listed in the side column. The nouns that are always plural usually constitute a pair of something or an object made up of parts working together.

SINGULAR   **Physics explains** how you win a tug of war.
PLURAL   **Are** your **eyeglasses** too weak or too strong?

SINGULAR   **Statistics is** a tough course in college.
PLURAL   **Statistics are** the basis of this report.

SINGULAR   **Is politics** an interest of yours?
PLURAL   How **do** the **politics** affect the seating chart in the class?

Some Collective Nouns

audience	flock
class	group
club	herd
committee	pair
crowd	(the) press
family	(the) public
	team

Singular

mathematics	news
measles	physics
mumps	

Plural

binoculars	scissors
eyeglasses	shorts
pants	stairs

Singular or Plural

acoustics	statistics
politics	series

EXERCISE 9 Choosing the Correct Verb

Underline the verb in parentheses that agrees with the subject.

1. Statistics (support, supports) the conclusions in her study.

2. If the audience (applaud, applauds), take a deep bow.

3. The press (tend, tends) to frustrate celebrities. *accept* tend

4. A pair of new speakers (cost, costs) more than I can spend.

5. The Rangers together with their coach (agree, agrees) on a strategy.

6. (Has, Have) mumps become a problem in the child-care center?

7. Those pants (look, looks) vintage but fashionable.

8. These binoculars (work, works) well for bird-watchers.

9. Where (do, does) the club sell books at this sale?

10. (Is, Are) the crowd cheering for the Oscar-winning actress?

EXERCISE 10 Writing Complete Sentences

Write a sentence using each word listed below as the subject. Make sure that the verb in each sentence agrees in number with the subject. Write your sentences in the present tense. Students' sentences will vary.

EXAMPLE   politics
The politics in the race for mayor are nasty and embarrassing.

1. news   6. mathematics

2. acoustics   7. scissors

3. stairs   8. crowd

4. class   9. measles

5. flock   10. club

EXERCISE 11 Write a Description
Students' descriptions will vary.

On a separate piece of paper, write a brief paragraph in response to the question below. Support your response with facts, reasons, and examples. Check to make sure you're using proper subject-verb agreement.

Refer to **Composition**, Lesson 2.4, for tips on writing a descriptive paragraph.

You are performing at a school fund-raiser with a heavy-metal rock group. The auditorium is packed with students, the school and local press, teachers, and parents. How would the audience and various members of it react to your performance?

In your writing, use collective, plural, and singular nouns to describe the action and reactions on stage and in the audience.

Other Problems in Agreement

Here are other situations in which subject-verb agreement may become problematic.

▶ For subject-verb agreement in an adjective clause, look for the antecedent of the relative pronoun. The antecedent is what determines whether the verb is singular or plural.

> She is one of those **athletes** who **compete** hard and **win** often. [The verbs agree with *athletes*.]
> This is the **game** that **tests** her strength. [The verb agrees with *game*.]

For more on adjective clauses, see **Grammar**, Lesson 8.2.

▶ The title of a work of art (painting, movie, literature, or music) is always a singular subject and takes a singular verb.

> *The Thirty-Nine Steps* **is** my favorite Hitchcock movie.
> *The Birds* **is** coming to the local movie theater.

▶ Use a singular verb with a third-person subject that names a single amount or time. Use a plural verb with a third-person subject that refers to multiple items.

> **Two-thirds is** the answer to the division problem.
> [a single amount]
> **Three dollars is** not enough to buy an entire pizza.
> [a single amount]
> These three **dollars are** damaged. [multiple items]
> **Two weeks** of vacation always **passes** too quickly. [a single time period]
> **Six months equals** half of a year. [a single time period]
> These dark winter **days are** passing slowly. [multiple items]

EDITING TIP

Use a singular verb when *many a(n)* and *every* comes before a compound subject.

Many a student **and** tutor **meets** at the coffee shop.

Every Monday **and** Wednesday **is** soccer practice.

▶ Use a singular verb with names of organizations that are plural in form.

> **The Campfire Girls is** an organization for young females.

Exercise 12 Choosing the Correct Verb

Write the correct form of the verb in parentheses on the blank to complete each sentence.

1. (say) I agree with the speakers who ____say____ people should read.

2. (boast) *Luck Strikes* ____boasts____ a cast of happy actors and actresses.

3. (tell) *Green Hills and Winding Roads* ____tells____ a story about eighteenth-century Virginia.

4. (shine) The cars that _____shine_____ in the showroom window are the most expensive models that the dealership sells.

5. (pitch) The campers who _____pitch_____ their tents under a tree are sheltered from rain.

6. (begin) "Talk Counts," a radio show, _____begins_____ at 3 P.M.

7. (represent) Three months _____represents_____ the length of a season.

8. (seem) Three-eighths _____seems_____ to be the right answer.

9. (listen) Many a boy and girl _____listens_____ to tales told aloud.

10. (be) _____Is_____ every first and third Monday a regular business day for our health club?

11. (help) Health Matters _____helps_____ millions of people control their eating.

12. (sponsor) On the Fourth of July, the Teamsters _____sponsors_____ the town parade.

13. (quarrel) Nearly every brother and sister _____quarrels_____ over borrowing the car.

14. (make) Two weeks _____makes_____ up a fortnight.

15. (grow) Many a flower and shrub _____grows_____ best in the sun.

16. (equal) Fourscore years _____equals_____ eighty years.

17. (be) *Wuthering Heights* _____is_____ my favorite novel.

18. (work) My sister, who _____works_____ as a nurse, is coming to visit.

19. (become) Every nook and cranny _____becomes_____ filled with mud after a flood.

20. (scorn) Howard is one of the many who _____scorn_____ bottled water.

Working Together

Exercise 13 Create Your Own Exercise

On a separate piece of paper, write two sentences as examples of each of the four rules about subject-verb agreement in this lesson. Then, rewrite the sentences using the same format as in Exercise 12 above. Exchange papers with a classmate, and complete the sentences with the correct verb forms. Exchange papers again to check the sentences, and discuss questions you or your partner might have about subject-verb agreement. Answers will vary.

Revising and Editing Worksheet 1

Improve the following draft by revising for ideas, organization, word choice, and sentence variety. After revising, edit the draft for errors in spelling, capitalization, punctuation, and usage. Write your revised and edited version on a separate piece of paper. Compare your changes with those of a writing partner.

Students' revisions will vary. Subject-verb agreement errors are corrected.

¹ Is
~~Are~~ Yoknapatawpha County a real place? ²Many a fan and critic
wonders
~~wonder~~ about this while reading the novels of William Faulkner (1897–1962). ³A
takes
series of novels by this author ~~take~~ place in this fictitious county, modeled after Jefferson County, Mississippi, Faulkner's real home.

reflect
⁴The politics of Yoknapatawpha County ~~reflects~~ the politics of the real Mississippi in the century after the Civil War. ⁵The aristocracy of the South
clings
~~cling~~ to its pride with difficulty. ⁶The poorer members of society
hold
~~holds~~ on to the value of life with great difficulty.

comes
⁷Faulkner himself ~~come~~ from a well-to-do Mississippi family. ⁸The political and commercial exploits of his great-grandfather, Colonel William
were
C. Falkner, ~~was~~ legendary. ⁹The twentieth-century author's ancestor, who
was
lived life with great flair and style, ~~were~~ killed by one of his political rivals.

love
¹⁰Today, many still ~~loves~~ the characters from Yoknapatawpha County~~.~~
and admire
¹¹~~Many still admires~~ Faulkner's unique writing style. ¹²Almost all of
are
Faulkner's novels—after his third novel—~~is~~ set in this place. ¹³One of them
includes   focus
~~include~~ a map. ¹⁴All his novels ~~focuses~~ on the psychology of people. ¹⁵The
present
early novels ~~presents~~ views that are different from those of the later ones.

¹⁶An earlier novel like *Sartoris*, which was written when Faulkner was a
reveals
young man, ~~reveal~~ his more negative views about people. ¹⁷But by the time he won the Nobel Prize for Literature (1949), the mature Faulkner said, "Man will not merely endure; he will prevail."

is
¹⁸Which of the books written by William Faulkner ~~are~~ your favorite?

C **CCSS** Language 1, 2. (See pp. T14–T15.)

Revising and Editing Worksheet 2

Improve the following draft by revising for ideas, organization, word choice, and sentence variety. After revising, edit the draft for errors in spelling, capitalization, punctuation, and usage. Write your revised and edited version on a separate piece of paper. Compare your changes with those of a writing partner.

Students' revisions will vary. Subject-verb agreement errors are corrected.

¹Casey, a book critic for the local newspaper, together with other journalists

eats

~~eat~~ lunch at the same café each day. ²A friend and Casey ~~begins~~ *begin* to talk about

Have

books. ³"~~Has~~ there been many books written about the experience of Native

Americans in the recent past?" the friend, Amanda, asks. ⁴As a reviewer of

knows

current books, Casey ~~know~~ the answer immediately.

write

⁵"One of those authors who ~~writes~~ memoirs is William Least Heat Moon,"

write

Casey answers. ⁶Then, he continues, "Some, like this author, ~~writes~~ about

tells

unique experiences. ⁷*Blue Highways* ~~tell~~ about William Least Heat Moon's travels

around the United States in the 1970s."

⁸Casey explains how the author leaves a college in Columbia, Missouri. ⁹The

has

author ~~have~~ taught English and literature courses at the college. ¹⁰William Least

known

Heat Moon is also ~~know~~ as William Trogdon. ¹¹William Least Heat Moon heads

out to small towns throughout the United States. ¹²Either *Leaves of Grass* or

becomes

Black Elk Speaks ~~become~~ the author's reading companion as he travels. ¹³One

is

book ~~are~~ a series of poems; the other book is a Native American memoir.

represents

¹⁴Three months ~~represent~~ a small part of his coast-to-coast trip to places such

as Dime Box, Texas, and Ninety-Six, South Carolina. ¹⁵Neither Igo nor Ono,

fades

California, ~~fade~~ from the author's memory because of their odd names.

attracts

¹⁶Casey tells Amanda that a community ~~attract~~ the author because William

Least Heat Moon thinks he might find out something about his own ancestry.~~-~~

, which

¹⁷~~His ancestry~~ is part Native American. ¹⁸Several of the book's chapters ~~shows~~

show

how willingly people share their personal histories with a stranger such as

William Least Heat Moon.

Chapter Review

EXERCISE A Choosing the Correct Verb

Choose the verb in parentheses that agrees with the subject.

1. (Is, <u>Are</u>) the employer and her employees in a meeting?

2. Mathematics (cause, <u>causes</u>) many students to seek out tutors.

3. This bulletin board, not that pencil sharpener, (stay, <u>stays</u>) here.

4. Somebody on these school teams (<u>has</u>, have) many trophies.

5. Any of these books (<u>belong</u>, belongs) on the library reserve shelves.

6. How (<u>is</u>, are) the public responding to the new mayor?

7. Neither the dogs nor the cat (<u>has</u>, have) vaccination tags.

8. (Is, <u>Are</u>) the book, magazine, and pamphlet free?

9. Joe, as well as Mike and Tami, (create, <u>creates</u>) recipes.

10. Sal and Beth (is, <u>are</u>) among those students who (<u>get</u>, gets) high grades.

EXERCISE B Proofreading a Paragraph

For each mistake in subject-verb agreement in the following paragraph, cross out the incorrect verb, and write the correct verb above it. **Hint:** Not every sentence contains an error; one sentence has more than one error.

¹Because our school has students from many foreign countries, a special welcome committee ~~greet~~ greets newcomers. ²Some of the foreign students are children of diplomats who ~~works~~ work in embassies. ³Alida and Sarkis speak languages other than English. ⁴Russian and Armenian as well as English ~~is~~ are spoken in their homes. ⁵The parents of Akeem ~~works~~ work for a Nigerian newspaper. ⁶Each of his parents ~~write~~ writes a column about the United States. ⁷The international press ~~have~~ has many representatives in our city; therefore, the children ~~attends~~ attend our schools. ⁸International Kids ~~are~~ is the name of a club in our school that everyone is welcome to join. ⁹The group ~~consist~~ consists of students from four continents, including the United States. ¹⁰Every boy and girl ~~take~~ takes turns presenting something special about his or her language and culture.

EXERCISE C Writing Complete Sentences

On a separate piece of paper, write a complete sentence for each numbered item, beginning your sentence with the given word or group of words. Use present tense verbs, and check your sentences for subject-verb agreement.

Students' sentences will vary.

1. Both you and I . . .

2. Three ingredients in the soup . . .

3. The only reason that counts . . .

4. A flock of birds . . .

5. No one . . .

6. Few . . .

7. Neither English nor other languages . . .

8. The Forest Rangers of America . . .

9. She is one of those dancers who . . .

10. The public . . .

11. Each of us . . .

12. Either the judge or the jury members . . .

13. None of the contestants . . .

14. Anybody in the crowd . . .

15. The television show *The Honeymooners* from the 1950s . . .

16. National politics . . .

17. Every car, truck, and van . . .

18. Which . . .?

19. Thirty-eight dollars . . .

20. *The Adventures of Huckleberry Finn* by Mark Twain . . .

Write What You Think

Answers will vary. Give students full credit if they have stated an opinion and attempted to support their opinions. Look for grammatically complete sentences that begin with a capital letter and end with an appropriate end punctuation mark.

On a separate piece of paper, write a paragraph in response to the statement below. Support your opinion with reasons and examples. Be sure to revise and edit your work.

Today's young people spend so much time playing computer games and surfing the Internet that they ignore the beauty and grandeur of nature. Schools should make sure their students spend a minimum of four hours a week outdoors doing physical activities such as hiking, playing sports, and even gardening while they learn about the environment. Such activities are just as important as English or math.

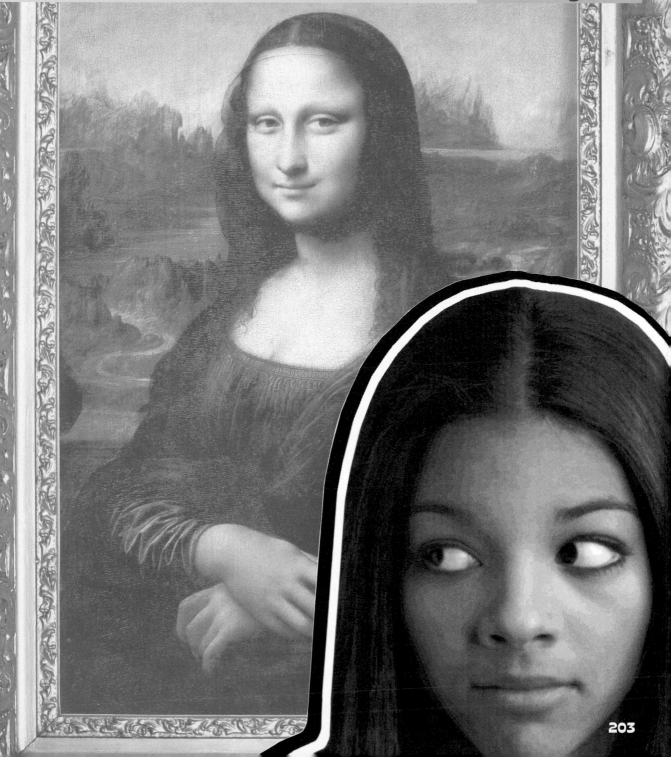

Using Pronouns

STUDENT WRITING
Narrative Essay

Team Captain
by Adele Grundies
high school student, La Mesa, California

Direct students to www.grammarforwriting.com for chapter-specific portfolio projects.

My first thought was "Cool: something for my college application." When I was appointed captain of my high school tennis team, I had no idea how much responsibility the new title would hold. After practice that first day, my coach asked me if I had any ideas about uniforms that year. Uh-oh. I had no clue what this job would consist of.

After practice every day, I was already worn out and did not need the additional burden of having to drive from one sports store to the next for tennis skirts. By the time I got home at 5:30 and tried to order shirts, I realized that all silk-screening stores had already closed. I also didn't realize that a white T-shirt cost $3 while a white tank top cost $25, a fact that was difficult to explain to the rest of the team.

Finally, we needed some kind of fund-raiser. In the hot days of September, with thirty energetic girls, I decided to have a car wash. I made up dozens of flyers, piles of tickets, and lists for people to bring buckets, signs, soap, sponges, and towels. The first weekend was so successful that we had a second car wash. Seeing everything come together was amazing because everyone was working together and having fun.

All of this work wore me down, but it also gave me the excitement of responsibility, which I loved. During our daily runs, instead of joking around with complaints of exhaustion, I would push myself to be a good example to the rest of the team, and I yelled my encouragement whenever possible. As the other seniors took their cue from me and began acting in the same manner, I saw the team come together in a way that had never happened in the past three years that I'd been on it. I felt like a captain.

Adele Grundies's essay is effective because she concisely explains a challenge she faced, how she confronted the challenge, and the effect it has had on her. As you write essays for college applications or other purposes, think about how these qualities can strengthen your own essay.

Reread the essay, and pay particular attention to Adele's pronouns. How many different kinds of pronouns does she use? How do they help create her casual style? In this chapter, you'll practice using pronouns correctly in various writing exercises.

Allow time for students to discuss the student writing. Suggest that they identify its strengths and propose possible improvements. Use the model to introduce the concepts in the chapter.

Using Subject Pronouns

This chart shows you subject pronouns. Notice that the second-person pronoun *you* is the same in both the singular and plural forms.

Subject Pronouns	
SINGULAR	**PLURAL**
I, you, he, she, it	we, you, they

➠ Use a **subject pronoun** when the pronoun functions as the subject (s) of a sentence or clause. Most mistakes are made when the pronoun is part of a compound sentence element.

       s   s
The artist and **I** took part in a panel discussion. [The pronoun is part of a compound subject.]

         s   s
The sculptor **whom you** and **I** met in the museum is famous. [The pronouns are subjects of the adjective clause.]

➠ Use a subject pronoun when the pronoun functions as the predicate nominative (PN) of a sentence or clause.

Remember: A **predicate nominative** is a noun or pronoun that follows a form of the verb *be* and renames or identifies the subject.

     PN   PN   PN
The volunteers were Sean, Yokiko, and **he**.

                PN   PN
The co-chairs of the committee are Terri and **I**.

EXERCISE 1 Choosing the Correct Pronoun

On a separate piece of paper, write a subject pronoun that correctly completes each sentence.

    EXAMPLE   The teens in the tennis tournament are
                    you and *she*.

1. Find out what year Venus Williams said that ___she___ and her sister were the top two female tennis players.

2. The sisters proved that ___they___ could rise through the ranks quickly.

3. If ___you___ were a talented player, would ___you___ compete professionally?

CCSS

Standards for this lesson focus on applying the conventions of standard English when using subject pronouns, as well as correctly applying the conventions of standard English capitalization and punctuation.

WRITING HINT

When someone on the phone asks, "Who is this?" you probably say, "It's me." But be sure to use a subject pronoun in writing or on grammar tests when the pronoun comes after a form of *be*: "It's **I**" or "It is **we**."

STEP BY STEP

Use these steps to choose the correct pronoun in compound subjects:
Allie and (me, I) plan to run the marathon.

1. Say the sentence with just the pronoun:
   Me plan to run the marathon. [sounds wrong]
   I plan to run the marathon. [sounds right]

2. Use the pronoun that sounds right:
   Allie and **I** plan to run the marathon.

4. The girls' mother said in an interview that ___she___ acted as coach and manager, too.

5. Their father calls them during tournaments because ___he___ can't attend their matches.

6. The exciting rivalry between Martina Hingis and Venus kept ___them___ both in top form.

7. Martina was ranked number one until ___she___ lost to Venus.

8. As a strong tennis player, Venus believes that ___she___ can beat any man.

EXERCISE 2 Editing a Paragraph

Edit the following paragraph to correct all errors in pronoun usage. **Hint:** Two of the sentences contain no errors.

¹Someone asked if Jeff and ~~me~~ [I] want to become professional athletes. ²Jeff and ~~me~~ [I] said, "No, thank you." ³Articles about teen athletes explain how ~~them~~ [they] have to practice for hours after school. ⁴Take professional tennis players or ice skaters. ⁵~~Them~~ [They] must travel all the time while practicing and continuing an education. ⁶Would Jeff and ~~me~~ [I] like to live in hotels, away from friends and family all the time? ⁷A tennis player such as Martina Hingis, formerly ranked number one in the world at sixteen, may not have liked the lonely hotel life, but she must have enjoyed the success. ⁸Venus Williams and ~~her~~ [she] needed strong support from their families. ⁹Both players say that ~~them~~ [they] depended on their parents for coaching and personal guidance. ¹⁰Would Jeff or ~~me~~ [I] like to be at the top of the athletic world?

CONNECTING Writing & Grammar

Refer to **Composition**, Lesson 4.2, to find strategies for writing persuasively.

Write What You Think

On a separate piece of paper, write a one-paragraph response to the following statement. Support your opinion with facts, reasons, and examples. Be sure to revise and edit your writing.

Young athletes who compete professionally run the risks both of sustaining serious injuries to joints and bones that are not fully developed and of missing out on educational and social opportunities that are part of growing up. With this in mind, a rules committee has proposed the following rule: No one under the age of eighteen may compete professionally in tennis, figure skating, gymnastics, baseball, basketball, football, or hockey.

Answers will vary. Give students full credit if they have stated an opinion and attempted to support their opinions. Look for grammatically complete sentences that begin with a capital letter and end with an appropriate end punctuation mark.

Using Object Pronouns

This chart shows you object pronouns. Notice that the second-person pronoun *you* is the same in both the singular and plural forms, and it is the same for both subject and object pronouns.

Object Pronouns	
SINGULAR	**PLURAL**
me, you, him, her, it	us, you, them

▐▐▐➤ Use an **object pronoun** when the pronoun functions as the direct object (**DO**) or indirect object (**IO**) of a sentence or a clause. Most mistakes occur with compound-sentence structure.

>   DO   DO
> As part of the play, Derek pushes **you** and **me**.
>
>   IO   IO   DO
> Nadine showed the **boys** and **us** her **souvenirs**.
>
>   IO   IO   DO
> Ian asked **you** and **him** a difficult **question**.

▐▐▐➤ Use an object pronoun when the pronoun functions as the object of a preposition (**OP**) in a sentence.

>   OP   OP
> Please stand behind **Roger** and **him**.
>
>   OP
> Besides **me**, nobody has the combination to the safe.

▐▐▐➤ Use an object pronoun when the pronoun functions as an object complement (**OC**). (See Lesson 6.8 for more on object complements.)

>   DO   OC
> The street mime made his **audience us**.
>
>   DO   OC   OC
> I consider the **winners you** and **me**.

When an object is a compound object, use the step-by-step approach you learned on page 205. Test each pronoun alone, and say the sentence aloud to yourself. Let your ear help you decide the correct pronoun to use.

EDITING TIP

Be sure to use an object pronoun when the pronoun functions as an object of a preposition. Avoid these common errors:

                         me
This is just between you and ~~I~~.

I gave the tickets to Carly
    him
and ~~he~~.

Be especially alert with pronouns in a compound object.

STEP BY STEP

To decide whether to use a subject pronoun or an object pronoun:

1. Decide what function the pronoun performs in the sentence.
2. If the pronoun is a subject or a predicate nominative, choose the subject pronoun.
3. If the pronoun is a direct object, an indirect object, an object complement, or the object of a preposition, choose the object pronoun.

EXERCISE 3 Choosing the Correct Pronoun

Underline the pronoun in parentheses that correctly completes each sentence.

1. Both Tran and (I, me) read a book about treasures on the *Titanic*.

2. The movie about the *Titanic* scared Raymond and (he, him).

3. Money and jewels on board the *Titanic* went down with (she, her) when (she, her) sank.

4. Between you and (I, me), I prefer the book to the movie.

5. The *Monitor*, the Civil War shipwreck, interested my father and (I, me).

6. J. L. Worden, the captain of the *Monitor*, was a hero to (us, we).

7. According to (he, him), Worden was wounded during a battle between the *Monitor* and the *Merrimack*.

8. My father and (me, I) talked about the battle between the *Monitor* and the *Merrimack*.

9. (She, Her) and her friend gave an oral book report about the sinking of the *Monitor* in 1862.

10. Recently, a naval officer showed (we, us) pictures (he, him) had taken of the wreck of the *Monitor* on the sea floor.

EXERCISE 4 Writing Sentences with Object Pronouns

Correct the following sentences. Each one includes a subject pronoun or an object pronoun. Cross out each incorrect pronoun, and write the correct one above it. If the sentence is correct, write *C* after it.

EXAMPLE   ~~Her~~ *She* and her friend went to the butterfly exhibits.

1. Jeff and ~~him~~ *he* got up early for the Christmas bird count.

2. When they got to the park, they saw Tom and ~~I~~ *me*.

3. ~~Him~~ *He* and ~~me~~ *I* had coffee at the boathouse.

4. Between you and ~~I~~ *me*, we counted fifty different birds.

5. For Norma and him, it was a high count. C

Who or Whom?

Here are some tips to help you use the subject pronoun *who* and the object pronoun *whom*.

Subject Form	Object Form
who	whom

▐▌▶ Use the subject pronoun *who* when the pronoun functions as a subject or as a predicate nominative in a sentence or in a clause.

Who painted the mailbox turquoise? [*Who* is the subject.]

Robbie is **who** gave the party. [*Who* is the subject of the clause. The clause functions as a predicate nominative.]

The carpenter **who** repaired the mailbox also painted it. [*Who* is the subject of the adjective clause *who repaired the mailbox*.]

▐▌▶ Use the object pronoun *whom* when the pronoun functions as a direct object, an indirect object, or the object of a preposition in a sentence or a clause.

Whom do you trust? [*Whom* is the direct object.]

You handed **whom** the keys? [*Whom* is the indirect object of a sentence.]

For **Whom** the Bell Tolls is one of Ernest Hemingway's greatest novels. [*Whom* is the object of the preposition *for*.]

P.S. Almost nobody uses *whom* today in everyday speech because it sounds so formal. However, in formal writing—and on grammar tests—follow the rules listed here and use *whom* as indicated.

In deciding whether to use *who* or *whom* in a sentence, try substituting *he/she* or *him/her* for *who/whom*. If *he* or *she* sounds right in the sentence, use the subject pronoun *who*. If *him* or *her* sounds right, choose the object pronoun *whom*. To do this for a question, flip the question around to make it a statement.

(**Who**, **Whom**) did you speak with? [Change the question into a statement.]

You spoke with (**who/whom** *or* **she/her**).

[The object pronoun **her** is correct, so use the object pronoun **whom**.]

Whom did you speak with?

▐▌▶ Use *who/whom* to refer to people and *which* or *that* to refer to objects.

Sam was the one **who** played first base.

That was the ball **that** went over the wall.

C ccss

Standards for this lesson focus on applying the conventions of standard English, including recognizing that usage of *whom* has changed over time.

WRITING HINT

For issues of complex or contested usage, consult a reference guide or grammar Web site.

WRITING HINT

When choosing between *who* and *whom*, use *whom* if you can replace the word with *him*.

STEP BY STEP

When you need to choose between *who* and *whom*:

1. Decide what function the pronoun performs in the sentence.
2. Use *who* if the pronoun functions as a subject or a predicate nominative.
3. Use *whom* if the pronoun functions as a direct object, an indirect object, or the object of a preposition.

EXERCISE 5 Choosing the Correct Pronoun

Complete each sentence by writing the correct pronoun form of *who* or *whom* in the blank.

1. Alexander Graham Bell, ____who____ invented the telephone, didn't work alone.

2. The person with ____whom____ he worked, Tom Watson, discovered how speech travels through wires.

3. Bell worked with people ____who____ were hearing impaired.

4. Bell also worked with his father, ____who____ had created a system of speech through signals.

5. Bell was the first scientist ____who____ believed speech could travel by electricity.

6. The first person to ____whom____ Bell spoke by telephone was Watson.

7. In 1876, people discovered ____who____ Bell was when he unveiled his new invention.

8. It was Bell ____who____ fought the hardest for his new invention.

EXERCISE 6 Editing a Paragraph

Work with a partner to edit the following paragraph to correct all errors in pronoun usage.

          Who
[1]~~Whom~~ do you think would make a great inventor? [2]Is it only a student
who
~~whom~~ gets good grades in science? [3]Do all students ~~which~~ do well in science

think of themselves as future engineers or inventors? [4]A recently developed
          who
program, "Invention and Design," encourages students ~~whom~~ might become
      who
inventors. [5]A person ~~that~~ taught high school physics guided the students
          whom
through the program. [6]Program developers decided who would work with ~~who~~

on each team, based on students' verbal, math, and artistic abilities. [7]Students
   who
~~whom~~ participated said that teamwork was the most difficult and the most
      who
rewarding aspect of the program. [8]Teams ~~whom~~ failed in their first invention
      who
often succeeded with their second try. [9]The second attempt often showed ~~whom~~
   who
persisted. [10]This hands-on program inspired students ~~whom~~ participated to

comment: "It was inspiring; I plan to do more in this field" and "It was

challenging, and that made it more exciting."

Appositives and Incomplete Constructions

An appositive is a word or phrase that identifies or explains the noun or pronoun that comes right before it. (See Lesson 7.2.)

▶ For a pronoun appositive, use a subject pronoun if the word that the appositive refers to is a subject or a predicate nominative. Use an object pronoun if the word that the appositive refers to is a direct or indirect object or the object of a preposition.

> The Wright brothers, Wilbur and **he**, made aviation history.
> [*He*, a subject pronoun, refers to *brothers*, the sentence subject.]
> The aviation pioneers are the Wright brothers, Wilbur and **he**.
> [*He* refers to the predicate nominative *brothers*.]
> Aviation history was made by the Wright brothers, Wilbur and **him**.
> [*Him* refers to *brothers*, the object of the preposition *by*.]
> The historian praised the Wright brothers, Wilbur and **him**.
> [*Him* refers to *brothers*, the direct object.]

▶ When the pronouns *we* or *us* are followed by a noun appositive, choose the pronoun form you would use if the pronoun were alone in the sentence.

> The era in which an event takes place matters to **us** historians.
> [You would say, "The era . . . matters to *us*."]
> Next, **we** athletes will participate in a state competition. [You would say, "Next, *we* will participate. . . .
> The dog brought **us** teenagers the bone. [You would say, "The dog brought *us* the bone."]

▶ In an incomplete construction, choose the pronoun form you would use if the sentence were complete. An incomplete construction omits some words, which are understood. Usually, an incomplete construction appears at the end of a sentence and starts with the word *than* or *as*. In the following sentences, the omitted words appear in brackets.

> Marly is a faster sprinter than **she** [is].
> Jerome solves algebra equations as quickly as **he** [solves them].

▶ Be consistent in your choice of pronouns; don't shift pronouns unnecessarily.

> INCORRECT **One** should research **your** family tree.
> CORRECT **One** should research **one's** family tree.
> CORRECT **You** should research **your** family tree.

EDITING TIP

Pronouns ending in -*self* or -*selves* cannot be used as subjects. Use personal pronouns as subjects.

Victoria and ~~myself~~ *I* read

that book.

Has anyone sung better than ~~youself~~ *you*?

EXERCISE 7 Choosing the Correct Pronoun

Underline the pronoun in parentheses that correctly completes each sentence.

EXAMPLE   The composers of the song, Dana and (<u>she</u>, her), won the prize.

1. Why aren't the winners, Gena and (<u>he</u>, him), accepting the awards?

2. The M.C. handed Dana and (I, <u>me</u>) the microphone.

3. (<u>We</u>, Us) student council members won't vote for a longer school day.

4. Shannon and (<u>she</u>, her) are the hardest workers.

5. Yoko understands chess better than (<u>I</u>, me).

6. Nelson believes that when one reads, (<u>one's</u>, your) world opens up.

7. Jimmy played the sonata as well as (<u>we</u>, us).

8. It's not for (<u>us</u>, we) to decide.

9. Did anybody do better on that test than (<u>you</u>, yourself)?

10. It is (<u>he</u>, him) we trust.

Working Together

EXERCISE 8 Create Your Own Exercise

Write five sentences on any subject, using an appositive with a pronoun in each sentence. Try to use appositives as different parts of a sentence, such as the subject, predicate nominative, direct object, indirect object, object complement, or object of a preposition. Then rewrite the sentences using the format in Exercise 7 above. Exchange papers with a classmate, and underline the pronoun that completes each sentence correctly. Check your answers with your partner.
Students' sentences will vary.

EXERCISE 9 Editing Sentences

Read each sentence for errors with pronouns. Cross out a pronoun that is incorrect, and write the correct pronoun above it. If a sentence is correct, write *C* after it.

EXAMPLE   Jefferson is as smart as ~~me~~. _I_

Students may also change *one doesn't* to *you don't*.

1. If one doesn't forget the facts, ~~your~~ _one's_ papers will need fewer corrections.

2. Was it Anne who sang in as high a key as I?   C

3. Let me remind you that ~~us~~ _we_ citizens vote every November.

4. The mayor gave the teachers, Mr. Wiecker and ~~she~~ _her_, an award.

5. It was the twins, Alaine and she, who greeted you.   C

6. Asher and ~~me~~ _I_ would like to do this for our mother.

7. Why don't ~~us~~ _we_ students have a seat on the school board?

8. If only our candidate could speak as well as ~~her~~ _she_, we'd win.

Agreement with Antecedent

The word a pronoun refers to is its **antecedent**. Pronouns must agree with their antecedents in **gender** (male or female) and **number** (singular or plural). You may wish to review Lessons 10.2 and 10.3 on subject-verb agreement with indefinite pronouns and compound subjects.

||||▶ Use a plural possessive pronoun to refer to two or more antecedents joined by *and*.

> Therese, Carolina, and Michael enjoyed **their** mountain hike.

||||▶ Use a singular possessive pronoun to refer to two or more singular antecedents joined by *or* or *nor*.

> Neither Max nor Tony sent **his** stories to the magazine.

||||▶ Use a singular pronoun when the antecedent is a singular indefinite pronoun: *anybody, anyone, each, either, everybody, everyone, neither, nobody, no one, one, somebody, someone*.

> Someone in the girls choir sang **her** solo off key.
> Neither of the boys remembered **his** homework.

Use the expression "his or her" when a singular indefinite pronoun refers to both males and females.

> Each of the writers will read **his or her** story tomorrow.
> Nobody in the group wanted to voice **his or her** opinion.

||||▶ When a compound antecedent joined by *or* or *nor* contains a singular word and a plural word, use a pronoun that agrees with the nearer antecedent.

> Suzy or the **boys** volunteered **their** help.
> The dogs or **cat** played in **its** yard.

||||▶ Use *it* to refer to animals when the animal's gender is unclear. Otherwise, use *he/him* or *she/her*.

> Keep that tiger away from me! **It**'s dangerous! [gender unclear]
> My cat Marisa always licks **her** paws. [gender clear through name]

EXERCISE 10 Choosing the Correct Pronoun

Underline the pronoun in parentheses that agrees with its antecedent. **Hint:** First, find the antecedent(s).

1. One of the students refuses to do (<u>his</u>, their) assignment.

2. Matt, Karan, and Ed edit (her, <u>their</u>) school magazine.

3. Was either Tony or Nestor sitting in (<u>his</u>, their) assigned seat?

Possessive Pronouns

my	our
your	your
his	their
her	
its	

TEST-TAKING TIP

When checking that a pronoun and antecedent agree in gender and number on a standardized-test item, be sure to check that they also agree in person. See item 16 on page 311.

WRITING HINT

To avoid having to repeat the phrase "his or her" too often, try either to use an article instead of a pronoun or to rephrase the sentence.

Nobody gives away ~~his or her~~ ^a locker combination. Most people don't tell their locker combination.

4. Princess enjoys burying (its, <u>her</u>) bones.

5. Anyone who reads (<u>a</u>, their) story receives extra credit.

6. None of the women gave (her, <u>their</u>) secret password away.

7. Each one of my friends has (<u>his or her</u>, their) own point of view.

8. Will the boys or that girl give me (<u>her</u>, a, their) pass to the library?

9. Jay and Jane wrote (his or her, <u>their</u>) play about life on Mars.

10. Janet and Dena ran to the park after (her, <u>their</u>) class was over.

EXERCISE 11 Editing Sentences

Edit the following sentences for errors with pronouns. Cross out a pronoun that is incorrect, and write the correct pronoun above it. If a sentence is correct, write *C* after it.

1. Kim and Sara left ~~her~~ their notebooks in the library.

2. Neither fathers nor mothers want their children to fail.   c

3. Can Marcia or John give ~~her~~ his report before lunch?

4. Somebody in the earth science class eats ~~their~~ his or her lunch outside.

5. Each of the boys uses his calculator to add large numbers.   c

6. Someone has left ~~their~~ his or her homework on the bus.

7. Each of my aunts and uncles volunteered ~~his~~ his or her time.

8. Felix, Bob, and Rayna buy ~~her~~ their lunch in the cafeteria.

9. Peter, Paul, and Mary harmonized ~~his or her~~ their parts.

10. Several members of the chess club will discuss ~~his or her~~ their strategies.

EXERCISE 12 Writing Sentences

Work with a partner to write a sentence using the words given below as the subject. Use a correct possessive pronoun in each sentence you write.

Students' sentences will vary.

1. Each of the singers

2. Everybody on the team

3. Antony and Cleopatra

4. Mrs. Murray or Mr. Fleury

5. Neither Cheryl nor Annette

6. The circus elephant

7. Our dog King

8. Neither of the runners

Clear Pronoun Reference

Personal pronouns must always agree with their antecedents in gender, number, and person.

▌▌▌➤ Avoid confusing or unclear pronoun references.

UNCLEAR Alba and Zoe worked on the project until **she** had to go home. [*Who* had to go home? The pronoun reference is unclear.]

CLEAR Alba and Zoe worked on the project until **Zoe** had to go home.

UNCLEAR The collector admired the Elvis lamp on the table and bought **it**. [*It* could refer to either the *table* or the *Elvis lamp*.]

CLEAR Because the collector admired the Elvis lamp that was sitting on the table, she bought it. [*It* clearly refers to the *Elvis lamp*.]

UNCLEAR The cat chased the mouse and the hamster and caught **it**. [*It* could mean either the *mouse* or the *hamster*.]

CLEAR The cat chased the mouse and caught it; the hamster got away. [*It* clearly indicates the *mouse*.]

▌▌▌➤ Avoid inexact or weak references, especially when a pronoun doesn't have a definite or clear antecedent.

A sentence that contains a weak pronoun reference is difficult for readers to decipher.

UNCLEAR Rashid wrote tons of stories on a science fiction theme, but none of **it** was ever published. [What does the pronoun *it* refer to?]

CLEAR Rashid wrote tons of science fiction stories, but none of **his writing** was ever published.

UNCLEAR You missed both the party and the dinner, **which** was good. [What does the pronoun *which* refer to?]

CLEAR You missed both the party and the dinner. It was a delicious meal.

▌▌▌➤ Avoid using *it*, *they*, and *you* in a vague, general way when a sentence has no clear antecedent.

UNCLEAR **They** say that exercise helps the mind as well as the body. [What or who does *they* refer to exactly?]

CLEAR **Fitness researchers** say that exercise helps the mind as well as the body.

UNCLEAR The music was so loud, **you** couldn't hear yourself think.

CLEAR The music was so loud, **we** couldn't hear ourselves think.

CLEAR The music was so loud, **concert-goers** couldn't hear themselves think.

> **WRITING HINT**
>
> Certain phrases are correct, even though pronouns appear without clear references—for example, *it's raining, it's late, it seems.*

Working Together

EXERCISE 13 Writing Sentences with Clear Pronoun References

Edit the following numbered items so that pronouns have clear references. Cross out words you want to replace, and write the replaced words above them. You may also need to change the order and wording in sentences for clarity. If a sentence has no errors, write a *C* after it. **Hint:** Some sentences have more than one error.

EXAMPLE   *The candidates*
~~They~~ do whatever it takes to win an election.

1. In some countries, ~~you~~ *citizens* can only praise but never criticize the government.

2. He really believes in art, but he doesn't believe that genius can be taught. C

3. We waited outside the actors' dressing rooms but didn't meet a single ~~one~~ *actor*.

4. In the boardroom, ~~they~~ *marketing executives* make all kinds of decisions about how products will be advertised.

5. Pull the weeds and the carrots from the garden and wash ~~them~~ *the carrots*.

6. Ralph and Denton shared the course materials before ~~he~~ *Ralph* had to return ~~it~~ *them* to the college professor.

7. Marc told Luther ~~he~~ *that Luther* was in line for an award.

8. Elaine made rabbits disappear, coins appear, and her own hat twirl in the air. ~~This~~ *These tricks* delighted the audience.

9. Don and Juanita always composed songs, but ~~none of it was ever performed~~ *they never performed any of them*.

10. Did ~~they~~ *the doctors* tell you to take this medication three times a day?

EXERCISE 14 Editing a Paragraph

Rewrite the paragraph below on a separate piece of paper. Use accurate and clear pronoun references in your edited paragraph.
See Answer Key at www.grammarforwriting.com.

[1]They say the best cars are the old ones. [2]My friend Mike restored a 1969 Mustang. [3]That car had a shiny black paint job. [4]It was the kind with sparkles, so it shone and glittered when you saw him drive by. [5]The interior was immaculate. [6]Its upholstery was leather, and it crinkled with age. [7]It was a polished and gleaming dashboard. [8]When Mike turned the key, it made a low insistent rumble. [9]It was hard not to look at that beautiful car when it drove past.

C CCSS Language 1, 2. (See pp. T14–T15.)

Chapter 11

Usage

Revising and Editing Worksheet 1

Improve the following draft by revising for ideas, organization, word choice, and sentence variety. After revising, edit the draft for errors in spelling, capitalization, punctuation, and usage. Write your revised and edited version on a separate piece of paper. Compare your changes with those of a writing partner.

Students' revisions will vary. Sample revisions are given.

¹Many people think only of Ellis Island in New York Harbor when ~~it comes~~ they think about

~~to~~ immigration‸some also think of Angel Island in San Francisco Bay. ²The   but

island processing centers for ~~immigrants~~ were both in operation until 1940.   immigration

³Chinese, Japanese, and other Asian immigrants ~~whom~~ passed through this   who

Western center between 1910 and 1940 told ~~his~~ stories to immigration officials   their

on Angel Island.

⁴More than 100,000 Chinese and other Asian immigrants ~~that~~ passed   who

through Angel Island suffered discrimination and internment. ⁵One Chinese

immigrant ~~write~~ on the walls of the detention center‸ ~~⁶The immigrant wrote~~   wrote of the American officials

~~of the American officials,~~ ". . . They mistreat ~~we~~ Chinese." ⁷~~Him~~ and others   us   He

had ~~his~~ poems and pictures discovered by a California park ranger in 1970.   their

⁸A book of these poems, titled *Island*, has been published. ⁹The English

versions of the poems may be just as powerful as ~~them~~ in their original   they are

~~language~~. ¹⁰~~A person whom~~ reads this book will find that ~~their~~ understanding   languages   One   who   one's

of the Asian immigrant experience begins to deepen.

¹¹From 1863 to 1962, the American government and military services

decided ~~whom~~ would use angel Island. ¹²The government and ~~them~~ chose to   who   they

use the island ~~as an army post, known as Fort McDowell.~~ ¹³During World   for a number of purposes.   It was home to Fort McDowell, an army post.

War II, a number of American guards and POWs spent ~~his~~ war years on Angel   their

Island. ¹⁴Before the island became a state park in 1962‸ ¹⁵~~Angel Island~~ served   it

as a missile base.

¹⁶If the ground on Angel Island could speak, ~~the land~~ would spin endless tales of   it

tragedy, suffering, and heartache.

Students should write complete sentences, fix fragments and run-ons, plus correct errors in pronoun usage.

C **ccss** Language 1, 2. (See pp. T14–T15.)

Revising and Editing Worksheet 2

Improve the following draft by revising for ideas, organization, word choice, and sentence variety. After revising, edit the draft for errors in spelling, capitalization, punctuation, and usage. Write your revised and edited version on a separate piece of paper. Compare your changes with those of a writing partner.

Students' revisions will vary. Sample revisions are given.

¹Many of the Kennedy clan have contributed to american government. ²The
second son of Joseph and Rose Kennedy was John Fitzgerald ~~Kennedy~~, ~~whom~~ [who]
was president from 1961 until 1963. ³On November 22, 1963, he was
assassinated. ⁴The parents of JFK and all his siblings gave ~~his~~ [their] support to John's
political ambitions. ⁵As president, John chose ~~whom~~ [who] would be his attorney
general without hesitation. ⁶He chose his younger brother Robert. ⁷The tragic
fate of assassination was shared both by John and ~~he~~ [him].

⁸When one thinks about John F. Kennedy, ~~your~~ [one's] focus also turns to his wife,
Jacqueline. ⁹John F. Kennedy or ~~her~~ [she] always delighted the public with ~~their~~ [his or her]
dynamic personality. ¹⁰~~Her~~ [She] and ~~their~~ [her] children Caroline and John Jr. remained
in the public eye long after JFK's death. ¹¹Later in Jacqueline's life~~, she took on~~
the job of editing books for a publisher~~,~~ ~~showing~~ [showed] her to be a talented individual,
not just a famous one.

¹²The father of John, Robert, and Edward ~~were~~ [was] as prominent as ~~them~~ [they]. ¹³Joseph
Kennedy rose from rags to riches in business and government. ¹⁴As ambassador
to England, he served President Franklin D. Roosevelt.~~–¹⁵~~Before World War II.
¹⁶~~Joseph Kennedy believed~~ [Kennedy's belief] that the United States should not intervene in the
war and ~~approved~~ [his approval] of talks between England and Nazi Germany; subsequently, [were viewed negatively back home]
he was urged to resign ~~their~~ [his] post. ¹⁷Rose and Joseph encouraged their children to
participate in government. ¹⁹Both of ~~they~~ [them] felt enormous pride when ~~her~~ [their] son became
the first Irish American and the first Catholic president of the United States.

Chapter Review

EXERCISE A Using Subject and Object Pronouns

Fill in each blank with the correct form of a pronoun that makes sense in the sentence. Make sure that the word you add is a pronoun, not a noun. The first answer is supplied.

¹Members of the Famous Arkansans Committee are Felicia, Wayne, and __I__ .

² __We__ are preparing an oral report for a class presentation. ³Felicia developed a research and organization plan for __us__ . ⁴The plan is to come up with a list of famous people from Arkansas. ⁵When __we__ accumulate fifteen names, __we__ will divide them between the three of us for further research. ⁶For Felicia, Wayne, and __me__ , this plan sounds good. ⁷To begin, Felicia tells __us__ several names of important, contemporary people from Arkansas. ⁸ __She__ lists President Clinton, the forty-second U.S. president; Maya Angelou, an author and poet; and Johnny Cash, a country-western singer. ⁹Wayne admires prominent people from the past, so __he__ places Sequoyah, a Cherokee who helped develop an alphabet for his language, on the list. ¹⁰Between Felicia, Wayne, and __me__ , there are fourteen names on the list; that means that __we__ must come up with just one more.

EXERCISE B Choosing the Correct Pronoun

Underline the pronoun in parentheses that correctly completes each sentence.

1. (<u>Who</u>, Whom) painted *Portrait of the Artist's Mother*, known as *Whistler's Mother*?
2. The man (<u>who</u>, whom) painted (she, <u>her</u>) is James Whistler.
3. It was Whistler (<u>who</u>, whom) coined the phrase "Art for art's sake."
4. Would you consider (he, <u>him</u>) a modern painter?
5. London, the city in which he settled in 1859, never fully accepted (<u>him</u>, he).
6. Whistler's writing mentions painters (who, <u>whom</u>) he admired.

7. Whistler also noted the critics with (who, <u>whom</u>) he quarreled.

8. Whistler raged against John Ruskin, the English critic (<u>who</u>, whom) had attempted to ruin (he, <u>him</u>).

9. French, Spanish, and Japanese painters were among those (<u>who</u>, whom) influenced (he, <u>him</u>).

10. It was (<u>they</u>, them) he turned to for inspiration.

EXERCISE C Correcting Pronoun Errors

Correct all pronoun errors in the following sentences.

1. The casting director gave the main roles to Nathan and ~~I~~. *(me)*

2. Raquel and ~~her~~ used their own zoom lenses. *(she)*

3. The prop person worked with Tracy and ~~she~~. *(her)*

4. Marta told the director that the editors have more work than ~~them~~. *(the set designers)*

5. The film producers were ~~us~~ three sisters. *(we)*

6. The title, "Three Sisters," amused ~~we~~ actors. *(us)*

7. The costume designer is as creative as ~~her~~. *(she)*

8. Is Morley a more experienced actor than ~~him~~? *(he)*

EXERCISE D Using Correct Pronouns

Fill in each blank with a pronoun that agrees with its antecedent(s).

1. Each of the women brought ___her___ child to the park.

2. Anyone in this group can present ___his or her___ report.

3. The neighbors had ___their___ block-association picnic.

4. Fourth-grade boys and a second-grade boy recited ___their___ poems.

5. Either the students or Mr. Morano will present ___his___ views.

6. It was either Matt or Ben who forgot the words to ___his___ poem.

7. Everyone who reads ___his or her___ report aloud will get extra points.

8. Three cheerleaders and Marlene share ___their___ locker in the gym.

9. Either Mel or Arthur makes ___his___ multimedia presentation today.

10. Neither the king nor the queen wore ___his or her___ crown outside.

Using Modifiers

STUDENT WRITING
Expository Essay

Driving: Teen Rite of Passage
The Benefits and Pitfalls of Teenage Driving Revealed
by Suzanne O'Kelley
high school student, Eugene, Oregon

Looking at the packed parking areas around South, one sees that driving is a major factor of student life. Though some students manage to remain oblivious to the call of the driver's seat, many fall prey and are captured by the ups and downs of driving.

The allure of the automobile hits as freshmen turn fifteen and attempt to pass their driver's permit test. Not knowing what to expect, nervous teens wait in the Department of Motor Vehicles building. Finally, the first nerve-racking driving test is over, and new drivers flood onto the open road . . . usually, still in the passenger's seat.

Parents seem to have a hormone that releases when their child can drive, forcing them to ruin the experience in every way possible. Their fingers lock in a white-knuckled position and their feet pound on an imaginary brake pedal as their son or daughter putters around a parking lot at the breakneck speed of ten miles per hour.

Driver's education is another infamous aspect of driving that parents say is "for the child's own good." The in-class sessions are filled with '80s videos worse than *Footloose,* but hey, there's no better remedy for insomnia. The behind-the-wheel courses are expensive and embarrassing, unless it suddenly becomes cool to drive two miles under the speed limit in a car covered with "Student Driver" signs. The only benefit from these classes is an insurance discount.

For most people, the actual driver's license test is a blur. But when the time comes to drive alone for the first time, all the hassles and worries of the past year of student driving vanish. Now there are new things to worry about. . . .

For those without a car, there's nothing more appealing than a new set of wheels. Less appealing, however, is the hundreds of hours put into buying and caring for a car, but as long as the car is still on the distant horizon, the problems that accompany a car are both out of sight and out of mind.

When a car is finally available, problems arise. Gas money, insurance money, parking money, and repair money flow out of wallets. Friends want rides, parents want errands, but drivers just want freedom.

> The audience for Suzanne O'Kelley's essay about driving is her high school peers. Her humorous tone and witty descriptions hold a reader's attention and encourage him or her to read on. In addition, Suzanne discusses several aspects of her topic, including parents' reactions, driver's education classes, and car ownership.
>
> As you reread the essay, pay attention to the modifiers—the adjectives and adverbs. Modifiers add color and freshness to your writing. As you do the writing exercises in this chapter, you'll practice adding modifiers to your own work.

Allow time for students to discuss the student writing. Suggest that they identify its strengths and propose possible improvements. Use the model to introduce the concepts in the chapter.

Forming the Degrees of Comparison

When you make comparisons, you use three **degrees of comparison**: the **positive**, the **comparative**, and the **superlative**. Imagine three days in a row without rain or snow, starting on Friday.

POSITIVE   On Friday, the sky was blue and the sun was **bright**.

COMPARATIVE On Saturday, the sun was **brighter** than on Friday.

SUPERLATIVE On Sunday, the sun was the **brightest** of all three days.

Here are some rules for forming comparative and superlative degrees.

> **One-syllable modifiers** Add *-er* and *-est* to one-syllable modifiers.
>
> short, short**er**, short**est**   great, great**er**, great**est**

> **Two-syllable modifiers** Add *-er* and *-est* to most two-syllable modifiers.
>
> simple, simpl**er**, simpl**est**   shiny, shin**ier**, shin**iest**

When an *-er* or *-est* ending for a modifier sounds clumsy, use *more* and *most* before the positive degree.

> eager, **more** eager, **most** eager

> ***-ly* adverbs** Use *more* and *most* for all adverbs that end in *-ly*.
>
> rapidly, **more** rapidly, **most** rapidly

However, be careful since not all *-ly* words are adverbs.

> ugly, ugli**er**, ugli**est**

> **More than two syllables** For modifiers of three syllables or more, use *more* and *most* to form the comparative and superlative degrees.
>
> capable, **more** capable, **most** capable
>
> unappealing, **more** unappealing, **most** unappealing

> **Decreasing degrees** For all modifiers, use *less* and *least* for decreasing degrees of comparison (regardless of the number of syllables).
>
> humble, **less** humble, **least** humble
>
> bravely, **less** bravely, **least** bravely

> **Irregular modifiers** The modifiers listed in the side column form their degrees of comparison irregularly.

Irregular Degrees of Comparison

good	better	best
well	better	best
bad	worse	worst
badly	worse	worst
ill	worse	worst
many	more	most
much	more	most
little	less or lesser	least
far	farther further	farthest furthest

STEP BY STEP

To form the comparative and superlative degree of modifiers:

1. Count the number of syllables.
2. Apply the appropriate rule:
   one syllable = *-er* and *-est*
   two syllables = Check a dictionary if in doubt whether to use *-er*, *-est* or *more*, *most*.
   three syllables = *more* and *most*
   -ly adverbs = *more* and *most*
3. Memorize the modifiers with irregular degrees of comparison.

EXERCISE 1 Proofreading a Paragraph

Cross out any incorrect modifiers and write the correct form in the space above it.

[1]If you want to find a ~~gooder~~ (good) ranch, where would you look? [2]You'd probably expect to find the ~~authenticest~~ (most authentic) ranches in a place like Texas. [3]But can you imagine a less ~~predictabler~~ (predictable) place for a ranch than England? [4]In truth, it might take a ~~longest~~ (longer) time to get to Laredo, England, than to Laredo, Texas. [5]In Laredo, England, though, just 5,139 miles from its namesake, you'll find a ranch ~~trulyer~~ (more truly) Western than ranches from frontier days in Texas! [6]In Westphalia, Germany, one of the ~~most strange~~ (strangest) places you could visit would be Lubbock Town, named after another Texas cowboy location. [7]Cowboy clubs have become popular throughout Germany, where people more ~~thoroughlyer~~ (thoroughly) enjoy experiencing the American West in re-created towns. [8]The Munich Cowboy Club sponsors a Western museum, which exhibits one of the ~~most rare~~ (rarest) autographed photographs of Buffalo Bill Cody. [9]From among the clubs and re-created towns that exude cowboy charm, Germans show ~~more keen~~ (keener) interest in cowboys and the frontier days than people from other foreign countries.

EXERCISE 2 Forming the Comparative and Superlative

Write the comparative and superlative degrees for each modifier.

1. beautiful — more beautiful — most beautiful
2. highly — more highly — most highly
3. good — better — best
4. bad — worse — worst
5. plain — plainer — plainest
6. cautious — more cautious — most cautious
7. courageously — more courageously — most courageously
8. industrious — more industrious — most industrious

EXERCISE 3 Writing a Travel Advertisement

You are a travel writer who has just taken an assignment to write a one-paragraph description of a great place to visit. On a separate piece of paper, write this paragraph, which will be included in a letter mailed to people interested in taking a trip. You may write about a real place or a made-up place. Use at least five comparative and superlative modifiers in your paragraph to make readers of this letter want to visit the place you're writing about.

Using the Degrees of Comparison

Use the following rules to help you use the comparative and superlative forms of modifiers correctly.

▐▐▐▶ Use the **comparative degree** to compare two things. Use the **superlative degree** to compare three or more things.

COMPARATIVE   The San Francisco cable cars were a **better** means of transportation than the buses.

SUPERLATIVE   Our visit to Muir Woods was the **best** day of our trip.

In dialogue, you'll often hear the superlative used in a comparison between two things. In writing, though, use the comparative.

INCORRECT   Of the two places we visited, I liked the Golden Gate Bridge **best**.

CORRECT   Of the two places we visited, I liked the Golden Gate Bridge **better**.

▐▐▐▶ **Avoid double comparisons.** Use either *more* (or *most*) or *-er* (or *-est*) but never the word and the suffix together.

INCORRECT   I tried to run **more faster** to gain on my opponent **more sooner**.

CORRECT   I tried to run **faster** to gain on my opponent **sooner**.

> ### EDITING TIP
>
> Avoid misusing *less* and *fewer*. *Less* indicates "how much" and is used to modify a singular noun. *Fewer*, which specifies "how many," is used to modify a plural noun.
> fewer
> Boyd read ten ~~less~~ books than Rita did. [*Books* is a plural noun that can be counted.]
> Boyd eats **less** food when he isn't exercising. [*Food* is a singular noun that cannot be counted.]

EXERCISE 4 Editing Sentences

Edit these sentences for the correct use of modifiers. If the sentence has no errors, write *C* after it. If you find an error, cross out the incorrect word(s), and write the correct form of the modifier above the line.

EXAMPLE   The Sound Surround pays students ~~higher wages than~~ *the highest wages of* any place else in town.

1. Of all the people I know, Stephanie has the ~~more~~ *most* interesting job.

2. Nestor and Michelle work in a store that sells the ~~most~~ latest music.

3. Between rock and jazz, Michelle likes jazz ~~best~~ *better*.

4. Nestor is the ~~more~~ *most* knowledgeable about music among all his friends.

5. The Clothes Horse hires ~~less~~ *fewer* high school students in winter than in summer.

6. The Sports Shack is the ~~more~~ **most** difficult place in town for students to get work.

7. Of the two debates, the one about jobs was more relevant. C

8. Lemar has ~~fewer~~ **less** time in his schedule for studying now that he's working.

9. Deciding whether or not to work after school is one of the ~~more~~ **most** difficult decisions students must make.

10. The law should be more flexible about the hours students work. C

EXERCISE 5 Editing a Paragraph

Improve the following paragraph by correcting all the incorrect modifiers.

¹People think that scooping ice cream during the summers would be the most ~~funnest~~ **fun** job. ²However, these people don't think about the hazards of the job. ³First, pushy tourists have to consider every flavor before they choose the ~~more better~~ **best**. ⁴They can get nasty if you are not the ~~more~~ **most** patient of all the servers. ⁵Second, on the ~~hotter~~ **hottest** day of the summer, an ice-cream shop is packed with customers looking for quick service. ⁶Finally, even if you thought that the ~~most~~ tastiest food was ice cream, you'll never enjoy it after scooping it all day.

EXERCISE 6 Writing Sentences with Comparisons

On a separate piece of paper, write a paragraph in which you compare two or more objects, people, places, or activities. Here are some possible topics:

three books	two states	three parks
two famous people	three sports	three advertisements

Include at least four comparative or superlative forms in your paragraph, and underline each one. Students' paragraphs will vary.

Write What You Think

On a separate piece of paper, write a paragraph in response to the statement below. Include reasons and examples to support your opinion. Be sure to revise and edit your writing.

Students should not be allowed to work after school or during the summer until they are at least eighteen years of age. Answers will vary. Give students full credit if they have stated an opinion and attempted to support their opinions. Look for grammatically complete sentences that begin with a capital letter and end with an appropriate end punctuation mark.

Illogical Comparisons and Double Negatives

IIII➡ Avoid illogical comparisons. Use the words *other* or *else* to compare something with others in its group.

ILLOGICAL	Chicago is larger than any city in the Midwest. [Chicago is a city in the Midwest. Chicago can't be larger than itself.]
LOGICAL	Chicago is larger than any **other** city in the Midwest.
ILLOGICAL	Molly can run farther than anyone on the track team.
LOGICAL	Molly can run farther than anyone **else** on the track team.

IIII➡ Avoid unclear comparisons. Add whatever words are necessary to make a clear comparison.

UNCLEAR	Eduardo is more interested in writing stories than Judy.
CLEAR	Eduardo is more interested in writing stories than Judy is.
CLEAR	Eduardo is more interested in writing stories than he is in Judy.

IIII➡ Avoid using two negative words together. Only one negative word is necessary to express a negative idea. Count the contraction *-n't* (for *not*) as a negative word.

Note that there is more than one way to correct a double negative. Use the correct form that sounds best to you and fits the tone and style of your writing.

INCORRECT	I haven't never read a science fiction story that I didn't like.
CORRECT	I've never read a science fiction story that I didn't like.
CORRECT	I haven't yet read a science fiction story that I didn't like.
INCORRECT	Ryan didn't have no room for nothing except a small suitcase.
CORRECT	Ryan didn't have room for anything except a small suitcase.
CORRECT	Ryan had no room for anything except a small suitcase.

Did you notice that you sometimes need to change words when correcting a double negative? For example, you change *nobody* to *anybody*, *nothing* to *anything*, *never* to *ever*, *no one* to *anyone*, *nothing* to *anything*, and *none* to *any*.

Below you'll find examples of ways in which two negatives may be used correctly in one sentence. These kinds of situations occur infrequently.

I wouldn't not read a book by Sigrid Nuñez just because I've never heard of her.

Jamie couldn't not go to his sister's recital after she practiced so hard.

WRITING HINT

Some modifiers must stand alone because they are at the highest degree of comparison already. For example, how can something be more perfect than perfect?

That is a ~~very most~~ unique hairstyle.

Tacos are my ~~most~~ favorite food.

EDITING TIP

In colloquial speech, some people say *ain't* as a contraction for *am not*, *is not*, and *are not*. In standard English, however, *ain't* is widely considered to be inappropriate.

EXERCISE 7 Editing Sentences for Double Negatives

Working Together

In the following famous quotations, fix all the double negatives. Eliminate or change words as necessary.

1. Nothing ~~can't~~ [can] be created from nothing. —Lucretius, 99–55 B.C.

2. He ~~hasn't never~~ [has not] aquired a fortune; the fortune has acquired him.
   —Bión, 325–255 B.C.

3. I ~~couldn't not~~ [could not] know whether I was then a man dreaming I was a butterfly, or whether I am now a butterfly dreaming I am a man. —Chang-tzu, 369–286 B.C.

4. His only fault is that he ~~hasn't~~ [has] got no fault. —Pliny the Younger, c. A.D. 100

5. An argument doesn't need ~~no~~ [a] reason, nor a friendship. —Ibycus, c. 580 B.C.

6. What ~~ain't~~ [is no] good for the swarm ~~ain't~~ [is] no good for the bee.
   —Marcus Aurelius Antonius, A.D. 131–180

EXERCISE 8 Proofreading a Paragraph

Correct all errors due to illogical or unclear comparisons and double negatives in the paragraph below.

¹As classical composers, Beethoven (1770–1827) and Mozart (1756–1791) stand out from everyone [else] in the eighteenth century. ²No one ~~couldn't never~~ [else could ever] come close to their musical brilliance or popularity. ³Their home of Vienna, Austria, boasted more musical talent than any [other] European city of its day. ⁴Nobody ~~never~~ [ever] had a father as supportive of his talent as Mozart's. ⁵Leopold Mozart didn't let ~~nobody~~ [anybody] important in Europe accept his son as less than a child prodigy, or genius. ⁶On the other hand, Beethoven's childhood was more ~~difficulter~~ [difficult] than Mozart's. ⁷Beethoven's father ~~hadn't none of the~~ [had no] desire to help his son; instead, he used the boy's talent for his own gain. ⁸There wasn't ~~nothing~~ [anything] as lucky for the young Beethoven as his support by Count Waldenstein of Bonn, Germany. ⁹This aristocrat was more interested in Beethoven than his father [was]. ¹⁰Both composers spent their final years in the ~~most~~ saddest of circumstances. ¹¹Mozart ~~didn't have~~ [had] no money, which made his life harder than [other] people's lives. ¹²Beethoven became deaf and ~~couldn't~~ [could] hear no music, forcing him to compose from memory.

Misplaced Modifiers

If a sentence is not written correctly, a modifier may accidentally modify the wrong word. A **misplaced modifier** is a word, phrase, or clause that's in the wrong place. It modifies a word that is different from the one it's meant to modify.

▯▶ Correct a misplaced modifier by moving it as close as possible to the word it is meant to modify.

MISPLACED Smiling with delight, the trophy was handed to Jenine.

CORRECTED The trophy was handed to Jenine, who was smiling with delight.

MISPLACED They imagined an extraordinary space trip in their classroom.

CORRECTED In their classroom, they imagined an extraordinary space trip.

MISPLACED From the ocean floor, Andy gave me a seashell.

CORRECTED Andy gave me a seashell from the ocean floor.

MISPLACED Fidgeting and fussing, the nurse calmed the sick child.

CORRECTED The nurse calmed the sick child, who was fidgeting and fussing.

EXERCISE 9 Editing Sentences

Correct the misplaced modifiers in each sentence below.

1. On her way to work, My sister saw the girl climbing the mountain on her way to work.

2. As a baby, my mother sang lullabies to me. as a baby.

3. Gliding on air currents, she observed two hawks. gliding on air currents.

4. From the top bookshelf, he read *Green Mansions*, a long-forgotten book. from the top bookshelf.

5. In the canoe, We enjoyed watching the lake in the canoe.

6. Lumpy and sour, my father baked the loaf of bread incorrectly. lumpy and sour

7. Rufus only hides under the bed during a thunderstorm. only

8. In her studio one day, Sara drew a cartoon of a rhinoceros in her studio one day.

9. Loud and shrill, Max turned off the car alarm. loud and shrill

10. At the age of twelve, Zoe's parents took her to the Everglades. at the age of twelve.

WRITING HINT

Always check that the word *only* modifies the word you really intend it to modify in a sentence. Place *only* before the word or phrase it modifies.

MISPLACED
I **only** play tennis on Tuesdays. [This implies that you do nothing else but play tennis on Tuesday.]

CORRECTED
I play tennis **only** on Tuesdays. [Now it's clear that when you play tennis, it's on Tuesday.]

TEST-TAKING TIP

An error on a standardized-test item may appear in the form of a misplaced or dangling modifier. Correct such an error by moving the modifying phrase to a location where it makes better sense or by adding words to the sentence to clarify meaning. See item 4 on page 313 and item 13 on page 315.

Working Together

EXERCISE 10 Editing a Scene from a Play

Work with a partner to correct misplaced modifiers in this passage from a play.
Write your revision on a separate piece of paper. Compare your changes with
those made by other pairs of classmates.

SCENE 1: ¹Elisa, the main character, thinks about her future ~~in the moonlight.~~ [*In the moonlight,*]

²In the background ~~howling,~~ her father tries to quiet Bailey, the family dog. [*who is howling.*]

³~~Flying in the dark,~~ Elisa and her father see a bat. [*flying in the dark*] ⁴Elisa's ideas about her

future are at once forgotten ~~inside the house.~~ [*Once inside the house,*]

ELISA

⁵~~At the age of four,~~ you gave me Bailey, remember? [*when I was four*]

FATHER

⁶You always drew pictures of dogs ~~in your bedroom~~; so I [*In your bedroom,*]

had to give you a real one.

(⁷Scared, Elisa closes the door to keep the bat outside.)

ELISA

⁸Dad, I was thinking about my future career; but I forgot all [*with the fresh night air surrounding me,*]

about the career I'd like to pursue ~~with the fresh night air~~

~~surrounding me.~~

FATHER

⁹~~As a clever girl,~~ my journal is full of your ideas about what [*clever*]

you will do one day. ¹⁰You will find some old entries in my [*Inside a desk drawer,*]

journal about your aspirations to become a veterinarian.

~~inside a desk drawer.~~

Dangling Modifiers

Sometimes, a modifier appears that isn't logically attached to any word in a sentence. A **dangling modifier** is a word, phrase, or clause that doesn't connect to or logically modify any word in the sentence.

DANGLING	Refreshed but hungry, the fried egg tasted great.
CORRECTED	I got out of bed refreshed but hungry, and the fried egg tasted great.

⫸ Correct a dangling modifier by rewording the sentence. Add a word or words that the phrase or clause can modify.

DANGLING	Walking home from school, the wind blew over a pine tree.
CORRECTED	Walking home from school, we saw the wind blow over a pine tree.

In the corrected sentence, the phrase *walking home from school* modifies the noun *we*.

DANGLING	Struggling to complete the marathon, an ankle was sprained.
CORRECTED	Struggling to complete the marathon, Greta sprained her ankle.

In the corrected sentence, the phrase *struggling to complete the marathon* clearly modifies *Greta*.

DANGLING	Using DNA evidence, the suspect was proved innocent.
CORRECTED	DNA evidence proved that the suspect was innocent.

The corrected sentence makes it clear that it was not the suspect who was using the DNA evidence.

EXERCISE 11 Editing Sentences

Rewrite each sentence to correct the dangling modifiers. If a sentence is correct, write *C* after it. **Hint:** You may want to use the second-person pronoun *you* to rewrite sentences that contain dangling modifiers.

EXAMPLE   To become an architect, ~~the study is hard.~~ *you must study hard.*

1. After ~~circling~~ the stadium for an hour, a parking spot opened up near
   we circled
   the west entrance.

2. ~~Stuck between the sofa cushions,~~ he lost the remote control. *between the sofa cushions*

C CCSS

Standards for this lesson focus on applying the conventions of standard English, including recognizing that usage, which may vary in written and spoken expression, is a matter of convention.

WRITING **HINT**

Some dangling modifiers used in everyday speech are acceptable as introductory phrases. Examples include *generally speaking, strictly speaking, considering the alternative, to tell the truth*, and *to be perfectly frank.*
Generally speaking, cats make good pets.

Cats can't speak, so the phrase *generally speaking* is technically a dangling modifier.

For issues of complex or contested usage, consult a reference, such as *Merriam-Webster's Dictionary of English Usage* or *Garner's Modern American Usage.*

you
3. To tell the truth, my stereo is secondhand. *Students may also mark this C.*
^

As we were
4. Strolling along the beach this afternoon, the sun set.
^

As I was   my
5. Bicycling up Tug Hill, ~~the~~ tire went flat.
^

you should find it
6. By paying close attention to your surroundings, ~~it's~~ easy to write a good story.

I saw
7. While walking in the woods, two long-eared owls fly overhead.
^

my keys   ^   I never lose them.
8. By always putting ~~them~~ in the same place, ~~my keys are never lost.~~

to the west
9. ~~Looking to the west,~~ the moon rose over Cleopatra's Needle.
‗   ^

I was
10. While talking on the phone, my mother knocked on my door.
^

EXERCISE 12 Revising a Paragraph

Revise the following paragraph from a biography by correcting dangling modifiers. Write your revised biography on a separate piece of paper. **Hint:** Some sentences may include introductory phrases that are acceptable English even though they are also dangling modifiers. Consider using second-person pronouns when you rewrite sentences with dangling modifiers. You may need to add words as well as change arrangements of words in some sentences.

Students' revisions will vary. A sample revision is given.

you study
[1]To understand great architects, Frank Lloyd Wright (1867–1959) ~~is one of the~~

you discover
~~most famous modern architects.~~ [2]Visiting Chicago and its suburbs, many of his

designs ~~are evident in various structures.~~ [3]By following the lines of nature, ~~the~~

the prairie style of architecture
~~prairie style of~~ Frank Lloyd Wright's ~~architecture was~~ invented. [4]Attempting to

Wright removed
create an open feeling in homes, unnecessary walls ~~were removed in Wright's~~

homeowners welcomed   as a
~~homes.~~ [5]Considering the alternative, open spaces ~~were a welcome~~ change

~~for homeowners.~~ [6]Using his ideas for construction, ~~Taliesin,~~ Frank Lloyd Wright's

built Taliesin, his   experiencing fire twice,
own house, ~~was built~~ in Spring Green, Wisconsin. [7]Although ~~destroyed twice~~

Wright constructed
~~by fire,~~ Wright rebuilt Taliesin both times. [8]Concerning Taliesin, a second

structure, Taliesin West, ~~was constructed~~ in Scottsdale, Arizona. [9]For learning

architecture students use
about design, this building ~~is used~~ as a school ~~for architecture students~~ today.

the Guggenheim family erected
[10]Upon selecting Wright's architectural plans, a unique, circular museum in New

York City ~~was erected and is called the Guggenheim Museum.~~

Revising and Editing Worksheet 1

Improve the following draft by revising for ideas, organization, word choice, and sentence variety. After revising, edit the draft for errors in spelling, capitalization, punctuation, and usage. Write your revised and edited version on a separate piece of paper. Compare your changes with those of a writing partner. Students' revisions will vary. Sample revisions are given.

¹This report is on waves of energy. ²Light waves may travel fastest [faster] than

sound waves, but the principle by which all waves of energy travel is the

same. ³To understand this idea, you don't have to do nothing [anything] more

complicated than experiment with a rope. ⁴To create a rope wave, a hand is [move your hand]

moved while holding onto one end of the rope. ⁵The high and low spots on

the rope waves are no different from the crests and troughs of water. ⁶The

more harder you move the rope, the more greater the amount of energy

created that travels through the wave. ⁷The gentler [more gently] you move the rope, the

lesser [fewer] number of waves you create.

⁸Can you name more kinds of waves than anyone? [else you know] ⁹After reading this

selection, you wouldn't not [would] include light waves, sound waves, rope waves,

and water waves on a list of waves of energy; but think more harder to make

your list more longer. ¹⁰Did you consider musical instruments?

¹¹Vibrating wildly, a musician's plucked guitar strings are a source of [vibrating wildly]

sound waves. ¹²Those strings don't never [ever] stay still when you hear music.

¹³Think about your favoritest [favorite] singers in the world. ¹⁴To make their music,

vocal chords are vibrated [they vibrate their vocal cords]. ¹⁵Waves of energy from the vocal cords are what [, which we hear as the human voice,]

we enjoy listening to as the human voice from a stage.

¹⁶There aren't [are] scarcely no [any] instruments that don't send out no waves of

energy, from air blown through wind instruments to strings vibrated [vibrating] on

string instruments. ¹⁷Some people enjoy the waves of energy produced by

surfaces being tapped on percussion instruments most [more] than any other instruments

ever invented.

Students should use modifiers correctly in complete sentences.

C CCSS Language 1, 2. (See pp. T14–T15.)

Revising and Editing Worksheet 2

Improve the following draft by revising for ideas, organization, word choice, and sentence variety. After revising, edit the draft for errors in spelling, capitalization, punctuation, and usage. Write your revised and edited version on a separate piece of paper. Compare your changes with those of a writing partner.

¹This biographical sketch is ~~on~~ [about] the Shawnee leader Tecumseh (1768?–1813)~~,~~ [;] he led one of the most surprising and ~~baddest~~ [worst] raids against American forces in the War of 1812. ²Why couldn't he ~~not~~ side with the Americans? ³Being forced to live like white people in North America~~,~~ Shawnee beliefs ~~were threatened~~ [threatened].

⁴No less than five times during Tecumseh's childhood did his people confront white soldiers. ⁵While fighting for Shawnee land around the Ohio River, Tecumseh's father and two of his brothers were killed. ⁶[Through a dream he had,] Tecumseh hoped to unite all Native Americans in a multitribal alliance ~~through a dream he had~~. ⁷The ~~dreamed-of~~ alliance wouldn't let ~~no~~ [any] tribes be moved from their land or be denied their way of life. ⁸Letting his brother, known as the Prophet~~,~~ or Tenskwatawa, address fellow Native Americans~~.~~ ⁹~~The alliance was strengthened~~ [strengthened the alliance]. ¹⁰Tenskwatawa's style of speaking was more ~~fiercer~~ [fierce] than Tecumsehs [,] [style of speaking]. ¹¹Some listeners thought of him as wiser but stranger than any [other] speakers that came before him. ¹²In addition, Tenskwatawa didn't preach ~~no~~ nonviolence~~.~~ ¹³[I]n the fight for independence from the United States.

¹⁴Young Native Americans ~~knowed~~ [knew] of Tecumseh's ~~capturing~~ [capture of] Detroit during the War of 1812 before he was fifty. ¹⁵At Tippecanoe, in 1811, ~~a battle was lost by Tenskwatawa~~ [Tenskwatawa] [lost a battle]. ¹⁶The British hadn't ~~never~~ [ever] intended to support Tecumseh or his brother. ¹⁷The British eventually trapped Tecumseh in a ~~more~~ brutal battle at Moraviantown, Canada. ¹⁸There, Tecumseh ~~only~~ died with [only] his dream of Native American unity and independence.

Students' revisions will vary. Sample revisions are given. Students should use modifiers correctly in complete sentences, fix fragments and run-ons, plus combine subjects, verbs, and simple sentences into compounds whenever appropriate for sense and the flow of ideas.

Chapter Review

EXERCISE A Using Degrees of Comparison

Proofread the following sentences for the correct use of modifiers. If you find an error, cross out the word or phrase, and rewrite it correctly in the space above. If a sentence is correct, write C after it.

1. One of the ~~fascinatingest~~ *most fascinating* ways in which animals communicate is through pheromones.

2. A pheromone is one of the ~~most~~ best ways to signal location.

3. Pheromones are one of nature's more intriguing class of chemicals. C

4. In animals, the sense of smell is often the ~~more higher~~ *most highly* developed sense.

5. Animals can sense wind-borne pheromones from a ~~farthest~~ *far* distance away.

6. A bee sting that releases a pheromone causes more ~~aggressiver~~ *aggressive* behavior in nearby bees.

7. A bee sting's odor most ~~oftenest~~ *often* incites other bees to sting in the same place.

8. A bombardier beetle's pheromone is ~~least~~ *less* likely to cause harm than to attract a potential mate.

9. A skunk's pheromone-produced spray is the ~~less~~ *least* pleasant smell to me.

10. Chemists believe that pheromones are ~~the more~~ *a* better way to protect crops than artificial pesticides.

EXERCISE B Correcting Double Negatives and Illogical Comparisons

Correct problems with double negatives and illogical comparisons in the sentences below. Cross out words that aren't necessary, and add words that might be needed to correct each sentence.

1. Tony ~~hadn't~~ *had* hardly done anything unusual when his hard drive crashed.

2. Couldn't ~~nobody nowhere~~ *anybody anywhere* figure out how to fix his computer?

3. Marcia, who is better than anyone *else* with computers, fixed it.

4. Marcia hasn't ~~never~~ *ever* been stumped by a computer problem.

5. Her computer was ~~more old~~ *older* than mine.

6. Tony couldn't find ~~no~~ ^any^ Internet site to diagnose his problems.

7. Marcia suggested a library site, saying, "Well, maybe I'm ~~most~~ ^more^ interested in libraries ^are^ than you."

8. He tried ~~more~~ harder to find ~~more~~ better information through the site.

9. The library's electronic catalog didn't have ~~none~~ ^any^ of the information.

10. Then, Marcia chose a different database and found an article ~~more~~ better than anything Tony could find.

EXERCISE C Writing Sentences with Comparisons and Clear Modifiers

On a separate piece of paper, write five sentences about your experiences using a computer and the Internet. The sentences do not have to follow one another as they would in a paragraph. Use one comparison or clear modifier in each sentence. Students' sentences will vary.

EXERCISE D Revising a Paragraph

On a separate piece of paper, rewrite the paragraph to correct misplaced and dangling modifiers. **Hint:** You may need to change the wording or to add words to correct some modifiers. See Answer Key at www.grammarforwriting.com.

¹Roaring and leaping, Professor Michael Bleyman was not afraid of tigers or lions. ²To provide a home for abandoned or abused big cats, Bleyman founded a special farm in North Carolina. ³Named as the successor to Bleyman after his death, Nancy Schonwalter's old job as a video producer was abandoned. ⁴The Carnivore Preservation Trust is maintained by Schonwalter and only volunteers, without government funds. ⁵Wandering freely around the preservation, neighboring farmers aren't afraid of the big cats. ⁶Having escaped its cage, Bleyman once had to catch a tiger roaming around his neighbor's land when he began saving big cats. ⁷Now over twenty years old, a chain-link fence surrounds the animal preserve. ⁸Emaciated and tied to a tree, people from the Carnivore Preservation Trust once rescued a tiger found in downtown Houston, Texas. ⁹Newly rescued, Nancy Schonwalter might approach a tiger without fear in order to gain its acceptance. ¹⁰One of the problems for the Trust is only finding enough big-cat food for the animals, which costs around $350,000 a year.

CHAPTER REVIEW

C CCSS Language 1. (See pp. T14–T15.)

Cumulative Review

EXERCISE A Using Verbs Correctly

On a separate piece of paper, correct all the errors in verb usage in the following sentences. Look for incorrect verbs and verb forms, unnecessary shifts in verb tense, and unnecessary use of the passive voice. **Hint:** A sentence may have more than one mistake.

1. If I ~~was~~ (were) you, I would have screamed with joy when I ~~winned~~ (won) the award.
2. As the master of ceremonies ~~speaked~~ (spoke), I ~~holded~~ (held) my breath.
3. I might ~~has~~ (have) stayed ~~freezed~~ (frozen) in my seat at the idea of giving a speech.
4. You ~~do~~ (did) well to have ~~choosed~~ (chosen) a quotation from Shakespeare.
5. No one will ever ~~forget~~ (forget) the way you ~~had~~ thanked your drama coach.
6. To hear every word you ~~was~~ (were) saying, we ~~keeped~~ (kept) quiet.
7. Your poise ~~teached~~ (taught) me an important lesson.
8. You ~~rised~~ (rose) to the occasion and ~~gaved~~ (gave) credit to your fellow actors.
9. If I had ~~sit~~ (sat) in the front row, you could ~~had seed~~ (have seen) me smile.
10. When you ~~have~~ went back to your seat, you ~~was~~ (were) on cloud nine.

EXERCISE B Subject-Verb Agreement

Underline the verb in parentheses that agrees with the subject.

1. Astronomers (was, <u>were</u>) shocked to find evidence of water in space.

2. Conditions on Titan, a moon of Saturn, (resembles, <u>resemble</u>) those that led to the creation of life on Earth.

3. One of the scientists (<u>guesses</u>, guess) that life could emerge on Titan.

4. Researchers at a European Space Observatory (has, <u>have</u>) been using new techniques to study our solar system.

5. Water, a sign of life, (<u>has</u>, have) been spotted all over the cosmos.

6. Water apparently (<u>exists</u>, exist) where temperatures are extremely cold.

7. What (<u>is</u>, are) the source of this water among planets and stars?

8. Comets, some think, (has, <u>have</u>) brought water to the solar system.

9. (<u>Is</u>, Are) the United States or other countries conducting research about water?

10. The press often (writes, <u>write</u>) articles on the search for water.

CUMULATIVE REVIEW

EXERCISE C Using Pronouns Correctly

Underline the pronoun in parentheses that correctly completes each sentence.

1. Carson and (I, me) will be lifeguards this summer.

2. The beverage vendors at the lake will be Koko, Ali, and (he, him).

3. The store owner hired Otis and (I, me) as summer cashiers.

4. It's all right to call the dog (he, him) instead of *it*.

5. Was Ms. Chen the executive to (who, whom) you wrote?

6. Between you and (I, me), I liked the root beer better.

7. The best summer employees, Luz and (she, her), got a raise.

8. The employees gave the factory managers, Lily and (he, him), a gift.

9. Few realize how much (we, us) volunteer ushers enjoy the films we see.

10. The janitors and (her, she) cleared the displays from her classroom walls.

EXERCISE D Using Modifiers Correctly

On a separate piece of paper, edit the following sentences to correct all errors in the use of modifiers, including dangling modifiers. **Hint:** Some sentences have more than one error.

1. Which cuisine do you like ~~more~~ better, Chinese or Korean?

2. The ~~most fresh~~ freshest ingredients make the ~~bestest~~ best soup.

3. Of these four restaurants, the Pasta Palace is the ~~less expensivest~~ least expensive.

4. She cooked the ~~most~~ greatest meal of all time in her mind.

5. The Afghan Kebab House is smaller than any other restaurant in this city.

6. The chef worked ~~more~~ harder to create the ~~most~~ perfect dessert.

7. Didn't ~~nobody never~~ anybody ever tell you that the dish contained hot peppers?

8. While stir-frying the vegetables, ~~the recipe belonging to Dave was lost.~~ Dave lost his recipe.

9. ~~Floating in the soup, the customer spotted a clove of garlic.~~ The customer spotted a clove of garlic floating in the soup.

10. The ~~deliciouser~~ more delicious the dish, the ~~popularer~~ more popular it becomes on the menu.

Punctuation: End Marks and Commas

STUDENT WRITING
Expository Essay

Student Copes with Disability
by Alex Zane
high school student, Pottsville, Pennsylvania

To some students, walking to school, learning to drive, and running laps in gym class are all challenges; but to sophomore Robert Heffner, these "challenges" would be welcome.

Heffner, who attended the Intermediate Unit 29 in Mar Lin before attending Pottsville, has cerebral palsy, which leaves him unable to walk without the assistance of crutches.

This challenge may affect his walking ability, but it doesn't change his attitude, which always seems to be positive.

"With all that he is dealing with, he never complains, and he never tries to go home sick. Meanwhile, other students are always in my office trying to go home. I just think he is such a positive example of what people can overcome," PAHS school nurse Janine Tobash said.

Heffner's upbeat attitude can be seen in how he feels about this school. "PAHS is a very good school. The students and faculty help me sometimes by carrying my books in between classes and by helping me get my lunch," Heffner said.

Also, when the school elevator is running slowly and causing him to be late, his teachers "always understand."

An example of a student who helps Heffner can be found in senior Robert Yarnell, who helps out by getting and carrying Heffner's lunch every day—although Yarnell himself doesn't feel that the act deserves attention.

"Rob is a nice guy. I help him because he is my friend, not because I want to look like some Good Samaritan," Yarnell said.

Faculty member Ms. Lucy Portland noticed the atmosphere Heffner created when she had him in study hall during his freshman year. She noticed that wherever he was, fellow students were always there to give a helping hand, whether it was in class, at school dances, or at sporting events. "Rob has become an active member of the school community. People enjoy helping him because he is so personable. In study hall, students would clear the aisle for him and help him with his books," Portland said.

With an optimistic attitude, Heffner is able to create a cheerful atmosphere wherever he goes by showing students that it's possible to overcome anything.

Alex Zane's expository essay explains the qualities of a remarkable person. He has organized his essay logically, starting out with background information and including quotations from faculty members and friends.

Reread Alex's essay, and notice how he uses punctuation accurately in quotations, clauses, and phrases. In this chapter, you'll practice using commas and end marks accurately in your own writing.

Allow time for students to discuss the student writing. Suggest that they identify its strengths and propose possible improvements. Use the model to introduce the concepts in the chapter.

End Marks and Abbreviations

▐▶ Use a **period** at the end of a statement (declarative sentence). Use either a period or an exclamation mark at the end of a command (imperative sentence).

DECLARATIVE   The Metroliner takes you to the state capital**.**

IMPERATIVE   Take the Metroliner**.** It's coming**!**

▐▶ Use a **question mark** at the end of a direct question (interrogative sentence). An indirect question ends with a period.

DIRECT   Could you tell us which bus stops near the White House**?**

DIRECT   Wanda asked, "Which bus stops near the White House**?**"

INDIRECT   I wonder which bus stops near the White House**.**

▐▶ Use an **exclamation point** at the end of an exclamation (exclamatory sentence).

That's the president**!** He's walking toward us**!**

▐▶ Use a period after many abbreviations.

In general, avoid using abbreviations when you write a paper or report for school or work. Instead, spell out the word(s). The following chart shows the exceptions to this rule.

Periods in Abbreviations			
Initials and Titles	Dr. P. Tano Jr.	Tia F. Lyn, Ph.D.	Ms. E. Jones
Times	A.M. P.M. B.C. A.D.		
Addresses	83 Shadow Ave. P.O. Box 99 32-10 Elm Blvd.		
Others	Inc. Co. Assn. etc. vs.		

▐▶ Some abbreviations should not have a period. One familiar form of abbreviation is the **acronym**, a word formed from the first letter(s) of several words. Acronyms do not use periods.

RADAR   **Ra**dio **D**etecting **A**nd **R**anging

SCUBA   **S**elf-**C**ontained **U**nderwater **B**reathing **A**pparatus

A modern tendency is to omit the period following common abbreviations, such as *ft* (*foot* or *feet*) and *lb* (*pound*). State abbreviations used as postal addresses don't take periods (*NY*, *TX*, *CA*). Some other common abbreviations that don't take periods include *mph* (miles per hour), *AM* or *FM* radio, *TV*, *FBI*, and *IRS*.

P.S. Dictionaries differ in punctuating some abbreviations, including the abbreviations for United States (*US* or *U.S.*). Whichever style you choose, use it consistently throughout your writing.

EDITING TiP

When an abbreviation with a period, such as *etc.*, falls at the end of a sentence, don't use another period.

INCORRECT
We liked Washington, D**.**C**..**

CORRECT
We liked Washington, D**.**C**.**

However, don't omit a comma, question mark, or an exclamation point following an abbreviation.
Did the play begin at 8:00 P**.**M**.?**

WRiTiNG HiNT

Follow the style in a style manual for using periods, commas, and abbreviations in a bibliography.
Martin**,** John**,** and Samantha Schwartz**.** *Writing with the Reader in Mind***.** Englewood Cliffs**,** NJ**:** Prentice Hall**,** 1989**.** Print**.**

EXERCISE 1 Proofreading a Paragraph

Proofread the following paragraphs for problems with end marks and punctuation in abbreviations.

or US

¹By 5 P.M. on October 29, 1929, the stock market had plunged the US into the biggest banking crisis of its history! ²In 1932, Mr. Franklin D. Roosevelt was elected president. ³Roosevelt, or FDR, had a plan called the New Deal to help the nation recover from the Depression. ⁴His plan was to get people working again through ~~govt.~~ *government* programs. ⁵Some of his most successful programs still exist today. ⁶You've heard of the F.D.I.C., haven't you? ⁷That was a plan to protect bank deposits up to $5,000. ⁸Another program that still exists is Social Security. ⁹The ~~SS~~ *Social Security* Act was set up to provide retirement funds and unemployment insurance. ¹⁰If you live in ~~TN.~~ *Tennessee*, you have heard of the TVA, or the Tennessee Valley Authority. ¹¹This agency, which was begun under the New Deal, was designed to increase the productivity in, and prosperity of, the ~~T.N.~~ *Tennessee* Valley.

¹²One of the reasons FD.R was able to begin so many programs was that he hired a dynamic group of advisors. ¹³Among those on his panel were Dr. Raymond Moley, Rexford G. Tugwell, Ph.D., and Dr. Adolph A. Berle, Jr. ¹⁴In addition, Ms. Frances Perkins was appointed as secretary of labor. ¹⁵All contributed to solving the ~~natl.~~ *national* crisis of the Great Depression.

Refer to **Composition,** Lesson 2.4, for tips on writing an expository paragraph.

EXERCISE 2 Writing an Expository Paragraph

On a separate piece of paper, write a paragraph that explains the functions of a club or organization in your school. You may choose to talk about a group that you might join, such as the student council or the marching band, or one that operates as part of the school administration, such as the teachers' union or the guidance center. In your explanation, be sure to identify the leaders and administrators of the group. Use abbreviations correctly, and end all sentences with an appropriate end punctuation mark.

Answers will vary. See teacher pages for assessment rubrics.

C CCSS Language 2. (See pp. T14–T15.)

Lesson 13.2
Mechanics

Commas in a Series

You know what a period means when you're reading: You've come to a complete stop, one that signals the end of a complete idea. A **comma** is trickier because it represents a slight pause within a complete sentence. The next few lessons will help you review the most important rules for commas.

▐▶ Use commas to separate items in a series. A series contains three or more similar items in a row.

> We fished, hiked, and biked in Idaho.
> I want mushrooms, peppers, and sausage on the pizza.

See also Lesson 14.2, which explains when to use semicolons rather than commas in a series.

▐▶ When a coordinating conjunction (such as *and* or *but*) connects a series of items, phrases, or clauses, *don't* add commas. Commas are needed between independent clauses.

> Tony dived for the ball **and** caught it **but** dropped it when he tried to throw it to first base.
> Tony dived for the ball, **and** he caught it.

▐▶ Use a comma to separate two or more adjectives that precede and modify the same noun.

> The **tall, majestic** mountain appeared in the distance.

However, don't use a comma when the last adjective in a series is really part of a compound noun. You can tell if one of the adjectives belongs to the noun if you can't reverse the position of the adjectives.

> My **favorite second** cousin lives in Tulsa, Oklahoma. [*Second cousin* is a compound noun.]

STEP BY STEP

To decide whether to put a comma between two adjectives preceding a noun:

1. Put *and* between them. If *and* makes sense, use a comma.

   They walked to the old, [and] spooky building

2. If *and* doesn't make sense, don't use a comma.

   The fat ~~and~~ mother hen clucked wildly.

EXERCISE 3 Proofreading Sentences

This student writer forgot to use commas in sentences. Insert all necessary commas. If a sentence is already correct, write C after it.

1. It can be called the Midwest the bread basket the Middle West or the heartland.

2. People think of the Midwest as endless amber fields of grain.

3. Others focus on the wild͵destructive storms that rip through the Midwest.

4. East of the Mississippi are endless cornfields. c

5. Enormous͵black clouds gather over the Midwest and bring frequent torrential downpours.

6. Crop destruction can result from a tornado͵a hailstorm͵or a blizzard.

7. Willa Cather͵Carl Sandburg͵and Sinclair Lewis set their poems and stories in the Midwest.

8. The soil͵the climate͵and adequate rainfall create good farming conditions.

9. South Dakota's vast͵endless͵open space is featured in the movie *Badlands*.

10. Does *The Wizard of Oz* take place in Kansas͵Ohio͵or Idaho?

EXERCISE 4 Proofreading a Paragraph

Proofread the following paragraph. Insert commas where they are needed, and correct end punctuation marks. When you are finished, exchange your work with a classmate, and check each other's work for correct punctuation.

¹The last word that is spelled correctly at the Scripps Howard National Spelling Bee determines the winner each year? ²The winning words from 1966͵ 1983͵and 1984 were no more than six letters. ³Those words were *ratoon͵Purim͵* and *luge!* ⁴Have you ever heard of these words? ⁵Some winning words are words for health conditions or bacteria͵such as *narcolepsy͵staphylococci͵* and *eczema.* ⁶Others are familiar words that have tricky spellings͵such as *kamikaze͵ sarcophagus͵*and *croissant.* ⁷How about *chihuahua* and *incisor?* ⁸Even my kid brother can spell those words!

Compound Sentences and Introductory Elements

IIII➤ Use a comma before a coordinating conjunction that joins two independent clauses.

The coordinating conjunctions (*and, but, or, nor, for, so,* and *yet*) join independent clauses to form a **compound sentence**.

> The children wanted to stay at the beach, **but** the sun had set.

IIII➤ Use a comma in compound interrogative or imperative sentences in which the subject either does not appear first or is an implied *you*.

> Finish writing your report now, or the teacher won't accept it.
> What did your parrot say, and how did you train it?

IIII➤ Use a comma after an introductory participle or participial phrase.

> **Alerted,** the firefighters raced to the cineplex.
> **Alerted by 911,** the firefighters raced to the cineplex.

IIII➤ Use a comma after an introductory infinitive or infinitive phrase.

> **To relax,** Claire does needlepoint.
> **To swim the English Channel,** you'll need to train for over a year.

IIII➤ Use a comma after an introductory adverb clause.

> **When you give a speech,** look at your audience.

See also Lesson 13.5 for how to use commas following introductory words such as *yes, no,* and *well.*

IIII➤ Use a comma after an introductory prepositional phrase or a series of introductory prepositional phrases.

> **With regrets,** I turned down Justin's invitation.
> **By four o'clock on Thursday,** I'll be at the beach.

P.S. A comma is not always necessary after a short, introductory prepositional phrase. However, your meaning will be clear if you use a comma after most introductory prepositional phrases, and the comma will be correct in most cases.

Exception: Don't use a comma after an introductory prepositional phrase if it is immediately followed by the verb of the sentence.

>   V   S
> Inside the bag on the bedroom door **is** the **flashlight**.

According to some grammar books, a comma may sometimes be omitted between two short main clauses; however, in this book, grammar rules are kept as simple and as consistent as possible.

EDITING TIP

Don't confuse a compound sentence with a sentence that has a compound subject or a compound verb. You don't need a comma between parts of a compound subject or a compound verb.

COMPOUND VERB
The party started at 7 P.M. and ended by midnight. [no comma]

COMPOUND SENTENCE
Tina will marinate the chicken, and Tony will grill it. [comma]

Exercise C Revising Sentences

Revise each sentence by inserting the words shown in parentheses at the caret mark. Add commas where necessary. Check to see that your sentences are punctuated correctly. See Answer Key at www.grammarforwriting.com.

1. The Chicago Symphony Orchestra ^ was founded in 1891. (which is the third-oldest symphony in the United States)

2. Samuel Barber wrote music for the poems of Pablo Neruda. ^ (the Chilean poet)

3. The cymbals are considered percussion instruments. (not only the drums) ^

4. David Del Tredici ^ wrote many pieces of music based on *The Adventures of Alice in Wonderland*. (who studied music in California and New York)

5. Pablo Casals ^ founded a yearly festival in Puerto Rico. (not only became a master cellist but also)

6. Yo-Yo Ma ^ gave his first recital at six years of age. (the famous cellist)

7. *Rhapsody in Blue* ^ was written by George Gershwin in the 1920s. (the first musical composition to combine jazz with classical music)

8. The classical concert pianist ^ was Vladimir Horowitz. (whom many consider to be the greatest of the twentieth century)

Exercise D Proofreading a Paragraph

The following mess of words is a puzzle for you to figure out. Make it into a paragraph by separating it into sentences on a separate piece of paper. Add commas, periods, and other end punctuation marks. Be sure to begin each sentence with a capital letter. See Answer Key at www.grammarforwriting.com.

How can you demonstrate that light travels faster than sound well do you experience thunder or lightning first most people will say lightning and they're correct you may not know it but thunder and lightning occur at the same time yet light travels faster than sound doesn't it consequently we see the lightning bolt which strikes first before we hear the crash of the thunder to discover how far away lightning is striking you can use a formula first you count the seconds between a lightning strike and the sound of thunder that follows next you divide by three your quotient tells you the approximate distance to the lightning in kilometers

Punctuation: All the Other Marks

Direct students to
www.grammarforwriting.com
for chapter-specific
portfolio projects.

STUDENT WRITING
Narrative Essay

One Teen Can Make a Difference
by Emily Broxterman
high school student, Overland Park, Kansas

I had an amazing surge of energy that morning as I leapt from my bed. It was still dark, and I looked forward to the rising sun. I quickly showered and dressed and anxiously waited for my parents to drive me to City Hall in downtown Topeka.

As I arrived, I saw hordes of students ready to begin the day. When my partners on the executive planning committee saw me, they ran to me screaming, "Today's the day!" I smiled back. "Let's do it!" I said.

We had planned all year for the first annual Smoke-Free Teens Are Rising (STAR) Rally, and it was finally going to happen. It was an idea that grew from wanting to educate other students about the legislative process and the detrimental effects of tobacco use.

A few months before we conceived of the rally concept, I testified before the Kansas legislature on behalf of the Smoke-Free Class of 2000 (SFC2000) in support of a bill that would limit youth access to tobacco. My fellow SFC2000 members and I continued to rally in support of this bill (I even called one of the senators at home!) until the bill was finally signed into law in May 1996. I learned so much from that experience about policy making, legislation, and advocacy. Most important, I learned that with persistence and dedication, I could make a difference. I wanted to share these important lessons with other kids my age.

The STAR Rally program of events lasted all day, beginning with mock Senate hearings and ending with over seven hundred students marching to the capitol, where the governor of Kansas greeted us. He praised our efforts and wished us well.

In retrospect, the first rally was definitely fulfilling. Since that day three years ago, we have held two more rallies and are planning our fourth. I had originally hoped that STAR participants would feel empowered to fight tobacco in their own communities. As my peers come out in droves each year and as the size of the rally continues to grow, I know they are realizing the strength of the message: One teen *can* make a difference.

Emily Broxterman's narrative essay describes events that have made a big impact on her life. Her title and her ending message help explain the significance of the events.

As you reread the essay, notice how Emily has used punctuation around quotations and abbreviations. In this chapter, you'll practice using punctuation accurately in your own writing.

Allow time for students to discuss the student writing. Suggest that they identify its strengths and propose possible improvements. Use the model to introduce the concepts in the chapter.

Colons

A **colon** (:) indicates that a list, a long quotation, or a formal statement will follow.

▶ Use a colon before a list of items, especially after the words *the following* or *the following items*.

> Henry James wrote about Americans living in Europe in the following novels: *The Portrait of a Lady*, *The American*, and *The Ambassadors*.

▶ Use a colon before a formal statement or quotation and before a long quotation that is set off as a block (any quotation of more than three lines).

> A book reviewer pointed out how Henry James's view of the United States is embodied in his characters: "The innocence of a young America is reflected in the almost foolish innocence with which James's American characters make decisions in Europe."

> **EDITING TiP**
>
> Don't use a colon before a list when the list follows a verb, a preposition, or the phrases *such as*, *including*, or *especially*.
> Henry James's novels take
> place in London, Venice, and Rome.
>
> My favorite authors are Mark Twain, F. Scott Fitzgerald, and Ernest Hemingway.

A long quotation of more than three lines is indented and set off as a block. Don't use quotation marks for block quotations.

> In the following passage from *The Europeans*, Robert Acton tries to impress a baroness from Europe:

> > Acton wished her to think highly of American scenery, and he drove her great distances, picking out the prettiest roads and the largest points of view. . . . It seemed to the Baroness very wild, as I have said, and lovely; but the impression added something to the sense of the enlargement of opportunity, which had been born on her arrival to the New World.

▶ Use a colon to emphasize a word or a phrase.

> Some people describe Henry James in one word: snob.
> The James family produced three brilliant writers: Henry (literature), William (psychology and philosophy), and Alice (a journal writer).

▶ Use a colon in the following situations: (1) between the hour and minutes, (2) between the chapter and verse in a reference to the Bible, and (3) after the greeting of a business letter.

> 7:45 P.M.   Genesis 12:1–3   Dear Dr. Demar:

Depending on the style you choose for bibliographical references, you may need to use colons in your Works Cited list. Refer to a model in **Composition** Lesson 4.5.

EXERCISE 1 Adding Colons to Sentences

Insert colons where they are needed in the following sentences. If no colon is needed, write *C* after the sentence.

1. Tyrone liked the following books by Edith Wharton: *The House of Mirth, The Age of Innocence,* and *Ethan Frome.*

2. The first paragraph of *Ethan Frome* begins as follows: "In a sky of iron the points of the Dipper hung like icicles. . . ."

3. Ruby starts reading *Ethan Frome* at exactly 8:30 every evening.

4. Edith Wharton picked the perfect name for the setting of *Ethan Frome*: Starkfield.

5. Ethan Frome, a farmer, finds himself crushed by many forces: the cold, the isolation, and the small-town prejudices.

6. Two women complicate life for Ethan Frome: Mattie and Zeena.

7. *Ethan Frome* was a departure for Edith Wharton; her usual subject was high society. C

8. Edith Wharton owned two stately homes: one in Lenox, Massachusetts, called "The Mount," and another in Newport, Rhode Island.

9. Edith Wharton spent time in the following cities: New York, Paris, and London.

10. Chapter 3 opens with a description of farmwork: "There was some hauling to be done at the lower end of the wood-lot, and Ethan was out early the next day."

EXERCISE 2 Writing a Travel Diary Entry

Imagine that you could visit any region of the United States that interests you, such as New England, the Southwest, the Pacific Northwest, or the Gulf Coast. What would a day be like during this trip? Jot down what you would do during the day, beginning each entry with the time. This is called an *itinerary*. Write in complete sentences. Answers will vary. See teacher pages for assessment rubrics.

EXAMPLE   6:45 A.M. I wake up and have breakfast on the patio, enjoying the view of the sun over the Sandia Mountains.
8:00 I make a list of what I will visit: Tío Pepe's restaurant, Old Town in Albuquerque, Georgia O'Keeffe's adobe house.

Semicolons

Use a **semicolon** (;) for a pause that's longer than one signaled by a comma but shorter than one signaled by a period or colon.

▶ Use a semicolon to join independent clauses in a compound sentence that doesn't have a coordinating conjunction.

> Minneapolis is a city in Minnesota; its twin city is St. Paul.

▶ Use a semicolon between independent clauses joined by a coordinating conjunction if either clause contains commas.

> We'll visit Chicago; **but** first we'll stop in Gary, Indiana.

▶ Use a semicolon before a conjunctive adverb or a transitional expression that joins independent clauses. A comma follows the conjunctive adverb or transitional expression.

> Kansas City is located on the Kansas border; **however,** a portion of the city lies on the Missouri border.
> I need to get to Kansas City; **that is,** I need to get to Kansas City, Missouri.

▶ Use a semicolon to separate items in a series when one or more of the items contains a comma.

> Tina lives in Ovid, New York; Wanda lives in Rome, New York; and Tony lives in Ithaca, New York.

Some Common Conjunctive Adverbs

accordingly	meanwhile
also	moreover
besides	nevertheless
consequently	otherwise
furthermore	still
however	then
indeed	therefore

Some Common Transitional Expressions

as a result	in addition
for example	in fact
for instance	that is
from that point on	
in other words	
on the other hand	

EDITING TIP

Do not use a semicolon between an independent clause and a dependent clause or phrase.
I saw the Statue of Liberty, which is in New York Harbor.

EXERCISE 3 Using Semicolons and Colons

Some of the following sentences need a semicolon; others require a colon. Review the rules for colons in Lesson 14.1, and then add or correct punctuation marks in the sentences below. If a sentence is correct, write *C* after it.

1. Ada's ancestors immigrated from Kiev, Ukraine; Bari, Italy; and Warsaw, Poland.

2. Ellis Island processed immigrants landing in New York; that is, it processed them until 1954, when it closed.

3. Ellis Island was part of New York; now most of it belongs to New Jersey.

4. Respond to this statement: Ellis Island should belong to New York, not to New Jersey.

7. Ramón believes that the Spanish word <u>qué</u> means "what."

8. Freddie watched the TV show "Hike Pike's Peak" from the series called <u>Peak Experiences</u>.

9. The operator asked Tim, "Did you say your name began with a <u>D</u> or a <u>T?</u>"

10. Kate Riley, the author of the novel <u>Cold Water Flat</u>, admitted to the audience, "I write from my own experience."

EXERCISE C Adding Punctuation to Dialogue

Read the following dialogue. On a separate piece of paper, insert quotation marks, other punctuation marks, and new paragraphs where they are needed. You may want to review Lesson 14.5. See Answer Key at www.grammarforwriting.com.

¹Watch out for the spiders webs, Vladimir warned, this place is full of them. ²Lucy slowly turned the doorknob of the old fishing cabin, opened the creaky door, and exclaimed Wow! ³No ones been here for ages. ⁴Vladimir asked, Have you ever seen such old stuff before? ⁵No, never Lucy answered. ⁶She walked over to the bookshelves and looked at the dusty books on the shelves and said Theyre ancient. ⁷Vladimir opened one cracked, leather-bound book to page thirty three, where he found a handwritten note. ⁸He turned to Lucy and blurted out. ⁹This note says: the Vlonsky family that's my mothers maiden name came to this fishing cabin with their neighbors, the Nicholas family in 1965. ¹⁰Vladimir wondered aloud, Could it be that no one has been here since then?¹¹I can't believe it Lucy gasped. ¹²Then Vladimir said, my parents and grandparents often told me about this place. ¹³When Lucy picked up another book To The Memory of Childhood by Lydia Chukavskaya she found another handwritten note. ¹⁴She read aloud We, the Vlonsky family, have enjoyed our first American holiday in this cabin: Memorial Day May 30, 1965.

Capitalization

Direct students to
www.grammarforwriting.com
for chapter-specific
portfolio projects.

STUDENT WRITING
Narrative Essay

In the Corps Now:
Why I Am Set to Become a Marine
by Matisa Childs
high school student, Coral Gables, Florida

"Attention, forward march!" the sergeant yelled.

As I marched with other future recruits toward the South Dade Marine Recruiting Station, my heart ached with fear and confusion. I knew one thing: My mind was set on becoming a Marine.

After being scatterbrained throughout the past years of high school, the time came to figure out what I was going to do after graduation. I thought about college, but I did not know what to study. Then I began to joke about the military and finally decided to approach the recruiters on campus with an open mind. I figured it would not hurt. After learning of the benefits and career choices the military had to offer, I wanted in.

Being enlisted in the Delayed Entry Program (DEP) of the U.S. Marine Corps is a challenge. If I were going into the military, I wanted to be one of the best, so I chose the Marine Corps to earn respect and to gain pride.

After the first "poolee" meeting (a poolee is what the Marines call "to be" recruits), I realized this was not going to be an easy task. Poolee meetings are held at least once a month at Tropical Park; all-female poolee meetings are held every quarter at South Florida's main Marine recruiting station in Fort Lauderdale.

"Meetings" require poolees to get up at 5:30 a.m. on a meeting day and run, do crunches, pull-ups (flex hang for ladies), push-ups, and side-straddle hops (jumping jacks). Having been sore after this somewhat painful ordeal, we all seem to enjoy the chanting as we jog back to the recruiting station: "Hey Army, pick up your jets and follow me, we are Marine Corps proud to be; hey Navy, pick up your ships and follow me, we are Marine Corps proud to be; hey Air Force, pick up your jets. . . ."

Often, I ask myself why I want to be one of the few. The Marine Corps puts my mental and physical ability to the test to create discipline and a sort of humbleness. Because of this, my mind is set on becoming a Marine.

Matisa Childs's personal narrative explains why she has chosen to join the Marine Corps after high school. She gives background information and then tells about her experience in the preliminary training meetings.

As you reread the essay, notice how capital letters are used in words such as Marine Corps and Air Force. You'll review the rules for capital letters in the lessons and exercises in this chapter.

Allow time for students to discuss the student writing. Suggest that they identify its strengths and propose possible improvements. Use the model to introduce the concepts in the chapter.

Proper Nouns and Proper Adjectives

You've already learned (Lesson 5.1) that a **proper noun** names a particular person, place, thing, or idea. A **proper adjective** (Lesson 5.4) is the adjective form of a proper noun. Both proper nouns and proper adjectives are capitalized.

▶ Capitalize the names of people.
  Jack Johnson   Susan B. Anthony
  Frederick Douglass   Albert Einstein

▶ Capitalize geographic names.

PLANETS, CONSTELLATIONS	Earth Neptune Big Dipper
	Andromeda galaxy Milky Way
CONTINENTS	South America Europe Antarctica
ISLANDS	Windley Key Guam Manhattan
COUNTRIES	Vietnam South Korea Albania
STATES	Alabama New Mexico Oregon Idaho
CITIES, TOWNS	Houston Santa Fe Orlando Kansas City
BODIES OF WATER	Pacific Ocean Gulf of Mexico Lake Champlain
LOCALITIES, REGIONS	Black Hills Southwest the Everglades New England
	Rio Grande Valley the Pacific Northwest
STREETS, HIGHWAYS	Canal Street Route 66 Pacific Highway
BUILDINGS	Willis Tower Empire State Building the Eiffel Tower
PARKS, MONUMENTS	Yellowstone National Park Eleanor Roosevelt Memorial

Note: In the examples above, articles (*the*) and short prepositions (*of*) that are part of the name are *not* capitalized.

▶ In street names or any other place where numbers are spelled out, lowercase the second number of a hyphenated number.
  Eighty-fifth Street   Forty-second Stop Café

▶ Regions named after directions are capitalized, but compass directions are *not* capitalized.
  the deserts of the Southwest   northeast of Chicago

▶ Common nouns that refer to two or more proper nouns are *not* capitalized.
  Mississippi and Missouri rivers   Main and Grand streets

▶ Capitalize proper adjectives formed from proper nouns.
  Persian rug   Italian restaurant   Shakespearean sonnet

WRITING HINT

Foreign last names that consist of more than one word often follow the capitalization rules of the foreign language. Check a biographical dictionary or other reference book for accuracy.

Cecil B. DeMille

Robert De Niro

Ludwig van Beethoven

Leonardo da Vinci

Charles de Gaulle

Walter de la Mare

WRITING HINT

Sometimes, the dictionary gives two possibilities regarding capitalization. For example, both *brussels sprouts* and *Brussels sprouts* are correct. In cases like this, pick one and be consistent in your writing.

EXERCISE 1 Proofreading Sentences

Insert capital letters where they belong in the following sentences. To indicate a capital letter, use the proofreading symbol of three underscores beneath the letter: (t).

EXAMPLE   You'll find the bakery on the southwest corner of thirty-ninth street.

1. Christopher columbus crossed the atlantic ocean from spain to the americas.

2. leif ericson from norway and possibly voyagers from ireland successfully sailed to north america before columbus did.

3. Ancient people may have crossed the bering strait from asia to america on a land bridge that once connected siberia and alaska.

4. The southwest and west have many cities that once were missions, such as santa fe, san francisco, and san diego.

5. north america has geological features like no other place on earth.

6. settlers along the mississippi and columbia rivers lived with the threat of floods.

7. Immigrants traveling to the united states might have seen the statue of liberty on liberty island in new york harbor.

EXERCISE 2 Writing Sentences

Working with a partner, write ten sentences based on information given on the chart. Pick a statistic from the chart, and describe, explain, compare, or contrast it.
Students' sentences will vary.

Superlative U.S. Statistics		
Largest state	Alaska	591,004 sq. mi.
Smallest state	Rhode Island	1,212 sq. mi.
Largest county (excludes Alaska)	San Bernardino County, California	20,064 sq. mi.
Smallest county	Arlington County, Virginia	26 sq. mi.
Highest settlement	Climax, Colorado	11,560 ft.
Lowest settlement	Calipatria, California	-185 ft.
Longest river	Mississippi-Missouri	3,710 mi.
Highest mountain	Mount McKinley, Alaska	20,320 ft.
Lowest point	Death Valley, California	-282 ft.
Deepest lake	Crater Lake, Oregon	1,932 ft.
Rainiest spot	Mt. Waialeale, Hawaii Annual aver. rainfall 460 inches	
Tallest building	Willis Tower, Chicago, Illinois	1,454 ft.
Largest building	Boeing 747 Manufacturing Plant, Everett, Washington 205,600,000 cu. ft.; covers 47 acres	
Tallest structure	TV tower, Blanchard, North Dakota	2,063 ft.

Source: U.S. Geological Survey, U.S. Bureau of the Census

Titles

▐▶ Capitalize titles and abbreviations of titles when they are used before names. Also capitalize abbreviations of academic degrees after a name.

President Franklin D. Roosevelt
Justice Thurgood Marshall   Mayor Fiorello La Guardia
Edward Euing, M.D., a family-practice doctor

▐▶ Capitalize a word that shows a family relationship only when that word is used before a name but without a possessive pronoun.

Grandma Moses   Uncle Remus   my grandmother Alice   her grandfather

▐▶ Capitalize the first and last word and all important words in the titles of works.

Note: Unless they are the first word in a title, do not capitalize the following small words: articles (*a, an, the*), coordinating conjunctions, and prepositions with fewer than five letters.

BOOKS	*The Call of the Wild* *Of Mice and Men*
PERIODICALS	*The Brooklyn Eagle* *Atlantic Monthly*
STORIES, ESSAYS	"The Comforts of Home"
	"The Narrow Bridge of Art"
POEMS	"Mending Wall" "Song for the Rainy Season"
PLAYS	*The Importance of Being Earnest*
	The Glass Menagerie
TV SERIES	*All in the Family* *The Honeymooners*
WORKS OF ART	*Whistler's Mother* *American Gothic*
MUSICAL WORKS	"Bridge over Troubled Water" "Rock Around the Clock"
MOVIES	*Full Metal Jacket* *The Last Picture Show*
	Gone with the Wind

> **WRITING HINT**
>
> When you're not sure which words to capitalize or italicize in a title, check a dictionary, style manual, or handbook.
>
> *around the world in eighty days*

EXERCISE 3 Proofreading a Paragraph

Insert capital letters where they belong in the following paragraph. To indicate a capital letter, use the proofreading symbol of three underscores beneath the letter: (s̲).

¹Camille's assignment was to write an article about recycling for her school newspaper, *the midtown monitor*. ²She browsed through the *reader's*

guide to periodical literature and found an article entitled "collecting cans: house to house, block by block" from an issue of _the good news about garbage_. ³She also looked in the _new york times index_. ⁴On her way to the reference desk, she saw a copy of _a tale of two cities_. ⁵Her thoughts drifted to paris, france, where dickens's great novel takes place. ⁶She had enjoyed watching the Public Broadcasting Service (PBS) film version of the novel. ⁷Eventually, Camille snapped out of her daydream of faraway places when she heard a student reciting a poem called "wake up the day." ⁸Camille remembered her recycling report and, like reporters on _60 minutes_, she got to work.

Exercise 4 Writing About Research

On a separate piece of paper, write a few paragraphs about how you researched a subject for a report. You can base your paragraph on a real-life experience, or you can make up a story about doing research. Include titles of various works that you came across or thought about during your research experience. When you've finished writing, proofread your paragraph carefully to make sure you've used capital letters correctly. Students' paragraphs will vary. Refer to the writing rubrics in the teacher pages for help with assessment.

Exercise 5 Create Your Own Exercise

Work with a partner or small group. On a separate piece of paper, write ten sentences. In each sentence, include a title of a work or person's name with a title. (This paper will be your answer key.) You may choose books, magazine articles, stories, poems, plays, television series, works of art, musical works, or movies. Don't forget to include the titles of people (senators, kings, queens, doctors, coaches, etc.). You may also include geographic locations (such as Times Square) in your sentences. Try to vary your sentences by using a different kind of title in each sentence.

Rewrite your sentences on another piece of paper, this time without capital letters. Exchange papers with other student pairs or groups, and insert capital letters, where needed, by using the proofreading symbol of three underscores beneath the lowercase letter: (x). Students' sentences will vary.

First Words, Organizations, Religions, School Subjects

||||➤ Capitalize the first word in every sentence. Capitalize the first word in a direct quotation when the quotation either was originally a complete sentence or, as quoted, makes a complete sentence.

Do *not* capitalize the first word in an indirect quotation.

DIRECT QUOTATION   Waldo said, "This Web site contains Wallace Stevens's poem 'The Emperor of Ice-Cream.'"

INDIRECT QUOTATION   Waldo added that the site also contains biographical facts about Wallace Stevens.

If a quoted sentence is interrupted, begin the second part with a lowercase letter unless that second part is a complete sentence.

"I'm surprised," said Waldo, "that the poet Wallace Stevens was an insurance salesman."

Note: When you're quoting lines from literature, follow the writer's style. Some modern writers of fiction and poetry, such as E. E. Cummings or bell hooks, an African American poet, don't follow the usual rules for using capital letters.
Point out that bell hooks (intentionally lowercase) is the pseudonym of Gloria Jean Watkins.

||||➤ Capitalize the names of languages, nationalities, peoples, races, and religions.

In India, many languages are spoken, including Hindi and English.
The Baha'i faith is of Iranian origin and emphasizes spiritual unity.

||||➤ Capitalize the names of groups, teams, businesses, institutions, and organizations.

Amnesty International   Los Angeles Lakers   General Motors
Cornell University   The Red Cross   The Audubon Society
The Colorado School of Mines

||||➤ Capitalize the names of government agencies, groups (including the military), and organizations.

Environmental Protection Agency   Social Security Administration
The National Trust for Historic Preservation
U.S. District Court for Western Texas

||||➤ Capitalize the names of school subjects that are followed by a number.
Noah is taking Trigonometry 2, creative writing, United States history, and woodworking.

EDITING TiP

Capitalize the first word of a complete sentence in parentheses if the sentence stands alone. If a parenthetical sentence is part of another sentence, lowercase the first word.

Answer the questions. (Use a number two pencil only.)

Answer the questions in pencil (use a number two pencil only), and erase unwanted pencil marks thoroughly.

Some style books capitalize the terms *black* and *white* when referring to people's race; some do not. Whichever style students use, have them use it consistently.

Enriching Your Vocabulary

The verb *aspire*, as used in Exercise 6, means "to be ambitious; to yearn or seek." Derived from two Latin words—*ad*, meaning "to," and *spirare*, meaning "to breathe"—*aspire* has a connotation of reaching toward a lofty or grand goal.

EXERCISE 6 Proofreading Sentences

Insert capital letters where they belong in the following sentences. To indicate a capital letter, use the proofreading symbol of three underscores beneath the letter: (m̲).

1. Rory bragged, "it's easy to remember the famous first line of *moby-dick*: 'call me ishmael.'"

2. in israel, many jews and muslims speak hebrew, arabic, and/or english.

3. in some american cities, there are asian, african american, and hispanic cultural centers.

4. The new york stock exchange is in the financial district of new york city.

5. the united nations and the united states congress occasionally disagree.

6. new prescription drugs are tested by the food and drug administration (FDA).

7. aspiring doctors take chemistry 1 and 2, biology, and latin.

8. willa cather, author of *o pioneers!*, was a graduate of the university of nebraska.

EXERCISE 7 Create Your Own Exercise

Working with a partner, write one or more complete sentences in response to each numbered item. Students' sentences will vary.

1. Write about a school subject you would like to study.

2. Identify a favorite movie, and explain why you like it.

3. Share an expression or word from another language. Identify the language, and explain what the word or expression means.

4. Name a performing group you like and a song, dance, or play that it has performed or recorded.

5. Reproduce a direct quotation that someone you know said recently.

6. Take the same quotation you wrote in item 5, and turn it into an indirect quotation.

7. Choose a local organization, group, or agency in your town or neighborhood, and explain its purpose.

8. Write down a dialogue you had recently with a teacher, parent, or friend. Each character should speak at least three times.

I and *O*; Historical Events, Documents, and Periods; Calendar Items; Brand Names; Awards

⟫ Capitalize the words *I* and *O*.

The first-person pronoun *I* is always capitalized. The poetic interjection *O* is rarely used today. Instead, we use the modern interjection *oh*, which isn't capitalized unless it's the first word in a sentence.

> "O cursed ambition, thou devouring bird."—William Havard
> Oh, isn't it a beautiful morning.

⟫ Capitalize the names of historical events, documents, and periods.

> The Seneca Falls Declaration of Sentiments was first drafted at the 1848 Women's Rights Convention.
> Furniture from the Victorian Era is characterized by flowery carving and patterned upholstery.

⟫ Capitalize calendar items but not seasons.

| CALENDAR ITEMS | Passover | Presidents' Day | Monday, October 19 |
| SEASONS | | spring break | summer solstice | autumn leaves |

When you refer to a century, however, do not use capital letters.

> Coco Chanel changed the course of twentieth-century fashion.

⟫ Capitalize brand names for manufactured products.

> Toyota Camry   Kleenex   Xerox   Word for Windows

But do not capitalize the common noun that follows a brand name.

> Take a Kleenex tissue.   Use some Dial soap.

⟫ Capitalize names of awards.

> *Schindler's List* by the **prolific** Steven Spielberg won an Academy Award.

EXERCISE 8 Proofreading a Paragraph

Insert capital letters where they belong in the following sentences. To indicate a capital letter, use the proofreading symbol of three underscores beneath the letter: (p̲).

¹On december 10, people celebrate the anniversary of the death of

alfred nobel, the twentieth-century swedish chemist and inventor. ²The

nobel prize is awarded to individuals for their outstanding contributions

---

WRITING HINT

Some writers use capital letters for emphasis. Using all capital letters represents urgency.

The officer shouted, "STOP!"

WHY HAVEN'T YOU RETURNED MY MESSAGE?

Enriching Your Vocabulary

The adjective *prolific* means "fruitful or turning out many products of the mind." Artists such as writers, composers, painters, and choreographers, are called *prolific* if they produce many works of art.

in chemistry, physics, medicine, and literature. ³In 1968, a nobel prize for economics was added. ⁴Sometimes, an organization wins the prize; the nansen international office for refugees won the 1938 nobel peace prize for its efforts before the outbreak of world war II in europe. ⁵Writers in various languages have won the literature prize: octavio paz from mexico, who writes in spanish; wole soyinka from nigeria, who writes in english; and w. b. yeats from ireland, who also writes in english. ⁶The 1978 winner in literature was joseph brodsky. ⁷Brodsky was born in st. petersburg, russia, and immigrated to the united states in 1972. ⁸His poems were written in russian; then they were translated into english. ⁹The american academy and institute of arts and letters elected Brodsky as a member the year after he won the nobel prize.

Exercise 9 Proofreading a Dialogue

With a partner, make corrections in the use of capital letters in the dialogue below. Use the proofreading symbols of a slash to indicate a lowercase letter and three underscores to indicate a capital letter.

Spring = lowercase letter   friday = capital letter

1. marcy said, "i need one hundred copies of this poem by shakespeare."

2. "i can do that," martin kidded her, "As easy as Apple Pie."

3. "If you could," marcy smiled, "i would be as excited as a kid on the fourth of july."

4. Martin said, "i'll do it if the xerox machine is working."

5. Sipping her dr. pepper, Marcy replied, "i don't really need one hundred, but i could use at least ten for the potsdam poetry club meeting on tuesday."

6. Martin asked, "do you want me to copy the love poem with the line, 'How can it? o how can Love's eye be true?'"

7. "This is the line i like," marcy said, reading aloud. "'but, o my sweet, what labor is't to leave.'"

8. "what a beautiful line!" martin exclaimed. "everyone likes shakespeare."

Editing and Proofreading Worksheet 1

Edit the draft for errors in spelling, capitalization, punctuation, and usage. Write your edited version on a separate piece of paper. Compare your changes with those of a writing partner.

Students' answers will vary. Sample answers are given.

[1]the american poet wallace stevens (1879–1955) was born in reading, pennsylvania. [2]he went to college at harvard university on the banks of the charles river in cambridge, massachusetts. [3]after college, stevens studied law at new york law school. [4]After law school, he lived in new york city and was a reporter with the *new york herald tribune*. [5]beginning in 1916, he worked for the hartford accident and indemnity company and lived in hartford, connecticut. [6]in 1934, he was promoted to vice president of the company. [7]throughout his business career, he wrote poems. [8]when his volume *collected poems* came out in 1954, [9]he won the pulitzer prize for poetry. [10]The rich and successful businessman was now an esteemed american poet.

[11]in his poems, stevens attempts to create order out of chaos. [12]Read, for example, his poem "the idea of order in key west." [13]His search for solid ground is evident in his last volume of poetry, *the rock*. [14]wallace stevens also enjoyed a playful use of french, as in a poem title "le monocle de mon oncle." [15]Although stevens had a victorian upbringing, he was a modernist in his writing. [16]he had limited relationships with the most influential poets of his day, such as t. s. eliot and ezra pound.

[17]many students have read his poem "the emperor of ice-cream." [18]which appears in anthologies of american literature. [19](of course, stevens is not talking about breyers or edy's ice cream.) [20]today, many working poets and readers of poetry look to stevens for his wit, clear thinking, and philosophical approach to the world through his lyrical and very american poems. [21]In his own words, Stevens said, "poetry means not the language of poetry but the thing itself, wherever it may be found."

CCSS Language 1, 2. (See pp. T14–T15.)

Editing and Proofreading Worksheet 2

Edit the draft for errors in spelling, capitalization, punctuation, and usage. Write your edited version on a separate piece of paper. Compare your changes with those of a writing partner.

Students' answers will vary. Sample answers are given.

¹our story begins in the first half of the twentieth century, around 1920.

²many immigrants are arriving daily in the united states. ³they come from all over the world: europe, asia, and the caribbean. ⁴the family we will focus on comes from ukraine, which was then a part of russia. ⁵the popov family leaves russia to escape the terror that followed the 1917 russian revolution.

⁶when the family arrives in the united states, they travel across the country and settle in san francisco, california. ⁷the father, ivan, goes from door to door. selling
⁸He sells pots and pans. ⁹he struggles for many years ~~he is~~ finally ~~able to open~~ opens his own store. ¹⁰only then does he begin to feel at home in the united states.

¹¹the coming of the great depression causes trouble. ¹²Ivan holds onto his business. ¹³by earning extra income. ¹⁴~~He sells~~ selling brown cow milk products from door to door. ¹⁵his sons, dimitri and alexi, sell newspapers on street corners. ¹⁶to raise money for the family, too. ¹⁷by the early 1940s, success and security ~~arrives~~ arrive at the popov house. ¹⁸when Ivan invents an oven he calls the magic bake. ¹⁹the store can't sell enough of these amazing machines. ²⁰dimitri and alexi enlist in the u.s. army just as the United States enters world war II at the end of 1941.

²¹as always, the popovs ~~survives,~~ survive. Alexi comes home with a new wife, the former maria von klemp. ²²~~that~~ he met her in austria where he was a reporter for the army newspaper *stars and stripes*. ²³upon his dismissal from active duty in france, dimitri travels to ukraine. ²⁴he can ~~spoke~~ speak russian, and he wants to see where his parents came from. ²⁵He realizes during his visit how different his life would have been if his parents had not come to live in america.

Chapter Review

EXERCISE A Proofreading Sentences

Insert capital letters where they belong in the following sentences. To indicate a capital letter, use the proofreading symbol of three underscores beneath the letter: (w).

1. the oglala sioux lived in the black hills of south dakota.

2. the bronx and harlem rivers are now used for recreation.

3. the empire state building was once the tallest building on earth.

4. Will the senator from iowa become the president of the united states?

5. mrs. de la cruz owned an apartment on west end avenue.

6. we saw senator inouye interviewed on the television show *meet the press*.

7. "carried away" is my favorite story by the canadian writer alice munro.

8. My dog, fido, looked up and saw the ad for alpo dog food.

9. I called the environmental protection agency (EPA) about a gas leak.

10. we celebrated winter solstice in december by lighting candles in the snow.

EXERCISE B Writing Sentences

On a separate piece of paper, write a complete sentence as a response for each item. Use capital letters correctly. Students' sentences will vary.

1. Identify a town, city, state, region, or foreign country where a friend or relative lives.

2. What are the names of two streets near your home?

3. In what other state would you like your pen pal to live?

4. How would you describe two natural features of your environment in a letter to the pen pal?

5. Write a quotation based on something the pen pal from item 3 might write in a letter to you.

6. Now write the quotation from item 5 as an indirect quotation.

7. Write a sentence about a senator from your state, using the senator's exact name and title.

8. Write about an article in a newspaper that focuses on an organization or government agency, using the titles of both the article and the newspaper.

9. What club or organization would you like to volunteer for and why?

10. What company would you like to work for and why?

EXERCISE C Proofreading a Paragraph

Insert capital letters where they belong in the following sentences. To indicate a capital letter, use the proofreading symbol of three underscores beneath the letter: (d).

[1]During the first year of world war I, one of the most adventurous twentieth-century anthropologists and explorers was born—thor heyerdahl. [2]He grew up in norway, the northernmost scandinavian country, which borders the atlantic and arctic oceans. [3]He became famous after his 1947 trip across the pacific ocean from peru to the tuamotu islands of polynesia. [4]Along with five companions, he sailed on a primitive raft to prove his theory that the first polynesians were actually from south america. [5]The name of the raft, *kon tiki*, became the name of his famous book about this journey. [6]In 1970, heyerdahl set out to prove another theory about the way people migrate. [7]He believed that ancient people from the mediterranean could have sailed to the americas in reed boats. [8]He created a boat made from papyrus and sailed from morocco, which is located on the northwest coast of africa, to barbados, an island in the caribbean sea. [9]This journey became the subject for another book. [10]That book, entitled *ra expeditions*, was translated from his native Norwegian into english, and it was published in 1971.

EXERCISE D Writing a Paragraph

On a separate piece of paper, write a paragraph about an imaginary hot-air balloon trip you would make in the summer with two or three companions. In a paragraph or two, describe how you would travel and what route you would take. Include the sights you would hope to see on your trip, and, depending on where you live, name the geographical features and any landmarks or buildings you might see.
Students' paragraphs will vary. See teacher pages for assessment rubrics.

Spelling

Direct students to
www.grammarforwriting.com
for chapter-specific
portfolio projects.

STUDENT WRITING
Research Paper

Julia Morgan: Blueprint for Social Change
by Pia Lindstrom Luedtke
high school student, Pasadena, California

In the latter half of the nineteenth century, a fresh wave of pioneers and dreamers came to California on the newly built railroads. These people continued the state's tradition of exploration, discovery, and social innovation and brought with them distinctive ideas that rapidly redefined frontier California. This massive population influx was reflected in an increasingly urban state. . . .

In the midst of this transformation, two reform movements became prominent by the turn of the century. The first, the women's suffrage and rights movement, peaked between 1900 and 1920 and caused many women to question their traditional roles as wives and mothers. However, they often faced hostility when they strove for professional recognition and equality in a male-dominated world. The second, the Beaux-Arts movement, put the focus of architecture back on the individual. This was particularly significant because, during this time of expansion, architecture played an important role in the creation of the state's regional identity. Though seemingly different, both movements shared a belief in the freedom of personal expression.

Julia Morgan (1872–1957), an integral yet apolitical figure in both movements, had been the first of her gender to be accepted into the École des Beaux-Arts architecture school in Paris in 1898 and was California's first woman to receive a state architect's license. She was, in essence, a reflection of California's changing times. Though Morgan has been overlooked in the past, her determined and courageous response to the resistance to her entrance into a male-dominated profession made her one of the twentieth century's most significant California pioneers.

Reprinted by permission of *The Concord Review.*

The paragraphs above are the introduction to a research paper. Pia Lindstrom Luedtke builds her topic by supplying background information on the two movements that are relevant to her topic.

Can you find any misspelled words in Pia's essay? Look again. The essay is effective partly because it is error-free. In this chapter, you'll cover the rules and be given advice that will help you spell words correctly whenever you write.

Allow time for students to discuss the student writing. Suggest that they identify its strengths and propose possible improvements. Use the model to introduce the concepts in the chapter.

Using a Dictionary

If you have ever talked to a professional writer or journalist, you learned that such people use print and digital dictionaries on a daily basis. No matter how much you write or read, the dictionary will always be your most trusted guide to spelling. Remember that spelling counts—and not just in school. In the work world, correct spelling is essential. When you write cover letters to prospective employers, always check your spelling. On the job, make it a lifelong habit. You want your writing to be a positive, not a pejorative, reflection of who you are.

▶ If you're in doubt about how to spell a word, use a dictionary.

Besides showing each entry word's definition and etymology (word history), a dictionary offers many kinds of spelling help.

Entry word with syllable breaks
Pronunciation
Past tense with alternate past; and past participle with alternate

in·doc·tri·nate \in-'däk-trə -,nāt\ *vt* **-nat·ed;**
-nat·ing [prob. fr. ME *endoctrinen*, fr. AF *endoctriner*,
fr. *en-* + *doctrine* doctrine] (1626) **1 :** to instruct
esp. in fundamentals or rudiments : TEACH **2 :** to
imbue with a usu. partisan or sectarian opinion,
point of view, or principle — **in·doc·tri·na·tion**
\(,)in-,däk-trə -'nā-shən\ *n* — **in·doc·tri·na·tor**
\in-'dak-trə -,nā-tər\ *n*

Related words

Part of speech

strive \'strīv\ *vi* **strove** \'strōv\ *also* **strived** \'strīvd\;
striv·en \'stri-vən\ *or* **strived;** **striv·ing** \'stri-viŋ\
[ME, to quarrel, contend, fight, endeavor, fr. AF *estriver*
to quarrel, fr. *estri, estrif* strife—more at STRIFE] (13c) **1 :**
to devote serious effort or energy: ENDEAVOR <~to finish
a project> **2 :** to struggle in opposition : CONTEND
syn see ATTEMPT—**striv-er** \'stri-vər\ *n*

—from *Merriam-Webster's Collegiate Dictionary*, Eleventh Edition

P.S. People often ask, "If I can't spell a word, how can I find it in the dictionary?" It's not as hard as you think. Try sounding out the word and looking it up according to the sounds of each syllable. If you don't find it at first, try imagining what other letter or combinations of letters form the sound(s) of the word, and scan up and down the dictionary page. As a last resort, ask someone else for help.

CCSS

Standards for this lesson focus on applying the conventions of standard English, including spelling correctly.

Enriching Your Vocabulary

The adjective *pejorative* means "having a disparaging effect or force." This word casts a negative feeling over whatever it's applied to. My brother used the *pejorative* phrase "What a clown!" to refer to his opponent.

EDITING TIP

1. When you come across a new or unfamiliar word, check its meaning, spelling, and pronunciation.

2. If a word looks similar to another word, write down both words with their meanings.

3. When you're learning to spell a new word, learn it syllable by syllable or by word parts.

4. Add the words you misspell to your proofreading log, and use that log as a quick reference. Underline the letter or letters that cause you trouble.

EXERCISE 1 Using a Dictionary to Check Spelling

Work with a partner to write the letter of the correct spelling in the blank. If you're not sure of the correct spelling of a word, take turns looking up the word in a dictionary to check the correct spelling.

_b_ 1. (a) portible   (b) portable   (c) portibel   (d) portabel

_b_ 2. (a) resonably   (b) reasonably   (c) reasonabley   (d) reasonibly

_a_ 3. (a) murmur   (b) mermur   (c) murmer   (d) mermer

_a_ 4. (a) circumference   (b) curcumfrence
      (c) cercumference   (d) circumfrance

_c_ 5. (a) piculiar   (b) paculiar   (c) peculiar   (d) peculier

_a_ 6. (a) minimum   (b) minamum   (c) minemum   (d) minimem

_b or c_ 7. (a) jugement   (b) judgment   (c) judgement   (d) judgemint

_b_ 8. (a) recomendation   (b) recommendation
      (c) reccomendation   (d) reccommendation

_c_ 9. (a) sycology   (b) psycheology   (c) psychology   (d) physcoligy

_d_ 10. (a) temprament   (b) tempurment   (c) tempurament   (d) temperament

EXERCISE 2 Using a Dictionary

Answer the following questions. If you're not sure about how to spell your answer, look up the word in a college dictionary.

1. What is the plural of *thesis*? _theses_

2. Assume that you have to break the word *permeable* with a hyphen at the end of a line. Show all the points where you could place a hyphen. _per-me-a-ble_

3. How do you spell the plural of the noun *millennium*? _millennia or millenniums_

4. How do you spell the middle day in a school week? _Wednesday_

5. How do you spell the past tense and past participle of the verb *sink*? _past: sank or sunk; past participle: sunk_

6. When a word has alternate spellings, the one listed first in a dictionary is preferred. Underline the preferred spellings.

   a. <u>jujitsu</u> or jujutsu

   b. cargos or <u>cargoes</u>

   c. <u>dialogue</u> or dialog

   d. theatre or <u>theater</u>

   e. marvellous or <u>marvelous</u>

   f. <u>appendixes</u> or appendices

Spelling Rules

As you know, irregular spellings are not uncommon in English. But by learning a few simple rules, you'll always have guidelines to follow. Although these rules may have exceptions, with practice the exceptions will become second nature.

▐▐▐▶ Write *i* before *e* except after *c*.

Note that most of these words have a long *e* sound.

I BEFORE E	achieve	believe	chief	niece	piece
AFTER C	ceiling	conceit	deceive	receive	receipt
EXCEPTIONS	either	neither	leisure	seize	weird

▐▐▐▶ Write *ei* when these letters are not pronounced with a long *e*, especially when the sound is a long *a*, as in *neighbor* and *weigh*.

	height	their	foreign	forfeit	surfeit
SOUNDS LIKE AY	eight	freight	neighbor	reign	
	sleigh	veil	weigh		

▐▐▐▶ For words of more than one syllable that end with the sound /sēd/, only one word is spelled with *-sede*. Three words end in *-ceed*. All other /sēd/ words end in *-cede*.

-SEDE	supersede				
-CEED	exceed	proceed	succeed		
-CEDE	concede	intercede	precede	recede	secede

▐▐▐▶ Spell out the words for numbers between one and one hundred when writing sentences. Numbers that are compound words between twenty-one and ninety-nine are hyphenated.

> She watched Hitchcock's *The Thirty-Nine Steps* on Channel **fifty-seven**.
> Middle-aged people like to joke that **fifty** is the new **forty**.

Note: Always spell out a number that begins a sentence.
> **One hundred** schools volunteered in the clothing drive.

When a sentence begins with a large number, reword the sentence to avoid spelling out the number.

> *A total of 467*
> ~~Four hundred sixty-seven~~ students donated money to Doctors Without Borders.
> *It was in 2012*
> ~~Two thousand twelve was the year~~ that I learned the meaning of giving.

C CCSS

Standards for this lesson focus on applying the conventions of standard English to spell and hyphenate words correctly.

WRITING HINT

A good way to remember something is to make up a mnemonic, or memory, device. Here is a nonsense sentence to help you remember some of the exceptions to the *i*-before-*e* rule:

Neither weird dog can **seize either** bone at its **leisure**.

EDITING TIP

Many electronic word-processing applications can check your spelling. Automatic spell-checkers are helpful, but don't rely on them exclusively. Spell-checkers cannot determine whether you should use *their* or *there*, for example. You need to do that.

Newspapers and some magazines write out numbers from one to nine only; ten and up are written as numerals. Either style is correct as long as it's used consistently.

Working Together

EXERCISE 3 Remembering Spelling Rules

Work with a partner or small group to complete each item below. Write your answers on a separate piece of paper. Then compare your answers with those of other student pairs or groups in your class.

1. What rule does this mnemonic device help you remember: "The weight of this freight train equals eight sleighs?" Write *e* before *i* when the letters are pronounced with a long *a* sound.
2. Make up your own mnemonic device (a sentence like the one either in item one or in the Writing Hint on page 295) to help you remember the three words that end in *-ceed*. Answers will vary. If you *succeed* as a writer, you can *proceed* to *exceed* your wildest dreams.
3. Write all the two-syllable words you can think of that end with *-cede*. Check your list with a partner or small group. Possible words include *concede*, *precede*, *recede*, *secede*.
4. Write a sentence that tells something about the number of students in your class. Use the number in the sentence. Answers will vary. Twenty of the thirty-two students in this class have brown eyes.

EXERCISE 4 Proofreading a Newsletter

The person who wrote these brief articles for a community newsletter needs a proofreader. Find and correct all of the spelling mistakes below. Write the corrected articles on a separate piece of paper.
See Answer Key at www.grammarforwriting.com.

[1]**Wierd Sounds**

[2]Niether the city police cheif nor the residential nieghbors of the Tip Top Bread Factory can locate exactly where a wierd, high-pitched sound is coming from. [3]A group of Tip Top employees has decided to interceed in the investigation. [4]These employees will report thier findings in the next issue or conceed defeat.

[5]**Procede Without Caution**

[6]Without a doubt, the hieght of our success as a community is demonstrated in the way we spend our liesure time together. [7]To acheive this goal, our citizens place no cieling on what they can do to succede in creating fun activities for everyone, young and old. [8]So, on Saturday, don't receed into the background and riegn as a couch potato king or queen, or make an excuse like "My neice is visiting." [9]There's no reason to wiegh your options carefully, eiether. [10]Sieze the moment and join one of eight community groups—from the foriegn film club to the woodworking club (which made the sliegh for last year's winter parade) to the bongo club.

Prefixes and Suffixes

A **prefix** is a group of letters added to the beginning of a word; a **suffix** is a group of letters added to the end of a word. Adding a prefix or a suffix changes a word's meaning.

▐▐▐▶ Adding a prefix does not change the spelling of a word.

uncertain   **dis**trust   **mis**guided   **il**legitimate

▐▐▐▶ If a word ends in -*y* preceded by a consonant, change the *y* to *i* before adding a suffix.

	glorious	saltiness	loneliest	shininess
EXCEPTIONS	dryness	shyly		

Keep the *y* when adding the suffix -*ing*, as in *trying* or *staying*. Keep the *y* when adding the suffix -*ly* or -*ness* to one-syllable adjectives, such as *shyness* and *wryly*.

▐▐▐▶ If a word ends in -*y* preceded by a vowel, keep the -*y*.

	buoyant	destroyer	betraying	employable
EXCEPTIONS	daily	said		

▐▐▐▶ Drop a word's final silent -*e* before adding a suffix that begins with a vowel.

	retrievable	enclosure	cringing	adorable
EXCEPTIONS	mileage	canoeing	hoeing	acreage

Note: American dictionaries give *likable, lovable, movable,* and *sizable* as the preferred spellings but also include *likeable, loveable, moveable,* and *sizeable*. The preferred spelling is always listed first in your dictionary.

▐▐▐▶ Keep a word's final silent -*e* before adding a suffix that begins with the vowels *a*- or *o*- when the word ends in -*ge* or -*ce*.

advantageous   noticeable   changeable   courageous

▐▐▐▶ Keep the final silent -*e* before adding a suffix that begins with a consonant.

	statehood	falsehood	boredom	management
EXCEPTIONS	argument	ninth	truly	wisdom

Note: American dictionaries list *judgment* and *acknowledgment* as the preferred spellings but also include *judgement* and *acknowledgement*.

C **CCSS**

Standards for this lesson focus on applying the conventions of standard English to spell words correctly when adding prefixes and suffixes.

EDITING TIP

Some exceptions help you distinguish between two different words to which a suffix has been added.

sing + -ing = singing and *singe + -ing = singeing*

die + -ing = dying and *dye + -ing = dyeing*.

WRITING HINT

Use hyphens with prefixes before a proper noun or adjective. Examples include *un-American, sub-Sahara, pro-Vietnam*.

Sometimes, hyphens are used after a prefix to distinguish it from a word that looks just like it.

The **recreation** group teaches tennis. I participated in a **re-creation** of the Battle of Gettysburg.

▐▐▐➡ Here are the rules for doubling a final consonant before adding a suffix that begins with a vowel.

When the suffix begins with a vowel, double the final consonant in one-syllable words that end in a consonant preceded by a single vowel.

> *pegged, strapping, planning, skimmed, baggage*

Double the final consonants in words of more than one syllable when the word ends in a single consonant preceded by a single vowel and the new word is accented on the next-to-last syllable. Don't double the final consonant when the new word is not accented on the last syllable.

DOUBLE CONSONANT   *beginner, occurrence, referral*

SINGLE CONSONANT   *preference, reference*

Exercise 5 Adding Prefixes and Suffixes

Combine these words with their prefixes or suffixes (you may use a dictionary).

1. outrage + -ous ___outrageous___
2. un- + able ___unable___
3. re- + enter ___reenter___
4. dye + -ing ___dyeing___
5. live + -ly ___lively___
6. reply + -ed ___replied___
7. employ + -able ___employable___
8. state + -ly ___stately___
9. prefer + -ed ___preferred___
10. contrite + -ness ___contriteness___
11. flip + -ing ___flipping___
12. anti- + French ___anti-French___
13. sub- + continent ___subcontinent___
14. retrieve + -able ___retrievable___
15. amaze + -ment ___amazement___
16. post- + trial ___posttrial___
17. occur + -ence ___occurrence___
18. singe + -ing ___singeing___
19. control + -er ___controller___
20. anti- + establishment ___antiestablishment___

Exercise 6 Writing New Words

With a partner, write as many words as you can that contain one of the prefixes or suffixes (or both) listed below. Try to use at least four different prefixes and suffixes. Compare your list with those of other groups, and classify words together with the same prefix or suffix. Try to define your words. **Hint:** Look up the prefix or suffix in a college dictionary for help. See Answer Key at www.grammarforwriting.com.

PREFIXES   anti-, pre-, post-, un-, sub-, re-

SUFFIXES   -ment, -er, -able, -ence, -ness, -ous

Noun Plurals

There are several guidelines for forming noun plurals. Most are straightforward and easy to follow. As shown below, you start with the singular noun form and then follow the directions to form the plural.

Making Nouns Plural		
KINDS OF NOUNS	**WHAT TO DO**	**EXAMPLES**
Most nouns	Add -s to the singular.	cat**s**, car**s**, pencil**s**
Nouns that end in -s, -x, -z, -ch, -sh	Add -es to the singular.	mass**es**, tax**es**, waltz**es**, bench**es**, dish**es**
Family names	Follow the two preceding rules.	the Burton**s**, the Marx**es**, the Ruiz**es**, the Ross**es**
Family names that end in -y	Add -s to the name.	the Kennedy**s**, the Brady**s**
Nouns that end in -y preceded by a consonant	Change the -y to i, and add -es.	flurr**ies**, worr**ies**, observator**ies**
Nouns that end in -y preceded by a vowel	Add -s.	turkey**s**, valley**s**, guy**s**, replay**s**
Most nouns that end in -f or -fe	Add -s.	bluff**s**, sheriff**s**, belief**s**, proof**s**, safe**s**
A few nouns that end in -f or -fe	Change the f to v and add -s or -es.	shel**ves**, li**ves**, wol**ves**, thie**ves**, wi**ves**, lea**ves**
Nouns ending in -o preceded by a vowel	Add -s.	radio**s**, cameo**s**, scenario**s**
Most nouns ending in -o preceded by a consonant	Add -es.	hero**es**, tornado**es**, tomato**es**, innuendo**es** **Exceptions:** memos, silos
Most musical terms ending in -o	Add -s.	soprano**s**, alto**s**, solo**s**, piano**s**, piccolo**s**
Compound nouns	Make the most important word plural.	editor**s**-in-chief, passers**by**, bill**s** of sale, father**s**-in-law, merry-go-round**s**
Letters, numbers, and words referred to as words	Use an apostrophe (') + -s.	P**'s**, 4**'s**, no if**'s**, and**'s**, or but**'s**
Irregular plurals, foreign plurals, and words that stay the same for both singular and plural	No rules apply! Memorize these forms.	men, children, mice, geese, feet, oxen, teeth, crises, series, parentheses, species, sheep, curricula, fungi

CCSS

Standards for this lesson focus on applying the conventions of standard English to spell words correctly when forming noun plurals.

EDITING *TIP*

Many word-processing software applications can check your spelling. However, don't rely solely on these spell-checkers. They cannot determine whether you should use *to*, *two*, or *too*, for example. Only you can do that.

A few nouns have two acceptable forms: hoof**s** or hoo**ves**, scarf**s** or scar**ves**, dwarf**s** or dwar**ves**.

A few nouns have two acceptable forms: volcano**s** or volcano**es**, mosquito**s** or mosquito**es**, flamingo**s** or flamingo**es**, memento**s** or memento**es**.

Enriching Your Vocabulary

In geography, *promontory*, used in Exercise 7, means "a peak of high land that juts out into a body of water; headland." In anatomy, it refers to "a prominent body part." From the Marin Headland *promontory*, you can see the Golden Gate Bridge.

EXERCISE 7 Forming Plural Nouns

Write the plural form of each noun. Check a dictionary if you're unsure. If the dictionary doesn't list irregular plurals or alternate plural forms, follow the rules in the chart on page 299.

1. Estavaz ___Estavazes___

2. mouse ___mice___

3. hanger-on ___hangers-on___

4. employee ___employees___

5. dynamo ___dynamos___

6. kazoo ___kazoos___

7. staff ___staffs___

8. convoy ___convoys___

9. promontory ___promontories___

10. alibi ___alibis___

11. Horowitz ___Horowitzes___

12. giraffe ___giraffes___

13. loaf ___loaves___

14. ratio ___ratios___

15. zero ___zeros *or* zeroes___

16. Murphy ___Murphys___

17. genius ___geniuses___

18. tooth ___teeth___

19. fungus ___fungi *or* funguses___

20. *ABC* ___ABC's___

21. cupful ___cupfuls *or* cupsful___

22. stadium ___stadia *or* stadiums___

23. medium ___mediums *or* media___

24. brother-in-law ___brothers-in-law___

25. virtuoso ___virtuosos *or* virtuosi___

26. memo ___memos___

EXERCISE 8 Writing with Plural Nouns

Imagine a pair of identical twins who go to your school. Write a paragraph or two about the twins who have two of everything and who go everywhere and do most things together. Students' paragraphs will vary. See teacher pages for assessment rubrics.

EXAMPLE   Timmy and Tommy received watch**es** for their birthday**s**.

Remember to use two of every item. When you've finished writing, check to see that all noun plurals are spelled correctly.

Editing and Proofreading Worksheet 1

Edit the draft for errors in spelling, capitalization, punctuation, and usage. Write your edited version on a separate piece of paper. Compare your changes with those of a writing partner.

WANTED ¹~~Typeist~~ for either [Typist]
Tuesday or ~~wenesday~~ afternoons. [Wednesday]
²~~Inter-national busness~~ company. [International business]
³Student ~~applicationes accepted~~. [applications accepted]
⁴~~Foriegn languageses~~ a plus in all [Foreign languages]
employees! ⁵~~Aplications~~ should be [Applications]
~~submited~~ by March 20. [submitted]

LOST ⁶Diamond ring on ~~nineth~~ [ninth]
of ~~febuary~~, near ~~sub-way entrence~~ at [February] [subway] [entrance]
Eighty-sixth street ~~dureing~~ snow [during]
~~fluries~~. ⁷Information from ~~passerbys~~ [flurries] [passersby]
or people in ~~nieghboring~~ buildings [neighboring]
appreciated. ⁸Contact this
newspaper's ~~managment~~ with ~~writen~~ [management] [written]
description of ring for ~~referal~~ to [referral]
~~hopful~~ owner. [hopeful]

RENT ⁹~~Amazeing~~ value! ¹⁰Award- [Amazing]
~~wining~~ house builder to rent model [winning]
home. ¹¹~~Luxuryous viewes~~ of [Luxurious views]

~~mountaines~~ and ~~vallies~~ from second [mountains] [valleys]
story ~~windowes~~. ¹²This model [windows]
contains ~~noteable improvments~~ over [notable improvements]
~~earlyer~~ models. ¹³All real ~~estates~~ [earlier] [estate]
~~agent~~ as well as possible renters [agents]
welcome. ¹⁴Sorry, ~~niether~~ cats nor [neither]
dogs allowed.

INTERESTED? ¹⁵Unusual ~~liesure~~ [leisure]
vacations for both ~~childs~~ and adults. [children]
¹⁶See ~~videoes~~ of ~~extremly beautyful~~ [videos] [extremely] [beautiful]
vacation ~~Islandes~~ or ~~fascinateing~~ [islands] [fascinating]
hikes up ~~snowey~~ mountains. ¹⁷All [snowy]
kinds of ~~tripps availible~~. ¹⁸We are [trips available]
a long-time provider of fun for
~~familys~~. ¹⁹Write to request an [families]
~~outragous brosure~~ of our many, [outrageous brochure]
~~varyied~~ trips. ²⁰Each ~~brosure~~ is [varied] [brochure]
~~writen~~ by our preeminent travel [written]
~~writeing~~ staff. [writing]

C **CCSS** Language 1, 2. (See pp. T14–T15.)

Editing and Proofreading Worksheet 2

Edit the draft for errors in spelling, capitalization, punctuation, and usage. Write your edited version on a separate piece of paper. Compare your changes with those of a writing partner. Students' answers will vary. Sample answers are given.

¹Langston Hughes (1902–1967) spent his teenage ~~yeares~~ [years] between the ~~citys~~ [cities] of

Detroit and ~~c~~leveland [Cleveland]. ²After high school and one year of college, Langston

Hughes began his ~~traveles~~ [travels], ~~experienceing~~ [experiencing] Paris ~~france~~ [France], Washington, D.C., and

other ~~locationes~~ [locations]. ³Wherever he lived, his ~~righting abilites~~ [writing abilities] were ~~unstopable~~ [unstoppable].

⁴Some of his early work appeared in African American ~~anthologys~~ [anthologies]. ⁵One of

Hughes's ~~earlyest~~ [earliest] essays ~~appearred~~ [appeared] in the magazine *The Nation*. ⁶Through the

support of a wealthy fan, Amy Spigarin, Hughes ~~recieved~~ [received] funds to complete his

~~collage educatshun~~ [college education]. ⁷Around the same time, his ~~poemes~~ [poems] were published in a

volume entitled The Weary Blues (1926). ⁸His novel *Not without laughter* (1930)

~~iestablished~~ [established] his reputation, ~~giveing~~ [giving] him the title "the bard of Harlem."

⁹As a popular writer, Langston Hughes ~~siezed~~ [seized] the ~~oportunity~~ [opportunity] to ~~activly~~ [actively] speak

out ~~for~~ [about] the African American ~~experiance~~ [experience] and to voice his ~~beliefes~~ [beliefs] in ~~raciel~~ [racial]

justice and workers' ~~writes~~ [rights]. ¹⁰~~Dew~~ [Due] to his political ~~believes~~ [beliefs] he went to the soviet

union. ¹¹In the 1930s, where he studied ~~they're policees~~ [the Soviets' policies]. ¹²Hughes later ~~rote~~ [wrote]

that he was pro~~A~~merican, ~~denieng~~ [denying] that he was ~~un-patriotic~~ [unpatriotic].

¹³Langston ~~Hughes~~ [Hughes's] books line the ~~shelfs~~ [shelves] of ~~librarys~~ [libraries] and universities and

range from poetry to ~~storys~~ [stories] for ~~childrens~~ [children]. ¹⁴He hoped his work would help the

march toward civil rights ~~precede~~ [proceed] for African Americans. ¹⁵He included

everyday speech and the evocative language of the blues in poems such as

"Mother to Son," a work in which the mother speaks this ~~unforgetable~~ [unforgettable] line:

"~~l~~ife [Life] for me ain't been no crystal stair."

Chapter Review

EXERCISE A Proofreading a Letter

The newspaper that published the following letter needs a better proofreader.
Find and correct all of the spelling mistakes in it.
See Answer Key at www.grammarforwriting.com.

> [1]Dear Editer:
>
> [2]As a citazen, let me sieze this oportunity to thank you for your peice on recycleing aluminum cans. [3]I have ofen attempted to interceed in my nieghborhood's recyleing plans—but without sucess. [4]For people to suceed with this kind of environmental effort, they must be truely dedicated to thier cause. [5]Our local eforts to recycle have been less than enthusiastic, if not down right distresing. [6]You're article in last Wenesday's paper opened people's eyes to the importence of provideing new stratagees for saving and re-using natural resources. [7]Let me comend you on some of your recomendations. [8]In particuler, I endorse the exciteing idea of enlisting ninty-five student volunteeres during summer vacations.
>
> [9]I look forward to the next reciept of my newspaper, which I hope unviels more information on this importent subject.
>
> [10]Sincerly yours,
>
> *E. L. Wichester*
>
> E. L. Wichester

EXERCISE B Using a Dictionary

Answer the following questions. If you're not sure about how to spell your answer, look up the word in a college dictionary.

1. Which is the correct spelling: *pecular, peculir, peculiar, peculair?* _____peculiar_____

2. What do you call a person who owes a *debt*? _____debtor_____

3. How do you spell the past tense and past participle of the verb *ride*? _____rode, ridden_____

4. When you need to make a skirt or pants a couple of inches longer, what do you do to the skirt or pants? _____lengthen them_____

5. Underline the preferred American spelling for the following words:

   a. judgement or <u>judgment</u>   c. <u>mementos</u> or mementoes

   b. <u>canceled</u> or cancelled   d. <u>cooperate</u> or co-operate

6. How do you spell the present participle of the verb *singe*? __singeing__

7. "Three feet deep" tells the depth. "Four feet high" tells the __height__. "Eight feet wide" tells the __width__.

8. What is the plural of *thesis*? __theses__

9. At forty miles to the gallon, my car gets good gas __mileage__.

10. Hyphenate the word *fundamentally*. __fun-da-men-tal-ly__

EXERCISE C Adding Prefixes and Suffixes

Write the word that results when the following prefixes or suffixes are added.

1. like + able __likable *or* likeable__

2. please + ant __pleasant__

3. ninety + th __ninetieth__

4. anti + social __antisocial__

5. pre + paid __prepaid__

6. emancipate + -tion __emancipation__

7. liquefy + -ing __liquefying__

8. allot + -ed __allotted__

9. ir- + reversible __irreversible__

10. lonely + -est __loneliest__

EXERCISE D Writing Plurals

Complete each sentence by writing the plural form of the word in parentheses.

1. Claudia tried on three different (scarf) __scarves *or* scarfs__.

2. Two working (radio) __radios__ will be more than enough.

3. Many (observatory) __observatories__ are open only to scientists.

4. Until the calf injury heals, please use those (crutch) __crutches__.

5. The alpha male is the strongest member in a pack of (wolf) __wolves__.

6. Did you know that this house on Cape Cod belonged to the (Kennedy) __Kennedys__?

7. Environmental (crisis) __crises__ happen all over the world.

8. The violin and piano (virtuoso) __virtuosos *or* virtuosi__ performed a duet.

9. The (alumnus) __alumni__ association met at noon.

10. You lengthened the (cuff) __cuffs__ of my pants perfectly.

Cumulative Review

EXERCISE A Using Commas and End Marks Correctly

In the following sentences, insert all missing commas, periods, and other end punctuation marks.

1. Have you ever viewed a planet star or comet through a telescope and have you ever been to a planetarium

2. News of the sighting of a possible planet in TMR-1 an outer space system was reported in a May 28 1998 newspaper in Miami Florida

3. In fact the dot or what might be a planet shows similarities to Jupiter

4. Jupiter also known as a gas giant can't sustain life

5. Incidentally the dot which was viewed through the Hubble telescope was 450 light-years from Earth

6. This possible planet turned out to be debris spun off from a developing star a common process

EXERCISE B Adding Punctuation to Dialogue

Add punctuation, capital letters, paragraph breaks, and any other changes necessary to the following dialogue. Write your corrected version on a separate piece of paper. See Answer Key at www.grammarforwriting.com.

[1]Steve asked Laura have you read The Red Badge of Courage the civil war novel by Stephen Crane. [2]Laura answered "No but I have read two of his short stories *The Open Boat* and The Blue Hotel. [3]"Do you know anything about Crane"? Laura asked "because I'd like to know". [4]Steve opened their textbook and read aloud Stephen Crane was born on November 1 1871 and died on June 5 1900. [5]His short life was full of questions and mysterys. [6]At times he lived the high life, other times he was penniless. [7]Scholars and readers are continually interested in his life, which few completely understand".

[8]Laura was interested in what Steve read. [9]You know Laura said I have a music CD called The Open Boat. [10]Steve asked "Is the name taken from the Stephen Crane story"? [11]Laura exclaimed "I bet it is"! [12]Steve stated "Writers titles should remain there's alone, I think unless they give the title to someone else.

EXERCISE C Proofreading a Paragraph

Proofread the paragraphs on the following page for the correct use of capital letters. Use the proofreading symbol of three underscores to indicate a capital: (m)

Mechanics

[1]No one ever won a nobel prize for building a skyscraper, but the people who built the empire state building in 1930 deserve one. [2]On September 17, 1930, governor alfred e. smith of the state of new york laid the cornerstone. [3]It was on this site that the elegant waldorf-astoria hotel had stood. [4]In its place, the architects—shreve, lamb & harmon associates—along with the builders—starrett brothers & eken, inc.—created a 102-story building that stood 1,472 feet tall up to the top of the antennae.

[5]This skyscraper is made out of indiana limestone and granite. [6]Marble from france, italy, belgium, and germany lines the interior. [7]The construction cost was originally estimated at $50 million; but because of the great depression, the cost actually went no higher than $25 million.

[8]Construction took one year and forty-five days. [9]On may 1, 1931, in washington, d.c., president herbert hoover pressed a button to turn on the building's lights to celebrate its completion.

EXERCISE D USING A DICTIONARY TO CHECK SPELLING

Work with a partner to write the letter of the correct spelling in the blank. If you're not sure of the correct spelling of a word, take turns looking up the item in a dictionary to check the correct spelling.

_a_ 1. (a) achievement (b) acheivement (c) achievment (d) acheivment

_b_ 2. (a) disapoint (b) disappoint (c) dissapoint (d) dissappoint

_c_ 3. (a) preecede (b) preeceed (c) precede (d) preceed

_b_ 4. (a) annonymous (b) anonymous (c) anonimous (d) anonymis

_c_ 5. (a) hight (b) hieght (c) height (d) heite

_d_ 6. (a) embarasment (b) embarrasment (c) embarassment (d) embarrassment

_a_ 7. (a) mistakable (b) mistakeable (c) mistakible (d) mistakeible

_a_ 8. (a) buoys (b) bouys (c) buoyes (d) bouyes

_d_ 9. (a) ocurence (b) ocurance (c) ocurrence (d) occurrence

_b_ 10. (a) comodites (b) commodities (c) commodites (d) comodities

Standardized Test Practice: Grammar and Usage

In addition to an essay component, standardized writing tests include a multiple-choice component that tests your understanding of standard written English. In this section of Level Green, you will find four multiple-choice formats in four different sections. (For additional practice in standardized test formats with grammar feedback, go to www.grammarforwriting.com.) The four formats include:

- SAT Practice: Identifying Sentence Errors
- SAT Practice: Improving Sentences
- SAT Practice: Improving Paragraphs
- ACT Practice

Following these four sections is a practice test in which items from three formats are combined.

IDENTIFYING SENTENCE ERRORS

In this type of multiple-choice item, a sentence will have four words or phrases underlined and labeled **A** through **D**. Your task will be to identify an error, if there is one, and fill in the corresponding answer oval. If there is no error, your answer choice will be **E**, which is "No error."

IMPROVING SENTENCES

In this section, your task will be not only to spot mistakes but fix them, too. In each test item, a sentence will be all or partly underlined. You must spot and fix an error, if there is one, within the underlined portion. Choices **B** through **E** each rephrase the underlined portion, serving as a possible replacement for it. Choice **A** repeats the underlined portion exactly as it is originally given. Choose **A** if you think the item is correct as is.

IMPROVING PARAGRAPHS

The test items in this section have the same structure as the ones in the Improving Sentences section but are keyed to a passage instead of an individual sentence. The items test your ability to revise and combine sentences within the context of an essay and improve its unity, organization and coherence, and word choice.

ACT PRACTICE

As its title suggests, this section is standardized test practice in ACT format. It includes two passages with grammar and usage items keyed to them. Like the Improving Paragraphs section, the test items ask you to revise and combine sentences within the context of an essay and improve its unity, organization and coherence, and word choice.

SAT Practice: Identifying Sentence Errors

Directions: In each item, one of the underlined words or phrases may contain an error in grammar or usage. If there is an error, choose the underlined part that must be changed to make the sentence correct, and fill in the corresponding oval. If the sentence has no error, fill in oval E. In selecting answers, follow the requirements of standard written English.

Example

Of the many seniors <u>who</u> <u>are planning</u> to audition for the
              A   B

part of Juliet, the <u>most experienced</u> actors are Lianne and
                C

<u>her</u>. <u>No error</u>
D   E

The correct choice is **D**. *Lianne and she* is a compound predicate nominative that requires the subject pronoun *she*, not the object pronoun *her*.

---

1. Four basic methods <u>of preserving</u> <u>all kinds</u> of food <u>is</u> drying, heating,
                 A   B   C

<u>refrigerating</u>, and using chemicals. <u>No error</u>
   D   E

2. According to one ancient Greek storyteller, King Minos <u>imprisoned</u>
                                            A

the architect Daedalus and his son Icarus in the labyrinth <u>that</u>
                                             B

Daedalus <u>had builded</u> to house the Minotaur, a man-eating creature
         C

<u>that was half bull and half man</u>. <u>No error</u>
       D   E

STANDARDIZED TEST PRACTICE

3. Among those who were most influential in achieving the vote for
      A   B   C

American women was Susan B. Anthony and Elizabeth Cady
          D

Stanton. No error   Ⓐ Ⓑ Ⓒ ⬤ Ⓔ
       E

4. Phillis Wheatley was the first female African American poet to have
              A   B

her work published. Although she was not the earliest American
  B   C   D

poet. No error   Ⓐ Ⓑ ⬤ Ⓓ Ⓔ
    E

5. If you're interested in recovering more quick from a cold, rest and
    A   B

plenty of liquids are your best medicines. No error   Ⓐ ⬤ Ⓒ Ⓓ Ⓔ
         C   D   E

6. One of America's finest Southern writers, Eudora Welty, who's father
              A   B

came from the North, was born in Jackson, Mississippi, in 1909.
  C   D

No error   Ⓐ ⬤ Ⓒ Ⓓ Ⓔ
  E

7. Carole and me were surprised to find that the Pacific Ocean is about
         A   B

twice as large as the Atlantic Ocean and has a greater average depth.
      C   D

No error   ⬤ Ⓑ Ⓒ Ⓓ Ⓔ
  E

8. Known for both its strength and its endurance, the donkey is smaller
   A   B   C

than a horse and lives about twice as longer as a horse. No error   Ⓐ Ⓑ Ⓒ ⬤ Ⓔ
  C   D   E

9. Maria's report is about Robert Scott, the Scottish explorer <u>who</u>
A

reached the South Pole in January 1912 only to find that the

Norwegian Roald Amundsen, <u>whom</u> he considered his rival,
B

<u>had gotten</u> there before <u>him</u>. <u>No error</u>
C   D   E

10. In 1890, at Wounded Knee Creek in South Dakota, when U.S.

soldiers <u>hear</u> a shot, they started <u>shooting; when</u> the battle ended,
A   B

they <u>had killed or wounded</u> as many as 300 Sioux, <u>including women</u>
C   D

<u>and children</u>. <u>No error</u>
D   E

11. Neither Julio nor his sister <u>are</u> free until three o'clock when their
A

classes <u>end; by then</u>, it will be <u>too late</u> for them to meet <u>their aunt</u> at
B   C   D

the airport. <u>No error</u>
E

12. After <u>visiting</u> the zoo, Jessie and her family hurried to catch the last
A

train home, but <u>they missed it</u> <u>unless</u> their bus <u>was delayed</u> by rush
B   C   D

hour traffic. <u>No error</u>
E

13. Clouds <u>are made up</u> of tiny particles of water or ice <u>floating in the air</u>
A   B

and gathered together until <u>it forms</u> a cirrus, cumulus, nimbus, or
C

stratus cloud, <u>which are</u> four common types of clouds. <u>No error</u>
D   E

14. Oahu, the third <u>most largest</u> and the <u>most densely</u> populated of
                                  A   B

Hawaii's islands, <u>has</u> no active volcano, but <u>there are</u> two active
                   C   D

volcanoes, Mauna Loa and Kilauea, on the Big Island. <u>No error</u>
                                                           E

Ⓐ Ⓑ Ⓒ Ⓓ Ⓔ

15. Between 1892 and 1954, <u>more than twelve million</u> men, women,
                                       A

and children <u>enter</u> the United States through Ellis Island in
                 B

New York City's <u>harbor, which was</u> the main entry point for
                           C

<u>European immigrants.</u> <u>No error</u>
       D   E

Ⓐ Ⓑ Ⓒ Ⓓ Ⓔ

16. According to an article in *Money*, <u>there are</u> at least three <u>sound</u>
                                       A   B

<u>reasons</u> why you <u>should start saving</u> your money in a retirement
  B   C

fund now to prepare for <u>one's eventual retirement.</u> <u>No error</u>
                               D   E

Ⓐ Ⓑ Ⓒ Ⓓ Ⓔ

17. The periodic table of the elements <u>is</u> a chart that <u>shows</u> all of the
                                 A   B

chemical elements, <u>their atomic numbers, their symbols,</u> and
                              C

<u>the number that tells what their atomic weight is.</u> <u>No error</u>
                       D   E

Ⓐ Ⓑ Ⓒ Ⓓ Ⓔ

18. <u>Began</u> in the third century B.C., the Great Wall of China winds
  A

<u>its way</u> for about 4,000 miles across the northern plains; <u>it was built</u>
  B   C

as a protective defense <u>to stop northern invaders.</u> <u>No error</u>
                       D   E

Ⓐ Ⓑ Ⓒ Ⓓ Ⓔ

SAT Practice: Improving Sentences

ONLINE COMPONENTS
www.grammarforwriting.com

SAT and ACT practice worksheets with grammar feedback are available online.

Directions: In each of the following items, all or part of the sentence is underlined. Beneath each sentence are five ways of phrasing the underlined part. Choice (A) is the same as the original; the other four choices are different. Select the answer choice that best expresses the meaning of the original sentence. Your goal is to produce the most effective sentence, one that is clear and not wordy. Choose (A) if the original sentence is better than any of the other answer choices.

Example

The American poet E. E. <u>Cummings, who's poems have no capital letters</u> or end punctuation marks, cared about how his poems look on the page.

(A) Cummings, who's poems have no capital letters

(B) Cummings, whose poems have no capitol letters

(C) Cummings, whose poems has no capital letters

(D) Cummings, whose poems have no capital letters

(E) Cummings whose poems have no Capital Letters

The correct choice is **D** because it has the correct spelling of the possessive pronoun *whose* and the word *capital* and also has the plural verb *have*, which agrees with the subject *poems*.

---

1. A fifteen-member mayoral task force has made forty-nine recommendations to combat the spread of <u>graffiti, one is</u> to hold parents responsible for their children's behavior.

   (A) graffiti, one is

   (B) graffiti, one among which is

   (C) graffiti, one of which is

   (D) graffiti, and one of which is

   (E) graffiti; because, for example, one of which is

2. Although the research paper was assigned weeks ago, neither of my two best <u>friends or I have finished writing their first draft</u>.

   (A) friends or I have finished writing their first draft

   (B) friends or I have finished writing his or her first draft

(C) friends nor I have finished writing their first draft

(D) friends nor me have finished writing our first draft

(E) friends nor I have finished writing our first draft

3. Simon <u>dived into the pool and swim</u> the 100-meter freestyle, setting a new school record.

(A) dived into the pool and swim

(B) dived into the pool and swam

(C) dived into the pool and had swum

(D) had dived into the pool and had swam

(E) dove into the pool and swim

4. <u>When reading Emily Dickinson's poems, her imagination</u> and powerful, clear ideas are amazing.

(A) When reading Emily Dickinson's poems, her imagination

(B) When reading Emily Dickinson's poems, the poet's imagination

(C) When I read Emily Dickinson's poems, I find that her imagination

(D) When Emily Dickinson's poems are read, her imagination

(E) When my class reads Emily Dickinson's poems, her imagination

5. The "separate but equal" doctrine of racial segregation, in place since <u>the 1890s, that doctrine was overturned</u> by the Supreme Court's 1954 ruling in *Brown v. Board of Education.*

(A) the 1890s, that doctrine was overturned

(B) the 1890s; that doctrine was overturned

(C) the 1890s. That doctrine was overturned

(D) the 1890s, was overturned

(E) the 1890s, and it was overturned

6. No one could read hieroglyphics, the ancient Egyptian system of picture writing, until 1822, when Jean François Champollion <u>discovers that the Rosetta stone contained the same passage</u> in three different languages: hieroglyphics, Greek, and demotic.

(A) discovers that the Rosetta stone contained the same passage

(B) discovered that the Rosetta stone contained the same passage

(C) had discovered that the Rosetta stone contained the same passage

(D) had discovered that the Rosetta stone had contained the same passage

(E) had been discovering that the Rosetta stone contained the same passage

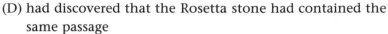

7. The Trans-Alaska Pipeline System, completed in 1977, carries crude oil 800 miles from Prudhoe Bay on the Arctic Ocean to Valdez, an ice-free port on the <u>southern coast. Where the oil is shipped in tankers</u>.

(A) southern coast. Where the oil is shipped in tankers

(B) southern coast. Where tankers ship the oil

(C) southern coast, where the oil is shipped in tankers

(D) southern coast, where tankers are shipping the oil

(E) southern coast: where the oil is shipped in tankers

8. According to Greek legend, the person who was able to loosen the Gordian knot would rule all of Asia; that turned out to be Alexander the Great, who cut the knot with his sword <u>after failing to untie it</u>.

(A) after failing to untie it

(B) after having tried but having failed to untie it

(C) despite the fact that he had failed to untie it

(D) as a direct consequence of, unfortunately, failing to untie it

(E) after being one of the many persons who had failed to untie it

9. An oxymoron is a figure of speech made up of two apparently contradictory <u>words, such as "sweet sorrow," "cold fire," and another</u> one is "genuine imitation."

(A) words, such as "sweet sorrow," "cold fire," and another one is "genuine imitation."

(B) words: such as "sweet sorrow," "cold fire," and another one is "genuine imitation."

(C) words, such as "sweet sorrow," "cold fire," and another example is "genuine imitation."

(D) words, such as "sweet sorrow," "cold fire," and "genuine imitation."

(E) words, for example, such as "sweet sorrow," "cold fire," and "genuine imitation."

10. Ramon or her usually lead a class review before the chemistry test.

(A) Ramon or her usually lead

(B) Ramon or her usually leads

(C) Ramon or her are usually leading

(D) Ramon or she usually lead

(E) Ramon or she usually leads

11. If you can locate the Big Dipper in the northern constellation Ursa Major, you can find Polaris, the North Star, a line drawn through the two stars at the far end of the dipper's bowl points to the North Star.

(A) the North Star, a line drawn through

(B) the North Star, because a line drawn through

(C) the North Star and a line drawn through

(D) the North Star, although a line drawn through

(E) the North Star, of course a line drawn through

12. Elvira performs that dance really good, much better than me.

(A) really good, much better than me

(B) real good, much better than I

(C) really well, much better than I

(D) really well, much better than me

(E) really good, much better than I

13. Driving home from school, the lost dog was seen by Lorna.

(A) Driving home from school, the lost dog was seen by Lorna.

(B) Driving home from school, Lorna was seen by the lost dog.

(C) Driving home from school, Lorna saw the lost dog.

(D) The lost dog, driving home from school, was seen by Lorna.

(E) Lorna saw the lost dog, driving home from school.

14. In Jonathan Swift's *Gulliver's Travels*, the humanlike Yahoos are gross, disgusting brutes, however the gentle, civilized Houyhnhnms, their masters, which are horses.

(A) brutes, however the gentle

(B) brutes; as a result, the gentle

(C) brutes, in contrast with the gentle

(D) brutes, and the gentle

(E) brutes, the gentle

SAT Practice: Improving Paragraphs

Directions: The passage that follows is an early draft of an essay. Some parts need to be rewritten. Read the passage carefully and answer the questions that follow. Choose the answer that most clearly and effectively expresses the writer's intended meaning. In making your decisions, follow the conventions of standard written English. After you have chosen your answer, fill in the corresponding oval.

(1) Democracy is the form of government in which the people rule. (2) By electing representatives to do their business for them. (3) Elections are held to elect mayors, city councils, judges, governors, state representatives and senators, U.S. congressional representatives and senators, and presidents. (4) There are also, especially at the state and local levels, referendums (yes-no votes) on important issues. (5) There are lots and lots of elections each year. (6) Unfortunately, the United States has been plagued by voter apathy, a low turnout of eligible voters.

(7) You can't just walk up to a polling place and vote. (8) You have to be registered. (9) That means you have to formally apply and meet certain requirements: prove that you are a U.S. citizen and over eighteen, that you have lived at a certain address for the required amount of time, and that you are who you say you are. (10) Among American voters, the turnout has, in the past, been about fifty percent. (11) That means that fifty percent of the people who are eligible to vote actually vote. (12) Senior citizens have far and away the highest voter turnout; the lowest turnout has been among young people.

(13) For example, eighteen-year-olds can register to vote at their high school. (14) Under the "motor voter program," you can register to vote in most states when you apply for a driver's license. (15) You can even register online, to the tune of rock music. (16) MTV's "Rock the Vote" campaign signed up 1.4 million new young voters during the 2004 presidential campaign.

(17) In a democracy, people have not only the right to vote but also the *responsibility* to vote. (18) The idea that "my one vote doesn't count" just isn't true—look at all the extraordinarily close elections that happen each year. (19) Remember that in dictatorships around the world, people *can't* vote. (20) So don't let your vote go down the drain. (21) First register; then vote in every election you can.

1. Which of the following is the best way to revise and combine sentences 1 and 2 (reproduced below)?

   Democracy is the form of government in which the people rule. By electing representatives to do their business for them.

   (A) Democracy is the form of government in which the people rule, and by electing representatives to do their business for them.

(B) Democracy is the form of government in which the people rule by electing representatives to do their business for them.

(C) Democracy is the form of government in which the people rule although electing representatives to do their business for them.

(D) In a democracy the people rule; usually they elect representatives to do their business for them.

(E) Democracy is the form of government in which the ruling people elect representatives to do their business for them.

2. To improve the first paragraph, what should be done with sentence 5 (reproduced here)?

There are lots and lots of elections each year.

(A) Leave it as it is.

(B) Delete the sentence.

(C) Change "lots and lots" to "plenty."

(D) Insert "being held around the country" after the word "elections."

(E) Move the sentence to precede sentence 1.

3. Which of the following is the best word or phrase to insert at the beginning of sentence 7 (reproduced below)?

You can't just walk up to a polling place and vote.

(A) To begin with,

(B) Consequently,

(C) As a result,

(D) On the contrary,

(E) In conclusion,

4. Which of the following is the best way to revise and combine sentences 7 and 8 (reproduced below)?

You can't just walk up to a polling place and vote. You have to be registered.

(A) You can't just walk up to a polling place and vote, and you have to be registered.

(B) Although you can't just walk up to a polling place and vote, you have to be registered.

(C) To begin with, you can't just walk up to a polling place and vote; you have to be registered.

(D) You can't just walk up to a polling place and vote; although you have to be registered.

(E) You can't just walk up to a polling place and vote; as a result, you have to be registered.

5. Which of the following is the best revision of the underlined portion of sentence 12 (reproduced below)?

Senior citizens have far and away the highest voter turnout; the lowest turnout has been *among young people.*

(A) (Leave it as it is.)

(B) most highest voter turnout; the lowest turnout has been

(C) highest voter turnout, except that the lowest turnout has been

(D) higher voter turnout. The lower turnout has been

(E) highest voter turnout despite the fact that the lowest turnout has been

6. Which of the following is the best sentence to insert at the beginning of paragraph 3 (before sentence 13)?

(A) Many young people are turned off by politics and negative campaigning or think their vote doesn't count.

(B) To get more people to vote, new ways have been tried.

(C) In recent years, several strategies have been tried to get young people to register to vote.

(D) The Twenty-Sixth Amendment, ratified in 1971, lowered the voting age to eighteen.

(E) Young people can vote in different ways.

7. The primary effect of the final paragraph (sentences 17–21) is to

(A) give more information about voter apathy

(B) describe the effects of voter apathy

(C) compare and contrast democracy with a dictatorship

(D) persuade the reader to register to vote and then actually vote

(E) persuade the reader to keep informed about election issues and candidates

ACT Practice

ONLINE COMPONENTS
www.grammarforwriting.com

SAT and ACT practice worksheets with grammar feedback are available online.

Directions: You will find two reading passages in the left column and questions in the right column. In each of the passages, some words and phrases are underlined with a number underneath. The numbers refer to the questions at the right. Most questions ask you to choose the answer that best expresses the idea in standard written English or in the style of the passage. If you think the original wording is best, choose answer A, "NO CHANGE."

Other questions, indicated by a small number in a box, ask about the passage as a whole or about a particular section of the passage.

For each question, choose what you think is the best answer, and fill in the corresponding oval at the bottom of the page. Sometimes you will need to read several sentences beyond the numbered point in the passage to answer the question correctly.

Passage I

Emily Dickinson: Reclusive Genius

[1]

Emily <u>Dickinson, acknowledged as</u>
                    1
one of America's greatest poets, achieved fame long after her death in 1886. While she was alive, Dickinson shared her poems with only a few people, and only seven were published. She sent several to the editor of the *Atlantic Monthly*, asking for criticism.

1. **A.** NO CHANGE
   B. Dickinson is acknowledged
   C. Dickinson—acknowledged
   D. Dickinson whom is acknowledged

I. Ⓐ Ⓑ Ⓒ Ⓓ

STANDARDIZED TEST PRACTICE

[2]

Dickinson grew up in Amherst,
Massachusetts. She was the daughter of a
prosperous lawyer. He later became a
congressman. She seemed a happy,
normal child, yet somewhat shy and
reserved when she went off to boarding
school. Something happened when
Dickinson was a young woman; biogra-
phers speculate that she fell in love with
a married pastor, who she called her
mentor and inspiration.

[3]

In her late twenties, she began to
withdraw from society. Soon she was
living as a recluse, dressing all in white,
seeing no one but her family, avoiding
friends, and she never would leave her
father's house. You can visit that house
today—it's called the Homestead—in
Amherst and see her room and her careful
preserved white dresses.

2. What is the best way to combine the first three sentences in paragraph 2?

  A. Having grown up in Amherst, Massachusetts, Dickinson is the daughter of a prosperous lawyer, who later had became a congressman.

  B. Dickinson grew up in Amherst, Massachusetts, the daughter of a prosperous lawyer who later became a congressman.

  C. Dickinson, who was the daughter of a prosperous lawyer and later became a congressman, grew up in Amherst, Massachusetts.

  D. Dickinson grew up in Amherst, Massachusetts, and she was the daughter of a prosperous lawyer who later became a congressman.

3. A. NO CHANGE

  B. pastor, who was called by her

  C. pastor who she was in the habit of calling

  D. pastor, whom she called

4. A. NO CHANGE

  B. friends, who never would leave

  C. friends, and never leaving

  D. friends, because she never left

5. A. NO CHANGE

  B. her careful, preserved

  C. her careful and preserved

  D. her carefully preserved

2. Ⓐ Ⓑ Ⓒ Ⓓ   4. Ⓐ Ⓑ Ⓒ Ⓓ
3. Ⓐ Ⓑ Ⓒ Ⓓ   5. Ⓐ Ⓑ Ⓒ Ⓓ

[4]

Dickinson died at 55, her family was
surprised to discover more than a
thousand poems neatly bundled in her
dresser. Family and friends undertook to
publish the poems, but they tampered
with them. They altered her punctuation
(Dickinson used mainly dashes) and
capitalization, they substituted words
and phrases that they felt improved
on what she had written. Although they
tried to make her poems more
conventional by eliminating irregular
rhyme and meter. Not until 1955 did an
editor and scholar, Thomas H. Johnson,
publish her poems just as she had written
them.

6. A. NO CHANGE
   B. When Dickinson died at 55, her family were surprised
   C. When Dickinson died at 55, her family was surprised
   D. Dickinson's death at 55 surprised her family

7. A. NO CHANGE
   B. capitalization, also they substituted
   C. capitalization: they substituted
   D. capitalization; they substituted

8. A. NO CHANGE
   B. Also, they tried
   C. Consequently, they tried
   D. Despite the fact that they tried

9. A. NO CHANGE
   B. just as she had wrote them
   C. in the exact same way that she had put them down on paper
   D. in the way Dickinson had originally written them in the first place

6. Ⓐ Ⓑ **C** Ⓓ
7. Ⓐ Ⓑ Ⓒ **D**

8. Ⓐ Ⓑ **C** Ⓓ
9. **A** Ⓑ Ⓒ Ⓓ

STANDARDIZED TEST PRACTICE

[5]

Her poems are unique—brief, yet high-ly imaginative. Through startling imagery and figurative language, they express powerful feelings. An innovator, Dickinson was among the first to use slant rhyme and irregular meter. If you don't know her poems, try reading two of her best: "I heard a Fly buzz—when I died" and "Because I could not stop for Death." 10

10. Which of the following is the best sentence to insert at the beginning of paragraph 5?

A. Restored to the author's original texts, we can see that her poems are the work of a genius.

B. It's great to read the original text of her poems.

C. Thomas Johnson's *The Complete Poems of Emily Dickinson* is a remarkable volume.

D. Now that we have her poems in their original form, we can see that Dickinson was indeed a genius.

Question 11 asks about the preceding passage as a whole.

---

11. The writer wishes to add the following sentence:

Mostly, however, her audience was a select few relatives and friends, who discovered a poem tucked into a letter or a basket of cookies.

This sentence would most logically be placed:

A. at the end of paragraph 1

B. at the beginning of paragraph 2

C. at the beginning of paragraph 3

D. at the end of paragraph 3

10. Ⓐ Ⓑ Ⓒ ●

11. ● Ⓑ Ⓒ Ⓓ

Passage II

Hawaii: <u>The Land and It's People</u>
<u></u>   12

[1]

Hawaii is an archipelago, a chain of volcanic islands, <u>that stretch more than</u> 1,500 miles in the middle of the north Pacific. The coral <u>reefs, which surrounds the islands, makes</u> for excellent scuba diving and snorkeling. Over time, Hawaii's volcanic rock has broken down into rich soil. This has helped to make subtropical Hawaii an island paradise.

[2]

There are only two species of mammals native to the islands—the monk seal and the hoary bat. The first Hawaiians were Polynesians who arrived sometime between A.D. 200 and 500, bringing with them dogs, chickens, pigs, and, unfortunately, rats. These first settlers planted coconuts, bananas, yams, and <u>a plant called taro; sugarcane,</u> bamboo, coffee, pineapples, and mangoes came later. ⬛16

12. A. NO CHANGE
   B. Land and Its' People
   C. Land and Its People
   D. Land & Its People

13. A. NO CHANGE
   B. that stretch further than
   C. that stretches more then
   D. that stretches more than

14. A. NO CHANGE
   B. reefs which surround the islands, makes
   C. reefs that surround the islands makes
   D. reefs surrounding the island make

15. A. NO CHANGE
   B. taro and sugarcane,
   C. taro because sugarcane,
   D. taro; sugarcane,

16. Which is the best sentence to insert at the beginning of paragraph 2 to tie together the first two paragraphs?
   A. Hawaii has lots of very beautiful animals and plants.
   B. In this isolated paradise, most of the mammals and many plants have been imported.
   C. In this paradise, many plants and animals live.
   D. Taro is a plant used to make a food called poi.

17. A. NO CHANGE
   B. members of his crew, were
   C. members of his crews were
   D. members of his crew have been

---

12. Ⓐ Ⓑ Ⓒ Ⓓ   15. Ⓐ Ⓑ Ⓒ Ⓓ
13. Ⓐ Ⓑ Ⓒ Ⓓ   16. Ⓐ Ⓑ Ⓒ Ⓓ
14. Ⓐ Ⓑ Ⓒ Ⓓ   17. Ⓐ Ⓑ Ⓒ Ⓓ

When Cook and his men landed in Hawaii in 1778, he named the islands the Sandwich Islands for his benefactor, the Earl of Sandwich. Cook, along with the <u>members of his crew, was</u> warmly greeted by the indigenous Hawaiians. <u>The two</u>
17
<u>ships were resupplied, they</u> explored the
18
islands, and introduced European diseases that quickly decimated the native population. 19

[4]

[1] Then it became a stable monarchy until Sanford Dole, an American, <u>led a coup</u> in 1893, forcing Queen
20
Liliuokalani from power. [2] When Cook discovered the islands, Hawaii was a feudal society ruled by warring kings. [3] By 1898, Hawaii <u>had became</u> a U.S. territory.
21
[4] In 1959, the eight Hawaiian islands became the fiftieth state in the United States. 22

18. **A.** NO CHANGE
    B. Having been resupplied, the two ships explored
    C. The two ships were resupplied, exploring
    D. Cook and his men resupplied their ships, explored

19. Which of the following is the best sentence to place at the beginning of paragraph 3?
    A. Europeans had no idea that these islands existed.
    B. The English explorer Captain James Cook was the first European to set foot on Hawaii.
    C. The native Hawaiians existed in happy isolation.
    D. Hawaii was discovered in 1778.

20. **A.** NO CHANGE
    B. leads a coup
    C. lead a coup
    D. leading a coup

21. **A.** NO CHANGE
    B. will have become
    C. had become
    D. becomes

22. What is the most logical order for the sentences in paragraph 4?
    A. NO CHANGE
    B. 2, 3, 4, 1
    C. 2, 1, 4, 3
    D. 2, 1, 3, 4

18. Ⓐ Ⓑ Ⓒ Ⓓ
19. Ⓐ Ⓑ Ⓒ Ⓓ
20. ⬤Ⓐ Ⓑ Ⓒ Ⓓ

21. Ⓐ Ⓑ Ⓒ Ⓓ
22. Ⓐ Ⓑ Ⓒ ⬤Ⓓ

Practice Test

Time—25 Minutes (1 question)

You have 25 minutes to write an essay on the topic below.

DO NOT WRITE AN ESSAY THAT ADDRESSES ANY OTHER TOPIC. AN ESSAY ON A DIFFERENT TOPIC WILL NOT BE ACCEPTED.

Plan and write an essay on the assigned topic. Present your thoughts clearly and effectively. Include specific examples to support your views. The quality of your essay is more important than its length, but to express your ideas on the topic adequately, you will probably want to write more than one paragraph. Be sure to make your handwriting legible.

Consider the following statement. Then write an essay as directed.

In July 1944, Anne Frank, a German Jewish teenager, wrote the following in the diary she kept while her family was in hiding from the Nazis during World War II:

"It's difficult in times like these: ideals, dreams and cherished hopes rise within us, only to be crushed by grim reality. It's a wonder I haven't abandoned all my ideals, they seem so absurd and impractical. Yet I cling to them because I still believe, in spite of everything, that people are truly good at heart."

—from Anne Frank, *The Diary of a Young Girl: The Definitive Edition*

Assignment: Write an essay in which you agree or disagree with the statement above, using examples from history, current events, science, art, music, or your own experience to support your position.

WRITE YOUR ESSAY ON A SEPARATE SHEET OF PAPER.

Part B

Time—35 minutes (55 questions)

Directions: In each item, one of the underlined words or phrases may contain an error in grammar, usage, word choice, or idiom. If there is an error, choose the underlined part that must be changed to make the sentence correct, and fill in the corresponding oval. If the sentence has no error, fill in oval E. In selecting answers, follow the requirements of standard written English.

Example

Road repairs, <u>which are taking place</u> all over the county, <u>are</u>
　　　　　　　　　　A　　　　　　　　　　　　　　　　　　B

<u>causing</u> tremendous traffic jams but <u>will eventually make</u>
　B　　　　　　　　　　　　　　　　　　　　　C

commuters' rides <u>faster and more smoother.</u> <u>No error</u>
　　　　　　　　　D　　　　　　　　　　　　E

1. Neither Alonzo nor <u>her</u> <u>has asked</u> their grandmother about what
　　　　　　　　　A　　B

<u>her life was like</u> when she <u>was growing up</u> in Honduras. <u>No error</u>
　　　C　　　　　　　　　　　D　　　　　　　　　　　E

2. <u>Because of</u> the <u>unseasonably warm</u> weather in Washington, D.C., the
　　A　　　　　　　B

Japanese cherry, Bradford pear, and magnolia trees <u>are bursting</u> into
　　　　　　　　　　　　　　　　　　　　　　C

blossom several weeks <u>more earlier</u> than usual. <u>No error</u>
　　　　　　　　　D　　　　　　　　　E

3. On August 6, 1926, American Gertrude Ederle, the first woman

<u>to swim</u> across the English Channel, <u>swum</u> the 35 miles from France
　A　　　　　　　　　　　　　　　　B

to England in stormy seas in 14 hours and 31 minutes, <u>beating</u> the
　　　　　　　　　　　　　　　　　　　　　　　　C

<u>men's record</u> by two hours. <u>No error</u>
　D　　　　　　　　　　E

4. Just <u>between you and me</u>, I'm sure that Carlos and <u>she</u> are the

              A   B

<u>most likeliest</u> of <u>all the contestants</u> to win this year's senior class

      C   D

talent show. <u>No error</u>   Ⓐ Ⓑ ● Ⓓ Ⓔ

          E

5. Amber, a yellowish-brownish gem used to make jewelry, is actually

the <u>fossilized form</u> of ancient tree resin, or sap, from extinct

      A

evergreen <u>trees, that is</u> why <u>one</u> can sometimes see <u>air bubbles</u>,

           B   C   D

<u>insects, and bits of leaves</u> in amber. <u>No error</u>   Ⓐ ● Ⓒ Ⓓ Ⓔ

       D   E

6. Roller hockey—<u>like</u> ice hockey, soccer, basketball, and many other

              A

team sports—<u>requires</u> <u>its</u> players to have strength, stamina, and

             B   C

<u>the ability to be accurate.</u> <u>No error</u>   Ⓐ Ⓑ Ⓒ ● Ⓔ

       D   E

7. All living plants and animals <u>are composed</u> of cells that <u>contain</u>

                               A   B

genes <u>made up</u> of DNA (deoxyribonucleic acid), which <u>transmits</u> the

      C   D

hereditary characteristics of each organism. <u>No error</u>   Ⓐ Ⓑ Ⓒ Ⓓ ●

                                            E

8. Grandma <u>Moses, whose real name</u> was Anna Mary Robertson Moses,

                   A

was a farmer's <u>wife who began</u> painting <u>until</u> she was in her late

               B   C

<u>seventies; her popular paintings</u> depict everyday scenes of farm life

         D

in an "American primitive" style. <u>No error</u>   Ⓐ Ⓑ ● Ⓓ Ⓔ

                                     E

9. Members of groups <u>that are affiliated</u> with the modern animal rights
A

movement, which <u>began</u> in the early 1970s, <u>protest</u> the use (they
B$$C

say abuse) of animals for medical research, for testing cosmetics, and

<u>they object to the killing of animals for fur.</u> <u>No error</u>
D$$E

Ⓐ Ⓑ Ⓒ ⬤ Ⓔ

10. When a dispute is settled by arbitration, the opposing parties

<u>present their case</u> and <u>submit there evidence</u> to an arbitrator (usually
A$$B

an attorney or a retired judge), <u>who reaches</u> a decision, which the
C

parties <u>have agreed beforehand to abide by.</u> <u>No error</u>
D$$E

Ⓐ ⬤ Ⓒ Ⓓ Ⓔ

11. In Chapter 1 of *Alice's Adventures in Wonderland* (1865) by Lewis

Carroll, a girl named Alice <u>falls</u> down a rabbit hole when <u>she follows</u>
AB

a White Rabbit <u>who is hurrying</u> <u>very quick</u> because he is late for an
C$$D

appointment. <u>No error</u>
E

Ⓐ Ⓑ Ⓒ ⬤ Ⓔ

12. Dinosaurs, <u>whose name</u> <u>comes</u> from two ancient Greek words
AB

<u>meaning "terrible lizard,"</u> lived during the Mesozoic Era (from 65 to
C

205 million years ago), and no one who has studied their fossils

<u>know for sure</u> what caused them to become extinct. <u>No error</u>
D$$E

Ⓐ Ⓑ Ⓒ ⬤ Ⓔ

13. The person <u>who</u> you need to talk to about taking an advanced
            A

placement class in calculus is Mr. <u>Grippo, who</u> <u>has been</u> out of
                                      B   C

school for a week because of his surgery to repair a torn rotator

cuff, <u>which he got</u> while lifting weights. <u>No error</u>   Ⓐ Ⓑ Ⓒ Ⓓ Ⓔ
          D   E

14. Cuneiform, <u>which was developed</u> by the Sumerians about 4000 B.C.,
                      A

<u>is</u> a writing system made up of wedge-shaped symbols <u>incised in clay</u>
B   C

and then <u>dried, each symbol</u> stands for an object, an idea, or a
              D

sound. <u>No error</u>   Ⓐ Ⓑ Ⓒ Ⓓ Ⓔ
          E

15. Frans van Mieris, a seventeenth-century Dutch painter, is <u>most</u>
                                                                    A

<u>famous</u> for his ability to depict everyday life in small paintings
  A

<u>so finely executed</u> that none of his brushstrokes <u>is</u> <u>visible; he is also</u>
        B   C   D

<u>known</u> for his masterful rendering of textures. <u>No error</u>   Ⓐ Ⓑ Ⓒ Ⓓ Ⓔ
  D   E

16. Because Max and Jonathan <u>are</u> fraternal (not identical) twins, each
                                   A

one <u>looks</u> <u>different</u> and has <u>their</u> own personality. <u>No error</u>   Ⓐ Ⓑ Ⓒ Ⓓ Ⓔ
        B   C   D   E

17. If you <u>wear</u> eyeglasses, <u>one</u> can choose from a variety of special
               A   B

coatings for your lenses <u>that are designed</u> to prevent scratching,
                              C

<u>reduce glare</u>, and protect your eyes from ultraviolet rays. <u>No error</u> Ⓐ Ⓑ Ⓒ Ⓓ Ⓔ
  D   E

18. Coming in for a landing, the sunset was the most spectacular
        A   B

display of colors (intense shades of blues, reds, and golds) and

was much more beautiful than any other sunset I had ever seen
        C   D

before. No error   Ⓐ Ⓑ Ⓒ Ⓓ Ⓔ
      E

19. No one among the parents and teachers whom I've talked to knows
              A   B   C

the current status of the proposed and extremely controversial bill to
                                              D

extend the school year to a full twelve months. No error   Ⓐ Ⓑ Ⓒ Ⓓ Ⓔ
                                        E

Directions: In each of the following items, all or part of the sentence is underlined. Beneath each sentence are five ways of phrasing the underlined part. Choice (A) is the same as the original; the other four choices are different. Select the answer choice that best expresses the meaning of the original sentence. Your goal is to produce the most effective sentence, one that is clear and not wordy. Choose (A) if the original sentence is better than any of the other answer choices.

20. The rising prices of oil and gasoline has made consumers increasingly interested in buying hybrid cars, which get far more miles per gallon than conventional cars.

(A) has made consumers increasingly interested

(B) has interested consumers increasingly

(C) have made consumers increasing interested

(D) have made consumers increasingly interested

(E) have interested made consumers increasingly   Ⓐ Ⓑ Ⓒ Ⓓ Ⓔ

21. Kristen and I should of left the house earlier; we almost missed our plane.

(A) Kristen and I should of left the house earlier;

(B) Kristen and me should have left the house earlier;

(C) Kristen and I should have left the house earlier because

(D) Kristen and me should have left the house earlier, however,

(E) Kristen and me left the house earlier although

22. In a speech he give in Detroit in 1963, Dr. Martin Luther King Jr. said, "If a man hasn't discovered something that he will die for, he isn't fit to live."

(A) In a speech he give in Detroit in 1963,

(B) In a speech he had gave in Detroit in 1963,

(C) In a speech he had been given in Detroit in 1963,

(D) In a speech he gave in Detroit in 1963,

(E) In a speech he has given in Detroit in 1963,

23. It's been an extremely mild winter so far without hardly no snow.

(A) without hardly no snow

(B) with hardly no snow

(C) with hardly any snowing

(D) with hardly any snow

(E) with hardly no of snowing

24. The largest city in Nebraska is Omaha, named for a tribe of Native Americans, the state capital is Lincoln.

(A) largest city in Nebraska is Omaha, named for a tribe of Native Americans, the

(B) largest city in Nebraska is Omaha, named for a tribe of Native Americans; the

(C) largest city in Nebraska is Omaha, named for a tribe of Native Americans: The

(D) largest city in Nebraska is Omaha, named for a tribe of Native Americans, despite the fact that the

(E) larger city in Nebraska is Omaha, named for a tribe of Native Americans; the

25. <u>Anyone who is shopping for a new car,</u> it's important to be informed about the dealer's costs so that you can negotiate a fair price.

(A) Anyone who is shopping for a new car,

(B) If you are shopping for a new car,

(C) If one is shopping for a new car,

(D) Shoppers who are looking for a new car,

(E) If anyone is shopping for a new car,

26. The French Impressionist Edgar Degas is best known for his paintings and drawings <u>of horse racing and young women who were dancing at the ballet.</u>

(A) of horse racing and young women who were dancing at the ballet.

(B) of horse racing and young women who are dancers at the ballet.

(C) of horse racing and ballerinas.

(D) of horses, racers, and of dancers.

(E) of horse racing and young women who are ballerinas.

27. Everyone in the family <u>who were watching the championship game cheered</u> whenever the home team scored a point.

(A) who were watching the championship game cheered

(B) who was watching the championship game cheered

(C) whom was watching the championship game will have cheered

(D) whom would have been watching the championship game cheered

(E) who will have been watching the championship game cheered

28. Ghana's major exports are agricultural products, such as cacao and coffee; minerals, such as gold and <u>diamonds, and timber is also an important export.</u>

(A) diamonds, and timber is also an important export.

(B) diamonds, and they also export important timber.

(C) diamonds, for example, and timber.

(D) diamonds; and also exported timber.

(E) diamonds; and timber.

29. Photosynthesis <u>is the process by which green plants transform</u> the sun's energy into chemicals (carbohydrates), using carbon dioxide, water, and sunlight with the aid of chlorophyll.

(A) is the process by which green plants transform

(B) is the process: by which green plants transform

(C) is the process, and green plants transform

(D) is the unique process, which green plants transform

(E) is the process which green plants, as an example, transform

30. The person <u>who Elena and I have been trying to reach</u> to ask about specially priced concert tickets for students has not returned our calls.

(A) who Elena and I have been trying to reach

(B) to whom Elena and I have been trying to reach

(C) whom Elena and I have been trying to reach

(D) who Elena and me have been trying to reach

(E) whom Elena and me have been trying to reach

31. Please e-mail this photo of my cousin to <u>Mike and he, so they and my cousin, who</u> they've never met, can recognize each other at the airport.

(A) Mike and he, so they and my cousin, who

(B) Mike and he, so they and my cousin, whom

(C) Mike and him, so they and my cousin, whom

(D) Mike and him, so them and my cousin, whom

(E) Mike and him, so they and my cousin, who

32. <u>The reason why the right whale got it's name is because whalers</u> preferred to hunt these whales, which float when dead and yield lots of whale oil and whalebone.

(A) The reason why the right whale got it's name is because whalers

(B) Because whalers named the right whale the right whale, they

(C) The right whale got its' name as a result of whalers having

(D) The right whale got it's name because of the fact that whalers

(E) The right whale got its name because whalers

33. After hitting an iceberg, more than 1,500 people died when the R.M.S. *Titanic* sunk on the night of April 14–15, 1912.

(A) After hitting an iceberg, more than 1,500 people died when the R.M.S. *Titanic* sunk

(B) More than 1,500 people died when the R.M.S. *Titanic* hit an iceberg and sank

(C) After hitting an iceberg, the R.M.S. *Titanic* sunk, killing more than 1,500 people,

(D) More than 1,500 people, after hitting an iceberg, died when the R.M.S. *Titanic* sank

(E) More than 1,500 people died after hitting an iceberg, when the R.M.S. *Titanic* sunk

34. "Not Waving But Drowning" is the title of a poem by Stevie <u>Smith, its about a swimmer</u> who tried but failed to get the attention of someone onshore.

(A) Smith, its about a swimmer

(B) Smith, and its about a swimmer

(C) Smith about a swimmer

(D) Smith: and it's about a swimmer

(E) Smith, for example, it's about a swimmer

35. Tae kwon do is a Korean martial art that many adults and children enjoy because it <u>improves your strength, agility, and your balancing abilities.</u>

(A) improves your strength, agility, and your balancing abilities

(B) improves their strength, agility, and balance

(C) improves there strength, agility, and balance

(D) is possible to improve your strength, agility, and one's ability to balance

(E) improves their strength and their agility and their balance

36. The main ingredients in falafel is pita bread, chickpeas, tahini (ground sesame paste), and salad.

   (A) The main ingredients in falafel is pita bread,

   (B) Falafel's main ingredient is pita bread,

   (C) Pita bread is one of the main ingredients in falafel, also you need

   (D) A list of the main ingredients in falafel would have to include pita bread;

   (E) The main ingredients in falafel are pita bread,

37. Jody and him have joined a bowling league and bowl regularly every Saturday.

   (A) Jody and him have joined a bowling league and bowl regularly every Saturday.

   (B) Every Saturday Jody and him have joined a bowling league, so they bowl regularly.

   (C) Jody and he have joined a bowling league, so they bowl regularly every Saturday.

   (D) Because Jody and he have joined a bowling league, they bowl regular every Saturday.

   (E) Although they bowl regularly every Saturday, Jody and he have joined a bowling league.

Directions: The passage that follows is an early draft of an essay. Some parts need to be rewritten. Read the passage carefully and answer the questions that follow. Choose the answer that most clearly and effectively expresses the writer's intended meaning. In making your decisions, follow the conventions of standard written English. After you have chosen your answer, fill in the corresponding oval.

(1) It's Saturday afternoon, and I want to go to the beach, but you want to see a movie. (2) We argue passionately. (3) Each of us tries to convince the other that we are right. (4) We try to persuade the other person. (5) We give all the reasons we can think of, but neither of us budges from our position. (6) What can we do? (7) We can compromise.

(8) The word *compromise* comes from the Latin *com-*, "together," and *promittere*, "to promise." (9) As far back as Roman times apparently, two people made a mutual promise to really do whatever an arbitrator says they should do. (10) *Compromise* is both a noun, referring to the agreement reached, and a verb, referring to the process of reaching that agreement.

(11) When the disagreement is between individuals, an arbitrator isn't necessary; the individuals can manage to sort out the problem themselves. (12) For instance, there are several possible solutions to our beach-versus-movie conflict. (13) We could go to the beach this afternoon, we could go to a movie after dinner. (14) Or we might go to the beach today and go to the movies next Saturday. (15) Or we could forget about the movies and the beach entirely and do something today that we both can agree on—maybe going Rollerblading or going on a picnic or a hike.

(16) The art of compromise isn't world-shakingly important when it comes to Saturday afternoon activities. (17) In business, law, and family life, it's essential to know how to reach a compromise. (18) For example, when a city's sanitation workers or transportation workers go on strike, how do labor and management reach an agreement that ends the strike when they have diametrically opposed positions?

(19) You can actually learn strategies that will help you to negotiate a compromise. (20) In a best-selling book titled *Getting to Yes: Negotiating Agreement Without Giving In,* the authors discuss several strategies for reaching agreements in difficult situations. (21) Three of these strategies are respecting the other party, listing all the possible options, and they also try to find common goals.

38. In order to strengthen the first paragraph, what is the best thing to do with sentence 4?

(A) Delete sentence 4.

(B) Move sentence 4 to precede sentence 1.

(C) Move sentence 4 to follow sentence 7.

(D) Change "the other person" to "each other."

(E) Add "that we are right" to the end of sentence 4.

39. What is the purpose of paragraph 1?

(A) to describe a personal experience that was important to the writer

(B) to introduce the subject and grab the reader's attention

(C) to persuade the reader not to argue with friends

(D) to inform the reader about strategies for reaching a compromise

(E) to define the word *compromise*

40. Which of the following is the best revision of the underlined portion of sentence 9 (reproduced below)?

As far back as Roman times apparently, two people made a mutual promise to really do whatever an arbitrator says they should do.

(A) (Leave it as it is.)

(B) to do whatever an arbitrator says they should really do

(C) to do in reality what an arbitrator decides for them

(D) to abide by an arbitrator's decision

(E) to do everything exactly the way the arbitrator tells them to

41. What is the purpose of paragraph 3?

(A) It continues the true story begun in paragraph 1.

(B) It gives an ancient Roman arbitrator's decision about the situation in paragraph 1.

(C) It gives the writer's opinion about the best possible compromise to the situation described in paragraph 1.

(D) It lists several options for reaching a compromise in the situation in paragraph 1.

(E) It involves the reader in deciding on the best possible compromise.

42. In the context of paragraph 3, what is the best revision to sentence 13 (reproduced below)?

We could go to the beach this afternoon, we could go to a movie after dinner.

(A) (Leave it as it is.)

(B) We could go to the beach this afternoon: we could go to a movie after dinner.

(C) We could go to the beach this afternoon, or we could go to a movie after dinner.

(D) We could go to the beach this afternoon and then go to a movie after dinner.

(E) We could go to the beach this afternoon; in contrast, we could go to a movie after dinner.

43. Which of the following transitional words or phrases should be inserted at the beginning of sentence 17 to logically connect the ideas in sentences 16 and 17 (reproduced below)?

(16) The art of compromise isn't world-shakingly important when it comes to Saturday afternoon activities. (17) In business, law, and family life, it's essential to know how to reach a compromise.

(A) In conclusion,

(B) Therefore,

(C) Consequently,

(D) As a result,

(E) However,

44. What is the best possible revision of the underlined portion of sentence 21, (reproduced below)?

Three of these strategies are respecting the other party, listing all the possible <u>options, and they also try to find common goals</u>.

(A) (Leave it as it is.)

(B) options; and also they try to find common goals

(C) options, and creating another list of the goals that are common to both parties

(D) options, and they are attempting to itemize common goals

(E) options, and trying to find common goals

45. Which of the following would make the best concluding sentence (sentence 22) at the end of the last paragraph?

    (A) So the next time you're involved in a dispute that seems impossible to resolve, apply these strategies, and try to negotiate a compromise.

    (B) You can learn a lot from reading this book.

    (C) Learning to negotiate compromises is an important social skill.

    (D) Everyone should practice learning how to negotiate a compromise.

    (E) So learn how to negotiate a compromise, and you can get what you want more often.

Directions: In each item, one of the underlined words or phrases may contain an error in grammar, usage, word choice, or idiom. If there is an error, choose the underlined part that must be changed to make the sentence correct, and fill in the corresponding oval. If the sentence has no error, fill in oval E. In selecting answers, follow the requirements of standard written English.

46. The plumber who <u>came</u> to fix the cold water faucet that wouldn't
                    A

turn off seemed to <u>deliberately</u> dawdle and <u>as a result</u> <u>has ran</u> up a
                B   C   D

bill that was far too high. <u>No error</u>
                      E

47. Nikola, Myra, and <u>them</u> are planning a surprise pizza party for Mrs.
                    A

Applegate, <u>their</u> science teacher, <u>who's</u> retiring after thirty-five years
        B   C

of teaching <u>biology, physics, and chemistry</u> to Shaw High students.
                    D

<u>No error</u>
  E

48. In Japan, many types of sea vegetables, such as kelp, nori, and hijiki,

<u>are</u> <u>commercially</u> <u>grown; often</u> they are dried and seasoned before
 A   B   C

<u>being</u> used in cooking. <u>No error</u>
 D   E

Ⓐ Ⓑ Ⓒ Ⓓ **Ⓔ**

49. When she was eight years old, Sayeeda <u>learned</u> <u>herself</u> to ride her
                                     A   B

brother's adult-sized bicycle by <u>repeatedly</u> going to the top of her
                                   C

hilly street, riding downhill, and falling dozens of times until she

finally <u>was able to ride</u> a two-wheeler. <u>No error</u>
          D   E

Ⓐ Ⓑ Ⓒ Ⓓ Ⓔ

Commonly Confused Words

▐▐▶ **accept, except** *Accept* is a verb that means "to receive" or "to agree to." *Except* is a preposition that means "but."

> The committee decided to **accept** the senator's proposal. All the committee members **except** the senator from Iowa voted in favor of it.

▐▐▶ **adapt, adept, adopt** *Adapt* is a verb that means "to make fit or modify for use." *Adept* is an adjective that means "very skilled or proficient." *Adopt* is a verb that means "to make one's own; to take by choice."

> If you **adopt** a dog, you'll have do **adapt** your schedule to walk it.
> Soon, you'll become **adept** at teaching the dog tricks.

▐▐▶ **advice, advise** *Advice* is a noun that means "an opinion, or a recommendation regarding a decision." *Advise* is a verb that means "to give advice or counsel."

> Brian usually listens to the counselor's **advice**.
> I **advise** you to drive slowly around the curve.

▐▐▶ **affect, effect** *Affect* is a verb that means "to influence." The noun *effect* means "the result of an action." The verb *effect* means "to cause" or "to bring about."

> Drinking coffee **affects** my sleep.
> An **effect** of the oil shortage is the rising gas prices.
> The new school dress code has **effected** major changes in the classroom.

▐▐▶ **all ready, already** *All ready*, an adjective, means "completely ready." *Already*, an adverb, means "previously" or "by now."

> I have **already** seen *Romeo and Juliet*.
> The room is **all ready** to be painted.

▐▐▶ **all right** *All right* is always two words. The word *alright* is not acceptable in formal written English.

> Is it **all right** to invite her?

▐▐▶ **all together, altogether** *All together* means "in a group." *Altogether* is an adverb that means "completely" or "in all."

> I worked on the school newspaper for four years **altogether**.
> I kept the papers **all together** in my drawer.

▐▐▶ **amount of, number of** Use *amount of* when you write about a general quantity of something. Use *number of* to refer to something that can be counted.

> The **amount of** food Gary consumed surprised me.
> The **number of** laps Helena swims every day is impressive.

▓▶ **anywheres, everywheres, nowheres, somewheres** These words are all spelled incorrectly. None of them should be spelled with an -s at the end.

> **Everywhere** we went on vacation, it rained.
> **Nowhere** did it pour as it did that day in Portland.

▓▶ **bad, badly** Use *bad*, which is always an adjective, after a linking verb such as *be*, *seem*, and *feel*. Use *badly*, an adverb, to modify an action verb.

> Even though it was a **bad** connection, I told Ming Yen how **badly** I missed her.
> Hector felt **bad** about missing Kathy's call.
> Fortunately, Peg's trailer wasn't **badly** damaged in the storm.

▓▶ **beside, besides** *Beside* means "by the side of." *Besides* as a preposition means "in addition to." *Besides* as an adverb means "moreover."

> **Beside** the reservoir is a small grove of locust trees.
> **Besides** joining the soccer team, I joined the drama club.
> It's too cold to swim; **besides**, the pool is closed.

▓▶ **between, among** Use *between* to compare two people or things. You may also use *between* when comparing three or more items if the sentence implies that only two of them will be compared at a time. Use *among* to refer to a group or to three or more people or things.

> **Between** shrimp and lobster, I'll take shrimp any day.
> Do you know the difference **between** a crustacean, a bivalve, and a fish?
> **Among** fishermen, crabbing is considered an art.

▓▶ **borrow, lend, loan** *Borrow* means "to take something temporarily that must be returned." *Lend*, the opposite of *borrow*, means "to give something temporarily with the expectation that it will be returned." *Loan* is both a verb and a noun. As a noun, it's the thing that is *lent*.

> Ali will **lend** you his copy of *The Martian Chronicles* to read.
> He already **borrowed** another science fiction novel from Hank.
> Was that Isaac Asimov book you gave me a **loan** or a gift?

▓▶ **could have, could of** Always use *could have*; *could of* is incorrect.

> Natasha **could have** been a rock star.

▓▶ **different from, different than** In most cases, *different from* works better than *different than*. However, in certain instances, *different than* eliminates an awkward construction and streamlines a sentence.

> How are crocodiles **different from** alligators?
> The zoo looks **different than** it did ten years ago.

342 *Commonly Confused Words*

▐▐▐▶ **disinterested, uninterested** *Disinterested* means "impartial or lacking interest in something or someone." *Uninterested* means "bored, indifferent, showing no interest in someone or something."

> The lawyers selected only **disinterested** individuals for the jury.
> The defendant appeared strangely **uninterested** in the verdict.

▐▐▐▶ **emigrate, immigrate** *Emigrate* means "to leave one country and go to another." *Immigrate* means "to enter a country and live there."

> Gambrowitz, the writer, **emigrated** from Poland during World War II.
> She **immigrated** to Argentina and worked as a bank clerk.

▐▐▐▶ **farther, further** *Farther* refers to physical distance. *Further* refers to additional degree or time.

> Nevil walked **farther** on the Appalachian Trail than Joan did.
> His understanding of French goes **further** than I will ever know.

▐▐▐▶ **fewer, less** *Fewer* modifies plural nouns that can be counted. *Less* modifies singular nouns that can't be counted.

> Use **fewer** peppers in the sauce. **Less** Tabasco sauce would also improve the flavor.

▐▐▐▶ **imply, infer** *Imply* means "to hint or suggest." *Infer* means "to understand a hint or suggestion."

> I **infer** from your report that you enjoy cooking.
> Did she **imply** that she planned to become a chef someday?

▐▐▐▶ **inside of, outside of, off of** Don't use *of* after the prepositions *inside, outside,* and *off.* Also, use *from,* not *off* or *off of,* when you're referring to the source of something.

> You'll find a ring **inside ~~of~~** the box.
> He leapt **off ~~of~~** the diving board.
> Here's the calculator I borrowed **from** Tina.

▐▐▐▶ **kind of a, sort of a, type of a** Drop the *a*. Use *kind of, sort of,* or *type of.* But keep in mind that *kind (sort, type) of* can usually be omitted without changing the meaning of a sentence and, in fact, should be avoided unless truly necessary.

> The **kind of ~~a~~** guitar I most like is acoustic.
> The guitar I like most is acoustic.

➠ **lay, lie** *Lay* means "to set something down," and it takes a direct object. *Lie* means "to place oneself or remain in a horizontal position," and it does not take a direct object.

> Don't **lay** the blanket on the bed.
> Make sure you **lie** down and rest before the swim meet.

➠ **learn, teach** *Learn* means "to gain knowledge." *Teach* means "to instruct."

> Tim can **teach** Betty how to drive a car.
> She will **learn** to drive this summer.

➠ **like, as, as if, as though** Don't use *like* to introduce a subordinate clause. Use *as, as if,* or *as though.* Use *like* to express similarity, sameness, or near sameness.

> The dog runs **as if** it's being chased.
> He performed well, **as** I knew he would.
> Pat and Anna look **like** sisters.

➠ **raise, rise** *Raise* is a verb that means "to lift up," and it takes a direct object. *Rise* is a verb that means "to go up; to get up," and it does not take a direct object.

> I **raise** the shade when I **rise** in the morning.

➠ **real, really** *Real* is an adjective that means "actual." *Really* is an adverb that means "actually" or "genuinely."

> I **really** like movies based on **real** events or people.

➠ **set, sit** *Set* means "to place or put down," and it takes a direct object except when referring to the sun. *Sit* means "to occupy a seat," and it does not take a direct object.

> I will **set** the table before dark.
> We can **sit** down for dinner and watch the sun **set** in the west.

➠ **than, then** *Than* is a conjunction that introduces a subordinate clause. *Then* is an adverb meaning "therefore" or "next in order or time."

> The cougar leapt higher **than** the antelope.
> **Then** the cougar showed her prowess at tree-climbing.

➠ **who, whom, which, that** Each of these relative pronouns has its own job. Use *who* (a subject pronoun) or *whom* (an object pronoun) to refer to people. Use *which* or *that* to refer to animals and objects, not to people.

> The twins, **who** left their sandals in the hotel room, were the same teenagers **whom** we met in the lobby. Walking barefoot toward the pool, they dropped their goggles, **which** they needed for swimming.

Index

capitalization (*continued*)
of buildings, 279
of calendar items, 285
of cities, 279
of common nouns that refer to
two or more proper nouns, 279
of compound numbers, 279
of constellations, 279
of continents, 279
of countries, 279
in dialogue, 267
of essay titles, 281
of first words of quotations, 283
of first words of sentences, 283
of geographic names, 279
of highways, 279
of historical events, documents,
and periods, 285
of interjection *O*, 285
of islands, 279
of monuments, 279
of movie titles, 281
of names of awards, 285
of names of government
agencies, 283
of names of groups, teams,
businesses, institutions, and
organizations, 283
of names of languages,
nationalities, peoples, races,
and religions, 283
of names of people, 279
of names of school subjects
followed by a number, 283
of parks, 279
of periodical titles, 281
of planets, 279
of play titles, 281
of poem titles, 281
of pronoun *I*, 285
proofreading for, 18
of proper adjectives, 101, 279
of proper nouns, 95, 279
of regions named after
directions, 279
to show emphasis, 285
of states, 279
of story titles, 281
of street names, 279
of titles of musical works, 281
of titles of written works, 281
of towns, 279
of TV series titles, 281
of words showing family
relationship, 281
of works of art, 281
cause-and-effect relationship, 31

subordinating conjunctions
showing, 41
transitions to show, 28
-*cede*, spelling rules for, 295
-*ceed*, spelling rules for, 295
centuries, 285
chronological order, 26, 55
in narrative writing, 30, 55
claim
in analyzing fiction, 76
in analyzing nonfiction, 91
in essays, 33
in persuasive writing, 32, 60, 62,
64, 66
in research papers, 86
See also thesis statement
classification, 31
clauses
adjective, 153–54
adverb, 107, 155–56
dependent, 151
elliptical adverb, 155
essential, 153
punctuation rules for, 247
identifying, 151–52
independent, 151–52
main, 151–52
nonessential, 153
and use of commas with, 247
noun, 157–58
subordinate, 41–42 ,123, 151–52
clincher sentence, 22, 23
cluster diagram, 10–11
coherence in writing, 26–29
collective nouns, 95
and subject-verb agreement, 195
colons, 259–60
with quotation marks, 265
combining sentences. *See* sentence
combining
commas, 244–50
after abbreviations, 249
with adjective clauses, 247
with adjectives, 243, 247, 249
in business letters, 249
in combining sentences, 39, 123
in compound interrogative or
imperative sentences, 245
after conjunctive adverbs, 39
to introduce quotations, 265
after introductory elements, 245
in letters, 249
in punctuating dialogue, 267
with quotation marks, 265
to separate date and year, 249
in series, 243–44

to set off contrasting
expressions, 247
to set off direct quotations, 249
to set off introductory phrase,
135
to set off mild interjections, 107
to set off name followed by
abbreviation, 249
to set off nonessential
appositives/appositive phrases,
247
to set off noun of direct address,
247
to set off parenthetical and
transitional expressions, 247
to set off tag questions, 249
comma splice, 123
common nouns, 95
comparative degrees of comparison,
223, 225
comparison/contrast, 31
comparisons
avoiding double, 225
avoiding illogical, 227–28
degrees of, 223, 225
transitions to show, 28
complements
object, 129, 207
subject, 127–28
complete predicate, 117
complete subject, 117
complex sentences, 159
compound adjectives, 101
hyphens in, 271
compound antecedents, 213
compound-complex sentences, 159
compound nouns, 95
hyphens in, 271
compound prepositions, 105
compound sentences, 39, 151, 159,
245
changing run-on sentence into,
251
commas in forming, 39, 245
independent clauses in, 159
semicolons in forming, 261
compound subjects, 39, 245
agreement with, 193–94
with pronouns, 205
compound verbs, 39, 245
conclusions, 33, 34
drafting, 35
concrete nouns, 95
conjunctions, 107–9
in combining sentences, 39
coordinating, 39, 107, 123

gerund phrases, 141–42
  in combining sentences, 43
gerunds, 141–42

H

helping verbs, 99
"'Hoot' delivers message of
  empowerment to kids" by Ty Burr,
  64–65
hyphens, 271
  in compound adjectives, 101
  in compound nouns, 95
  proofreading for, 18
  when adding prefixes to proper
    nouns/adjectives, 297

I

ideas and unity, in revising, 15
-ie, spelling rules for, 295
illogical comparisons, 227–28
immigrate, emigrate, 343
imperative mood, 181
imperative sentences, 115, 121
  compound, 245
  punctuation after, 115, 241
  subject in, 121
imply, infer, 343
incomplete constructions, 211–12
indefinite articles, 101
indefinite pronouns, 97, 191, 269
  apostrophes to show possessive
    form of, 269
  plural, 191
  singular, 191
  subject-verb agreement with,
    191–92, 213
independent clauses, 151–52
  comma between, in forming
    compound sentence, 39
  semicolons between, in forming
    compound sentence, 261
indicative mood, 181
indirect objects, 125–26, 207
indirect quotations, 283
  punctuation for, 241
infer, imply, 343
infinitive(s), 143–44
  commas after introductory, 245
infinitive phrases, 143–44
  commas after introductory, 245
informative/explanatory writing.
  See expository writing; problem-
  solution essay; research papers
inside of, off of, outside of, 343
intensifiers, 103
intensive pronouns, 97

interjections, 107–8
  capitalization of *O*, 285
  commas to set off mild, 107
  exclamation points to set off
    strong, 107
interrogative pronouns, 97
interrogative sentences, 115, 121
  See also questions
  compound, 245
  punctuation after, 115, 241
  subject in, 121
intervening phrases, 189–90
intransitive verb, 125
introduction, in essays, 33
inverted sentences, placement of
  subject in, 121
irregular verbs, 173–76
italics, 263–64
items in series
  commas to separate, 243–44
  semicolons to separate, 261

K

kind of a, sort of a, type of a, 343

L

lay, lie, 175, 344
learn, teach, 344
lend, loan, borrow, 342
less, in degrees of comparison, 225
less, fewer, 343
letters. *See* business letters; friendly
  letters
letters as letters
  apostrophes to form plurals of,
    269
  italics for, 263
lie, lay, 175, 344
like, as, as if, as though, 344
linking verbs, 99, 127
list of items, colon before, 259
literary analysis, 74
  analyzing fiction, 74–77
  questions for, 76
  analyzing nonfiction, 89–92
literary present tense, 76, 177
literature, writing about, 74–77. *See
  also* evaluation; literary analysis;
  personal response essay
loaded words, supporting
  emotional appeals with, 61
loan, borrow, lend, 342
logical appeals, 60
logical order, 27
  in expository writing, 31

M

main clause. *See* independent
  clauses
main ideas
  in expository writing, 31
  in prewriting for research
    papers, 87
many a(n), and subject-verb
  agreement before compound
  subject, 197
misplaced modifiers, 229
mnemonics, 295
modifiers. *See also* adjective(s);
  adverb(s)
  dangling, 231–32
  irregular, 223
  misplaced, 229
  one-syllable, 223
  two-syllable, 223
mood, 30, 181–82
"A Move to Save Coral Reefs,"
  69–70
movie reviews, 67. *See also* critical
  reviews

N

narrative writing, 30–31, 53–57. *See
  also* personal narratives
negatives, double, 227–28
no, comma to set off, 249
nominatives, predicate, 127–28,
  205
none, as indefinite pronoun, 191
nonessential adjective clauses and
  commas to set off, 247
nonessential appositives, 137
nonessential clauses, 153
  and commas to set off, 247
noun(s), 95–96
  abstract, 95
  appositives as, 137
  capitalization rules for, 279, 281
  collective, 95, 195
  common, 95
  compound, 95
  concrete, 95
  defined, 95
  of direct address, 247
  forming plural, 299
  gerund/gerund phrases as, 141
  hyphens in compound, 271
  identifying, 96
  infinitive/infinitive phrases as,
    143
  plural, 299–300